GIAN PUBLISHING HOUSE
PUBLISHERS OF BOOKS ON HUMAN CIVILIZATION
29/6 SHAKTI NAGAR, DELHI-110007

First Reprint in India, 1986

*Printed at Goyal Offset Printers, Delhi-110035
and published by Smt. Gayatri Garg
for Gian Publishing House, Delhi-110007*

THE
PROBLEM OF THE INDIAN POLIT

BY

PRATAPAGIRI RAMAMURTI

WITH A FOREWORD
by

JOHN McKENZIE

Gian Publishing House

29/6 SHAKTI NAGAR · DELHI-110007 · INDIA

THE PROBLEM OF THE INDIAN POLITY

loose thinking which is at the root of so much disharmony in the world of human relationships. It is the hope of Science that a disinterested pursuit of truth will rally human beings round the banner of its eternal values; humanity might thus be brought together by recognising the common affinities and life-values underneath the seeming differences arising from regional and historical causes.

The problems of human life being various, the methods of approach are also many: philosophical, scientific and practical. In the series herewith presented, all these methods have been employed. There is a common purpose running through the labours of individual writers, however divided they may be on specific issues and details, however varied and even contradictory may be their conclusions. That purpose is to present the human problem in all its aspects carefully analysed and discussed.

Our ambition is to build up a body of systematic knowledge, at once scientific and of practical utility, which might help in the reconstruction of the future, and to organise a School of thought with an 'ethos' and a 'quest' uniquely its own. However partially the ambition and hope may be realised, we feel sure that what we are doing is worth doing, and that it is high time it should be undertaken by some of us in India.

The great dream of the Editor's teacher, Sir Patrick Geddes, was to build the City Beautiful, the New Jerusalem, as he called it. He is no more amongst us to dream, to survey, to build and to rebuild. But it is our hope and purpose that the master's wishes should be fulfilled, however fragmentarily and inadequately, by these humble efforts of those who have inherited a little the light of his spirit, and felt the urge of his indomitable will to strive, to labour, to plan and to achieve.

School of Economics and Sociology,
University of Bombay,
March, 1935.

N. A. THOOTHI.

GENERAL INTRODUCTION TO THE SERIES

This series of monographs embodies the results of researches conducted by students working under my direction in the Bombay University School of Economics and Sociology, and by myself. The studies bear upon problems of human life in its various aspects—regional, economic, institutional, cultural and philosophical— with a view to advance constructive suggestions concerning the complicated problems that confront us at the present day.

Such an undertaking necessitates the treatment of facts and ideas in a scientific spirit and manner. Only patient investigation can yield results that prove valuable for the guidance of life. Every problem has its practical bearings. Hence, to understand a problem we must study it with reference to its past as well as its present, in order that we may be enabled to estimate its future. Vague and unscientific endeavours and conclusions are worse than useless ; for they not merely vitiate human effort but frustrate purpose and aspiration, and paralyse our hope to shape the future.

And, in our own days, there is an urgent need for the kind of inquiries that the present series proposes to undertake and pursue. We are in the midst of an 'omnipresent anarchy of values' ; consequently, we are in a drift which bids fair to sweep the world to disaster. If equilibrium has to be regained and maintained, there must be a clear and adequate understanding of the fundamental facts, purposes, values and difficulties of human life. The humble aim of this series is to study and understand the various aspects of the human problem, and discover and formulate, or may be, rediscover and reformulate, a scheme of values that may become the basis of a more equitable and stable human order. One of our objects is to prevent

EDITOR'S NOTE

The present study of Prof. R. Pratapagiri, is the result of his four years' work under my supervision during 1927-31 at the Bombay University School of Economics and Sociology.

The author starts with the conviction that the problem of Hindu Polity needs thorough reconsideration, overhauling and revision, even if that may lead one to fundamental and revolutionary changes. This attitude compelled him to go to the roots of things Hindu. Previous workers in the field of Hindu Polity have hinted at the relationship between Dharma and polity; others have even partially worked at these roots and have realised and located them as imbedded in the central concept of Hinduism, viz., Dharma; but Professor Pratapagiri may rightly claim to be the first to coordinate the conceptions and aspects of Hindu Polity as a whole in the light of Dharma, as the undersigned has done in the first volume of this series with reference to human life as a whole as manifested in a particular region.

Further, Professor Pratapagiri compares the concept of Dharma with Western ideals, and interprets and estimates the shortcomings and failures of Swa-dharma in the light of those ideals. This process of analysis leads Professor Pratapagiri to the following conclusions: (1) That on the whole, in the course and as a result of human evolution in history, human experience has not been merely deepened but also widened as regards the possibilities for choice in life; (2) that therefore most of our values, particularly Hindu, have lost their survival utility; (3) and that consequently the chaos in the Hindu life of modern times is due to the conflict between the constant insistence on old values and the demands of the new and strange tendencies and aspirations of the life within and the possibilities of the blossoming and fulfilment which Dharma-sanctions, mechanically applied, seem to thwart.

In view of this, the author suggests that the old walls that kept our forefathers safe, and within which they were content to move and have their being, must go, and that the boundaries must be extended within which human thought, effort, endeavour, and the spirit of adventure and experiment might have freer play than they have been allowed upto now. The debris of old blind walls must be swept away ; and out of the synthesis of the totality of human values, out of a world-experience wherein the ancient Hindu values may be allocated their due place, new landmarks and guide-posts must be constructed. And he goes on to urge that, if necessary, we must even be prepared to completely discard and disown our past heritage, for the sake of a fuller and more telic expression of the human spirit.

Professor Pratapagiri employs the philosophical method, in that he tries to understand facts in terms of a system of values. Facts are not detached entities to be measured and weighed by themselves ; they are part and parcel of a complicated whole which is the expression of a telesis.

If many of the problems and contradictions relating to the subject-matter of this interesting volume were considered on the canvas of a pluralistic universe full of varieties and possibilities called regions, as suggested by me in another place, it may be that most of them could not merely have been explained but even solved in a concreter way, so far as may be, than that provided by an implicit reliance on the idealism which the author of this learned volume postulates as the ultimate and infallible solvent of our difficulties.

FOREWORD

Professor Pratapagiri has made a real contribution to political thought in this study of Indian Polity. He has undertaken a task which, so far as I know, has not been essayed with the same thoroughness and comprehensiveness by any previous thinker. He has sought to present the problem of Indian Polity in relation to the life of the whole people. He has done well to take us back to the spiritual roots of the life of India, for no one will ever understand any part of the life of India without reference to them. There are many of those who to-day are influencing most deeply the thought and the activity of Indian youth, to whom the spiritual quest of the past, with all its philosophies and religions, is something simply to be deplored, and to whom the whole system of *dharma* with its marvellous definition and distribution of human duties is a simple anachronism. Whatever one may say about this attitude, this at least seems to be certain, that ignorance of India's past is a most serious disqualification in any one who would plan for India's future. For the past is not dead, and it cannot die so long as the spirit of the people who made it continues to live.

In the constructive part of his work Professor Pratapagiri is concerned with ideals rather than with details of political organisation. He has valuable things to say regarding the spiritual foundations which must be laid for the building of the India that is to be. I trust that what he has said will be pondered by those who desire to see India taking her rightful place in the life of the world.

John McKenzie.

PREFACE

The main aim of the present treatise is to understand the philosophical bases of the Ancient Indian Polity. Scholars of eminent repute have studied the problem mainly in its political aspect, following the trend of traditional historiography. The results they have obtained, valuable in themselves, are so far likely to present incomplete views. That accounts to a certain extent for the opinion generally held that the Ancient Indian State was purely secular and positive in nature, and that the State was unaffected by the social conditions of the time. I hold, that political institutions cannot exist in a vacuum, and therefore the ideas and ideals of our ancients were bound to mould the nature of the Polity. For, the Polity is the complex-reflex, in institutional terms, of the content of philosophical thought which is expressed not only in the speculation of a few thinkers, but which also determined the very life the people lived. For, in India, philosophy was not mere study, but practice; it embodied the Spirit of the Time. It is the vital interpenetration of the various aspects of life that is generally lost sight of. The main effort of this treatise is to grasp the nature of the Polity as a whole, as influenced by its philosophical bases.

The Ancient Indian State, far from being secular, was itself a socio-politico-religious institution. And as such, no study would be complete without an adequate inquiry into the foundations of the Polity, religious, social and political. My method of approach is mainly philosophical and the problem of the Indian Polity, as I envisage it, is primarily to discover the present value of our ancient ideals, in our attempt to formulate the bases of the Polity of the future.

I have not offered any definite solution to the problem of the Indian Polity. The necessity is to visualise it properly, and also indicate the direction future research should take.

I would consider that my labours have not been in vain if my work would induce other students to undertake a similar study of the Ancient Indian Polity. Every aspect of that Polity admits of detailed and specialised investigation. And I am happy to note that another book in the same series in dealing with "Political Organisation in the Hindu State" carries forward some of the ideas more generally discussed in this work.

I take this opportunity of expressing my gratitude to Dr. N. A. Thoothi for his kind guidance. My thanks are also due to the Rev. Dr. J. McKenzie who has laid me under deep obligation by writing the Foreword to this work. I have also to acknowledge the help I have received from Prof. R. D. Choksi, who has kindly gone through most of the proof-sheets.

Some errors may have crept in, owing to my anxiety not to delay publication; should a second edition become necessary, I shall endeavour to eliminate them.

I may add that the authorities of the University of Bombay very kindly gave a substantial grant towards the cost of this publication.

Wilson College,
Bombay.

Pratapagiri Ramamurti.

CONTENTS

ERRATA

N = Notes.

Page & Line.	*For.*	*Read.*
13 N ; 27.	Complain	Complaint
19 ; 1	of destiny	or destiny
19 ; 3	No purpose	a purpose
19 ; 17	Huttington	Huntington
20 ; 1-2	" there has been through the ages of oscillation and gradual ascent "	" there has been through series of oscillation a gradual ascent "
20 ; 16	To discern	We discern
24 ; 26	Paul Dewssen	Paul Deussen
26 ; 11	throughout bear in mind	throughout, bear in mind
35 ; 4	ourselves,	ourselves
41 ; 12	much value	such value
42 ; 7	metaphysic	metaphysics.
44 ; 5	vivrithi	nivrithi
51 ; 17	contain within	contains within
53 ; 14	practice	practise
56 ; 3	escheatology	eschatology
67 ; 20–21	self possessed	self-possessed
79 ; 5	knowldge	knowledge of
83 ; 31	insits	insists
112 ; 7	renumeration	remuneration
132 ; 24	iof	of
170 ; 31	suculent	succulent
179 ; 6	ethic	ethics
181 ; 23	rituality	ritualistic
182 N ; 33	tend	ten
195 ; 2	perfectability	perfectibility
229 ; 12	diagonised	diagnosised
260 N ; 31	more	move
283 ; 2	acquiescense	acquiescence
285 ; 26	Revolutions	Revolution
291 ; 27	special	spatial
293 ; 12	external	extreme

294	; 18–19	The relegated to	The State cannot be relegated to
295	; 26	legislative	legislate
309	; 10	displomacy	diplomacy
309	; 20	kingship	kinship
311	; 7	actua	actual
312	; 18	deluge the country	deluge the country.
312	; 18–20	with the it again to the fundamental idea of the Indian Polity of the Mughals	The fundamental idea of the Polity of the Mughals
319 N	; 35	Muirhead and Hether-ington	Hetherington and Muirhead
323 N	; 35	Greene	Green
328	; 6	Greeks State	Greek State
332	; 8	someties	sometimes
335 N	; 35	Taittviigaka	Taittiriyaka
371	; 19	interia	inertia
371	; 24	form a millions	form millions
372	; 5	there some	there are some
377	; 17	release of deliverance	release or deliverence
381	; 33	Mareus	Marcus
382	; 11	fellows	fetters
382	; 16	Epaminondes	Epaminondas
383	; 25–26	When, indeed is the knowledge if bi at the eternal is not obtained	What, indeed, is the knowledge, if by it the eternal is not obtained
385	; 17	leisure in	leisure is
394	; 13	far and wider	far and wide
410	; 10	monarchical	monarchy
426	; 1	become	becomes
435	; 7	And it understood it in	And if understood in
443	; 3	tresspasses	trespasses

CHAPTER I

THE APPEAL TO HISTORY

"History is the light of Truth".

CICERO

"Yet I doubt not through the ages
One increasing purpose runs,
And the thoughts of men are widened
With the process of the Suns."

TENNYSON

The institutions of the Ancient Indian Polity cannot be studied, divorced from considerations of value. They are a phase of the universal process in which we live and have our being. To interpret them we have to appraise them as the concretised expressions of the perpetual attempt at the adventure of living. They must, therefore, be understood in terms of life, its hopes, ideals and aspirations which they embody however imperfectly. It is an irresistible demand of the human spirit that so long as imperfection remains, there shall be no limit to striving. For an imperfection that has perfection for its end must go through an infinite process of fulfilment. It is the unlimited hope, the promise of the future, a vision of the Holy Grail man is in search of, that impels him on and on ; and instinctively he travels towards the goal.

It is the same age-long quest to reach out to something beyond, yet something intimately bound up with man's life, as the rhythm in the movement of the song. He touches a chord here and there, but not yet has he discovered the key which would harmonise discordant notes and yield that soft music which he vaguely remembers to have heard long ago, as in a dream. It is the memory of that Summer Song that urges him, ever and anon, to the eternal quest. So long as he has not found,

P

the object of his search he will never cease in his effort. There will ever remain the "divine discontent."

This quest of man is expressed in whatever he does. He embodies it in his Polity. He might or might not be conscious ; but all the same he impresses his idea on the institution he moulds. Institutions, as we hold, are primarily ideas ; they are concretised purposes. Imperfect institutions are the expressions of imperfect ideas. As is the man's idea, so is his handiwork. The more perfect the vision of the life he wishes to live, the nearer will be his institutional fulfilment to the City of God. His failure, so far, to realise the ideal Polity is the outcome of his limitations. It is essential to know his failings in order to avoid them in future. A knowledge of his mistakes in the past will help him to rise towards the blue vaulted skies, and succeed even in the face of defeat. He will be enabled to find what is missing and to plan his future with confidence.

That is why we appeal to history. The nature of the problem before us can only be grasped by a reference to India's past. The story of this country has been unlike that of any other known to the world's history. To understand it, it is not enough to watch the destinies of royal dynasties, the rise and fall of kingdoms and empires. India has been the home of philosophers, and to this day the spiritual motive dominates her life. "It is the intense spirituality of India and not any great political structure or social organisation that it has developed that has enabled it to resist the ravages of time and the accidents of history."[1] We cannot, indeed, help being filled with sorrow at the panorama of suffering and travail that the picture of our past unfolds. The most flourishing empires that the genius of man has erected are now mouldering ruins, choked-up aqueducts, crumbling palaces,

[1] Radhakrishnan: *Indian Philosophy*, Vol. I, pp. 24-25.

and deserted cities. Inexorable Time has laid its heavy hand on everything mortal,—a witness and a portent perhaps, warning us to fix our gaze on abiding issues. Enduring a mental torture we glance back into that gloomy picture; and our perturbed soul sinks into the deepest melancholy and profoundest sadness. The perusal of mere events and records, of wars and crimes, thus misleads and leaves behind the impression that our history is the mausoleum of dead issues.[1] We shall ever remind ourselves, in the discussions that follow, that the history of our land abounds with ideals and beliefs, with the achievements of the soul.[2] India has revelled in things of the spirit; and her history is the record of the mind, of the thought that expresses its endless quest, "ever old, ever new". The flame of her spirit can never be extinguished.

It is necessary hence to dive below the surface of political events to discover the life of the people.[3] The ordinary histories that we have, are "generally treated in a one-sided manner. They give no insight into the true state of society." Our appeal to the history of our past is not to such writings though it may be necessary to refer to them. Fortunately India has a splendid heritage, vast and rich, bequeathed to us through the accomplishments of the human mind, and in the results of human art. These reveal life itself, in its manifold colours and shades.

[1] Gibbon says that "History is little more than the register of the crimes, follies and misfortunes of mankind."

[2] See Shailer Mathews: *The Spiritual Interpretation of History*, p. 29.

See also Tagore's *Nationalism*, pp. 5-7.

[3] See Marvin: *Living Past*, p. 5.

Macaulay: *Essay on History* (*Selections* ed. by Sir Otto Trevelyan, pp. 355-361).

R. C. Dutt: *Civilisation of India*, p. 97.

Murasaki Shikib: *Genji Monogatari*, p. 6.

See G. P. Gooch: *History and Historians in the Nineteenth Century* for his description of the scope of History, p. 573.

Through them we come to know how people have felt and lived, their hopes, fears and aspirations. We discover how closely we are related to them, though so far removed in distance of time. We are enabled to discern the connective tissue of civilisation, the continuous force which binds age to age, "the link in the chain of organic beings connecting the past with the future."[1] Life is a continuous process; a lengthening chain. Engrossed in the past we fail to grasp this huge linkage. The social structure is continuous. Emerson had said that man is a quotation from the past; it would be truer to say that he is the epitome of all the ages. We inhale as our spiritual atmosphere the experience and knowledge of the past. "Man has been," writes Graham Wallas, "increasingly dependent on his social heritage." We are what we are because of our social heritage. We are what we are because our fathers were what they were. "They are largely the stuff of which our present selves and our present world are made."[3] Our speech, our religion, our polity, our very problems are their legacy. It is only the savage that recognises not the rock from which he is hewn, the pit from which he is dug.[4] We should delve with reverence[5] into the pregnant archives of our past, if we wish to seek to know the ground we stand on, the road we travel, and the reason why. "All our hopes of

---

[1] Maudsley: *The Physiology and Pathology of the Mind*, p. 73 quoted by Bagehot: *Physics and Politics*.

[2] *Our Social Heritage*, p. 19.

[3] J. A. Smith in: *Unity of Western Civilisation*, p. 72.

[4] "The power of regarding the past and of understanding the causes which have produced the present form of affairs is one of the greatest tests of Civilisation". Sir Flinders Petrie: Article on "Discovering the Unknown Past" in *Harmsworth's Universal History*.

[5] This reference is one of the most peculiar traits of the Indian. See S. Radhakrishnan: *Indian Philosophy*, Vol. I, pp. 46-47.

Carlyle: Bohn's Standard Library, p. 40.

the future", as Frederick Harrison has said,[1] "depend on a sound understanding of the past." For, "of man above all other beings it is true that to know what he is, we must know what he has been."[2] To understand our present Polity and to visualise its future, it is therefore necessary to trace its past history through the ages. What is must be understood in the light of what has been.[3] That is why we appeal to history.

But our appeal to history is to a branch of study which is not to be understood in its conventional sense. Or we shall be told that it is a "hybrid form of experience, incapable of any considerable degree of 'being or trueness' ";[4] and that the doctrine of Historical Necessity negates the freedom of the Human Will.[5] If man's Will is free and determines itself, his volitions "are not properly speaking the effects of causes, or at least have no causes which they uniformly or implicitly obey."[6] We cannot enter into an elaborate discussion of the problem raised here. We would only point out that the doctrine of Historical Necessity, if properly understood, is very remote from Fatalism; neither is it that of Pre-determination. We shall have reason, more than once, in the subsequent pages to protest vehemently against the principle of inexorable determinism. It is this principle that has vitiated our attitude to life, resulting in a deadening inertia. By Historical Necessity we only mean the interpretation of

---

[1] *The meaning of History*, p. 6.

[2] John Caird: *An Introduction to the Philosophy of Religion*, Ch. X.

[3] It is also possible to interpret the Past by the Present. See Crozier J. B. *Civilisation and Progress*, p. 35.

[4] Bosanquet: *Principle of Individuality and Value*, pp. 78-79. Refer also to J. M. Baldwin's article in the Dictionary of Philosophy and Psychology, and Allen Johnson's *Historian and Historical Evidence*.

[5] Froude Vol. I, p. 12.

[6] J. S. Mill: *A System of Logic*, p. 547 ff.

experience which tells us that given certain set of conditions certain consequences may be expected to follow. We never claim, however, that identical set of circumstances can be repeated at will. Man's life is essentially dynamic and manifests a process of development.[1] Upward growth and progress, Turgot proclaimed long ago, is the law of human life. It would not be possible to draw too close analogies from past behaviour.[2] What we claim is only a certain degree of probability in human calculations. The fundamentals of Human nature being what they are, in every clime and age,[3] it is quite in the scope of human understanding to predict with a high degree of accuracy from given antecedents to consequents.[4]

We do not, however, enter into the controversy whether history is a science or not.[5] Here we are concerned with simply asserting that there is no antagonism between free will and historical necessity. "In spite of certain

---

[1] Muller Lyer: *The History of Social Development*: *Preface;* also pp. 254-255.

[2] Morley: *Notes on Politics and History*, pp. 58-60.
See also Spengler: *Decline of the West*, pp. 3-50.
Christopher Dawson: *Progress and Religion*, pp. 31-46.
Theodore Roosevelt's *Biological Analogies in History*.

De Tocqueville says: "History is a picture gallery containing few originals and great many copies". *The State of Society in France before the Revolution of 1789.*

[3] See James Bryce: *Modern Democracies*, Vol. I, pp. 16-22.

[4] cf. Buckle: *Civilisation of England*, Vol. I, pp. 15-16.

[5] Schopenhauer had denied to history the character of science on the ground that it teaches only the particular and nothing of the universal. "The science", says he, "in that they are systems of concepts speak entirely of universals. History speaks of particulars which betokens a contradiction.".

It is indeed difficult to have an exact science of man; but it is quite possible, however, to have coherent and systematic knowledge.

See Urwick: *Philosophy of Social Progress*.

appearances wrongly understood, History is not a school of Fatalism ; it is one long pleading in favour of liberty''.[1]

Unfortunately the past is often presented in our every-day experience as a reactionary force, concentrated in the yoke of custom, and manifested in meaningless ceremonials, which are a mere drag on our free initiative. We have realised that ''progress is impossible without a painful disturbance of cherished customs and beliefs.''[2] Freedom has, thus, come to mean emancipation from the shackles of the past. We are instinct with the spirit of revolt. We see men in titanic conflict with tradition and environment. It is the hope that the future will not be like the present or the past that sustains these ardent souls. ''Is it'', they ask, ''that we can see nothing in the long vistas of coming ages that we should needs rivet our bark to the moorings of a dead past?'' They would brush aside the leavings of what constituted once for life, and seek real life, the efflorescence of their vital aspirations. It is the heart-rending anguish of the human soul to find its wings, the spiritual urge to rise from the grovelling dust to ethereal heights—the longing for a higher expression and a nobler life—the call of the Divine.

The note of this call is echoed in and through history. Its poignant thrill goes back reverberating through the ages. What is History but the enfranchisement of the Human Spirit, the eternal striving after Freedom ! Hegel is profoundly true when he says : ''The History of the world is none other than the progress of the consciousness of Freedom ;'' and ''the question of the means by which Freedom develops itself into the world conducts us to the phenomenon of History itself.''[3] Far from there being

---

[1] Lanfrey: *History of Napoleon*, Vol. I, pp. 2-4.

[2] Prof. P. A. Wadia.

[3] *Philosophy of History*, Introduction.

any conflict between Necessity and Freedom, we thus realise that liberty is the necessary goal of the whole trend of History.

All our misgiving is due to our looking at the past as the "dead past". Of what use, we may be asked, is it appealing to history that has finished happening? History, it is commonly held is a record of facts or events that occurred in the past. So let the dead bury the dead. This, at any rate, is a very simple method of disposing of things, and we wish it could ease our problem too. If we could start each time we begin the adventure of life with a clean slate we could then depend on what would turn up hereafter, instead of troubling ourselves, diving into the limbo of forgotten things. But life is not so simple; and however we may try to plough unhampered, we do come across rocky impediments that stand and have stood mocking for centuries at the efforts of man. The slate that is passed on to us bears the indelible stamp of myriads of fellow-adventurers, who each tried to write the story of life in his own way, but could only just thrust his little mark in between an apparently chaotic picture of countless little monographs. It is the slate with the whole past engraved on its surface.

Thus, it is not something which is simply the past with which we are concerned in the appeal we make to history. History is not simply the past, and it is time we turn our backs on Realistic philosophers who want us to fit out a "real" past. Such a quest is as hopeless as the metaphysician's search after *things-in-themselves*. To think of the past as a *thing-in-itself*, a thing out of all relation to the knowledge of it, a thing existing in itself, and by itself, is a metaphysical absurdity. From the point of view of the Realist, the object of history appears simply as the "past, the sum total of events that have happened. But an event that has finished happening is just nothing, and has no existence at all. The past, simply as the past, is non-existent.[1] What we call the facts of the past must be capable of being taken in "at once", "not merely by virtue of remembered facts, but also as experienced facts." In other words we live all history in our own person. "There is no age, or state of society, or mode of action in history," says Emerson, "to which there is not somewhat corresponding in man's life. We must learn to read in the history of the whole human race something of our own history."[2]

But we are too much influenced by the Temporal aspect of Time to see that what is Eternal is a Unity. It is not fanciful to consider the Universe to be infinite and the past as perpetually present.[3]

Unfortunately we have come to differentiate so much between different periods of time and between men of varying cultural stages that we fail to grasp that quantitative differences do not point to qualitative distinctions. After all, as Ratzel insists, mankind is one whole, though variously cultured.[4] There is a fundamental identity underlying human nature, in all times and places. If it were not so, we could not explain the quick response of the modern man to the play and interplay of elemental human instincts as they appear in one form or another in ancient literature. What is, indeed, the foundation of our interest when we read of the deeds and thoughts of by-gone days? What but that we personally pass through all the periods of existence! We feel the reality of the past, as if we were ourselves alive in it, participating in the enactment, "spectators and sufferers in the

---

[1] See Collingwood's Article in the *Journal of Philosophical Studies*, Vol. III, No. X, April 1928.

[2] cf. Max Muller: *Selected Essays*, Vol. II, p. 11.

[3] See Benedetto Croce: *Theory and History of Historiography*, p. 11 ff. where he discusses that every true history is contemporary history.

[4] *History of Mankind*, Vol. I, p. 4.

event." As Carlyle exhorts,[1] we sweep away the illusion of Time. The past is transfused into the living actuality that it once was. As much as the poet, we become what we sing. We live along the whole line of Asokan Pillars and Taj Mahals. The whole pageant is conjured up, living full-blooded. How can we account for the perennial appeal of the Mahabharata, the Gita, the Upanishads, the Ramayan and Kalidas' Shakuntala? How can we explain the attraction the Ajanta frescoes have even after the lapse of centuries? How is it that even at this distance of time we are powerfully moved when we read the tales of Rajasthan? Do we not merge ourselves in the sad thoughts of the crowned philosopher who turning away in sorrow and disgust from the harrowing spectacle of warring creeds and contending beliefs, sought refuge in the conviction that slowly dawned in his soul that no single tune held the key to the Infinite! Shall we be wrong, therefore, in assuming that human nature has remained substantially the same all through the ages?

When, therefore, we are appealing to the past history of our land, we are essentially building upon the postulate that human nature is identical in all times and places; and that it is possible to work on the principle of analogy, wherever we find similar conditions. Here lies the human interest of the past. It is not the mere events that we would know. We wish to enter into the very spirit of the men and women of by-gone days; not only the visible men and women, but, as Taine[2] has said, the invisible men and women. In other words, it is the "subterranean world", the hidden sphere of the soul, the inward of which the outward humanity is the expression that we try

---

[1] *Sartor Resartus.*

[2] *History of English Literature*, **Introduction.**

to reach. History, thus, has for its theme the human epic. And it is the Living Past that we try to reach.[1]

History, thus, is not simply the past. Neither is it the event. The dominance of the "narrative" spirit has vitiated the whole outlook of our historians, and there is a haunting terror of shadows. The construction of narratives, chronologically arranged, is not all history. It is something more. Facts are mere dross, as both Ruskin and Macaulay hold, and it is from the thoughts, the abstract truth that the events and happenings embody that history derives its value. History is the thought that expresses itself, the mind that records; and mind is prior to fact. All history is, in a sense, in the mind of man; not as a pre-composed symphony, however, we hasten to point out, as our statement might be misunderstood.[2] It is the Law of man's Being; the Divine force in him; the idea in its potentiality; the universal in its spirit, even as Hegel would have it. In order that the Potential be translated into Actual, the Activity in man in the highest sense, the Human Will, is required. The resultant is History. Here is verily the synthesis of Necessity and Will, Law and Freedom. The past is no obstacle and burden; and "knowledge of the past is the safest and surest emancipation."[3]

The Past, therefore, simply regarded as the past, in the crude realistic sense, is wholly unthinkable. The past that we try to reach is not a world of *things-in-themselves*, a world that has ceased to be, and so an isolated fact. Such a fact can never be related to the present; the chain of linkage is severed into its links. To us the past of India is the living relic in the present, for the past has

---

[1] See J. A. Hammerton's Foreword to *Harmsworth's Universal History*.

[2] Lotze quoted by Ward: *The Realm of Ends. Pluralism and Theism*, p. 310.

[3] Acton: *Lectures on Modern History*, p. 4.

resulted into the present. The India of the past is a projection of itself into the India of the present. Or to express it in other words, the past of India is the present experience of it, taken in as a unity, "a synthetic unity" to borrow the expression of B. Croce, a unity that may reveal sequence in Space and Time; each unit of the sequence, however, not as an isolated fact, unrelated to others, but in organic relation manifesting the rhythm of the flow of real life. And whatever of the past goes into our present experience, that is History in the largest sense of the word.[1]

And in our appeal to the History of India, we imply whatever comes into our present experience from the content of the past. To us, therefore, the Rig-Veda or the Budhist Jatakas, the Epics, the Smritis and the Srutis are as much History as any other relic now possessed by us which professes to describe the political events of by-gone days. For what we want to know is not the fossil itself, but the living, thinking Man of whom the relic before us is the dead representative. In the search of the so-called authentic facts or events we are apt to run into the danger of missing all that is truly human.[2] The most formidable obstacle to the proper understanding of our past is just our tendency to restrict history to the construction of narratives; and where such a construction is impossible to assume a sceptical attitude and dissipate effort in trying to sift what is supposed to be the unquestionable fact from myth and legend. Where there are no records, it is usually assumed that there is no history

[1] Benedetto Croce: *Theory and History of Historiography*, p. 12 where he says that a past fact does not answer to a past interest," in so far as it is unified with an interest of the present life.

[2] We are not directly concerned with the question of the details of Historiography. We refer the reader to Langlois and Seignobos: *Introduction to the Study of History*.

either ; as if, historical truths are lost to posterity because their memory is not preserved in the form of chronologically connected narratives.[1] And even the records that have come down to us are not all of them accepted as valid, for the "being or trueness" of history is held to be its verified and verifiable certainty.[2] This is not the place to enter into a discussion of the veracity of historical evidence and history as a scientific study ; for it becomes irrelevant viewed from our conception of history. The word "History" originally meant "inquiry" and only secondarily came to be applied to the embodiment of the

---

[1] "The essence of history consists in the very fact of happening not in the recollecting and recording what has happened." Ratzel: *History of Mankind*, p. 5.

See also S. Matthews: *The Spiritual Interpretation of History*, p. 3; see also pp. 38-39.

Regarding the importance of chronology, we are of opinion that it has been somewhat overstated by historians. "A body of history so-called," writes Vincent Smith, "must be built upon a skeleton of chronology, that is to say, on a series of dates more or less precise." Even a philosopher like Prof. S. Radhakrishnan says that: "In the absence of accurate chronology, it is a misnomer to call anything history." We would like to point out, however, that these profound scholars are confounding the office of the annalist with the function of the historian. History is not putting bits of information, chronologically arranged together like beads on a string. How true is the complain of H. G. Wells that: "Historians are for the most parts very scholarly men nowadays. They go in fear rather of small errors than of disconnectedness; they dread the certain ridicule of a wrong date than the disputable attribution of a wrong value".

[2] We perfectly agree with Benedetto Croce in his remarks on the verifiability of historical evidence for "once the indissoluble link between life and thought in history has been effected, the doubts that have been expressed to the *certainty* and *utility* of history disappear altogether in a moment. How could that which is *present* producing of our spirit ever be *uncertain*? How could that knowedge be *useless* which solves a problem that has come forth from the bosom of life?" (*Theory and History of Historiography*, p. 15).

results of inquiry in the particular form of narrative. The Greek word for history is "historia" meaning 'search after truth'. In trying to unravel the threads of the working of the human mind in the past, we cannot help playing the part of the judge. For annals are not history. To deserve that title conviction is required. We have to sit in judgment and accept as "true" that which appeals to our conscience, and is approved by our intellect.—True not in the empirical sense that the Realists would have as something actually happened, but "true" in a higher sense considered from the criterion of human values, moral or ethical as satisfying our sense of right and justice.[1]

The whole of the past we therefore seek to embrace in its spiritual unity; and we shall assign each fact that is brought into our present experience, its fitting rank in the scale of social progress.[2] We shall not mind chronology in examining our past; for we cannot isolate and treat in isolation each fact from the series of temporal or spatial succession. Our present experience is a unity. For us, therefore, not the assignment of date, but the assignment of value is of supreme importance. The question of time leads us into the realistic meshes of the world of *"things-in-themselves"*. Any experience of ours is at once temporal and eternal, a unity with a serial succession. Only by embracing the unity can we comprehend the parts that go to make it. It is only those who are incapable of taking their stand on the elevated plane of the spirit who needs must have physically isolable periods

---

[1] "History," says Froude, "is a voice for ever sounding across the centuries the laws of right and wrong. Opinions alter, manners change, creeds rise and fall but the moral law is written on the tablets of eternity." (*Short Studies on Great Subjects*, pp. 27-28).

[2] We may speak of civilisation, in its widest sense, as a fact. See Guizot: *History of Civilisation*, Vol. I, pp. 4-6.

or stages. The Past, the Present and the Future as periods in temporal succession, have no separable or isolable existence and are realities only when comprehended in their spiritual unity.

Our conception postulates the necessity of conceiving the world as an organic whole. We appeal to the past of India, for a proper understanding of our problem, but it is to a past which is truly "living" in the larger sense of the term.[1] And those who would understand us will therefore excuse us if we start the investigation of the problem of the Indian Polity, with our own conception of history. We conceive that the mission of history is to give us the content of life ; and the appeal that we make to history is to that which would serve as a common tribunal, being above contention. History, so to say, must be loyal to truth ; "truth" not in the realistic sense, but in the higher sense that does not exclude earnestness of conviction ; and so essentially moral or ethical. We should, indeed, be impartial ; but our impartiality is not that of the mirror which merely reflects.[2] The attitude of detachment is psychologically impossible and untenable. Open-minded we shall be, but "open-mindedness does not mean mental vacuity".[3] We cannot clean our mind as we would a slate. Just as every scientist, we also select a theme and we cannot but start with our own theory. In short we make use of hypotheses as much as other investigators. We see, as Charles Darwin did,

---

[1] History, in other words, must be a resurrection, "a blush of life in dead limbs."

See Lecky: *Historical and Political Essays* for a discussion of the place of literary element in Historiography.

See Lanfrey on the Mission of History: *History of Napoleon.*

[2] See Temperley's "J. B. Bury", *Selected Essays*, pp. 70-71.

[3] Allen Johnson: *The Historian and Historical Evidence*, Chapter on the use of Hypotheses.

that all observation must be for or against some view if it is to be of utility of any kind. We cannot, as Bacon imagines we can, for a while, renounce conceptions and try to acquaint ourselves with things themselves. How to have any idea of "things themselves" without our own view of them is the problem for the historian as much as for the metaphysician! We do not, indeed, commit ourselves to a pre-judgment and then fit the facts into our theory. In the pages that follow we have carefully conformed to Lord Acton's advice that we should weigh our testimony. We have tried, as far as lies in our power, to be loyal to truth.

The reader will kindly be indulgent towards us, if we therefore set aside all received notions and begin with a novel approach. For, if our task is after all to compile another text-book on the Indian Polity on the lines of those already in existence, we shall be repeating and duplicating the narratives already extant. As Goethe has said: "History must from time to time be re-written, not because new facts have been discovered, but because new aspects come into view, because the participant in the progress of an age is led to standpoints from which the past can be regarded and judged in a novel manner."[1] Perhaps this is due to an unconscious factor which affects all historians, both ancient and modern. It has been said that the younger generation feels pleasure in tearing down

---

[1] See Teggart: *Theory of History*, p. 7 ff.
cf. V. A. Smith: *Oxford History of India*, p. 9; xxxiii.
Every generation, Mark Pattison said, requires the facts to be recast in its own mould, and demands that history be re-written from its own point of view. And result is often that each later historian as Polybius has remarked "makes such a parade of minute accuracy and inveighs so bitterly when refuting others, that people come to imagine that all other historians have been mere dreamers, and have spoken at random in describing the world; and that he is the only man who has made accurate investigations and unravelled every history with intelligence.

the idols of the old ;[1] and so what have been the ideas of one age are not those of the next.[2] If this were true, how then can we conceive of a purpose in historical processes? If history is a perpetual sifting about, like the rolling of the waves, if, in other words, history is the mere record of change, how can we have a coherent idea that will justify our appeal to history?

The question that we have raised here goes to the root of our problem. For those who are accustomed to look upon the world-process as a series of changes occurring in mere succession, may hold that the future must necessarily differ from anything evolved or achieved so far.[3]

---

[1] See Pritchard: *Essays of To-day*, pp. 14-15.

Ben Lindsey's: *The Revolt of Modern Youth.*

Especially see C. E. M. Joad's *The Present and Future of Religion* where the writer analyses what this spirit of revolt involves, particularly in its reactions on religious beliefs.

[2] cf. Muller Lyer: *The History of Social Development*, pp. 254-255; 319-331.

See also the preface where he talks of "Lines of direction of Progress."

[3] Students of European history know how literally Turgot's conception of "Progress" was understood by the thinkers who followed, and applied by the enthusiasts of 1789. His hypothesis of progress, of upward growth would imply that the future would be unlike the past, that the new is ever substituting the old. Accordingly history would be the embodiment of imperfection, and to gain perfection we have to escape away from history. That is why Condorcet thought that the world would be emancipated by burning its records, though Turgot was himself innocent of such extravagance. The revolutionists of 1789 applied the law of Innovation and tried to break away from the France of History, and symbolised their new era by dating their calendar from the First year of the Republic. But we know how far the attempt succeeded. After the revolutionary fever subsided, there was a general desire to return to the "good old time", and as many institutions and ideas as could be resuscitated were dug up from the ruins. It was this singular phenomenon that De Tocquieville has described in his famous book: *The State of Society*

History is assumed to be the embodiment of imperfection; and so to gain perfection we should break away from history. In India, especially, there is a growing tendency to maintain that progress is incompatible with the past and that the time to use the surgical knife has come, to cut ruthlessly without ever entertaining the idea of sewing. It is necessary, hence, to understand the implications of the philosophy of change.

In spite of appearances change is not fortuitous. And in the evolution of human thought almost the first to conceive of Law as applied to Universe and existence were the Rig Vedic seers. They recognised that natural phenomena obey a higher "law" which they tried to comprehend by the term "Rta". We shall return to a consideration of this term later. What we want to insist here is that in India, from the very earliest times, when thought becomes conscious of itself an intelligible principle is sought to explain the relationship between the Temporal and Eternal, Appearance and Reality, Change and Permanence. The opposition is, however, got over, not by reconciliation in a higher synthesis, but in the ultimate negation of any opposition in the light of monistic interpretation of Reality. This conclusion has far-reaching consequences on the Indian Polity, as we shall see in the following pages. Change is only true of the phenomenal world, the world of "Maya". In the ultimate there is no change and all "pairs of opposites" are transcended. If Empirical Existence is impermanent, unsubstantial and changing, and in the last analysis, verily, unreal, then the "End" of human striving can nowhere be placed in the empirical life. This changing world would not reveal a "purpose" which man is to embody in his works. His end would be to realise an Absolute, behind and beyond, transcending all experience of life as such.

---

in France before the Revolution of 1789 and the causes that led to that event.

The moment, however, we postulate a goal of destiny towards which this life, here and now, is travelling, we can conceive of no purpose, realisable in and through life. We could then feel real zeal in life, and in spite of change, the phenomenal world would present an intelligible principle which shall be the pivot on which it turns. It is no longer mere flux, no drift, no meaningless becoming. History would reveal development, and its process a huge linkage. The life of humanity is a continuous chain. As Lord Acton has said,[1] "the dense web of the fortunes of man is woven without a void". And what is more, our very awareness of change, or succession in Time is itself the strongest proof of the reality of Unity; for, to be conscious of, a succession, in time or in space, is to experience the whole in its Unity.

And thus the idea of change, applied to history must be very carefully interpreted.[2] Huttington has called all history a record of pulsations. Stated thus, it is possible to ignore the real significance of life. The question is if these pulsations are merely automatic, or are they related to a purpose. To interpret historical purpose in terms of pulsations is very mechanical; and it fails to satisfy our moral and rational needs. History is something more than the record of mere impulse; it manifests the working of Law. And the Law takes into account the multiple facts of movement and change; and is the expression of unity, which seeks to embrace this pluralistic world. And further, this Law is not the mere interpretation of change; but is the manifestation of development. Dr. Muller Lyer accepts "Progress" as a fact of social development and even tries to indicate what he calls "lines of direction of Progress". And ever since the publication of the "Origin of Species", the idea of evolution has been gaining

---

[1] *Inaugural Lecture on the Study of History.*

[2] *The Pulse of Progress*, p. 318.

ground, and also the idea that "there has been through the ages of oscillation and gradual ascent".[1]

The facts of our nature, thus instinctively require "a solid and permanent background for this universal flow of events, an unchanging subject of change, which shall bind the multiplicity into a real whole and give us a definite something to grasp and rest upon, that shall not be for ever slipping from us." We feel that the universe does present a design and so is not a brute fact or collocation of facts; otherwise, it would appear that it is ruled by blind Fate. We arrive at this catastrophic conclusion if we assume that the universe is mere flux. In such a world change itself would mean something fortuitous.

For us the Universe is the embodiment of Reason and Life is Purposive. To discern the design of Providence, the fulfilment of God. "We obtain", as Flint truly says, "a veritable increase of our knowledge of God's character and ways". We see Him manifest in the manifold things around us—in every leaf of the verdant trees, in the ceaseless roar of the waters and the sighing of the winds. In spite of the differences, that seem to loom large, there is a fundamental Unity, which is the expression of the Divine Principle—the Unity which is the spiritual meeting-place of seemingly irreconcilable ideas, the principle which is the rhythmic harmony of Life and Universe.

The aim of human effort is to completely realise this principle. We have so far only partially realised it and hence our "Divine Discontent". We seek to be perfectly in tune with the Infinite; and this is our End all through the ages. It is the same Holy Quest for Humanity in the different walks of life—a quest, ever new, yet ever old! It is the Eternal Problem; and mankind is still solving it.

---

[1] Bodin, quoted by Bury: *The Idea of Progress*, p. 39.

It is only, in the limited sense, therefore, that the problems of one generation are not those of the next. Problems change, but the "Problem" remains ever the same; or, to express it in other words, the Problem is always the same: only the methods of approach change with the course of ages. Viewed from particulars we can never understand this principle of Spiritual Unity. The chaotic mass of details fall in into their ordered spheres, when we try to grasp the nature of a thing as a whole.

In our appeal to the history of our country we have tried to comprehend the "past" in its spiritual Unity. And the spiritual unity that the history of our past presents to us "is essentially one of spiritual aspiration and obedience to the law of the Spirit, which were regarded as superior to everything else".[1] And it is this Spiritual Unity that we have been seeking all through the ages. So far it is still a unity of endeavour, but not of fulfilment. It shall be our aim in the following pages to examine the cause of failure; we shall see why we could not realise completely our purpose in the institutions of our Polity. Our study of India's past has convinced us that our ancestors tried to solve the problem of Life, by a wrong understanding of Human Values; and the End, they tried to attain was at best partially true, inasmuch as it led them into abstractions, vague and dreamy. The solution they sought in the midst of political and racial diversity was to turn away from the illusion of the phenomenal to the Reality to be realised in the "Atman". There were indeed, attempts at political and racial unification; but they were doomed to fail, as they were partial, because the attitude to life itself was partial.

Our plea in this work is for a truly synthetic outlook.

THE AGE-LONG QUEST WHICH WE PARTIALLY EMBODY IN OUR POLITY SHOULD BE SOUGHT FOR IN

---

[1] Prof. S. Dasgupta: *History of Indian Philosophy.*

LIFE AS A WHOLE AND THROUGH LIFE AS A WHOLE. IT IS BY RADICAL REVISION OF OUR TRADITIONAL ATTITUDE TO LIFE THAT WE CAN HOPE TO EXIST. OUR CONTRIBUTION TO THE PROBLEM OF THE INDIAN POLITY IS THE IDEALIST'S VISION OF LIFE.

By the appeal to History, to the Content of Life it reveals, we shall be enabled therefore to understand the ideals and aspirations of our ancients, which they tried to translate into institutional terms in their Polity. A study of political institutions by themselves will not be of great use. We shall study also the idea-systems of our people as well. After all men become what they think; and they cannot help expressing themselves, consciously or unconsciously in whatever they do. We shall, therefore, examine the End they placed before themselves constantly, the Supreme Purpose they sought to attain. We shall find that this End influenced and determined their attitude to life.

And the ancient Indian Polity we hold is the reflex of the thought and aspirations of the people. It was a concretised embodiment of their scheme of life. It admirably suited their temper; and it was the guarantee of their Social Order. It maintained and fostered the "ethos" of their culture. The religious beliefs and tenets of the times affected characteristically the nature of the State. And so long as these beliefs continue to possess the hold they have obtained on the Indian mind the Indian Polity also will continue to manifest the same general characteristics that it has possessed all through the centuries. We hold that these beliefs and conceptions are imperfect and extremely one-sided, that they will not serve us for the formulation of the ideals of life to be lived here and now, that they are non-social and "particularistic". Our problem is not merely to seek and find the best constitution and give it the sanction of Law. Simply by placing on the Statute-Book a scheme for the organisation of our Political life we will not be inaugurating a new era in our history. So long as the imperfections in our Social Order remain, so long as the intellectual life continues to be moulded by the characteristic ideas that have given it a one-sided emphasis, and so long as the spiritual effort and discipline impel man to turn away from life, Here and Now, so long, indeed, we cannot help importing into our Polity our imperfections and limitations. Merely by providing our country with an ideal constitution we do not insure its permanence. And again by giving it a constitution that shall be congruent with its religious ideas and the Social Order we shall be perpetuating those very influences that have conspired to keep the country static, non-progressive, ever feeding upon its own Past. Our Problem, therefore, is very complex and very difficult. India cannot be untrue to herself. Whatever the constitution provided for her, it must be the spiritual framework in which she could live and progress. It must be suited to her growing soul. It must seek to embody her ideals, indeed, which have for so many centuries moulded her being, giving her efforts a one-sided tendency, but the ideals re-shaped and re-formulated so as to refer to the Life, Here and Now, permeating human endeavour with a healthy influence. In other words, the age-long quest, instead of taking us on the elusive path leading us to the unknown and unknowable goal, in the distant Future, must lead us to seek for the Supreme Real in and through Life, Here and Now, as a whole, in the participation of life's experiences through sharing in the varied contacts and relationships that we form.

Our appeal to History is hence to the Content of Life it unfolds, to determine its present value in our efforts to build up the Polity of the Future.

CHAPTER II

PHILOSOPHY AND POLITY

"Every theory of the universe includes judgments on the relative values or worthlessness of objects and thereby secures an influence on our practical conduct. Every philosophical system therefore has an ethical side whether it be matured or not into a special ethical system; and it is precisely this side to which our feeling attaches so great importance that we are inclined to estimate the value of a philosophical theory of the Universe by the ethical consequences which have resulted or may be derived from it. We allow ourselves to be guided in these matters by the old adage,—"By their fruits ye shall know them." Even this saying however cannot be taken without limitations. For to continue the illustration employed by Jesus, it may happen that a tree is good and yet bears no, or no good fruit,—possibly because its blossoms are prematurely touched by the cold breath of the knowledge of the truth.

This may in fact have been the case in India. Eternal philosophical truth has seldom found more decisive and striking expression than in the doctrine of the emancipating knowledge of the Atman. And yet this knowledge might be compared to that icy-cold breath which checked every development and benumbs all life. He who knows himself as the Atman is, it is true, for ever beyond the possibility of immoral conduct, but at the same time he is deprived of every incitement to action or initiation of any kind; he is lifted out of the whole circle of illusory individual existence, his body is no longer his, his works no longer his, everything which he may henceforth do or leave undone belongs to the sphere of the great illusion, which he has penetrated, and is therefore of no account."

PAUL DEWSSEN

SECTION I—HISTORY AND PHILOSOPHY

The function of history, as we conceive it, is therefore, to examine the content of life. We have seen that life is not atomistic, in spite of appearances, but that it is purposive; that it is not a mere drift, but a striving. There is a definite tendency, underlying existence—a tendency to reach to perfection. Thus human endeavour is not ruled by mere conflict and diversity; there is a principle of unity which reveals a world of Reason. It is only a partial and sectional view that presents contradictions and inconsistencies. Thus, the materialistic view may insist upon the problem of economic existence as the motive force in history.[1] Class conflict, it will appear from such a conception, seems inevitable. Economic self-interest seems to be the sole factor in making or unmaking history. While admitting the importance of the economic motive, we would emphatically assert that to interpret life, in the ultimate, in terms of a struggle to fill empty stomachs, is dangerous. Nietzsche assumes that "all human actions and impulses are subordinate to the process of the material world that works unnoticed powerfully and irresistibly." Most of our economists would endorse his opinion; and maintain that "the ultimate cause and the great moving power of all important historic events," as Engels would put it, lies, "in the economic development of society." In the interpretation of India's past, however, we shall definitely reject the materialistic criterion, for our history discloses to us a general tendency towards spiritual ends. Life is, indeed, more than meat, and the body than raiment.

Spiritual interests have always dominated in Indian Society.[2] India has always been "A world of thinkers, a Nation of Philosophers."[3] It is only, as we have maintained, by comprehending the content of thought, by understanding the mind that recorded, that we shall be able to relate our past to our present. The content of life that our past unfolds is baffling in its variety and diversity. It is a complex phenomenon which can only be grasped by taking it in as a whole. We are perforce compelled to take refuge in philosophy which alone can lend to this

---

[1] See the works of Marx and Engels. Also the speeches of Nikolai Lenin, Trotzky, Zinovief, published by Maurice Williams in his *Social interpretation of History.*

Teggart: *The Process of History*, pp. 84-90. G. L. Dickinson: *Justice and Liberty*, p. 15.

[2] See Bishop Whitehead: *Indian Problems*, p. 3.

[3] Max Muller: *The Six Systems of Indian Philosophy*, p. 42.

world of particulars its significance, and thus would enable us to arrive at the principle of unity that will reconcile this apparently pluralistic universe. It is impossible to understand the past history and civilisation of India or the present political situation without some knowledge of the religious beliefs and customs that have so profoundly influenced the life and character of the people."[1] We shall therefore examine the philosophical tenets that were current in this country, at one time or another, to determine how far they have influenced the Polity of India. We shall, throughout bear in mind, that so far as India is concerned there was no divorce between philosophy and Religion; philosophy essentially pointed to the way of life to be lived.[2] In India, unlike other lands, philosophy was not merely an intellectual study but was something to be practised. Elsewhere, perhaps, the common rut of mankind may live on its own round of life, untouched by the doubts and fears, hopes and joys of the small groups of seekers trying to solve the problems of existence. In India, on the other hand, the tenets of the different systems of philosophy filtered slowly down to the various strata of society; and have become the general idea-content of the community at large. Sometimes, it might also be that what might have been held vaguely and loosely by the people themselves, would have been seized upon by some thinker of exceptional force, and given emphasis and definiteness. Metaphysical disputations and religious discussions have ever been the feature in India, and in a sense, the different philosophies are but streams that sprang from a common ancestral heritage, "an ancient reservoir of thought from which all

---

[1] Bishop Whitehead: *Indian Problems*, p. 3.

[2] See Lord Lytton's address to the first session of the Indian Philosophical Congress and H. H. Rajah Sir Rama Varmah's Opening address to the 4th session of the same.

could have drawn and drunk."[1] "Indian Philosophy," says Radhakrishnan, "has its interests in the haunts of men, and not in supra-lunar solitudes. It takes its origin in life, and enters back into life after passing through the schools—the Gita and the Upanishadas are not remote from popular belief. They are the great literature of the country, and at the same time vehicles of the great systems of thought. The Puranas contain the truth dressed up in myths and stories, to suit the weak understanding of the majority. The hard task of interesting the multitude in metaphysics is achieved in India."[2] That is why we seek to understand the different idea—systems of India. What was systematised in them was the common property of the masses. And their philosophic tenets have had an enormous influence on life, and especially in determining the nature of our Polity.

Very early in the development of thought in India we see it already rich and various, "unsurpassed in depth and comprehensive many-sidedness". The different currents of speculation seem to have practically exhausted all possibilities. An interesting passage in the Anugita gives us an idea of the innumerable streamlets that irrigated the expansive field of metaphysical thought. Our ancients fearlessly sought Truth and never shrank from their conclusions. In the expression of their opinions they are clear and consistent.[3] The supreme question before

---

[1] Max Muller: *Six Systems of Philosophy*, p. 8.

[2] *Indian Philosophy*, Vol. I, p. 25.

[3] See the interesting comparison between Eastern and Western thinkers by H. S. Chamberlain in *The Foundations of the Nineteenth Century*, Vol. I, pp. 48; 85-87.

Regarding the indebtedness of Greek thinkers to Indian Philosophy or vice versa, read discussions in A. B. Keith: *Samkhya System*, Ch. VI; *Religion and Philosophy of the Veda*, Ch. 29—Prof. Radhakrishnan: *Indian Philosophy*, Vol. I, pp. 23-24—Max Muller: *Six Systems*, pp. 77-78; *Selected Essays* and Garbe's Article in *Ency. of Rel. and Ethi.*

them, as before thinkers all the world over is "what is Reality?" Is this Reality a thing-in-itself, independent of knowledge, unrelated to the knowing mind, unknown and unknowable? Is our faculty of understanding competent to grasp the unconditioned, the unlimited, the Infinite? Is this Reality One or Many? If it is the One, what of the Multiplicity presented to us in the Empirical world. If the Reality be Many, is it bare plurality lacking reason? Is the comprehension of Reality by the affirmative, accumulative process of "It is this, it is this," and so ad infinitum? Or is it the negative, exclusive mode of expression "Neti, Neti"?

Western philosophers, of every school of thought, have taken kindly to the world and the Life, Here and Now. Our existence may have its imperfections and shortcomings; but on that score it was not to be rejected; it has, indeed, elements of value which cannot be ignored. Life, above all is a partnership; it is a great co-operative endeavour. It might be made richer and nobler by the sharing of experience. And it is the manifestation of the Divine. Reality could be realised in and through it. The End of Human Life could be attained through love and service, under the conditions that make this our complex earthly existence.[1]

The Indian philosophers, on the other hand, consider the world to be miserable; and anxiety and torment to be the lot of those born here. Our earthly existence seems almost a blunder. The content of men's lives was abandoned as worthless and painful. There is a universal disgust and all panted for an escape from this fleeting existence of heat and turmoil. The Spirit of India was in quest of Immortality. Sentient Life, on the other hand, was a phantasmagoria, its delusion alone being real. The

[1] It is especially in Browning that we get the best expression of this aspect of Western thought.

desire for the world is the desire for death ; why, therefore, go after that through which the Eternal Seat cannot be gained ! Thus speculation in India centred round the question, "what is Reality as apart from the false world we see around us ?" This life of our social relationships is ruled out ; by the very necessity of the Indian ideal. Sometimes the spirit may get bewildered why it gets entangled in the meshes of this false world. Is not the Soul, in itself, unaffected, as water adheres not to the leaf of a lotus-flower ? Yet, in actual life, we feel pain and misery. Is this our suffering real ? If only we could know that it is due to "Avidya", our ignorance of our real identity, we could emancipate ourselves from the endless round of births and deaths. The true knowledge of the Atman would reveal the unreality of the world ; and he who has attained to it, though alive in the world has gained Mukti.

Could we but realise what a tremendous influence this view of life must have had on the Polity evolved by our forefathers ! What sort of life did they want to live, and what was their attitude towards the world ? We shall be able, by the answers given, to understand the institutions that were a response to the complex of their ideals.

We shall, therefore, examine the different systems of philosophy in order to elucidate the attitude to life our ancients had.

SECTION II—THE PHILOSOPHY AND ETHICS OF THE VEDA

The Vedic Age was a period of incessant warfare and the Aryans had a strenuous time, fighting against the original inhabitants, or sometimes among themselves. Their foes quailed before their might and it was essentially an age of advance and expansion. The Aryans were spreading through the Punjab towards the interior to the Ganges ; their possessions were swelling with every new acquisition, and Nature was profuse in her generosity in their new habitation. They were therefore, prosperous and happy, and looked up to their gods with trust, their gods who never failed them when invoked in time of trouble. Full of the confidence that victory brings, they breathed a free spirit, of joy and contentment ; and their hymns reflect truly the spirit of their age.[1]

The Vedic gods are generally personifications of natural phenomena, Powers of Nature invested with life. Friendly forces become gods, the inimical demons. How far personal relationships were established between men and gods is very difficult for us to determine. We do have expressions of the feeling which hankers after personal touch in some of the hymns.[2] But, after all, the Vedic gods lack human touches, such as we find in the gods of the Hellenic Pantheon. If the relation between men and gods were personal, the idea of a Divine Personal Will as affecting or regulating human lives would gradually have developed an idea similar to that which the Israelites had of Jehovah.

It is very difficult to characterise the religion of these primitive times. The presence of a plurality of gods sometimes would lead us to think that Vedic religion is polytheistic. It has been variously characterised as Monotheism.[3] Henotheism[4] and so on ; but the Rig-Veda does contain germs which serve as foundations for all

---

[1] See for example, *Rig-Veda*, Book I, Hymn 130. (Griffith's Translation, Vol. I, p. 181.)

[2] See *Rig-Veda*, Book I, Hymns 1, 31 and 185.

[3] According to Dayananda Saraswati.

[4] A name coined by Max Muller, see his *Six Systems*, p. 53. Macdonell, however observes that Henotheism is only an appearance, rather than a reality, for the Vedic deities are not represented "as independent of all the rest".

the later systems of thought.[1] In the creation song,[2] the most important in the history of the philosophy of India,[3] we have already an expression of the spirit of doubt.[4] What is significant is that the Aryans, since their coming to India already manifest qualities of mind and spirit that sharply differentiate them from the rest of the peoples of the primitive world. We notice that their temperament begins to be moulded by the environment in which it finds itself. We see the beginnings of the tendency to turn away from action to a speculative bent. Scepticism, so far, is however a healthy symptom ; it expresses itself in the quest after Unity. This might have, in the course of ages, led to spiritual monotheism.[5] But as Deussen has rightly

[1] Book I, Hymn 164. In this hymn we have an idea which would lead to a monotheistic conception of God.

[2] Book X, Hymn 129.

[3] A. B. Keith: *Religion and Philosophy of the Veda*, p. 435.

[4] Max Muller is of opinion that in this hymn is embedded the thought that led to Monistic philosophy in the future. But we shall note one pleasant feature in this hymn which we shall seek for in vain in the later dogmatic statements of philosophic thought. "Its spirit of doubt", says Keith, "is wholly alien to the classical philosophical systems of India." (*Rel. and Phil. of the Veda*, p. 435). The poet honestly confesses the difficulties in the way of comprehending First Principles and Ultimate Causes and he does not make it a secret that his quest has not led to any satisfactory solution, satisfying even to himself—. It is not the confidence of certitude that we note in the Upanishads, but still the air of the genuine doubter, who seeks to comprehend the Universe, but finds that the task is beyond himself. We should not try to read into the thought of the poet more than he himself gives. And by his confession, who knows and who can declare whence this creation? Perchance even the Supreme Deity may not know !

[5] "The positive side of the tendency of the Rig-Veda", says Keith, "to dissatisfaction with the gods of tradition is to be seen in the assertion of the unity of the gods, and of the world" (*Rel. and Phil. of the Veda*, p. 434).

Prof. Radhakrishnan writes: "The gradual idealisation of the conception of God as revealed in the cult of Varuna, the logic

pointed out :[1] "In India they reached monism, though not monotheism." Other strains of thought may be discernible ; but monistic thought eclipsed all other currents. This is evidently the outcome of the emphasis of the intellect upon the emotion. The faith in Prajapati as a personal God is monotheistic, but in the increasing recognition of the ideas of Brahman and Atman lay the foundation of Monistic thought.

This search after Unity, as the correlation of recurrent natural phenomena, inherent in the nature of things, viewed as a system or order, gave birth to a conception of great consequence, that of Rta. We shall discuss this term more fully later. Here we shall only say that this Vedic Rta could well form the starting point of ethical systems based upon the view of the world as a moral order. We cannot sufficiently deplore the unhappy tendency which led to the displacement of this term Rta by two notions which have come to wield phenomenal influence in moulding the thought of India—Karma and Dharma. In the Rig-Veda, however, the ethical significance of Rta is still tribal. There is, indeed, an opposition between Rta and Anrta, but the moral element in the Vedic hymns is of small extent. Rta, as opposed to Anrta, has reference, not to Truth as identical with the "Good", but only to accuracy of statement or good faith in keeping promises.

In the Brahmana literature also, "in the strict sense of the word there is no theory of Ethics,"[2] for the question of right conduct never was interesting enough or

---

of religion which tended to make the gods flow into one another, the henotheism, the conception of Rta or the unity of nature, and the systematising impulse of the human mind all helped towards the displacement of a polytheistic anthropomorphism by a spiritual monotheism". (*Indian Philosophy*, Vol. I, p. 91.)

[1] *Outlines of Indian Philosophy*, p. 13.

[2] Keith: *Rel. and Phil. of the Veda*, pp. 468-481.

considered important enough to be the subject of philosophical speculation. The character of the gods themselves is not above blame. The conception of Truth has no moral content ; it only means, accuracy or exactitude in sacrifice, which is the reality "par excellence" for the Brahmans.

"The development which places the Brahman in the first place," writes Keith,[1] "is not achieved until the Upanishads, but it is in preparation during the period of the Brahmanas, and it is in entire harmony with this spirit that these texts do not develop any theory of morality. Indeed they do not normally inculcate morality even on merely empiric grounds." By the time we come to the late Vedic age the temper of the Aryan mind has already undergone change, and is bent towards speculation. So long as the Aryans were absorbed in a struggle for existence against the Aborigines in their new home, they could have little time for reflection. But continuous victories first brought rest and partial peace, and later the sense of complete security. Then came the time to brood over life and its mysteries, on the shortness of life, and the nature of the world and its origin. Along with the theories of cosmogony we begin to have other notions which we study in the following section ; for by the time of the Upanishads we already see Indian thought at its highest flight.

SECTION III—THE PHILOSOPHY AND ETHICS OF THE UPANISHADS

Indian thought reaches the loftiest heights in the Upanishads.[2] They have been termed the "products of the highest wisdom."[3] The various systems of Indian

[1] *Rel. and Phil. of the Veda*, p. 469.

[2] See A. B. Keith: *Religion and Philosophy of the Veda* (appendices) where he discusses Kshatriya and Dravidian influences on the Upanishads.

[3] Schopenhauer; See Max Muller, S. B. E. Vol. I, Part I, p. lxii.

Philosophy and the numerous sects that exist to-day appeal to these treatises as infallible.[1] They are guesses at truth and are not systematic philosophy.[2] It is not impossible, however, to arrive at the leading ideas expressed in them, though still in the germ.[3] In the Vedas the centre of interest was in the outward fact; the Reality was sought in the objective Universe. But already we find new developments in the Brahmanas and more especially in the Aranyakas. In the Upanishads the centre of interest is shifted to the realm of the innermost recesses of the Atman; it is felt to be futile to search for the Supreme in something outside of us. The quest after the Real leads away from the objective to the subjective, to the Self of man, not the empirical self, but the higher Self which is identical with the Real. The aim of inquiry is to understand the Self which is "free from sin, free from old age, from death and grief, from hunger and thirst."[4] This body being mortal, is always held by death. The Self is subject to pleasure and pain so long as it resides in the body. The pleasures of life are transient. Wealth cannot purchase happiness and by its delusion men perish.[5] It is difficult for the rich to prefer the good. By following after outward pleasures we fall into the snare of wide-spread death.[6] They only chain us and turn us away from our End. Short is the span of life of the

---

[1] See Radhakrishnan: *Philosophy of the Upanishads*, p. 14.

[2] See Keith: *Rel. and Phil. of the Veda*, pp. 497-498.

[3] We should not try to interpret the thought of the Upanishads by any single theory. Different strains of thought seem to be present, of Pantheism, Cosmogonism, even theism too. If in this brief review we happen to give pre-eminent notice to the doctrines of Yajnavalkya, it is only because of their great influence in after times.

[4] *Chand Upa.*, viii, 7-12.

[5] *Katha Upa.*, I. 2, 1-6.

[6] *Ibid.*, II, 4. 2.

mortal who slowly decays here below.[1] Sons, grandsons, maidens and music, our possessions, "only last till to-morrow". The Eternal can never be attained by the transient. Living long in ignorance we imagine ourselves, to be happy.[2] Ceremonial observances, the performance of sacrifices, will never lead to the imperishable. Foolish people trusting to them, to such "frail boats", are subject again and again to old age and death. Man becomes good by good work, says Yajnavalkya,[3] and bad by bad work. According as he acts and according as he behaves, so will he be. And according as his desires are, so is his will; and as is his will so is his deed; and whatever deed he does that he will reap. "To whatever object a man's own mind is attached, to that he goes strenuously together with his deed; and having obtained the end (the last results) of whatever deed he does here on earth, he returns again from that world (which is the temporary reward of his deed) to this world of action."[4] Yajnavalkya, thus asserts the doctrine of Transmigration as a moral truth.[5] We find the idea further developed elsewhere.[6] We have in the Chandogya Upanishad that "Those whose conduct has been good, will quickly attain some good birth, the birth of a brahmana, or a kshatriya, or a vaishya. But those whose conduct has been evil will quickly attain an evil birth, the birth of a dog, or a hog, or a chandala."[7] Thus we find that a man is a creature of will. According to what his will is in this world,

---

[1] *Ibid.*, I. I. 23-29.
[2] *Munda Upa.*, I. 2. 9.
[3] *Brihad Upa.*, III. 2,13.
[4] *Ibid.*, iv. 4. 2-6.
[5] See Keith: *The Samkhya System*, p. 17.
[6] *Brihad Upa.*, vi, 2.
[7] *Chand Upa.*, v. 10; cf. *Aitereya-Aranyaka*, II, 1-4, *Katha* II, Adhyaya 5, 6-7.

so will he be when he has departed this life.[1] This world in which we live is the place for the performance of Karma. Kama is the basis for Karma ; and Kama is the cause of re-birth. "He who forms desires in his mind is born again through his desires here and there."[2] The desire for sons is the desire for wealth, and the desire for wealth is the desire for worlds.[3] Full of desires and overcome by the fruits of what he has done, he enters on a good or bad birth. Fools living in darkness, we go round and round, staggering to and fro. Having no understanding, and unmindful, we are like blind men led by the blind ; thus we enter the round of births. And being born we become united with all evils.[4] Man thinks that his highest blessing is to be wealthy, lord of others, and surrounded by all human enjoyments. He desires women who excite the fire of love. He is led away by the delusion that wife, sons and wealth are dear in themselves. He does not realise that in this world he is "like a frog in a dry well".[5] He attaches himself to the pleasures of the world, to the delights of the body, not knowing that fed on them he is "seen to return (to this world) again and again."[6] What, indeed, is the use of physical enjoyments! Even if man gains the whole world with all its wealth there is yet no hope of immortality.[7] He must, therefore, not be attached to that by which he cannot become immortal. He must not care for this body—this offensive, pithless body, a mere mass of bones, skin, sinews, marrow, flesh, seed, blood, mucus, tears, phlegm,

---

[1] *Chand Upa.*, III. 14.
[2] *Mundaka*, III. 2. 2.
[3] *Brihad Upa.*, III. 5,1
[4] *Ibid.*, IV. 3. 8.
[5] *Maitrayana*, I. Prapatika, 4.
[6] *Ibid.*, I. 4.
[7] *Brihad Upa.*, IV. 5. The dialogue between Yajnavalkya and Maitreyi.

ordure, water, bile slime.[1] He must give up the worldly life, the state of the householder and take to the forest, to the life of the mendicant. The man who understands His Self can never wish or desire that he should pine after the body.[2] He will never wish for offspring, for as a mendicant he would leave home and wander about. Even the performance of good works will not lead us to the higher knowledge by which the indestructible is apprehended; for, after the reward reaped by good work is enjoyed we enter again this world or a lower one.[3] "But those who practise penance and faith in the forest, tranquil, wise and living on alms, through right knowledge and abstinence, these spotless anchorites gain the self, the Immortal Person.[4] Through cessation of all desires and severance of all ties of the heart here on earth is immortality gained.[5] The body is only the cart for the intelligent driver, the Self; and is cast away as the slough of a snake on an ant-hill.[6] The Self stands above like a passionless ascetic amid the objects of the world.[7] The man, therefore, who does not desire, and not desiring is freed from all desires, or desires the Self only, "being Brahman goes to Brahman, as his vital parts do not depart elsewhere.[8] Desires are destroyed by the right knowledge of the Self, the knowledge of the real identity of the individual Self with the Supreme Self.[9] It is only

---

[1] *Maitrayana*, 1-3; see also III. 4.

[2] *Brihad Upa.*, Upa., IV. 4. 12.

[3] *Mundak*, 1. 2. 10.

[4] *Ibid.*, 1. 2. 11; and III, 1. 5.

[5] *Katha Upa.*, 11. 6. Valli, 14-15. See also *Brihad Upa.*, IV. 4. 7.

[6] *Brihad Upa.*, IV. 4. 7. See also *Maitraya*, Second Prapatika, 4. 3.

[7] *Maitraya*, Second Prapatika, 4.

[8] *Brihad Upa.*, IV. 4. 6.

[9] "In the philosophy of Yajnavalkya the identity of the Supreme and the individual souls is carried to the extreme extent

when there is, as it were, duality that one sees the other, smells, tastes, touches, salutes, and knows the other; but when the Self only is all this how should he see, smell or know another? How should he know Him by whom he knows all this? The Atman, the knowing Self within us, can never itself become object for us, and is therefore itself unknowable. He can only be described negatively by "neti, neti".[1] He is incomprehensible, imperishable, unattached, unfettered. He alone is the real, the one without a second.[2] This Universe is only Appearance; or may be it might even be illusion.[3] We must pierce through it if we wish for immortality; and see the Self behind.[4] Empiric Reality is only the self-illusion of the Brahman. The Svetaswatara Upanishad has it: "Know then Prakriti (nature) is Maya and the

---

but at the same time the soul is deprived of any distinct meaning. The identity of the Soul of man and the absolute is due to the mere fact that, by reducing the soul to nothing save what may be termed the mere abstraction of subjectivity, or of the transcendental unity of apperception, the soul becomes nothing but an aspect of process"—A. B. Keith: *Rel. and Phil. of the Veda*, p. 551 ff.

[1] *Brihad Upa.*, IV. 5. 15. cf. III 7. Brahmana.

This means that Thought is incompetent to know Reality. The Absolute is unknowable, and cannot be defined by empirical predicates. We shall discuss later the question of the adequacy of Thought. Here we would like to point out that what Yajnavalkya is committing himself to is to the position that the existence of the Absolute "is a transcendental reality, which is essentially from the empirical point of view a nonentity."

[2] *Ibid.*, IV. 3. 23.

[3] To say that the Universe is Appearance is not to say that it is illusion. The one view may lead to Pantheism, and the other to Monism. So far as the Svetaswatara is concerned we do definitely get the idea of delusion or illusion. But we do not know how to define the position of Yajnavalkya with regard to Empiric Reality. He leaves us vague. It would be safe to assume that in his exposition, too, we have "the germ of the illusion theory."

[4] *Katha Upa.*, Second Adhyaya, Fourth Valli, 1.

great lord the Mayin; the whole world is filled with what are his members." This world, in other words, is not beside the Brahman,[1] for it is in Him that all come together, and it is in Him that all rest.[2] The objects and relations of the world are real, not in themselves, but in so far as they are our Self. If we know the Self, indeed, we know the whole Universe, for as Yajnavalkya tells Maitrayi, the Self is to be seen, to be heard, to be perceived, and to be marked, and "when the self has been seen, heard, perceived and known, then all this is known".[3] Therefore the Supreme Reality is to be sought for in the Self; self knowledge is the highest knowledge. Just as the sounds of a drum or a conch-shell or a lute cannot be seized externally, but the sound is seized when the drum, or conch-shell or lute is seized; in the same way this world, the other world, and all creatures can be known only by him who knows the Atman. And just as the sound of a drum or a conch-shell has no existence in itself, this world has no existence of its own. "As a mass of salt has neither inside nor outside, but is altogether a mass of taste, thus indeed, has that Self neither inside nor outside but is altogether a mass of knowledge".[4] As the flowing rivers disappear in the sea,[5] losing their name and their form, thus a wise man, freed from name and form goes to the divine "Person who is greater than the great".[6] The infinite alone is bliss and not the finite,[7] and it rests in its own greatness. It is immortal. "The knowing (Self) is not born, it dies not; it sprang from nothing, nothing sprang from it, the Ancient is unborn,

[1] See Dasgupta: *Hist. of Ind. Phil.*, p. 51.
[2] *Brihad Upa.*, II. 5. 15.
[3] *Ibid.*, IV. 5. 6. cf. *Mundaka Upa.*, 1. 1. 6. *Katha Upa.*, 1. 3. 15.
[4] cf. *Chand Upa.*, VI. 1 khanda.
[5] *Ibid.*, VI. 10. 1.
[6] *Mundaka Upa.*, III. 2. 8.
[7] *Chand Upa.*, VII, 23, 1.

eternal, everlasting; He is not killed, though the body is killed".[1] The Self is smaller than the small, and greater than the great. He who knows the Self truly passes over death; there is no other path to go.[2]

In the philosophy of the Upanishads, so briefly discussed above, with its attitude to life, let us see if we could get at any maxims that would help us to regulate our behaviour as members of the human society. In other words, what is the ethical content. This content, we agree with Keith in asserting, is "negligible and valueless"; for, as he says: "the total impression conveyed by the Upanishads is that of intellectual exercise, whose aim was the attainment, partly of immediate goods, normally the happiness of heaven which was often materially enough conceived, and there is made no attempt to make the theoretical philosophy a ground of morality of any sort. There are here and there, moral maxims enunciated, but these are of no consequence, and rise in no way above popular morality".[3] In the metaphysics of the Upani-

---

[1] *Katha Upa.*, 1. Adh. 2. Valli 18.

[2] *Svetha Upa.*, VI. 15.

"The attainment of emancipation by this knowledge", writes A. B. Keith, "which gives it and is it, results in the immediate cessation of every motion: how can man desire anything who knows himself to be all? How can he fear when there is no other? There can be no sorrow for him, nor pain: he is like a blind man who has gained his sight, a wounded man healed, a sick man made whole. All his works are annihilated, as they have meaning only for an individuality. Future works have no effect upon him, but evil he cannot wish to do, since he has no desires; he may, if he cares, live on for the full length of life or do any action so long as he does it disinterestedly a view which the Isa Upanishad offers, despite its paradoxical appearance, doubtless as a sop to those who did not wish to be denied the position of emancipation, but preferred also to enjoy the things of life. He cannot ever feel any doubt; he has the full and abiding knowledge for all time"—A. B. Keith: *Phil. and Rel. of the Veda*, p. 582-583.

[3] *Ibid.*, p. 584.

shads there is no possibility to conceive of moral ideas, for action and behaviour, having reference as they do to empirical existence, are simply transcended. As Deussen remarks, when "the knowledge of the Atman has been gained, every action and therefore every moral action also has been deprived of meaning".[1] If we critically study the ethical thought of the Upanishads, we are perforce, further, driven to the conclusion that "Truth" has no moral content as yet ; it begins to have metaphysical significance, as opposed to the Unreal.[2] The crucial test, as we believe it ought to be, of the value of ethical moral conceptions is that much value is to be assigned according as the content of human life is conceived. And here we are not left in doubt. We might not trace the extreme pessimism of later times in the Upanishads. But if life is not looked upon as all misery, it is equally certain that life itself is not given much worth. The true ideal is that of Renunciation, of turning away from the world. The quest after Reality, as we have seen, takes one away from the empirical world, where man forms relationships, of husband and wife, father and child, etc., to an unnatural effort of trying to grasp the Monadic Atman, which in its very nature is unknown and unknowable. Hence we will be justified in holding that neither the philosophy nor the ethics of the Upanishads can serve as adequate foundations for true social morality ; and so the End of life presented therein can never guide us in formulating the ideals of human progress. "From the point of view of ethics," Keith truly says, "the demerits of the system of the Upanishads are even more glaring than from the point of view of the intellect. It is doubtless impossible to arrive at certainty on questions of the ultimate nature of Reality,

---

[1] *Philosophy of the Upanishads*, p. 362.

[2] cf. Radhakrishnan who, however says that "Morality, according to the Upanishads expresses the true nature of things". *Indian Philosophy*, Vol. I, p. 243.

but it is an easier matter to establish some principles of moral obligation, and to bring them into harmony with a scheme of the Universe which if theoretical shall none the less be at any rate plausible. The defect of the Upanishads is that they render morality in the ultimate issue valueless and meaningless. We may reasonably assume that any complete metaphysic must seek to explain as essential ingredients of existence, truth, goodness, and beauty, and we may safely conclude that a system, which, like that of the Upanishads, regards beauty and goodness as nothing but hollow mockeries, is defective and essentially unsound in its theoretic bases"[1] And so in the theory of the Absolute of the Upanishads, there is no place for moral life; neither is there scope for political life. If the Absolute could be known and realised, Here and Now, through all the complex relationships that constitute earthly life, then Life itself would become a great co-operative and corporate Quest. Moral and political aspects, as much as the purely religious or theological, would attain the necessary dignity and importance for arousing the curiosity of thinkers to make them subjects of study. Furthermore, the Absolute, instead of being conceived without content, would include as its ingredients all these things that make life what it is; man could realise God even being man. We are reminded of the famous verse—

"Let us not always say,
"Spite of this flesh to-day,
"I strove, made head, gained ground upon the Whole!"
"As the bird wings and sings,
"Let us cry, 'All good things
"Are ours, nor soul helps flesh more now, than flesh helps soul!"[2]

---

[1] *Rel. and Phil. of the Veda*, p. 596.
[2] Browning: *Rabbi Ben Ezra.*

SECTION IV—THE PHILOSOPHY AND ETHICS OF THE SANKHYA SYSTEM

The Sankhya[1] is a Realistic doctrine[2] since it postulates that Purusha, the multitude of souls, are independent beings. We are presented with a dualism[3] between Prakriti or Pradhana, (also called Mula Prakriti—Primal Nature or Primordian Matter) and Purusha. There can be no possibility of mediation between them, although the Sankhya Karika asserts that, for the soul's contemplation of Nature and for its abstraction, the union of both takes place, as of the lame and the blind. By this "union" creation is framed.[4] The Spirit cannot act being removed from all action.[5] Nature is active[6] but unconscious. The riddle of the world which the Sankhya Philosophy has to solve, as Max Muller points out,[7] would then be no more than to account for the mistaken interest which the Self takes in the sensuously perceiving and perceived world. Prakriti is as real as the soul. The soul is eternally unchangeable,[8] while Matter is eternally subject to change. Creation results in the temporary union between the two. This union is said to arise from want of discrimination, Aviveka, and cannot therefore be real union, as it dis-

---

[1] See the definition of Sankhya given by Aurobindo Ghose: *Essays on the Gita*, Vol. I, p. 100.

[2] See *Indian Philosophy* of Radhakrishnan, Vol. II, pp. 303-307.

[3] Aurobindo Ghose, *Essays on the Gita*, Vol. I, p. 100-115.
See Garbe's Article: *Ency. of Rel. and Eth.*, Vol. II.
cf. *Sankhya Aphorisms*, Book I, Nos. 66-67.

[4] *Sankhya Karika*, 21.

[5] cf. *Sankhya Aphorisms*, Book I, Nph. 160-164.

[6] *Ibid.*, Book II, Nos. 1-11.

[7] *Six Systems*, p. 385-386.

[8] See Garbe's Article in *Ency. Rel. and Eth.*

appears again by discriminative knowledge (Viveka).[1] The unfolding of the misery of the world is necessary for the salvation of the Purusha. The Sankhya-Pravachana-Bhashya begins by defining its end to be the prevention of pain[2]—"Atha trividha-Dukha-'tyanta-vivrithi Atyanta-Purusartah".[3] It is self evident that the world is a condition of misery. Pain is of the very essence of bodily existence.[4] The wise man must therefore seek release from this bondage,[5] and the Sankhya aims at setting man free from the sufferings of earthly existence. The root of all evil is the want of "discrimination", and the only means of deliverance is thus the discriminative knowledge of perceptible Principles and of the imperceptible One of the thinking Soul.[6] The sentient soul experiences pain, arising from decay and death, until it is released from its person. It passes through innumerable transmigrations[7] until finally liberated. "By virtue is ascent above; by vice descent to a region below; by

---

[1] cf. The Vedanta Doctrine of Maya.

Vijnanabhikshu tries to identify the Upanishad doctrine of the illusory nature of the reality of Matter (prakriti) by an appeal to what he calls "Original Vedanta". Garbe observes that this would be mixing up many heterogeneous matters and that Vijnanabhikshu quite effaces the individuality of the several Philosophical systems.

See also Keith: *The Sankhya system*, pp. 88-100.

Max Muller: *Six Systems*, p. 378-9.

[2] The three sorts of pain are (1) evil proceeding from self, (2) evil arising from external beings, and (3) evil arising from Divine causes.

[3] *The Sankhya-Pravachana-Bhashya*, edited by R. Garbe, p. 5.

[4] *Sankhya Karika*, 55.

[5] This release is only phenomenal, since bondage does not belong to Purusha—See Radhakrishnan, *Ind. Phil.*, Vol. II, p. 311-314.

[6] *Sankhya Karika*, 1-2; cf. *Sankhya Aphorisms*, Bk. III, No. 75. Bk. I, Nos. 56-57.

[7] See Keith's *Sankhya System*, pp. 17-18.

knowledge is deliverance, by the reverse bondage".[1] By dissipation is absorption into Nature, by foul passion, transmigration; by power unimpediment; by the reverse the contrary.[2] The Spirit is compelled to wander from birth to birth so long as true knowledge, the knowledge that Spirit and Nature are really distinct is not attained.[3] And in its progress through various births, the Spirit with the psychic apparatus,[4] the Linga, gathers portions from the gross elements described as born of father and mother in order to assume a physical body. "The issue from father and mother are perishable".[5] The deliverance of each soul respectively is performed by the evolution of Nature. As a dancer having exhibited herself to the Spectator, desists from the dance, so does Nature desist, having manifested herself to soul.[6] Having succeeded at last in her object, like a shy girl in 'deshabille,' "once having been seen, she does not again expose Herself to the gaze of the Soul."[7] We thus see that it is not the soul itself that is bound,[8] is released or migrates,[9] but that nature alone, in relation to various beings, is bound, is released or migrates.[10] By seven modes Nature binds Herself by Herself; by one She releases Herself for the Soul's wish.[10] Through the study of Principles, the con-

[1] *Sankhya Karika*, 44.
[2] *Ibid.*, 45.
[3] See R. Garbe: *Art Ency. Rel. and Eth.*
[4] See A. B. Keith: *Rel. and Phil. of the Veda*, p. 533.
[5] *Sankhya Karika*, 39.
[6] *Ibid.*, 59.
cf. *Sankhya Aphorisms*, Bk. III, 69.
[7] *Sankhya Karika*, 61.
cf. *Sankhya Aphorisms*, Bk. III, 70.
[8] cf. *Sankhya Aphorisms*, Bk. III, 6.
[9] cf. *Ibid.*, Bk. I, 106-107.
[10] *Sankhya Karika*, 62.
Sankhya Aphorisms, Bk. III, Nos. 71-72.
See A. B. Keith, *Rel. and Phil. of the Veda*, pp. 533-534.

clusive incontrovertible, one only knowledge is attained that,—Neither I am, Nor is ought mine, Nor do I exist.[1] Possessed of Self-knowledge the soul contemplates at leisure and at ease Nature, thereby debarred from prolific change, and consequently precluded from the seven forms.[2] He desists because He has seen her. She does so because She has been seen. In their union there is no motive for Creation.[3] By attainment of Perfect knowledge, virtue and the rest becomes ceaseless. Yet the Soul remains awhile invested with body as the potter's wheel continues whirling from the effect of the impulse previously given to it.[4] When the separation of the Informal Soul from its corporeal frame at length takes place, and Nature in respect of it ceases, then is Absolute and Final Deliverance accomplished.[5] There is thus only one means by which Nature can succeed in freeing spirit from fancied dependence on her, though she makes efforts in diverse ways : of the eight psychic states which are seen in intellect seven merely keep fast in its bonds ; with the eighth, knowledge, however, release is achieved. Complete release we find is the condition of complete isolation of the spirit which is unending and free from any other characteristic.[6] "The Soul, therefore, abides eternally released from the delusion and sufferings of this world, as a Seer who no longer sees anything, a glass in which nothing is any longer reflected, as pure untroubled light by which nothing is illuminated."[7]

"The whole theory," as Keith observes, "is one mass

---

[1] *Sankhya Karika*, 64.
[2] *Ibid.*, 65.
[3] *Ibid.*, 66.
cf. *Sankhya Aphorisms*, Bk. III, Nos. 63-64.
[4] *Sankhya Karika*, 67.
[5] *Ibid.*, 68.
[6] cf. *Sankhya Aphorisms*, Bk. III, No. 65.
[7] See Oldenberg : *Buddha.*

of difficult paradoxes, despite its seeming elegance and simplicity of structure."[1] Final emancipation, as we have seen, is the knowledge of the freedom of the spirit from all individuality and consciousness. The individual souls to be liberated, "have nothing true about them save their subjectivity, a subjectivity which has no creative power and is not properly realised at all by having an objective content. On the contrary, it is only by error that the soul is in any way connected with the existing world, through its fancied connection with Prakriti, "nature."[2] In a philosophy of the kind there can be no grounds for religious belief or ethical ideals. Even the vague merging of individuality in an Unknown Absolute that we note as the goal in other schools of thought is absent here, for the aim is not union with the Absolute but isolation from Prakriti. Indeed the idea of the Absolute is entirely discarded. "The existence of God is not proven", says the Sankhya.[3] This almost amounts to the denial of God. "The traditional Samkhya," says Arobindo Ghose, "is to use our modern distinctions, atheistic."[4] Vijnanabhikshu, however tries to expunge atheism from this system, but he does so, says Garbe only by the strangest means. Garbe maintains that "Kapila not only rejected the Brahman, the All-Soul, but emphatically denied the existence of God."[5] Max Muller, on the other hand, asks us to mark Kapila's impartiality and the entire absence, in the whole of his philosophy, of anything like animus against a belief in God. He nowhere puts himself in a hostile attitude towards the Divine Ideal. "He simply says—and in that respect he does not differ much from

---

[1] *Religion and Philosophy of the Veda*, p. 533.

[2] *Ibid.*

[3] See *Sankhya Aphorisms*, Bk. I, 92-96; Bk. V, 10-12. Bk. VI, 2.

[4] *Essays on the Gita*, Vol. I, pp. 97-98.

[5] *The Sankhya-Pravachana-Bhashya*, Preface.

Kant—that there are no logical proofs to establish that existence, but neither does he offer any such proofs for denying it." This apology only strengthens our contention. A living faith must be based upon a reasoned Belief in the existence of God. A philosophy that seeks to discuss ultimate issues, indifferent, we might almost add sceptical, about the existence of the Almighty, is under the grave danger of degenerating into Materialism. Any disbelief, indifference, or vague uncertainty about the existence of God cannot but result in Materialism, at least so far as the Empirical life is concerned. Prof. Jacobi, indeed sees, in the Sankhya a philosophy based on Materialism. Garbe sees its origin in a reaction against the idealistic monism of the Upanishads. Both the opinions are a little over-stated. But, as Keith has said, it is clear that, "the Sankhya cannot be derived from materialism pure and simple ; it must be taken from Materialism supplemented by a belief in spirit."[1]

SECTION V—BUDDHIST PHILOSOPHY AND ETHICS

The Philosophy of life inculcated by the Buddha is very simple. "One thing only do I teach", he said, "Sorrow and the uprooting of sorrow."[2] He appeared at a time when the foundations of the ancient faith were being undermined. There was a spirit of unrest and religious belief presented a congeries of discordant systems. Life had become intolerable in the priest-ridden land, encircled by Brahmanism, harassed by the ties of ritual, sect and dogma. Buddha delivered the people from this thraldom,[3] and established the kingdom of the Norm.[4] He

[1] *The Sankhya System*, p. 22.
[2] cf. *Challavagga*, IX, 1. 4.
[3] This is the constant note in the songs of the theras.
[4] cf. *Theragatha*, 818-835.

broke the trammels that bound freedom of thought and action. And beginning as the reformer of the old, Gautama nevertheless is said to have founded a new religion.[1] It was Brahmanical speculation which, of course, prepared the way for the rise of Buddhism. On the old foundations Buddha raised the new superstructure.[2] He shared in common with other Hindu Philosophers the heritage of the spiritual ideas of transmigration[3] and belief in Karma.[4] It was his aim to provide the way of deliverance from the frightful round of existences. He would not allow himself to be drawn into metaphysical discussions about the Universal Self or the infinity of the world.[5] "Sadasad Vikaram na sahate", was his only reply. His philosophy was intensely practical. Oldenberg truly remarks that Buddhism "does not purport to be a philosophy which inquires into the ultimate ground of things; unfolds to thought the breadths and depths of the Universe. It addresses itself to man plunged in sorrow, and while it teaches him to understand his sorrow, it shows him the way to exterminate it, root and all".[6] Buddha's practical aim was to provide the way of escape from impermanence, suffering and unreality. "All is transitory, all is misery,

---

[1] The Buddah himself was not conscious of establishing a new religion. See Prof. Rhys Davids: *Buddhism*, pp. 83-84; and Prof. Radhakrishnan's article in the *Mind* of April 1926.

[2] See Mrs. Rhys Davids: *Buddhism*, p. 31; Max Muller: *Selected Essays*, Vol. 2, pp. 214-215; Prof. Radhakrishnan's article in the *Mind* as already cited, and his *Ind. Phil.*, Vol. I, p. 361; A. B. Keith: *Buddhist Philosophy*, p. 63 ff and *Rel. and Phil. of the Veda*, p. 535 ff.

[3] See *Theragatha*, 17.

[4] See *Vasetta Sutta*; *Anguttara Nikaya* II, 33; and Dr. W. M. McGovern: *Buddhist Philosophy*, p. 165.

[5] See *Buddhism in Translations*, Warren, pp. 111-116. Also *Ten Indeterminates*, Dialogues translated by Mrs. Rhys Davids.

[6] *Buddha*, pp. 204-205.

all is void, all is without substance."[1] Hence he would concern himself only with the world he knew. His observation revealed to him that it was in a state of perpetual change,[2] of growth, decay and dissolution. This view of the Empirical life is that which the sages of the Upanishads had also emphasised. The transience and unsubstantiality of the phenomenal world is the constant theme of Indian thought. But what is more peculiarly the special feature of Buddhist tenets is the complete absence of any Reality as such. We have seen how the Upanishads cling tenaciously to the reality of the One Absolute, though depreciating everything else. The Sankhya frankly refuses to take into consideration the Absolute ; but postulates the reality of a multitude of individual subjects, Purusha. When we come to Buddhist thought, if not of Buddha, at any rate of his later followers, there is no reality at all ; the absolute is ignored, the individual soul too is ignored. Nothing is permanent or self-existing. Everything is flux, a continuous flow, nisatta or non-entity, nijjiva or soullessness.[3] The world is a dream and maya. It is only by a process of constructing that the intellect seems to perceive objects.[4] Is there a perceiver and something perceived? Have outward facts an inner validity, relating to our ideas to which they correspond? The gist of the Pragna-Paramita is that what is to be known has no more real existence than he who has to know ; this is the highest wisdom. But as Burnouf points out, this extreme view would never have served as the basis of a popular religion. 'In the sutras the reality of the objective world is denied ; the reality of form is denied ; the reality of the individual or the "I" is equally denied. But the existence of a subject, of something like

[1] cf. *Theragatha*, 676; also 678.
[2] cf. *Ibid.*, 145.
[3] Prof. Radhakrishnan: *Indian Philosophy*, Vol. I, p. 380.
[4] See Dasgupta: *His. of Ind. Phil.*, Vol. I, pp. 148-150.

a Purusha, the thinking substance of the Sankhya philosophy is spared. Something at least exists with respect to which everything else may be said not to exist.'[1] But this something is itself the ephemeral product of various causes and conditions.[2] All that is, is Dhamma, or grouping of conditions. The Universe is Dhamma, and the individual, too, is Dhamma. Although separate, these elements or groupings of Dhamma are independent, linked together by the Law of Causation. As everything is ruled by the Law of Causation, everything again is subject to the Law of Destruction. All sentient existence is under the inexorable Law of Death.[3] The Dhammapada asks us to look upon the world as a bubble and a mirage.[4] The human body is to be regarded as froth, knowing it as a mirage.[5] It is an empty fleeting frame.[6] And this body,[7] as all corporeal things, being material, contain within itself, the germs of dissolution. And in all inheres suffering;[8] what is changing, is inconstant, is sorrow. Life is evil, because misery, sorrow, and pain are inseparable from all modes of existence.[9] Even pleasure turns out to be pain.[10] All this world's desires are,

---

[1] Quoted by Max Muller: *Selected Essays.*
cf. Poussin: *The way to Nirvana*, pp. 43-44.

[2] See *Tika Nipata* 61. P. T. S. ed. Vol. I, p. 173.

[3] cf. *Theragatha*, 448; see also Nos. 151, 776, 793.

[4] *Dhammapada*, 170; see also *Theragatha*, No. 717; *Buddhist Legends*, Part 3, Bk. 13, story 3.

[5] *Ibid.*, 46.

[6] cf. *Visuddhi Magga*, Ch. I.

[7] See the descriptions of the body in *Milinda Panha*, 73.
Theragatha, 393-398; 567-576.
Siksha Samucchaya, trans. by Bendall, p. 85.

[8] See the Buddha's First Sermon at Benares; *Vinaya, Maha Vagga*, i. 6. 17-22.

[9] cf. *Theragatha*, 677.

[10] cf. *Visuddhi Magga*, xvii.

therefore, transient.[1] All created things perish;[2] all created things are full of sorrow;[3] all forms are unreal.[4] Clinging to family life is, therefore, evil.[5] Each succeeding birth is "a prison full of untold misery".[6] And in despondent moods is the question asked: "Is life worth living?"[7] The remedy appears to turn away from it. The wearied Soul craves for eternal rest.[8] How then to find this way of escape or deliverance? It is necessary for this to go back to the origin of suffering. Decay and death (jara and marana) presuppose birth (jati). The present life has a previous life. The theory of Re-birth is accepted by Buddha as a fact. Taking it for granted, he asks: "what causes birth?" He answers "It is craving that leads to re-birth;[9] craving for sensual pleasures, craving for existence, craving for wealth."[10] The mission of Buddha was to emancipate mankind from the beginningless[11] round of existences. The motive of religious life is to seek Nirvana from the jungle or ocean of the frightful round of existences. Since craving is the cause of birth, and birth is suffering, suffering will cease when craving ceases.[12] The path to Nirvana lies through detachment from the things of this world. It is the path which leads to

---

[1] See *Theragatha*, 187-188; 1159-1161.

[2] *Dhammapada*, 277.

[3] *Ibid.*, 278.

[4] *Ibid.*, 279.

[5] See *Theragatha*, 72, 43, 57, 149-105, 107, also *Siksha Samucchaya*, p. 83.

[6] See the introduction to the Jataka Book.

[7] Buddhism is extremely pessimistic so far as its attitude to life, Here and Now is concerned. But with regard to Hereafter, it is maintained that it is optimistic enough. cf. *Theragatha*, 46-59; *Dhammapada*, 373; 197-200.

[8] Oldenberg: *Buddha*, p. 220.

[9] cf. *Theragatha*, 339; 183-184.

[10] *Mahavagga*, i. 6. 17-22.

[11] *Samyutta*, xv.

[12] *Mahavagga*, i. 6. 17-22. cf. *Dhammapada*, 283.

"the life that lay beyond the walls and bonds of household life."[1] Lacking spiritual health we cling to wife and children.[2] To live the other life we must go forth from home into the homeless life.[3] We must relinquish the sickle and the plough,[4] for the man who has eyes to see will not abide "where ought may hinder the quest supreme."[5] He will seek the lonely spot, "far away where noise scarce comes, the haunt of creatures of the wild,"[6] "to lead the life the Buddha praised".[7] Even the companionship of human beings must be avoided.[8] The seekers after Nirvana must dwell, each by himself, in the forest "like logs rejected by the woodman's craft."[9] And there in profound solitude, with zeal and ardour, should the recluse practice meditation to destroy craving which is the cause of birth and suffering. He must practise, "the road called straight", for, "straight is the name that way is called",[10] the Noble Eightfold Path,[11] whereby we may reach salvation. Extremes in religious life must be avoided.[12] The Middle Way leads to Nirvana,

---

[1] *Theragatha*, 107.
[2] *Ibid.*, 188; see also 72, 453-458.
[3] *Ibid.*, 73; also 46, 57, 135-136.
[4] *Ibid.*, 43.
[5] *Ibid.*, 105.
[6] *Ibid.*, 577.
[7] *Vinaya Texts*, ii, 312, 313.
cf. *Bud. Suttas*, p. 210, ff.
Sutta Nipata, verses, 34; 74.
Siksha Samucchaya, ch. xi.
[8] *Theragatha*, 1051.
[9] *Ibid.*, 62; also 245.
[10] Sam, i. 14; *Sisters Verse*, 361.
[11] To wit: Right Faith, Right Resolve, Right Speech, Right Action, Right Living, Right Effort, Right Thought, Right Self-Concentration.
[12] See the story of Jambuka, *Theragatha*, 283-286. cf. *Dhammapada*, 141.

the sacred Eightfold Path,[1] as it is called. The seeker after salvation must first accept the Four Noble Truths, and must observe the moral precepts in thought, word, and deed. Then through meditation he becomes an Arhat and obtains knowledge. Desire is destroyed by Sila, Samadhi and Panna. Panna is right knowledge of the Four Noble Truths. It is Avijja or ignorance which is the cause for the desire for existence.[2] This Avijja is due to the Asavas or depravities, of Kamasava, Bhavasava, Dittasava, and Avijjasava. These depravities or Asavas result in our Kilesas lobha, dosa, moha, mama, dittihi, Vicikichha, thina, udhacca, ahivika, anottapa. These kilesas and asavas must be destroyed in order to dispel Avijja or ignorance. The practice of Silam removes kilesas. Samadhi is the next stage which destroys the old roots of the old kilesas and removes Tanha or desire. By Panna the seeker after salvation attains Arhathood, "distaste, indifference, the mind possessed." Thus there are different stages through which the seeker has to pass and we find that the faith and practice of Buddhism have much in common with the other systems of Indian Philosophy. At last, as the natural result of the destruction of desires, the Arhat obtains final extinction of sorrow or Nirvana, the Summum Bonum, the Deliverance from the Round of Existence, the final Release from the flux of re-birth and mortality.

This is the philosophy of Buddha. It appealed, however, to the millions as a moral and religious ideal, not as a system of philosophy.[3] This is not the place to enter into a discussion of Buddhism as a movement of social reform ; we only wish to emphatically point out that Bud-

---

[1] *Theragatha*, 47-422.

[2] See Oldenberg: *Buddha*, pp. 237-241.

[3] The aim of Buddha was eminently of a practical nature.

dha was never a social reformer[1] and that Buddhism was never a social heresy. In judging, therefore, the influence of what has come to be called Buddhism on Indian life it is advisable to disabuse our minds at the very start, that Buddhism was a separate religion. What Buddha actually did was to emphasise the cardinal elements of the thought of his times, and re-state the popular notions, like Karma and Transmigration, with a view to the practical bearings required of an aspirant after Liberation. In Hindu spiritual experience there is a curious fact which words like Philosophy, Religion or Ethics can never adequately express. This is what is known as "Marga." Poussin[2] has endeavoured to comprehend its content by the word "Discipline", and the term may best serve our purpose. Buddha essentially pointed to the "discipline" or *Patha* one has to traverse. His is the Middle Way, the Noble Eight-fold Path, as contrasted with the extreme practices which he deprecated. The emphasis of intellect over popular religion, we have seen, resulted in the Upanishadic reaction from the ritualism of the Brahmanas. But this rationalisation tended to abstract man away from the facts of life which were there, for good or bad. It was no use trying to deny suffering and change. And so Buddha provided spiritual consolation ; and this he does by largely ethicising the ideas he inherited. Arhatship could only be attained by Right Conduct. The immense hold Buddhism had over the millions is especially due to its moral teachings.[3] The

[1] We agree with Prof. A. B. Keith, *Buddhist Philosophy*, pp. 120-122. It is wrong to think that either Buddha or his followers tried to destroy the caste system. Caste was recognised always in the lay followers. And we know that caste distinctions are transcended when a person joins either the order of Bhikkshus or that of the Sanyasis.

[2] *The way to Nirvana.*

[3] See what Max Muller has to say about Buddhist moral code: *Selected Essays*, Vol. II, pp. 207-209.

main ideas of Buddhism, as a close analysis would show, have burnt their way, deep into the heart of every belief and sect of this country. Ideas of ontology and escheatology might differ, but so far as the world-view is concerned, the Buddhist view of life is the same as the view of the innumerable other faiths of India. A religion that was supreme for two thousand years to simply vanish without leaving traces on life and thought is an impossible idea.

We have so far refrained from discussing the metaphysics of Buddhism, of the Nihilist and Idealist schools. We shall, however, examine briefly if there is the idea of the Absolute in Buddhist thought. Did Buddhism postulate any belief in the existence of God? What of the human soul? What was meant by Nirvana? We shall see that it is impossible to estimate the value of the ethics of Buddhism without answering these questions.

We have seen that the search after Unity led to the thinkers of the Upanishads to look for it in the Absolute. But the Absolute, at least, so far as Yajnavalkya is concerned, is conceived without any content whatsoever. There is no attempt to reconcile the empirical in the Absolute. The Sankhya, again, discarded the idea of the Absolute, postulating the reality of a multitude of thinking Substances. If we could translate the Upanishadic idea of the world-process into ontological language, we might say, that it is Apparent Becoming in Being, the Being alone being real. The Sankhya would express it as the coming together of the lame and the blind ; but this only in the phenomenal ; in the ultimate the Purusha are independent beings ; the conclusion, according to the Karika being,—Neither I am, Nor is aught mine, Nor do I exist. In the metaphysical tenets of Buddhism, there is no place for any Reality. There is, however, some vague thinking Substance that persists through the endless births and deaths. And if there is any Reality or Absolute, of-course using the terms in a peculiar sense, that would be the Law of Causality. If in the Upanishads we have Substance without Causality, here we have Causality without Substance. The ontological statement would be then, Becoming in Apparent Being. From the conception of all Empirical Existence as Appearance, the Absolute alone being Reality, it is perfectly logical to swing round to the opposite conception of all Existence being continuous flow, without reaching to an anchor anywhere. This sounds paradoxical; but no other result could be possible when the Absolute is deprived of all content; and is beyond knowledge. If nothing can be predicated of Being, we are at least, it is assumed, sure of our experience in life. All is suffering; however much we might try to ignore it, the reality of pain and misery is there. If it could be proved philosophically that life itself is void of content, even as the Absolute, then we could arrive at the state of mind which is complete rest—Nirvana.

The first step, then, is the denial of the Atman, the mysterious ego-entity which is supposed to reside behind empirical personality, behind bodily and physical activity. Buddhism "swept away from the field of its vision the whole of the great soul-theory which had hitherto so completely filled and dominated the minds of the superstitious and of the thoughtful alike."[1] Paul Carus[2] holds that Buddha did not deny the Self as such. But we do say that Buddha, by depriving the Self of all individuality practically denies the Soul. Personality is not a unit, but a grouping of Dhamma. The separate elements, the material body, consciousness, feeling, ideas, volitions[3] etc., are brought together as members in the chain of Causation. We are reminded of the Epicurean theory

[1] Rhys Davids: *Hibbert Lectures*, 1881, p. 29

[2] *The Gospel of Buddha*, Introduction.

[3] See Dr. W. M. McGovern's *Buddhist Philosophy*, pp. 81-82.

of the Universe, conceived as the resolving and dissolving of atoms. There is a danger involved in a view of this kind which we must guard against. Just as in the Pantheistic doctrine God may be submerged in Nature with the resultant materialism, here too the Atomic conception may confound man with his surroundings, ignoring true personality as such. We do not improve matters in any way my taking refuge in the Bergsonian conception of *Elan vital*, and of Evolution. Man, it is asserted, not only creates but is himself created every second. What he was a moment back, he is not now. According to Buddhism, too, man is a living continuous complex, and he does not remain the same person in any given space and time. We can understand how to the Buddhist Bhikkshu the human being appeared only as a fleeting frame. He could not take him in as a Spiritual Unity, but needs must analyse and decompose the body into blood, mucus, phlegm, etc. No wonder that there is a loathing for things of the world.

The next step is to deny the Being of the universe. Here again we have merely grouping of elements. The world is Dhamma. Buddha refuses to be drawn into more definite admissions. He does not state whether the world is finite or infinite, eternal or non-eternal. It is difficult to state if the external world has objective validity. From an agnosticism of this nature, it is natural to jump to the Nihilism of Nagarjuna. After all, the external Universe, Dhamma, may be the mere construction of the imagination. All phenomena have no essence of their own. The Madhyamika or Sunya system is the logical outcome of the agnosticism of Buddha himself.

The next and the last step is the leap into the dark Nirvana. We slip headlong into a bottomless abyss. Buddhism, if tested by its own canonical books, says Max Muller, cannot be free from the charge of Nihilism. The evidence we have before us is so tantalising in its emptiness about the existence of God in Buddhist thought, that we cannot but feel that Buddhism has ignored Him altogether, and is, indeed, atheistic too. The illusion theory that we have elsewhere in Indian speculation is carried out to its conclusion, here with logical precision. In the Prajna-Paramita it is stated that Buddha began to think that he ought to lead all creatures to Nirvaná. But on reflection he finds that there are no creatures to be conducted and creatures to conduct. Why? It is all illusion. Nirvana is but an empty word. Salvation is also illusion, for who is to be liberated! The human soul must be conceived as possessing at least a temporary reality and individuality, even if ultimately to be absorbed into the Brahman. But the Brahman, in Buddhism, is ignored. Nirvana cannot, therefore, be the merging of the human soul, whose existence is not conceived, with God or Brahman, who is not even noticed. What can it be then? As Poussin[1] says, the idea of Nirvana cherished by the Buddhists is "chiefly a negative one". Rhys Davids represents it as simple extinction. Max Muller has well said that "the human soul, when it arrives at its perfection", is blown out, if we use the phraseology of the Buddhists, like a lamp; it is not absorbed, as the Brahmans say, like a drop in the ocean. The Upanishadic conception of Final Emancipation is the apotheosis of the Atman. But, we have it in the dialogue between Buddha and Ananda, when the direct question "Is there the ego"?, is put to him, Buddha refuses to give any statement. As Oldenberg says, Buddha, in fact, disallows the question as to the ultimate goal. "The question of Nirvana is brought before him by Malukya as directly and definitely as could ever be possible; but Buddha evades the question, as knowledge of such things as whether the world is finite or Infinite, whether the saint

[1] Article in the *Encyclopadea of Religion and Ethics.*

lives on beyond death or not do not conduce to progress in holiness. He says, "whatsoever has not been revealed by me, let that remain unrevealed; and what has been revealed, let it be revealed".[1] The answer amounts to, as the answers of many other Indian philosophers, a dignified silence.

SECTION VI—THE JAINA PHILOSOPHY AND ETHICS

Jainism, like Buddhism, is regarded as heretical, and is distinguished from the orthodox systems in that it rejects the vedas as authoritative. Yet it has much in common with the other schools, the motive being the same, Emancipation or Deliverance. Like the Sankhya, it also assumes a dualism. The ontological theory, as stated by the Jains amounts to the statement of the "Indefiniteness of Being" (anekantavada), which has become famous as the Syadvada. We have seen that the Upanishads held that we have only qualities given in our experience. There is no Being as such. The Jains, on the other hand, hold that the "nature of being (sat) is neither the absolutely unchangeable, nor the momentary changing qualities or existences, but involves them both".[2] Being is not of a persistent, unalterable nature, but Being, "is joined to production, continuation and destruction."[3] In other words, a reconciliation is attempted between the Brahmanical conception of the Transcendental Being and the Buddhist doctrine of impermanence and unsubstantiality. Some substance remains the same though the state and form undergo mutilations, as for instance, the clay-matter out of which a jug is made. The same clay lump may be used to prepare any other article, like for instance, a

---

[1] *Buddha*, see pp. 267-285.

[2] Dasgupta: *Hist. of Ind. Phil.*, Vol. I, p. 175.

[3] Jacobi's Article on Jainism, *Ency. Rel. and Eth.*

statue. What happens in every case of change is that (1) some qualities seem to be permanent as for example clay in the above illustration (2) some new quality is created, that is the particular form of the product, and (3) some old qualities are destroyed, as for example the old clay-lump. But underlying the whole there is some permanent factor or matter which can take any shape or quality. And any judgment we make is only our point of view ; and points of view are as numerous as the aspects of looking at things. They are one-sided and contain parts of truth. No judgment, in other words, is absolutely true or false. This is the doctrine of the "nayas". All our judgments are true, are not true, unspeakable, inconceivable and indefinite. That is why every affirmation must be guarded with the proviso "may be".

All dravya (things or substances) are divided into jiva and ajiva (living and non-living). The principle of life is not the body and is distinct from it. The body seems endowed with life because of this principle. This principle is the soul. Unlike the Upanishadic view, it was held that "the Soul is directly perceived (by introspection) just as the external things are. It is not a mere symbolical object indicated by a phrase or a description".[1] There is not one soul but an infinite number of souls. They are eternal, being substances, and are endowed with intelligence. This intelligence can never be destroyed, though obscured. The soul in its pure condition, is perfect and infinite in its capacities of perception, knowledge, bliss and power. Ordinarily, however, the soul is not perfect because of the veil of karma which defiles it. In the mundane condition, the impurity of the Soul is said to be caused by subtle matter bound by karma-matter. There are kinds of souls ; even water, air, fire, earth, plants, etc., being supposed to possess souls. The whole Universe is

[1] See Dasgupta: *Hist. of Ind. Phil.*, Vol. I, p. 188.

full of these infinite groups of souls or "nigodas". Only an infinitesimally small fraction of a single nigoda supplies the vacancy caused by the liberation of all these souls which have reached Nirvana. Those who have attained Mukti "dwell in a state of perfection at the top of the Universe, and have no more to do with worldly affairs, they have reached nirvana (nivritti or mukti)."

The ajiva (or non-living) is divided into pudgalastikaya, dharmastikaya, adharmastikaya, akastikaya, Kala, Punya, Papa.[1] It is not necessary for us to go into further details. We shall only make a passing notice of the fact that Matter is held to be of two states, subtle and gross. Material things are produced by the combination of atoms ; but unlike the Buddhists (who held that the atoms are not in actual contact) the Jains held that contact is essential and proved by experience. We have already drawn attention to the Jain conception of change and permanence. From one aspect of view the atoms may be said to be destroyed in the process of losing some and gaining other qualities ; but from another aspect they are eternal.

In the brief sketch of Jain thought given above, we have not yet considered the existence of God. In fact, it was felt to be a hopeless task to try to justify the existence of God.[2] All arguments rest on mere hypotheses which may be discarded on a closer analysis. If it is held that the world is the "effect" either as a whole or in parts, the very hypothesis would apply to the hypothetical God. Since "his will and thought must be diversely operating at diverse times and these are contained in him ;" and as the agent He should have a body as an intelligent creator. Even His abstract existence is a contradiction. But supposing that a God wihout body could

---

[1] See Dasgupta: *Hist. of Ind. Phil.*, Vol. I, p. 195 ff.

[2] *Ibid.*, pp. 203-206 for Jain atheism.

create this world, what can be the motive to such creation? Personal caprice? Is it because He is merciful and wanted to plant a garden of happiness? The existence of misery gives the direct and eloquent lie. Is it in sport, that we could call creation His "lila"? If this were so, evidently, God must be childish. If, further, it is held that He is to award rewards and punishments, then God cannot be above the charge of prejudice and favouritism...... But why One God only? Might there not be a Society of Gods? Would they fall out with each other if there were no Chief God to preside over and settle disputes? Obviously the character of Gods even is unreliable, and not above human facilities and vices. From whatever angle of view it may be considered, the Existence of God is, indeed, an unwarranted hypothesis, and hence may be discarded altogether.

In a philosophy of this kind, it is impossible to find adequate grounds for moral ideals. The motive which guides man to seek liberation or Moksha is the usual desire to prevent pain and attain happiness. And here Jain ethics shares in common the ideas of Karma, transmigration etc. with the other Indian systems. The attitude to life is coloured by the same view of it that we get in the other religious beliefs. There is a panting to escape from worldly existence, the continuance of which only means the accumulation of Karma, entailing new births, with never ending suffering.

The religious seeker, however, has no certitude anywhere. He has no God with whom he could hope to unite himself. True faith, as such therefore, is impossible so long as a reasoned indefiniteness prevails with regard to things over which such vague uncertainty is morally dangerous. Everything may be or may not be.

The enumeration, moreover, of the rules of conduct will reveal the exaggerated nature of the whole scheme of life that the Jains hold. Everything is directed to abstract man away from worldly intercourse and rivet attention on a future state of absolute happiness, the hedonistic evaluation of which is magnified beyond credulity in proportion as life, here and now, is depreciated. And again, the naked animism that predominates in Jain thought, with the fantastic notion of trees and worms as possessing souls, only serves to insult the dignity and sanctity of Man. The concern that is felt for the lives of creatures like bugs, reptiles, snakes and lizards is strangely absent for human life, which is treated beneath contempt. Ahimsa, we are tempted to say, is to be observed only with regard to the lower creatures. Man is looked upon with scant humanity. Self-torture, sometimes even suicide, is permitted, as a legitimate discipline for the attainment of Mukti. Self-himsa is glorified. Capital punishments were awarded freely. The doctrine of Ahimsa evidently did not refer to human life.

We cannot help feeling that the zeal to preserve life should be regulated by a noble conception of the kind of life which is to be so preserved. We want not merely to live, but to live the noblest and best life.

SECTION VII—THE PHILOSOPHY AND EHTICS OF THE BHAGAVADGITA

The Bhagavadgita belongs prior to the system-making age of sanskrit philosophy. We have in it the germs of a system, but no system ready-made.[1] Its thought is, therefore neither pure Monism, nor Mayavada, nor qualified Monism, nor Sankhya since it avoids all such rigid determination.[2] We have in it a strong theistic element. Instead of the reflective spiritualism of the Upanishads which could not satisfy the deep-seated emotions and yearnings

[1] K. T. Telang: *Bhagavatgita*, S. B. E., p. 10.

[2] See Aurobindo Ghose: *Essays on the Gita*, First Series, pp. 5-10.

of the heart, the Gita enunciates a practical religion founded on Faith and Worship.[1] Lord Krishna holds out the promise of release from all sins to those who turn to him as the sole refuge.[2] The value of Bhakti is emphasised, and through the favour of the Deity is the eternal seat gained.

In this Song Celestial, Arjuna typifies the struggling soul trying to understand the mystery of existence and reach to the Infinite Reality. With eyes tear-dimmed, "in pity lost, by doubtings tossed", and thoughts distracted, the warrior prince turns to the Divine Guide seeking counsel. He will not fight convinced that nothing good could spring from mutual slaughter.[3] It is the revolt of the man hitherto satisfied with action and its current standards, who finds himself faced with a conflict of ideals, and with no principle of conduct to fall back upon. The bewildered Prince feels an internal void and quails before the conflict, having lost anchor of the valid laws of action. The Divine Charioteer essays to bring him back to the true idea of Dharma, and to recover him from "the inglorious trouble shameful to the brave, barring the path of virtue."[4] He tells him that that which irks is the "sense-life", subject to opposite elements like heat, cold,[5] sorrow and joy, but which is only "brief and mutable," and counsels him to take sorrow and joy indifferently. This world, and the life we live here are indeed unhappy and transient, "the place of pain, the home of woes."[6] And all worlds, even to the world of Brahma "roll back again from Death to Life's unrest."[7] The undiscerning

---

[1] *The Song Celestial*, p. 53. (see also p. 42.)
[2] *Ibid.*, p. 109.
[3] *Ibid.*, p. 4.
[4] *Ibid.*, p. 7.
[5] *Ibid.*, pp. 8-9.
[6] *Telang's Translation of the Gita*, p. 79; also p. 86.
[7] *Song Celestial*, p. 47.

ones get entangled in bewilderment, "deluded at time of birth,"[1] through ignorance, and the attachment to pairs of opposites "twain snares of Like and Dislike."[2] It is Kama or desire that is the enemy of man and is the cause of sin. The constant foe of knowledge, which deludes this embodied Self is passion which takes on numerous forms, "Fair but deceitful, subtle as a flame."[3] This world of things is "foiled, soiled, enclosed in this desire of flesh,"[4] and yielding to its maddening guile, men succumb to Epicurean materialism, imagining that Pleasure is the End of Life.[5] They little know that life is not brought to an end hereby, and sinking into impure hell, they are continually hurled down to these worlds, "only into demonaic wombs,"[6] deluded birth by birth. The Law that impels man to pass through infancy and youth and old age, thence to the acquisition of another body, just as an old cloth is cast off for a fresh one,[7] is the principle which is the expression of the qualities which cause birth in good or evil wombs. Such is the iron law that even good action does not open directly to the path of eternal bliss. For action is to be devoid of attachment. The motive should not be to the fruit thereof, if release from the shackles of repeated births and taint of delusion is sought.[8] The reward for a meritorious action is a passage to heaven, to the celestial region where godly pleasures are enjoyed until the merit is exhausted when the man returns to the mortal world, again to the round of existences, of "going and coming"[9] It is difficult for

[1] *Telang's Translation*, p. 76.
[2] *Song Celestial*, p. 43.
[3] *Ibid.*, p. 21.
[4] *Ibid.*, p. 21.
[5] *Ibid.*, p. 94.
[6] *Telang's Translation*, p. 116.
[7] *Ibid.*, p. 45.
[8] *Ibid.*, pp. 48-49.
[9] *Ibid.*, p. 84.

those who have not restrained their Self to obtain devotion.[1] It is only possible by a severe and constant discipline through indifference to worldly objects. And if one is not advanced in this process of abstraction, his imperfection, though it does not tend to ruin, for "none who performs good (deeds) comes to an evil end," will nevertheless compel him "to be born again and again to work for perfection."[2] He attains the worlds of those who perform meritorious deeds, "dwells there many measureless years," and is born again into a family of holy illustrious and talented devotees."[3] The man who is possessed of knowledge, and has devoted himself to abstraction, alone reaches the Deity at the end of many lives. The Ocean of Transmigration can only be crossed by the boat of knowledge. It is the fire that reduces all actions to ashes, and purifies the man. Through faith[4] and the restraint of the senses he gains knowledge and is released from ignorance and doubt. Works do not fetter such a man any more.[5] This world is fettered by action, but he who is not attached to worldly objects and is self possessed and has no interest whatsoever in the things and happenings of this world,[6] who "withdraws his senses from (all) objects of senses, as the tortoise (withdraws) its limbs from all sides" obtains the "happiness that is in (one's) self (with the Brahman) one obtains indestructible happiness."[7] For after attaining to the Deity, there is no birth again.[8] And there is no further grief and no further desire.[9] The knowledge that all ac-

[1] *Telang's Translation*, p. 71.
[2] *Ibid.*, p. 72.
[3] *Ibid.*, p. 73.
[4] See Chapter XVII for the three kinds of Faith.
[5] *Telang's Translation*, pp. 62-63.
[6] *Ibid.*, p. 54.
[7] *Ibid.*, pp. 50-66.
[8] *Ibid.*, p. 79.
[9] *Ibid.*, p. 128.

tions are in every way done by nature alone, and that self is not the doer,[1] becomes manifest; and man sees "all the variety of entities as existing in one, and (all as) emanating from that". Then he becomes one with Brahman. "This inexhaustible, supreme Self, being without beginning and without qualities does not act and is not tainted", though "stationed in the body. It is eternal, indestructible and indefinable." He kills not and is not slain. He is unborn and immortal, everlasting. He does not die "dead though the house of it seems." Birth and death cannot be for the birthless and the deathless. And he who knows himself the exhaustless, self-sustained, immortal, indestructible, will not say that he has killed or caused to kill a man. In the ultimate, all conceptions of morality, Right and Wrong, are thus simply transcended. And most of our observations regarding the ethical thought of the other Indian systems, can also be made of the content of the Gita. It is only the fear of repetition that prevents us from further elaboration. The Gita has no place for true Ethics, neither is it a true philosophy of Action, for the End, in the ultimate, is the abandonment of all action whatsoever.

SECTION VIII—THE YOGA SYSTEM OF PHILOSOPHY AND ETHICS

The Yoga philosophy is sometimes known as Sesvara-Sankhya (Theistic Sankhya). The two systems, Yoga and Sankhya, have much in common and in course of time might easily have amalgamated. The belief in the existence of Isvara is not a serious obstacle, for the End is not the absorption of the Soul into Isvara, but the Sankhya ideal of isolation. "Patanjali, like Kapila, rests satisfied with the isolation of the soul, and does not pry

[1] *Telang's Translation*, p. 65.

into the how and where the soul abides after separation."[1] Devotion to the Lord is mentioned as only one of the means to obtain liberation, "as one only out of many means, and not even as the most efficacious of all."[2] And Patanjali defines the Lord thus : "Iswara, the Lord, is a Purusha (Self) that has never been touched by sufferings, actions, rewards, or consequent dispositions." The difference between Iswara and the individual souls lies in that Iswara is never in bondage, whereas the individual souls are in bondage till liberated or isolated. The Iswara of the yoga system can never be God in our sense. The End of the yoga is hence not union with God, but Kaivalya,—the attainment of complete detachment, and release from worldly fetters by a vigorous control of human nature. Or, to express it in other words, emancipation would mean the state of perfect isolation and self-centredness. This is sought to be attained by Abhyasa, or the practice of austerities. Even as early as the days of the Rig-Veda, we find that religious exercises are considered as valuable. Tapas and Brahmacharya were ideas that had already acquired a hold. The object was to attain self-control ; for it was felt that human passions had to be curbed just as a spirited steed is controlled. By Abhyasa, Patanjali means steadiness or Sthiti, i.e. "that state of mind, when free from all activity (Vritti), it remains in its own character, that is unchanged. Such effort must be continuous or repeated, as implied by the term Abhyasa." We might be inclined to laugh at some of the Yoga practices, as mere gymnastics and acrobatism. We should remind ourselves, however, that the object of self-imposed discipline is to prevent distraction of thought and to acquire

[1] Rajendralal Mitra, quoted by Max Muller: *Six Systems*, pp. 405-406.

[2] Max Muller: *Six Systems*, p. 426.

Ekagrata. It was also believed that certain superior powers could be acquired by these exercises.[1]

The yoga discipline begins with the practices which are to purify the mind from ordinary impurities. This is the ethical preparation. Then follow bodily and psychic efforts at control. After freeing himself from all distractions the yogin begins contemplation which would lead him to Samadhi and Kaivalya. The whole process is the eightfold method of Yama, Niyama, Asana, Pranayama, Pratyahara, Dhyana, Dharana, and Samadhi.

As we are not directly concerned with the details, except in so far as they elucidate the view of life of the yoga system we shall consider its ethical aspects, in the light of Kaivalya which is the goal of life.

The Yama and the Niyama clear the way for yoga, by making the mind disinclined to worldly things.[2] This is Vairagya which is defined as "the consciousness of having overcome (the world) on the part of one who has no longer any desire for any objects whatsoever, whether visible or revealed." This idea of Vairagya is not confined to yogins only. It is something which has burnt its way to the consciousness of the man in the street. It rules

---

[1] See Radhakrishnan: *Indian Philosophy*, Vol. 2, p. 337.

[2] Yama constitute:—

(1) Ahimsa or Non-injury.
(2) Satya or Veracity.
(3) Asteya or Non-stealing.
(4) Brahmacharya or absolute sexual restraint.
(5) Aparigraha or Non-acceptance. This involves unworldliness or Renunciation, i. e. the attitude of Indifference to the world.

The Niyama constitute:—

Purification (External and internal).
Contentment of Mind.
Tapas (accustoming oneself to all privations, keeping body unmoved and maintaining of silence).
Swadhaya or study of Philosophy.
Iswara-Pranidhana or meditation on God.

the daily life of millions of Hindus. Their whole attitude to life is dominated by its spirit. The world leads only to suffering, and everything is transient, held in the grip of destruction. The Yoga is thoroughly pessimistic in its tone. Its treatment of sorrow "is the same as that of the four sacred truths of the Buddhists, namely, suffering, origin of suffering, the removal of suffering, and the path to the removal of suffering.[1] So also its treatment of the Samsara cycle. Avidya must be overcome or Samsara continues. Avidya is the ignorance of the Four sacred Truths, not to be confused, therefore, with the Vedanta avidya of Sankara. And yoga takes for granted the law of Karma. Karmas are of four kinds : (1) sukla, (2) krsna, (3) sukla-krsna, (4) asukla-krsna. The particular form and life that is assumed in a future birth is determined by the accumulated Karmas of the present life. Sometimes the fruits of Karma, good or bad, are enjoyed even in the present life. Rebirth need not necessarily be as a human being ; that depends on Karma. After the Karma is exhausted, he will be born again as a man. This cycle goes on repeating itself unless avidya is overcome. A man may attain emancipation even in this life. He is then a jivanmukta, and though he continues to live in the world, he is not of it. When the man attains to Kaivalya, there is no further Karma or suffering. This Kaivalya, as we have seen, is however not union with God, but a state of complete detachment, and absolute independence. We have no idea of how the jiva lives on in the liberated state. Kaivalya might not be nihilism as the Purusha, or the liberated soul, continues to exist, perhaps like the jivanmukta of the Vedantins. But in what condition, Patanjali does not essay to enlighten us. Kaivalya defies description. It is "what no eye has seen and what has not entered into the mind of man."[2]

[1] Dasgupta: *Hist. of Ind. Phil.*, p. 237.
[2] Max Muller: *Six Systems*, pp. 471-473.

SECTION IX—THE NYAYA VAISESHIKA PHILOSOPHY

The Vaiseshika is supposed to be founded by Kanada, and the Nyaya is usually associated with it. They "represent the analytic type of philosophy" unlike the other systems of Indian philosophy, and their method is that of science, of logical inquiry and criticism.

The Nyaya is a system of Logic, the literal meaning of the term being "that by means of which the mind is led to a conclusion." Thus it is concerned with the means of knowledge. The chief End, however, is the same as that of the other systems of philosophy, the attainment of salvation. This is through the removal of false knowledge and the acquisition of right knowledge. This is the knowledge of the sixteen categories or Padarthas. According to the Nyaya Sutra supreme felicity is gained thereby. Real knowledge belongs to the soul only ; it is an attribute of it. The soul is not the senses which it controls ; nor is it Manas (mind) which is only an instrument of knowledge, whereas the soul is the knower. The external world, the world of Nature, is independent of our knowledge of it and is "a composite of eternal, unalterable, causeless atoms." The bondage of the world is due to Mithya-jnana, the confounding of the Self with the Not-self. The subject and the object are separate. Consciousness is due to the causal action of the not-self on self. And knowledge is the property of the Self.[1] The body is not the Atman ; if it were, then with its dissolution everything would cease ; merit and demerit would not pursue the soul. The Soul is a "real substantive being," whose existence can be proved by means of inference. "The Soul is unique in each individual. There is an infinite number of souls ; if not, then everybody must be cons-

[1] See Radhakrishnan: *Indian Philosophy*, Vol. II, p. 133 ft.

cious of the feelings and thoughts of everybody else. If one Soul were present in all bodies, then when one experiences pleasure or pain, all should possess the same experiences which is not the case." 'The Soul is an eternal entity which is from time to time connected with a body suitable to its desert. The body has its source in the acts done by the person, and is the basis of pleasure and pain. The body is formed under the influence of the unseen force of destiny, and is the result of the persistence of the effect of the previous acts. Each man becomes endowed with a body fit for being the medium of the experiences which he has to undergo. The birth of a being is not a mere physiological process. Uddyotakara says, "The Karma of the parents who have to enjoy the experiences resulting from the birth of the child, as well as the Karma of the Personality which has to undergo experiences in the world, both these conjointly bring about the birth of the body in the mother's womb". The connection of the soul with the body is called its birth and its separation from it death. At the beginning of creation an activity is set up in the atoms by which they combine so as to form material objects. A similar activity arises in the minds of the souls, which brings about several other qualities consequent upon the past careers of the souls themselves. The concrete history of each soul embraces a number of lives. At any one moment its historically continuous existence is rooted in the past and embraces an outline of the future. Any one life is but a part of a historically conditioned series.[1] The Soul comes into this life, therefore, not in entire forgetfulness, but with some tendencies and the accumulation of desert acquired in a previous birth. The experience of life is painful. Gotama is convinced that even pleasure is full

[1] Quoted from Radhakrishnan: *Indian Philosophy*, Vol. II, pp. 149-150.

of pain. Even while we seem to enjoy it, it is not anything positive, and so is not valuable to counterbalance pain. Even death does not bring to an end sorrow and pain. The soul has to course from birth to birth, through the round of existences, to reap the fruits of deeds. Transmigration is thus accepted as a fact, though we are given no idea of what life after death is. With the exhaustion of man's desert, he attains Moksha. He is emancipated from Samsara, and obtains release from pain. Gotama calls the state of Mukti as "Nihsreyasa" "the non-plus ultra of blessedness". Vatsayana describes this state of blessedness as "consisting in renunciation" with regard to all the pleasures of this life, and the non-acceptance of, or indifference to, any rewards in the life to come, as being in fact what Brahman is without fear, without decay and without death.[1] This Brahmanhood, however, should not be the object of desire, since desire is the cause of bondage. Moksha is the destruction of bondage, and is to be attained by the removal of Mithya-Jnana or false knowledge. The Prameyas or objects to be known include, among others, some practical things; Pravritti, Dosa, Pratyabhava, Phala, Dukha, and Apavarga. Pravritti is activity which ceases with Apavarga. Dosa or fault consists of passion or desire, aversion, and confusion or error. It is the cause of egoism, i. e. Ahamkara. It is our moha or ignorance that is at the root of dosa like raga and dwesha. This can be removed by thinking of its opposite, Pratipakshabhavana, which is the true estimate of things. With the removal of mithya-jnana action ceases, and with it, birth and sorrow consequent therefrom.[2] The Apavarga state is free from Klesas, and is devoid of Pravritti. The Soul is released from pain. Just as a man in dreamless sleep is devoid of all feelings, in the Apa-

---

[1] Max Muller: *Six Systems*, p. 484.

[2] Keith: *Indian Logic and Atomism*, pp. 250-251.

varga state, the Soul is divested of all qualities, and "remains in its own inert state".

The Vaiseshika system begins, like the other systems of philosophy, with the promise of teaching the way to salvation. Salvation can be obtained by the knowledge of the Six Categories, which embrace the whole realm of knowledge. These are substance, quality, action, generality, individuality and inherence, (sometimes a seventh Category being included, that of Abhava, as also two more, that of potentia and similitude). It is from the fifth category, that of Visesha or species (Particularity) that this system takes its name. All substances consist of invisible atoms whose combinations result in mental and physical phenomena. The true personality of the Soul can be realised only in its atomic individuality. The theory of knowledge of the Vaiseshikas is only slightly different from that of the Nyaya and it is not necessary for our purpose to go into it. Because of particularity we are able to know things as distinct from each other. And as the Atoms are numberless, so also are the particularities. Supreme felicity is due to merit from which springs knowledge of the Padarthas. According to Kanada, this state of final release or Moksha lies in "the separation of the self from the body without entering another body in the absence of merit or demerit which would produce a subsequent embodiment."[1]

Prof. Dasgupta thus sums up the idea of Salvation of the Nyaya-Vaiseshika Philosophy : "The state of mukti according to Nyaya-Vaiseshika is neither a state of pure knowledge nor of bliss, but a state of perfect qualitilessness in which the self remains in itself in its own purity. It is the negative state of absolute painlessness in mukti that is sometimes spoken of as being a state of absolute happiness (ananda), though really speaking the state of

---

[1] Keith: *Indian Logic and Atomism*, p. 251.

mukti can never be a state of happiness. It is a passive state of self in its original and natural purity, unassociated with pleasure, pain, knowledge, willing, etc."[1]

Before we pass on to the consideration of the next system, we shall make a brief mention of the Nyaya-Vaiseshika view of God. The Nyaya Sutra makes only a casual mention of God whereas Kanada does not openly make reference to God. Can we assume, therefore, that Gotama and Kanada were atheists?[2] Some modern writers, like Garbe, have held that their system was atheistic. But such a verdict cannot be held valid in face of many frank statements of theistic belief that we come across in the expositions of the followers of the Nyaya-Vaiseshika school. Prof. Radhakrishnan's criticism very ably expresses the value of the theistic element, both in the Nyaya and the Vaiseshika systems. Of the Nyaya, he writes : "Even if we grant the validity of the arguments employed to establish the reality of God, the Isvara of the Nyaya philosophy is not the comprehensive spiritual reality of which we are the imperfect expressions. He is outside of us, and the world too, however much he may be said to cause, govern and destroy it. Reality is composed of a great number of particulars linked together by an external bond, even as a chord binds together a number of sticks. God is not the creator of atoms, but only their fashioner. His reason works on the elements of the universe from without, but does not operate as a power of life within. This conception of God as beyond the world, as outside the entire frame of Space, as divelling apart in eternal, self-centred isolation is arid and empty. We cannot maintain the dualism of an infinite creator on the one side, and the infinite world on the other."[3] And of the Vaiseshika view of God, Prof. Radhakrishnan

[1] *History of Indian Philosophy*, Vol. I, p. 366.

[2] See Keith: *Indian Logic and Atomism*, Ch. X.

[3] *Indian Philosophy*, Vol. 2, p. 172.

says[1] that it is practically the same as that of the Naiyayika, and is open to the same criticism. The world was originally regarded as a piece of mechanism, complete and self-sufficient, with atoms and souls held together in their place, by the principle of adrsta. The difficulties relentlessly pressed by the critics of the Vaiseshika, that an unintelligent principle could not keep together the *disjecta membra* of the world, forced the later Vaiseshika to accept a divine principle as a way out of the difficulty. God is not the creator of the world, since souls and atoms are co-external with Him. God is distinguished from the human souls by His omniscience and omnipotence which qualify Him for the Government of the Universe. He is never entangled in the Cycle of Existence. He sets the world under certain laws, and lets it go, but he does not interfere with its course. The world is a gigantic piece of clock-work, set in motion by its maker, and guaranteed to go without any further interference. But a non-interfering God does not help the actual life of the world, while an interfering God runs the risk of upsetting his own laws. God and the world exclude each other but, if we do not revise the original premises even "God" cannot help us. If we start with a plurality of entities unrelated to one another, we cannot correct their isolation by the mechanical device of a God who arranges things from outside. The world held together by the mechanical expedient of a foreign medium is a mere aggregate of things and not an organic whole."

SECTION X—THE MIMAMSA PHILOSOPHY

The most important writers of the Mimamsa school are Jaimini, Sabara, Kumarila and Prabhakara. Prabhakara, as the tradition has it, was the diciple of Kumarila, who

[1] *Indian Philosophy*, Vol. 2, pp. 227-228.

was a senior contemporary of the great Sankara. These scholars concerned themselves primarily with the task of ritual interpretation. A vast system of sacrificial worship had grown up based upon the Brahmanas which "came to be regarded as texts of incontrovertible accuracy."[1] With the elaborate growth of ritual and its diffusion over different parts of India, the Brahmanas came to be supplemented by Smriti literature. And there was oral tradition regarding the mode in which sacrificial worship should be performed. But there were divergences between the Brahmanas and the later Samhitas which could not be explained away ; and it was but natural that doubts should arise over the intricacies of sacrificial ritual. The growing need felt expressed itself in the systematic efforts at interpretation and compilation by various scholars, and thus we have the Mimamsa, which means attempts at rational inquiry.

The Mimamsa theory of knowledge is based upon the doctrine of Self-validity (Svatah-pramanya). Kumarila points out that knowledge is intrinsically valid ; otherwise no external power can make it so. If this criterion of validity is applied to the authority of the Veda, it is not surprising that it is emphatically asserted that the Veda is not a human convention ; nor is it the creation of God, for it was held that to posit the existence of God was not necessary. So the Veda is eternal and rests upon its own authority. In other words, it is self valid. Perhaps, as R. Garbe suggests, "the Mimamsa was compelled to propound this theory in order to protect the Veda from the suspicion of fallibility which attaches to all human works."[2] Men should accept it without questioning. Only when its sanction is thus rested on an unassailable foundation could the Veda fulfil its functioning of guiding

---

[1] Keith: *The Karma Mimamsa*, p. 1.
[2] Article in *Ency. Rel. and Eth.*

through its injunctions the performance of actions, "whence arose an invincible potency (apurva) leading to a desirable end, and, this potency was a thing which no person, save through the Veda, could have any knowledge."[1]

The necessity to perform actions according to Vedic injunctions for the attainment of Salvation, in itself, is a proof of the existence of the soul. If there were no soul to be liberated, the Vedic ritual would have no meaning. This soul is not to be confounded with the body and the organs of sense or *Buddhi*. It is eternal and omnipresent and "many, one in each body." But it is compelled to course through birth to birth because of Karma. The fruits of actions, good or bad, must be consumed. Salvation is the release from the round of existence. This could be attained only by the exhaustion of Karma, when there will be no further generation of new efforts. This state can be arrived at by the cessation of kamya-karma, i. e. action performed with some desire. The Nitya-Karma, (like the Sandhya etc.) which has no benefit, saves man from sin ; and its non-performance produces sin ; Salvation is the state when the Soul is completely released from the body, and is not impelled to rebirth, for Karma is completely consumed. Kumarila conceives of this state of Moksha as the state of Atman in itself, free from pain, not however, as experience of the bliss of Atman. Parthasarathy also favours this view. In other words, Liberation is a state free from both pleasure and pain.

In this doctrine of emancipation we find it difficult to find an intelligent place for God. The Mimamsa rejects the idea of God, either as creator or destroyer ; for He can have no motive. If the conception of creation is valid, then God himself would need a creator to create him. "So there is no God, no creator, no creation, no dissolu-

---

[1] Keith: *Karma Mimamsa*, pp. 36-37.

tion or Pralaya."[1] It is significant, however as Keith observes of the theistic tendency of Indian thought that "even the Mimamsa was not exempt from transformation." Despite its emphatic denial of the existence of a Supreme Lord, the end of man is conceived of as being obtained by "meditation upon, and worship of the Supreme Spirit which is manifested in each man, and authors such as Apadeva and Langakhi Bhaskara declare that if the sacrifice is performed in honour of Govinda or the Creator, Isvara, it leads to the highest good, basing this assertion on the authority of the Bhagavadgita."[2] But we may assume that this tendency to adopt the Mimamsa to theistic or pantheistic views is not in true keeping with the spirit of writers like Jaimini, from whom we must expect to find its true exposition. "The Mimamsa", says Garbe, "does not recognise the existence of God."[3] "Jaimini", says Radhakrishnan, "does not so much deny God as ignore Him. No detail of the Vedic religion requires the assistance of God".[4] Max Muller tries to explain away what he terms the "supposed atheism" of the Mimamsa by the anxiety of Jaimini to clear the Lord from the charges of cruelty etc. He says, "Jaimini would not make the Lord responsible for the injustice that seems to prevail in the world, and hence reduced everything to cause and effect, and saw in the inequalities of the world the natural result of the continued action of good or evil acts."[5] But this explanation is not convincing, and we know as a matter of fact that both ancient and modern scholars have looked

---

[1] Dasgupta: *History of Indian Philosophy*, Vol. I, p. 403. See also Keith's: *Karma Mimamsa*, Chapter on *God, The Soul and Matter*.

[2] Keith: *Karma Mimamsa*, p. 76.

[3] Article: *Ency. Rel. and Eth.*

[4] *Indian Philosophy*, Vol. 2, p. 424.

[5] *Six Systems*, p. 277.

upon the true Mimamsa as "atheistic". Kumarila himself was aware that it was treated as Lokayata, i.e. as an atheistical system, and Prabhakara, indeed, has openly treated it as such.

We cannot therefore accept the Mimamsa as a true basis for social ideals. As a philosophy it wholly fails to satisfy us. Its view of the Universe, whose reality is after all looked upon only as the constant principle of Karma, is incomplete. Its ethics, too, is too objective and formal to serve as a guide to human conduct. Duty, according to it, refers to mere prescriptive observance. What is true or right is not that which finds validity in moral evaluation, but only that which is in conformity with ritual action. Accuracy in sacrifice and ceremony is the sole criterion. This formalism we cannot but reject, as something unnatural, for it cannot find the acceptance of men as moral and spiritual beings. The Ethics of the Mimamsa, therefore, "was purely mechanical and its religion was unsound."[1]

SECTION XI—THE PHILOSOPHY AND ETHICS OF THE VEDANTA OF SANKARA

The Vedanta Philosophy is the most important of the Indian systems and in it human speculation seems to have reached its very acme. And it is claimed by more than one modern writer that as a system of thought Vedantism has not outgrown its importance and usefulness. It is no exaggeration to state that it is the one system that finds to-day almost universal acceptance in India. It is very necessary, therefore, to understand its significance.[2]

The Vedanta Philosophy claims to give an exposition of the philosophy inculcated by the Upanishads and sum-

[1] Radhakrishnan: *Indian Philosophy*, Vol. 2, p. 428.
[2] Sircar: *Comparative studies in Vedantism*, p. viii.

marised by Badarayana in his Brahma-Sutras. There are two currents springing from this common source, but they take widely differing directions, that of Sankara and that of Ramanuja. The one is Advaita or Non-Dualism, whereas the other is Modified non-dualism. Both these off-shoots are not only concerned with the problem of knowledge, but are, as much as other philosophical systems, the expressions of life to be lived, through their peculiar discipline and attitude towards the world.

Sankara, it has been said, has made Vedanta "the basis of every religious sect that India has known, so as to satisfy the needs of men of all shades of intelligence and bias,"[1] and his pre-eminence has so impressed all, that whenever we talk of Vedanta we usually mean Sankara's Philosophy. It is really very difficult to understand and claim to interpret with accuracy his teaching and thought. Our embarrassment is also enhanced due to the fact that his teaching has always two aspects. The highest philosophical truth he imparted only to the few, whereas he diluted to a very great extent the extremism of his ideas for the benefit of the populace. For instance, the great thinker who went beyond the conception of God as we understand Him, to the Supreme Cause which is the Sole Reality, a Reality which is the "synthesis", if we may use the term rather vaguely, of the "Tat" and the "Tvam" and comprehended by the famous text "Tat Tvam Asi", needs must, in his role as missionary, give his sanction to the institution of idol worship. The idols were to him sometimes as the symbols of the Infinite, and sometimes of the lower order of Divine Beings, Gods in the phenomenal sense, like Brahma, Indra, Vishnu, etc. These gods, he says: "must be

[1] C. N. Krishnaswamy Aiyer: *Life and Times of Sankara*, p. 9.

admitted to be corporeal, and though by their divine powers they can at one and the same time, partake of oblations offered at numerous sacrifices, they are still like ourselves, subject to birth and death." And the necessity thus to compromise between the higher and the lower, is due to his consciousness, perhaps, of the limitations of human nature,[1] and that is why, perhaps, we have in him, in a sense, ever present this dualism. And the rigorous monist cannot, therefore, get away from this dualism, when he tries to distinguish between what he calls the higher knowledge and the lower knowledge, between Nirguna Brahma and Saguna Brahma, between ultimate Reality and the world of phenomena, and so on. What he does not realise, however, is that Reality is one harmonious whole, the parts of which are not "things-in-themselves", or "appearances", but are real to the extent as parts they partake of the reality of the whole. They find their significance only when conceived in the larger spiritual unity. The needs of our deepest religious aspirations can never be served by setting up an abstract, impersonal, unknown and unknowable Reality. Nor can we be satisfied by granting a provisional reality to the world of our social relationships which mean so much to us. We can never fix on a purpose to be fulfilled in and through life, if we are told that this world is mere appearance, whose reality is only for the time being, and held due to Avidya ; and that the highest truth is Tat Tvam Asi, That art thou, the identity of Brahman and Atman, subject and object, and so on.

The Vedantist may retort saying that it is our theological outlook that insits upon the necessity of a God whom we could love as our Father, Protector and so on ;

[1] "If I", he says, "had not walked without remission in the path of works, others would not have followed my steps, O Lord!" Quoted by Max Muller: *Six Systems*, p. 217.

but such a God is true only in the phenomenal sense; and if we posit such a personal Divine Being we cannot but pass beyond Him to the Supreme Brahman. In fact, the distinction is made between the Material Cause and the Efficient Cause, between Saguna Brahma and Nirguna Brahma. Sankara, in many places, speaks of both the aspects of Brahman. Does this mean, as Kokileswar[1] Sastri insists, that Sankara held that the two aspects, that of transcendence and immanance, are inseparable and real? Is Reality as unity in Diversity? Or is it the Panthestic conception that all is Brahman? Does his non-dualism mean the ultimate transcendence of duality, or the ultimate negation of duality?

Sankara has been described by many writers as a "rigorous monist", and perhaps, such a phrase, as Urquhart points out, gives us most concisely the key-note of his teaching. "He asserts one reality and only one, for there is no such thing as plurality or difference anywhere and, therefore, no beginning and no ending, nothing but that nearest experience which comes to each one of us, the consciousness of the self, intelligent just because it is conscious, but essentially universal rather than individual. If we can merge all things in our consciousness and merge ourselves as individuals in the universal consciousness we shall reach the goal of all our striving, the solution of all our difficulties. If we can negate the world we shall find that the world is well lost, for there is really no world, no individuality to lose, nothing but the all-pervading, eternal, infinite Reality, the fundamental, self-luminous Being."[2]

Is the mood behind this attitude really negative? Or is it the dawning of religious consciousness which seeks to find consolation in the idea that much of the burden of this world is unreal; which finds its springs in the mystic's

[1] *Advaita Philosophy*, pp. 4-5.

[2] *The Vedanta and Modern Thought*, p. 55.

aspiration to merge himself in God, to become one with Him, and in the ecstacy of the movement forget all sense of difference. Unfortunately we are not in a position to take Sankara in this light. As one of the Sutras has it: "The Soul is a part of the Lord, on account of the declaration of difference." Sankara inserts the qualification, "as it were" and seeks to argue that individuality is wholly the result of nescience; and the highest truth is the identity of the individual Soul with Brahman, "Tat Tvam Asi." The realisation of this supreme truth is the highest knowledge. With its attainment our cognition of world-appearances ceases. There is no duality, no idea of mine and thine, no subject and object. The illusion of the world-process is at an end. "The world as such has no real existence at all, but is only an illusory imagination which lasts till the moment when true knowledge is acquired."[1] The world is false, the product of Maya.

If, therefore, it is held that Sankara asserts that the Saguna and Nirguna aspects of Brahman to be inseparable, does this mean that he accepts the reality of the qualitative Brahman? We are inclined to say that Sankara is inclined towards the negative aspect, to the idea of a qualitiless Brahman, of whom no predication is possible. If it is maintained, as Kokileswar Sastry seems to do, that Sankara held also the idea of Saguna Brahman to be real, and if God is the originating and material cause of the world, then the world being the effect must participate of the reality of the cause. Then the conception of Maya as enunciated by Sankara cannot be true. We are aware that Sankara does not deny the apparent multiplicity of the Universe and our empirical knowledge. We know how he fought against those ideas as expressed. Existence to Sankara has substantiality and reality. But this is only from the standpoint of the lower knowledge. The Atman

[1] Dasgupta: *History of Indian Philosophy*, p. 440.

is limited by Maya or illusion, but this limitation is not real. If it were real Sankara can never reject dualism. It is only from the point of view of the lower knowledge that illusion exists. The higher knowledge is the truth of the identity of Atman and Brahman ; and so dualism is simply negatived. Only one existence there is ; this is the one unity which is the Atman or Brahman. Sankara is therefore to be understood as an unflinching monist. "For him, only "the One remains". There is but one Infinite Self. "Thou art that." "Unity is the one true existence while manifoldness is evolved out of wrong knowledge". The Self is altogether without qualities and is absolutely changeless." As the temporal is changing, and because it has no continued existence, it is the denial of reality, which can be founded only in the eternal.

There is a great truth embedded in the view that the Self can only reach itself by expanding into the Self of all ; and that our Self is the focussing of the Universal Self. All this Universe is Brahman, and the Atman is Brahman. The Real is the one Unity which is at once real, thought and bliss (Sat, Chit, and Anand) understood in a special sense. In other words, the real is Pure Thought and Self Consciousness ; and the effort of man is to realise his real identity ; "Aham Brahma", not the arrogation of man as God, but the realisation of his divinity as such.

If we press further, however, we will not fail to grasp the real nature of Sankara's Philosophy With his invidious distinctions of the lower and the higher, of the Nirguna and the Saguna, of the esoteric and the exoteric, it presents a series of inconsistencies which cannot be explained away ; and through the stern logic employed to vindicate the non-dualistic idea, Sankara succumbs—a victim to false abstractions which were destined to drag into their vortex many a seeker after him. The absolute denial of difference, step by step, would lead to the Nihilist position. Absolute or bare Monism is a snare that appears inviting only from a distance. The moment, however, we have a nearer view the issues become so clear that the infatuation for it will automatically vanish.

To begin with, we must emphatically say that the notion of bare Monism is metaphysically absurd. If only the One remains, and the One alone exists, who is it that is aware of that One. For knowledge implies relations. If we talk of unity, then it cannot be unity in itself, but unity in diversity. Unity, therefore implies or presupposes diversity. Again, if we can have knowledge of Brahman, it can only be through the relation of subject and object. And any predication of Brahman involves diversity. But we are expressly told that there is no diversity in Brahman. It is pure Consciousness without any subject and object. And according to Sankara the subject can never be made the object of thought. But the moment we start on the endeavour to gain a knowledge of the same, what else are we doing but to bring in the very distinction that Sankara has ruled out? His absolute is a static Absolute transcending the operation of thought. Thought depends on the existence of something which is presented to it as object, but the Brahman is held to be beyond thought. Such a Brahman, unknown and unknowable, of which no predication is possible, which is pure thought without activity, how can Sankara so positively assert that it exists? As soon as he makes such a satement he is already predicating something of Brahman, and already using the faculty of thought which he rejected. Either Sankara must at the end confess to himself that he had embarked on an impossible quest, on the wrong path, or go a little further in the direction that his pitiless logic dragged him so far, and conclude that the Brahman, unknown and unknowable, of whose existence we have no possible faculty of understanding to know, indeed does not exist! "The final answer to the question of the nature of the Atman is that recorded for us in a legend by Sankara; Vaskali asked Bahva as to the nature of the Brahman. The latter remained silent, and on being pressed for an answer replied, "I teach you, indeed, but you understand not: silence is the Atman".[1]

If the ultimate Reality is qualitiless, and the external world, Maya, what place for Ethics can there be in a philosophy of this kind? Kokileswara Sastri[2] has tried to prove that Ethics has its place in the Vedanta, and so there is no endeavour to escape from the region of the ethical altogether. He may be right in condemning as erroneous the idea that the Vedanta has no room for works. But he assumes too much when he claims that Sankara's position is logically unassailable; and especially in view of the statement he himself makes that: "as the ultimate goal is transcendent, no mundane works or attributes can have power to directly produce it". An uncompromising dualism is assumed as between the mundane and the transcendent; and it would appear that the two worlds have no original relation whatsoever. "Ethics belong essentially to the sphere of duality, and is not in place in any sphere in which activity is denied or transcended." Everything depends on the answers to the questions raised by Urquhart,[3] whether "the Vendanta can assign that ultimate validity to ethics which could seem to be required if individual and social life is to reach and abide in perfection" whether it is "necessary to hold that the highest ethical state and the highest condition of the Soul must be different from each other." The dualism becomes evident in the Vedanta by maintaining that truth and practical life are irreconcilable; and that

---

[1] Keith: *Rel. and Phil. of the Veda*, p. 522.

[2] *Adwaita Philosophy*, Chapter IV.

[3] *The Vedanta and Modern Thought*, p. 175.

truth cannot be sacrificed because its recognition would disturb the ethical ideal.[1] According to Vedanta, ethical effort is merely to purify the mind and prepare man for the ultimate stage when morality is transcended. The performance of works is not with a view to reach to an End, or attain to the Supreme Good, which is itself the fulfilment of our Life, and so realisable in and through works, through the perfect embodiment of our aspirations and ideals. Such fulfilment of works is powerless to effect the emancipation of the Soul. In the attainment of the highest state, the sphere of Ethics must be left behind. Deussen is perfectly justified when he says: "Moral transformation remained foreign to Indian thought."

SECTION XII—THE PHILOSOPHY OF THE EPIC

We shall briefly consider the attitude to life as revealed in the Great Epic. It is not possible for us to study in detail, and we therefore restrict ourselves to the *Santi Parva*, the *Anugita* and the *Sanatsujatiya*.

The war that was waged on the plain of Kurukshetra was a war of nations, as momentous as the Great War of 1914, both in the issues involved and in consequences. Above all that titanic conflict stirred men's mind, and set them thinking of the real nature of things and of the value of life. None was more affected than Udhisthira himself who had fought the bloody campaign to acquire the sovereignty of the earth. It seemed as if the Universe had crashed to its dissolution. Humanity lay prostrate, bled white. The prize for which he had fought no longer attracted the victor, stained as it was with the blood of his nearest and dearest. Once before, when the fearful

[1] Kirtikar, V. J.: *Studies in Vedanta*, p. 106.

action was about to commence, his brother Arjuna had quailed before the terrible task, having lost hold of all valid principles of Dharma. Lord Krishna it was who called him back to the sense of his duty in his famous discourse, immortalised as the Song Celestial. This time it is the venerable Bhisma who tries to instruct Yudhisthira and bring him round to the right conception of Dharma. In a short speech,[1] instinct with pathos, Yudhisthira pours forth the sorrow pent up within ; and his words are a pathetic indictment of war. What troubles the king is the thought that numerous families had become extinct. The evils flowing from the extinction of a family are always considered to be heinous by the Hindu. "On the extinction of a family, the eternal rites of families are destroyed, impiety predominates over the whole family."[2] The consequences of impiety would be that the women become corrupt and inter-mingling of castes would set in. The necessary ceremonies of the offerings of libations would then fail, and the ancestors sink into hell. The necessity of procuring a "putra" is so imperious that the parents practice all sorts of vows and sacrifices to be blessed with a son. But in the great war, Yudhisthira saw that the young sons had all been killed before they could pay off the debts they owed to their fathers. He felt, therefore, that the blame is his ; and intended to expiate for the sin, by the practice of renunciation "disregarding all the pairs of opposites, adopting the vow of silence, and walking in the way pointed by knowledge."[3] Yudhisthira, however, is persuaded by the great men who still surround him to seek the counsel of Bhisma, who lay on his bed of arrows, calmly awaiting his liberation. Accordingly he approaches Bhisma who instructs him.

[1] *Santi Parva*, Chapter VII, 5-10.
[2] *Bhagavad-gita*, Ch. I, p. 41 (Telang's) (Dutt's Edn.)
[3] *Santi Parva*, Ch. VII, 38. (Dutt's)

The ideas expressed by Bhisma and Vyasa and others in the *Santi Parva* refer to many things in general. Those of a political nature we shall be discussing in a future chapter. In this section we shall confine ourselves to the philosophical notions about Life and the Universe.

The familiar ideas that we have been discussing in connection with the other philosophical systems are to be found in the *Santi Parva*, but sometimes modified by other ideas which are very important for us to take note of. The Doctrine of Karma, for instance, is enunciated in one place in the familiar old way ; but in another place it is profoundly influenced by another set of ideas. "Doing both auspicious and inauspicious acts here, a class of men," says Yudhisthira, "maintain their wives, children and kinsmen, all bound to them in relations of cause and effect. When the lease of their life expires, abandoning their weakened bodies, they take upon themselves all the effects of their sinful acts, for none but the actor is laden with the consequences of his own acts."[1] But elsewhere Vyasa says : "No one can acquire anything by his own deeds or by sacrifices and adoration. No man can give anything to another. Man gets everything through Time."[2] And the predominating tendency of the *Santi Parva* is towards predeterminism, and the consequent fatalism. "As a weapon made by a smith or carpenter is made under the control of the person who uses it, and moves as he moves it, likewise this universe, controlled by actions done in time, moves as those actions move it."[3] "The world is moved by time. Its works are settled by the course of time. Man does all his acts, good, bad, and indifferent, entirely under the influence of Time."[4] Indeed he cannot act otherwise than as he does. He may

---

[1] *Santi Parva*, Ch. IX, 30-31 (Dutt's).
[2] *Ibid.*, Ch. XXV, 5 (Dutt's).
[3] *Ibid.*, Ch. XXXIII, 22 (Dutt's).
[4] *Ibid.*, Ch. LXII, 10 (Dutt's).

imagine that he does many things, good and bad ; but all is really due to Destiny.[1] "The absence of what is pleasant, the presence of what is disagreeable, good and evil, happiness and misery, follow Destiny".[2] And existence is mere resolving and dissolving. "Forsooth, all creatures that are born show at first a union (of various ingredients and forces). Dissolution, however, overtakes them at the end. Like bubbles in water they come and go away".[3] "In this world a thousand sorts of relationships are made such as mother and father and sons and wife. In truth, however, whose are they and whose are we? No one can become any one's own, nor can anyone become anybody else own. Our union here with wives and kinsmen and well-wishers is like that of travellers at an inn in the road. Life and its surroundings are always revolving like a wheel, and the companionship of those who are dear is only for the time being. The union with brother, mother, father and friend is like that of travellers in an inn...... Man whose existence is so transitory, is compelled in course of Time, whether he will or no, to come upon this inevitable and broad path of all creatures."[4] And just as a person enters a new house, even so a creature enters successive bodies. The soul cannot be killed, so who is the slayer and who the slain? "Man acquires everything through Time...... All earthly things ripened by Time, suffer destruction. Some...... slay some men. The slayers again are slain by others. This is the language of the world. In reality, however, no one slays and no one is slain."[5] There is only sorrow and no happiness in the world. And there is no end to grief, for "grief

---

[1] *Santi Parva*, Ch. XXVII, 27 ff.
[2] *Ibid.*, Ch. XXVIII, 18.
[3] *Ibid.*, Ch. XXVII, 28.
[4] *Ibid.*, Ch. XXVIII (Dutt's).
[5] *Ibid.*, Sect. XXV (P. C. Ray's).

arises from happiness itself''.[1] And emancipation from this transitory and painful existence, deliverance from re-birth is conceived of as complete detachment and the severance of bonds that tie man to worldly life. And the state of salvation is variously described, but mostly in the language that we have become familiar with already. The means to gain the End also is conceived of sometimes as through action, and sometimes as through renunciation. There are two paths that lead to the goal, one through the performance of duties of the station in life, and the other through asceticism. But let it be noted that the life of action is not prescribed with any due recognition of the values of life. We are constantly told that action itself must be permeated through and through with the ascetic spirit.

Let us pass on to the examination of the ideas of life we get from the *Anugita*. The *Anugita* is a sort of recapitulation of the *Bhagavad-gita*. The leading ideas that we have noticed in the other systems of thought are also to be found in the *Anugita*. We have the Law of Karma with all its familiar characteristics. ''This world is the world of actions, where creatures dwell. All embodied (selfs) having here performed good or evil (actions), obtain (the fruit)''.[2] ''There is no destruction here of actions good or not good coming to one body after another they become ripened in their respective ways.'' There is no escape from the fruits of action which must necessarily be enjoyed. ''And freedom from action is not to be attained in this world even for an instant.''[3] And ruin goes always with action. This life in the world is always bound down by the pairs of opposites. Whatever little there is of happiness in this universe is all misery.[4]

---

[1] *Santi Parva*, Sect. XXV (P. C. Ray's).
[2] *Anugita*, Ch. II (Telang's).
[3] *Ibid.*, Ch. V (Telang's).
[4] *Ibid.*, Ch. III.

Worldly life is a fearful ocean, very difficult to cross. The human body is an unholy aggregate ; it is transient. The fearful effects of attachment and affection consist in pain and grief. The end of pleasure is ever grief and all action ends in destruction. And therefore "attachment to objects of desire is laid down to be the great delusion," and "the definition of the essence of darkness is that one sees the real in what is unreal."[1] It is only when everything is absorbed into the mind that the pleasures of worldly life are not esteemed. "The learned man who absorbs objects of desires from all sides, as a tortoise (draws in) his limbs, and who is devoid of passion and released from everything, is ever happy."[2] And so, "one who does no action and who has no desire, looks on this universe as transient, like an Asvattha tree, always full of birth, death and old-age."[3] And he would attain to be "Eternal Supreme Brahman, tranquil, unmoving, constant, indestructible", should free himself from "all impressions free from the pairs of opposites, without belonging", and should move, "among the collection of organs with penance." Then he "sees the Self in the Self".[4]

"Only by the mind (used) as a lamp is the great self perceived". Knowledge is the highest thing and renunciation is the best penance. And the true object of knowledge is the self, and the Self abides in all entities. He who has reached the emancipated state, sees the Self within the Self and "understanding everything, he sees the Self with the Self in all entities as one, and also as various changing from time to time."[5]

There are other ideas of a very interesting nature into which we cannot at present go, ideas like retribution and

[1] *Anugita*, Ch. XXI.
[2] *Ibid.*, Ch. XXVII.
[3] *Ibid.*, Ch. IV.
[4] *Ibid.*, Ch. IV.
[5] *Ibid.*, Ch. XXVII.

reward to be meted out in some hell and heaven and the conception of the wheel of life revolving with an inevitable impulse. We pass on to a brief notice of the *Sanatsujatiya*.

The *Sanatsujatiya* contains all the familiar ideas of Karma and the rest. It is through heedlessness and delusion that man develops desires which tempt him to travel in "devious paths ; and through egoism, he does not attain to union with the Self, and "being attached to the fruit of action" he undergoes death after death. By "contact with unreal entities his migrations are (rendered) inevitable".[1] But "he who pondering (on the self) destroys (the) fugitive (objects of sense), not even thinking of them through contempt (for them), and who being possessed of knowledge destroys desires in this way becomes as it were, the death of death (itself), and swallows it up". And by the acquisition of "primordial knowledge" "men cast off this mortal world." By the performance of action people conquer for themselves only "perishable worlds". But "the man of understanding attains by knowledge to the everlasting glory—for there is no other way to it."

SECTION XIII—THE DRAVIDIAN PHILOSOPHY AND ETHICS

The Dravidian philosophy, again, manifests the general features that we have been discussing. The Soul is conceived to be encased from eternity in a "Suksma Sarira" which persists through all its transmigrations. It is called "anu" (atom) because, as the *Siva Jnana Ratnavali* explains "the all pervading nature of the soul (atma) has become limited to an atom by its bondage. And from eternity the soul is associated with impurities,

[1] *Sanatsujatiya*: Ch. II.

or "malas", of "anavam", "maya", and "karma". Accordingly souls are classified, according to the extent of their defilement as (1) Vijnanakalars, (2) Pralayakalars and (3) Sakalars. The Vijnanakalars rank highest. For they are emancipated from the two impurities of "maya" and "karma", but not yet from "anavam" or the nature of the soul. Hence though freed from the necessity of future births or re-births, they await final release. The Pralayakalars are not freed from the impurities of "anavam" and "karma", and so are compelled to pass through births and re-births. The Sakalars are the lowest as they are defiled by all the three impurities, and to this class belong all the human beings, and even the ordinary "devas" or Gods. They are subject to sense perceptions, because they are corporal existences, wherein Karma has to be balanced. Deeds, or Karma must be ripened before *consumed*. All Karma is necessarily evil because it leads to re-births. The Soul, at death, only leaves its "Sthula Sarira" (or physical body), and goes either to hell or heaven to undergo its experiences and "forgetting such experiences, just as a dreamer forgets his experiences of the waking state, passes as an atom in its Suksma Sarira state into a suitable womb at conception, impelled thereto by the desire created by its previous karma".[1] It is in the phenomenal universe that the souls must "eat their Karma", and rid themselves of impurity in order to attain "Mukti". Thus a Cosmos must be evolved and Creation is the act of grace[2] of Siva for the benefit of the flock of souls. The *Tiru Arut Payan* definitely declares that it is not possible for release to take place until "the unequal good and evil become balanced".[3] But this release is to be obtained by the grace of Siva.[4] The ordinary Dravi-

[1] Nallaswamy Pillai, *Siva Jnana Bodham*, p. 13.

[2] *Siva Prakasham.*

[3] vi. I.

[4] cf. *The doctrine of Bhakti of the Bhagavad-gita.*

dian cannot find solace in the Aryan conception of non-duality or Advaita, and so it had to be toned down very near to the realistic idea of duality, Dvaita. God must be beneficient, all gracious, and willing to save souls from the terrible consequences of karma and re-births. And as there exists an eternal necessity for the cosmos to be created, Siva is held to be the ultimate cause by a reference to whom cosmos as the effect must be explained. The Saiva intelligence could not characterise this cosmos as unreal, as "maya". But there was even a greater reluctance to postulate Matter, as the Sankhya philosophy does, assuming an irreconcilable dualism. Accordingly there was postulated merely the existence of an underlying basis of creation, an essence, a form of matter, elemental abstract matter which is held to co-exist with Siva eternally, producing differentiated spheres of action for souls. Pure maya has, however, no connection with souls, which are associated with an impure form of elemental matter, (akin to the Sankhya Prakriti) known as impure (asuddha) maya. In this impure maya inhere the "malas", or impurities of souls—those of "karma" or deed, and "anavam", ignorance, the state or condition of the soul)[1] (anu). It is when the soul is freed from its malas and has gained knowledge by arousing the grace (arul) of the Deity that it can, as the *Siva Jnana Bodham* says, "see the truth of its oneness with Siva."[2] The triple bond or pasam of anavam, karma and maya, which fetters the Soul's intelligence must first be destroyed. It is because of anavam, a mala inherent in the soul, that it is unable to understand its true nature, its oneness with Siva. The *Siva Prakasam* declares[3] that final emancipation from the

[1] See R. W. Frazer's Article in the *Encyclopaedia of Religion and Ethics*. The present writer is largely indebted to that article.

[2] *Ibid.*, p. 4.

[3] Sutra, lxxvi.

pasam that fetters the soul can be attained only by the grace of Siva, the *para sakti* of pure knowledge. "The Lord, appearing as *guru* to the soul, which has advanced in charya, kriya, and yoga,—instructs him," says the *Siva Jnana Bodham*,[1] "that he is wasting himself among the savage five senses, and the soul understanding its real nature, leaves its former associates, and not being different from Him becomes united to His feet."[2]

SECTION XIV—PESSIMISM, KARMA, REBIRTH, AND MUKTI

The foregoing review of the philosophical and religious thought of India reveals certain ideas which are common to all the systems, though they differ widely from each other in other respects. The motive to speculation is always the same. An escape is sought from this existence of heat and turmoil. The world is looked upon as a prison of untold misery, held in the grip of disease, death and bondage. Life is full of pain. In the words of Schopenhauer,[3] "it is bad to-day, and will be worse tomorrow; and so on till the worst of all." We delude ourselves by thinking that pleasure outweighs pain. Even pleasure is pain, for while it lasts, there is the lurking terror that it may end in pain. So Kalidasa observes that "joy is half a sorrow".[4] The world's joy is but a mockery. It is a mirage after which we run and pursue. Life is a fleeting phantom, for :

> "........one thing is certain, that Life flies ;
> One thing is certain, and the Rest is lies ;
> The flower that once has blown for ever dies."[5]

[1] Sutravali.
[2] There is, however, no annihilation of the Soul.
[3] *Studies in Pessimism*, p. 13.
[4] Das Gupta and Lawrence Binyon: *Sakuntala*, p. 71.
[5] Omar Khayyam: *Rubaiyat*.

We are mere shapes of clay in the hands of the Potter. The world itself is the play of the Creator. He moulds human beings in different images, to stalk across the stage in the likeness of life, only to sink them back into the undistinguished clay from which he has called them into being. And the play itself, as Nanak said, "... lasts to-day and tomorrow." Could the Creator have shaped this life and this world for his enjoyment, and at the end of his labours, in supreme self-satisfaction saw "it was good?"[1] Evidently He must be cynical and capricious, if He created this miserable world "because he enjoyed doing it, and should then have clapped his hands in praise of his own work, and declared everything to be very good."[2] For, if God took to creation, through mercy, then there should have been pure happiness and blessedness; so that we could say, along with Hamlet, "there is a divinity that shapes our ends."[3] But if life is all misery, then we should say with the poet :

"Count o'er the joys thine hours have seen,
Count o'er thy days from anguish free,
And know, whatever thou hast seen,
'Tis something better not to be."

If a man's day of death is postponed, it does not mean that he is made happier thereby. "For life is made merely longer", says Seneca, "not pleasanter, by delay."[4] Would it not be better to escape from life by the sword, or the rope, or poison?[5]

The Indian thinkers generally set aside the suggestion of suicide because of the acceptance of determinism and karma. Things are held to be guided by Fate, and people resign themselves accordingly. The Doctrine of Karma

---

[1] *Genesis*: Chapter 1.
[2] Schopenhauer: *Studies in Pessimism*, p. 23.
[3] Act V, Sc. 2.
[4] *Seneca*, p. 78.
[5] See Lecky: *History of European Morals*, p. 91

tells them that even suicide is no escape, for they will be born again impelled by their actions. Thus they will be forced back into existence. They should therefore seek the path of "No Return". The true knowledge alone would dispel avidya, and lead to moksha.

Underlying the whole is the idea that the world is devoid of value. Every system of thought and belief in India is one in denouncing world's existence. Final Release is through detachment from empirical relationships. We have to burn worldly love and cut ourselves off. In a sense, we might say, the spirit of denial and renunciation is common to all religions. Pessimism, it would be found on a deeper analysis is inseparable from religious faith. Perhaps with a happy world, there would be no necessity for God. And to induce men to turn their minds towards the Eternal, it would be necessary to impress upon them the transcience and unsubstantiality of worldly enjoyments and objects. In contrast, the Hereafter is magnified in such brilliant hues that it would not fail to draw men's attention. St. Paul, in his Epistle to the Romans exhorts them not to be "conformed to this world". And all great saints have felt that true religious endeavour should be undivided; there should be concentrated effort to reach God. With regard to the attitude towards life, therefore, every religion is in a sense pessimistic. For the matter of that, nobody can be a thoroughgoing optimist, if he would not succumb to the dangerous influence of justifying the *Status Quo*. We cannot say that what is, is as it ought to be. The "divine discontent", a dissatisfaction with the order of things as they are, is the very condition of a continued life. For "men who are satisfied with life as it is, are mostly those who live in a healthy surface activity which keeps them from reflection."[1] Their optimistic temper could be maintained

[1] Edward Caird: *The Evolution of Religion*, Vol. II, pp. 105-106.

only so long as circumstances are favourable. It is the optimism of children. Reflection "brings to us the consciousness of our finitude" and sets "the infinite over against us, as that which is unattainable, and yet as that which alone can satisfy us". It causes us to "pine for what is not". The more we become conscious of the cleavage between the actual and the ideal, the deeper is our sense of want. And hence is the feeling of world-weariness and self-disgust. The very greatest of men, Goethe and Kant, as much as Schopenhauer, are all of them pessimists at one stage of their life or another.

But just as there is no thorough-going optimist, we must say that there is no thorough-going pessimist as well. And there seems to be only the time-element distinguishing between the two world-views. Pessimism looks upon the present as an evil, and seeks a way of escape into a future bright world. Optimism looks upon the present itself in bright hues, and as leading into the larger life. And it has been sometimes said that the Indian philosophers, though pessimistic with regard to life, Here and Now, are optimistic indeed with regard to the Hereafter. This would be quite true if the life of the Hereafter is conceived of as attainable by man, by leading a good life, Here and Now. But the goal of life, as conceived by Indian philosophers, appears to be placed so distant, and indeed as beyond knowledge, and the Law of Karma so inexorable, that all hope of a bright Hereafter seems illusory indeed. In the West the pessimistic influence was not strong enough to vitiate human efforts. Life has its imperfections, sufferings and disappointments. Loud complaints of this we, indeed, do hear. But on this account, the Western philosophers did not turn away from life. Nobody could be more optimistic than Homer ; yet he complains :

"For there is nothing whatever more wretched than men,

Of all things as many as breathe and move o'er the earth."

Hesiod, too, observes that the land and the sea are full of evil things. Sophocles says that "not to be born is the most reasonable". Aeschylus feels pity for the condition of mortals whose prosperity even a shadow can turn. And yet there is a fundamental difference between the Greek and Indian views. As the apostle of pessimism himself puts it: "Between the ethics of the Greeks and the ethics of the Hindoos, there is a glaring contrast. In the one case......... the object of ethics is to enable man to lead a happy life; in the other it is to free and redeem him from life altogether......"[1] And what is true of Greek life is also largely true of modern European life. Western philosophers are keenly alive to the shortcomings of life; but they only on that account all the more think of the ways and means of making life happy by the elimination of wrong and evil. Plato's *Republic* has had many a modern imitation. And of late the progress made in social philosophy definitely points to healthy anticipations.

Why did the Indian thinkers, then, turn away from life? This is a question which is very difficult to answer. Some have assumed that the geographical environment has much to do in moulding the Indian temper.[2] But we think that the influence of geography on man has been exaggerated. As a matter of history, we do know that the same geographical conditions, of zone and climate, manifest enormous differences in development. Moreover, pessimism and optimism are but phases of the human temper which are to be found almost everywhere. Plato, in the *Timaeus*, is an optimist, but elsewhere, as in *Phaedo*, sometimes in *Gorgias* and in the tenth book of the *Republic*, he seems to reveal strains of pessimism.

---

[1] Schopenhauer: *Studies in Pessimism*, p. 25.

[2] See Oldenberg: *Life of Buddha*, p. 11 ff.

And what is true of Plato is true of almost every other thinker. We also know how Malthus and Darvin transfer the pessimistic note into biological reasoning. In view of all this, it would be wrong to attribute pessimism to purely geographical considerations. Indian pessimism is essentially due to metaphysical speculations. It is the reasoned conclusion of hardened philosophers in possession of a sound mind, rather than the expression of the wearied spirit of a disappointed and beaten soul, weighed down by physical discomforts. In other words, it is due to the failure to interpret existence in truly ethical terms. The reality of this world of ours, the world of our manifold relationships is denied. Our experience itself is ultimately transcended in the conception of the ultimate. And nowhere do we get any idea of a formulation of human values. In the impossible attempt to negate experience, life, and the world, the human spirit is banished into a self-constituted universe of imagination from which everything of life is forced out. The emphasis of thought results in the suppression of action and emotion. And no wonder with this fundamental dislocation of the eternal harmony that is the reality of the world, it very often happens that self-realisation is confounded with self-repression which in fact it becomes. Man enters this world which he abhors as a prison, remains a stranger to it, all the while revetting his hopes on the path of escape from life altogether. There is no aspiration to better existence through human effort. For this implies desire to live ; bondage to Karma, to the perpetual Going and Coming.

And this Doctrine of Karma is one of those powerful factors that have given Indian civilisation its characteristic stamp for two thousand five hundred years. It expresses the inexorable law of moral causation, fulfilling itself in the history of each soul through its round of existences. The idea of Karma and Karma-vipaka, along with that of Samsara, pervades the whole thought of India, giving it its peculiar ascetic bent. It is held that action, good and bad, binds man to the process of Going and Coming. Release from this frightful round can only be obtained through the cessation of Karma, by following the path of renunciation. The life of the Sanyasi is always looked upon, as we shall just consider, to be the highest. Action, therefore, shapes a man's destiny, the course of his future lives. It also explains the present. Karma must be consumed. Evil deeds must be expiated; and good deeds must receive their reward. As old Karma is exhausted, new desert is acquired. The origin of suffering and the diversity we notice in human conditions are to be attributed to Karma. The present life had an endless series of lives before, and will have an equally endless series in future, so long as Karma attaches to it. The Soul is compelled to course through the endless round so long as defilement attaches to it. Liberation is the destruction of Karma; for it is not bad action alone that condemns the human being to worldly existence. Even good action has the same effect. In this respect it is interesting to contrast the Indian doctrine with the Egyptian.[1] According to the latter it is only the wicked that are doomed to transmigration. The Indian view has it that both the good and bad migrate; and the particular form and condition of a new life is determined by the past Karma. Perhaps it might be held that to some this doctrine of transmigration might have been an incentive to virtue. Ceasar tells us that this was one of the tenets of the Druids: "Souls do not die, but pass at death from one to another; and that this was a great incentive to virtue, for the fear of death was disregarded."[2] And originally the belief in transmigration may not have been Aryan. Even though

[1] See Herodotus, ii, 123.

[2] Rhys Davids: *Hibbert Lecture*, 1881, p. 76.

See Tylor's: *Primitive Culture*, Vol. II, pp. 1-10 for Transmigration.

Plato and Pythagoras allude to it, to them the doctrine is primarily of philosophical interest only. Whatever that may be, in this doctrine of transmigration or metempsychosis we are, perhaps as Bosanquet puts it, "offered chains of personalities linked together by impersonal transitions."[1] The conception of continuance, of the soul persisting through all its changes might lead us to the idea of personality. Of course there is the difficulty which Aristotle pointed out "of an identical soul animating wholly different bodies in succession." When we come to a closer examination of the theory we indeed find that this identity is wholly illusory. As a theory of punishment, it assumes that it is the same individual who committed a crime that is also punished. "As amongst a thousand cows a calf knows its mother, so the deed done before time finds out its doer."[2] We shall consider the ethical aspects of this retributive justice later. A mere glance at Buddhist metaphysics will be sufficient to dispel any expectation that we may entertain regarding the Doctrine of Karma and Re-birth as the foundation for the idea of Immortality. Buddha has nothing to say of the soul. According to the tenets of his followers there is no Reality anywhere and everything is a process of becoming; a grouping of conditions. There is no Ego or entity as such. Moreover, what you call the individual is not the same in time. What he is now is not what he will be next moment. If there is anything absolute within the limitations of Buddhist thought, it is the Law of Causation, complemented as it is by the Law of Continuity; to express the same in ethical terms, it is the doctrine of Karma. It is Karma that survives through the endless round of births and deaths. But this Karma does not pursue the same individual through a succession of lives;

---

[1] *The Value and Destiny of the Individual*, p. 267.

[2] Prof. A. G. Hogg: *Karma and Redemption*, p. 19.

such a view is impossible without positing the substantiality of the Soul. It is in fact a new sentient being that Karma determines. The theory of Karma, as Prof. Rhys Davids points out, rests on the necessity of justice and causality, but the Buddhists "have failed to see that the very key-stone itself, the link between one life and another, is a mere word this wonderful hypothesis, the individualised and individualising force of Karma."[1] So according to the Buddhist "the so-called reincarnate Self is really a new being."[2]

Thus we understand the real idea of Immortality involved in the ideas of Karma and Samsara. If what is meant is the continuous, conscious growth of the spirituality of the human being, so that every succeeding birth does not appear as an isolated unit, but a conscious, intelligible link in the chain of human endeavour after the attaining to realisable Immortality, whatever that condition might be, the theory may admit of possible acceptance. But as it actually is, it is supposed that the fruits of deeds, either good or bad, are inherited. Karma, in its juridical aspect means the enjoyment of the rewards for good action and expiation for evil action. And the penalty is to be paid to the last pice. The whole theory is based upon a wrong scheme of hedonistic calculus. Action or moral conduct is not conceived of as having a cumulative influence on character as a whole. Every deed must exact its own fulfilment.

But it is only when we can consciously connect punishment with crime can the punishment itself be justified. If just as we can remember our deeds of a week ago, or a year back, we could also recollect, through effort, our experience in our previous births, we would then be supplied with an intelligent basis to account for the parti-

[1] *Hibbert Lectures*, pp. 105-106; (quoted by Pringle-Pattison: *Idea of Immortality*, p. 113).

[2] Pringle-Pattison: *The Idea of Immortality*, p. 114.

cular form and condition our present life has taken. Our present life as an effect could then be traced to a knowable cause in a past birth. Leibnitz was perfectly right when he said that "immortality without recollection is ethically quite useless."[1] We are reminded of the famous Doctrine of Recollection of Plato. The Soul does not drink sufficiently deep of the stream of Lethe to quite forget everything.[2] The recognition of man's whence and where, in other words his destiny as a moral being, is not the same, however, as surrendering to the Law of Karma, which is primarily a scheme of rewards and punishments according to the action.

And the ethical bearings of the Law of Karma are so vital that we should carefully analyse what they involve. We suffer because we must. Not only must we reap what we sow, but we must have sown what we reap. Right and wrong are not moral ideas as we would understand them, but refer to actions which are supposed to produce merit or demerit. And most of these actions are non-moral, referring as they do to prescriptive observance. But whatever that may be, every action is supposed to yield fruit, either good or bad. The Law is inexorable. Sometimes it has been expressed in the language of Science that every effect must have had a cause. If we see a man born, say blind or lame, this must be attributed to some sin of his in his past birth. And translated into the language of the Law of Cause and effect, the Law of

---

[1] Quoted by Inge: *Philosophy of Plotinus*, Vol. II, p. 30.

[2] The Doctrine of Transmigration seems to have acquired confirmation of many great thinkers of all ages. Empedocles is said to have said that he had been "a boy, a girl, a bush, a bird, a fish". Origen denounces the doctrine which seems to have acquired a pretty wide acceptance in the Early Christian Church. Leibnitz and Lessing also discuss the doctrine. See Rhys Davids *Hibbert Lecture*, 1881, Appendix IV; see Plato: *Phaedo*, i, 457; *Republic* X, etc. (Jowett's Translation.)

Karma seems so tempting, and so satisfactory that even Poussin has said that it is a happy one, eminently moral and to a large extent a true one."[1] It is necessary at the very outset to assert that the Law of Karma instead of being "eminently moral" lays the axe at the very roots of morality. We may even go to the extent of saying that this law is positively immoral, and is moreover so couched in its general tenets as easily to become the apologia of injustice and fatalism.

We shall go even further and venture to challenge, along with Pringle-Pattison,[2] the whole conception of moral forces as working along uncommunicating lines in this fashion, each hypothetical series of lives being as it were self-contained, inheriting only its own deeds and expitiating only its own sins. This is certainly a "defect" at once in religious feeling and in speculative imagination. For we are all members of one body, and although vicarious suffering, in a judicial or legal sense, is nothing less than immoral, the redemptive suffering of the best is the deepest truth of religious experience. And the Law of Karma lays emphasis not on redemption but on retribution. The whole process becomes an endless one, and the final release from the meshes of the operation of Karma seems indeed too distant to be of any consolation. As Deussen says, the theory is "that life, in quality as well as in quantity, is the accurately meted and altogether fitting expiation of the deeds of a previous existence. But the life in which the expiation takes place necessarily involves further actions, and these afford fresh opportunities for errors, unwitting offences and sins : and such deeds must be expiated anew in a subsequent existence,

---

[1] Art. *Ency. Rel. and Eth.*

In recent times the Doctrine of Rebirth has gained the acceptance of many western scholars, notable amongst whom is Dr. McTaggart.

[2] *Idea of Immortality*, p. 114 ff.

so that the clock-work of requital, in running down, always winds itself up again, and so in perpetuity."

In fact emancipation is not through the path of works. Almost every philosophical system of India, places the ultimate End or Moksha, beyond the realm of action and experience, and as beyond the level of Ethics. Action will never effect release from the frightful wheel of Samsara. And what accounts for the hold that the Law of Karma still has over the educated Indian is just its resemblance to the Scientific Law of Cause and Effect. We are of opinion that every natural fact must be appraised in terms of value or at least, if the Law of Karma is to have any meaning for us, it should be interpreted as the law of Moral Causation. And it is just here that the Law fails to satisfy our sense of ethical justice. The scheme of awards and punishments, according to it, is primarily in terms of material well-being. We do not have either a progressive fulfilment of ethical perfection or a gradual deterioration of the moral man according as the nature of Karma is either good or bad. There is no cumulative effect on character. Each act exacts its own reward or punishment. An ideally perfect man must nevertheless suffer in this life for some supposed sin he had committed in a previous birth. Above all "the principle of the Spiritual harvest" is that payment should be in kind. "He that soweth to the flesh shall of the flesh reap corruption; but he that soweth to the spirit shall of the Spirit reap life everlasting"[1] The Law of Karma does not include this principle at all.

It remains to be seen if the Law of Karma does at least provide an incentive to virtue. If its working is inexorable, and if every good deed finds its reward, and an evil one its punishment, it is natural to expect that this would serve as a deterrent to evil doing. And if good

[1] Quoted by Pringle-Pattison: *Idea of Immortality*, p. 117.

deed is rewarded it is also natural to expect that people will try to do good always. But this view suffers under the fatal defect that it equates happiness with good or virtue. All through Indian thought pain and suffering are taken to be evil. Moreover virtue itself can neither be disinterested nor self-sufficing. The theory of retribution is not a healthy force to form character, for it does not appeal to any positive fact of one's will. The idea must be grounded upon the belief in a living God, God who is both Good and Perfect. "Be ye therefore perfect, even as your Father which is in heaven is perfect," is the injunction of Christ.

In Indian Ethics moral injunctions are not for the attainment of fellowship with God who is Good and Perfect ; but they are with a view to the autonomy of the Self. Hence Hindu Ethics is highly individualistic. We shall further on note some vital qualifications of the statement so generally made here. Here we are only concerned in pointing out the dangerous implications of the Indian view and in our opinion the warning cannot be too strongly given especially in view of recent influences on our life. The predominating characteristic of Hindu civilisation is individualistic ; it could not be otherwise based as it is on the ideas of Karma and "Swadharma". But so far individualism is only of the life spiritual, though its reaction on social values must have been considerable. But of late, with the growth of the industrial and commercial enterprise, and the consequent intrusion of the economic criterion in the judgment of the facts of life, our life is rapidly becoming highly individualistic on its material side too. We might say that we are reaching by rapid strides to the state which can be described as "individualism run mad." And unless we bestir ourselves in time we shall crash inevitably towards an awful cataclysm which would mean the material and moral collapse of the fabric of whose stability we have so often boasted. Our civilisation that has appeared to all acute observers as in its foundations deeply laid—in fact, to be static—will at last move from its hinges and slide down the depths of the abyss, to explode in smoke and ruins, as that of the West in the Titanic eruption of 1914.

It is therefore with an anxious care for our society, and not with any fault-finding temper that we have undertaken to present in this thesis an ideal of life which should form the foundations of our Polity. We said that Indian Ethics is based on the idea of Self-autonomy. The emphasis is laid on the Self and the End of Life is to realise this Self. But the path to this realisation lies in detachment from the world of social relationships :

> "Walk not—where many folk would
> make thee chief.
> Dizzy the mind becomes, and
> hard to win
> Is concentrated thought. And he who knows :
> 'Ill bodes the company of many folk,'
> Will keep himself aloof from haunts of
> crowds."

is the constant injunction before the spiritual aspirant. So the more you multiply social contacts, the more numerous would your bonds become which tie you down to the Cycle of Going and Coming. It is not right action that leads to Moksha ; what it does is to insure another life under better circumstances. It is the discipline that destroys Karma, when action is abandoned, that is looked upon as valuable. We will not be surprised that we find this strange ideal held up to mankind even in such a book as the Bhagavad-gita, which contains so much of genuine matter which serves for Faith and Worship. We are asked to renounce all Dharma and take refuge in the Bhagavan. The ethical ideal does not, and cannot find its end in the Supreme End, which can be realised by Virtue and Righteousness. The Supreme End is placed beyond Virtue and Righteousness and the conduct of man should be such as to enable him to transcend Virtue and Righteousness, right and wrong.

Is the Law of Karma an efficient solution of the problem of justice? We have said that it concerns itself with the scheme of rewards and punishments. Karma, good and bad deeds, have their renumeration and retribution. Before we go further, let us draw attention to a peculiar influence the rise of this doctrine of Karma had over other ideas which in course of time might have been certainly healthy in their influence. Hopkins has well observed that "Karma struck hard against the old belief in sacrifice, penance, and repentance as destroyers of sin," for it lays down : "As a man himself sows, so he himself reaps ; no man inherits the good or the evil act of another man The fruit is of the same quality with the action, and good or bad, there is no destruction of the action." In other words the Law of Karma is inexorable. A man will be punished in spite of the fact that he may repent. Retributive justice, the theory of punishment has no reference to the reformation of the guilty and the sinner. In other words, punishment becomes an end in itself. "For", as Rashdall makes plain,[1] "the moment we insist upon the effect produced upon the sufferer's soul by his punishment, the retributive theory is deserted for the reformatory or the deterrent." Or to express it as Kant does, "the penal law is a Categorical Imperative." And the scheme of rewards and punishments that Karma follows is something like Kant's third Postulate of the Practical reason advocated as a religious theory of the actual world. "The distribution of happiness in exact proportion to morality constitutes", said Kant, "the summum bonum of a possible world." Pringle-Pattison truly points out[2] the illu-

[1] *Theory of Good and Evil*, Vol. I, p. 285.

[2] *Idea of Immortality*, pp. 118-199.

sory nature of the whole theory resting as it does on the religious or ethical postulate of absolute justice. "Retribution", he says, "is, according to Karma, the essential business of the world; the cosmic process continues to exist for no other purpose than to keep the balance true; and, as the balance is continually being disturbed the process is interminable."

There is another aspect of the Law of Karma which we ought to note carefully. It seems to have the single aim of vengeance. It is the rigid application of the old Mosaic Law, "an eye for an eye, a tooth for a tooth"; in other words, blood for blood; no mercy, no quarter. Karma is the founding of the moral universe upon this crude and primitive *Lex Talionis*. The Universe would, from this theory, appear to be organised for vindictive justice. It appears "as primarily a place for the doling out of punishment", and so is degraded "to the level of a police-court." No wonder to Schopenhaur the world appeared to be a penal colony.

One fatal defect of the Law of Karma is that it has no place for forgiveness, and as we have just seen, punishment becomes an end in itself. The sinner may no longer be a sinner. He might be a genuine penitent. Still he must be punished, not because he should be reformed, which he is already being penitent, but because the Law must have its course. Shall we not say that such a conception of Law is barbarous, and if it were true, we would sooner turn atheists than continue to believe in a just and merciful Providence! But God is truly love and He is always prepared to forgive our trespasses, as we forgive the trespasses of our brothers. His is the constant message of the hope of salvation and redemption: "Repent ye: for the kingdom of heaven is at hand."

One peculiar fact we have left out of consideration so far. When we place a thief or a murderer on his trial at the bar, pronounce the sentence he has to undergo, we would, as far as possible, at least give him all opportunities to prove his innocence. Above all he knows for what definite crime he is being punished, and unless the crime is made known the criminal does not know why he is punished and so cannot make any effort to better his character. If the trying judge, for instance, passes a general sentence punishing the prisoner for all the offences, known and unknown, that he might have committed we will evidently think that the proper place for such a judge is the mental hospital. This is exactly what the Law of Karma implies. If you posit a God who awards punishments for the unconscious evil Karma of man, evidently that God is himself evil since his punishments seem to be mysterious and arbitrary. He does not make known to the sufferer for what particular sin he is made to suffer. If we do away with the hypothesis of God, and assert that man punishes himself for his former Karma, then too, we can only imagine man to be a strange creature, devoid of reason, a victim to himself. He does not know for what particular crime he is punishing himself. And we ask, what man would voluntarily inflict self-punishment, if the choice did really rest with him?

Thus in the last analysis, we find that if the Law of Karma is inexorable it is absolute, which cannot be God's for such an identification is revolting to our conception of a merciful father, and which cannot be in any sense identified with our own self either. It is a blind freak, in a moral sense, but seems to be endowed with a marvellous reason, in the sense a bloodhound is after the scent of its victim.

It is quite natural from this view of life that the world of our social relationships is ruled out. The End, the Summum Bonum or Moksha cannot be realised through any empirical instrument. This world as we see has only a negative value. It is the place where Karma is performed and has to be consumed. It appears to be a prison, "a penitentiary, a sort of penal colony" as Schopenhaur would describe it. What cursed Fate is it that has thrown us into this couldrum of sin and misery!

How we wish, therefore, that we had not been! Could we so discipline ourselves and regulate our life that we could turn away from this world of appearance! It is Kama that is the root of Karma; with the destruction of the root, its seed becomes barren. So let ethical life have one object in view, the suppression of desire. Whatever we do, we should do without desire. Karma must be Nishkama. It is only from detachment from the things of the world that one would reach to the Arhatship of Kaivalya or Moksha. The Here and Now can never be the foundation for the Hereafter. A life of action would only perpetuate our misery. Karma binds us down to Samsara. Complete Renunciation is the first condition to the hope of the Hereafter. The Indian view of life can only lead to asceticism i. e. Sanyasa, the path that leads to "No Return."

But, we might be reminded that this is the extreme aspect of the problem that we are emphasising. The Hindu ideal, it might be said, affords ample scope for the life to be lived in this world. The fourfold scheme of life, in its Varna and Asrama aspects, is an elaborate ordering of existence on its empirical side, giving opportunities to live according to Dharma. We shall examine if there is any truth in this contention in a future chapter. Here we shall treat of the idea this involves in a more general manner. Universally stated it would mean that Moksha can be attained through both the paths, of action and of knowledge; i. e. through Karma and Jnana, through participation in life by the performance of action, and through philosophical detachment from life by the acquisition of discriminating knowledge. Or we may use the two expressions to denote this, for they are familiar to almost every Indian—*Deva-Yana* and *Pitri-Yana*.

Deva-Yana and *Pitri-Yana* refer to the path of the Gods and to the path of the Fathers. "On these paths all that lives moves on, whatever there is between father (sky) and mother (earth).[1] These are the two well-known paths of which we get numerous references in Hindu literature. "They who celebrate sacrifices go by the Pitri-path, while they who want salvation, go by the celestial path."[2] Those who perform Vedic acts go to heaven by the southern path of the Sun. But the northern path is trodden by those who are devoted to Yoga. In the *Chandogya Upanishad*[3] we have an elaborate description of the kind of life reserved for the Soul in the realms of the Fathers and of the Celestials. There seems to be a crossing of two separate ideas, "two entirely distinct conceptions of retribution. There is the conception of retribution as attained in another sphere of existence, crossed by the conception of retribution in another life on earth."[4] What is most important for us, however, is to note that a life of works does not lead at all to salvation. They who "living in a village practise (a life of) sacrifices, works of public utility, and alms" go to the world of the fathers; and "having dwelt there, till their (good) works are consumed, they return again that way as they came."[5] Action only fetters the man. "Freed from the sinful fetters of action, one attains to the highest end".[6] A life of works, in other words, leads us by the path of the Pitris to an existence of temporary enjoyment. The *Deva-Yana* leads to the region of the celestials where we live in communion with the conditioned or qualitative Brahman. According to Sankara even this is not the

[1] *Brihad Upa.*, VI, 2.
[2] *Santi Parva*, Chapter XVII, 15 (Dutt's Edn.).
[3] V, 10.
[4] Principal McKenzie: *Hindu Ethics*, pp. 71-72.
[5] *Chand Upa.*, V, 10.
[6] *Santi Parva*, Chapter XVII, 17.

highest stage or Moksha. The ultimate End, according to him, is to be united with Para-Brahman, which is a state of complete identity without difference. And this state of Kaivalya or Moksha can never be attained through Karma-Kánda. "Endued with actions creatures come into this wheel of life that is continually turning like the wheel of a car." We should leave aside this world of human relationships, should give up worldly concern, "which is really a passing illusion although it looks permanent", and "freed from all attachments and snapping all fetters", desire to get "a permanent, eternal, and ever-abiding place."

The importance attached to action can, however, be explained with reference to one of the most characteristic beliefs of the Aryan peoples. It is not all action that is commended but only a particular kind of action. It has reference to the Dharma of the individual as determined by birth and station in life. We will be discussing this later. Here we are concerned with the special kind of action to be performed by those who follow the Pitri-Yana. And this action has reference to ritual observance. Above all it refers to the offerings of libations to Gods, Rishis and Pitris. The Pitris or Fathers or Pitri-devatas as they are called, have to be satisfied with clarified butter and funeral balls etc. This is commonly known as the Shradha ceremony. And this custom is to be found common among all the early Aryans. It is to be found among the Greeks and Romans. Fustel de Coulanges contends that the origins of property in land are to be traced to the peculiar religious beliefs of these early peoples. Religion and property were closely connected. In India too we have the two very closely related. The rights of inheritance are determined according to the eligibility of the claimant to continue the domestic religion of the family. The importance attached to male offspring is due to the anxiety to ensure the continuance of the domestic religion. Marriage, therefore, has special reference to this necessity; it is to see that the family is continued. A life of domesticity is enjoined only because of this consideration. We are told how the four different modes of life were at one time weighed in the balance, "when domesticity was placed on one scale, it required the three others to be placed on the other for balancing it."[1] The reason for this is immediately given: in domesticity, it is said, are acts, intended for Pitris, gods and guests." But the household life itself cannot bring us any nearer the ultimate End. We have only to duly pass through the four modes of life prescribed, and eventually take to the mode of the parivrajaka. And whatever we do in the grihastha stage must itself be permeated through and through with the spirit of renunciation. True renunciation is the casting off of internal and external attachments, and this could be practised by the householder. That is why sometimes we are told that "asceticism is attainable by leading the life of a householder."[2] But as soon as the grihastha is blessed with a putra, he should renounce the domestic stage and pass on to the next. Salvation is not through the performance of action[3] but through self-repression. "When one contracts all his desires like a tortoise drawing in all his limbs, then the native effulgence of his soul soon manifests itself."[4] We are therefore in

[1] *Santi Parva*, Sect. XI-XII (P. C. Ray).

[2] *Ibid.*, Chapter XI, 21. (Dutt's Edn.)

"Off all orders that of householders (is the first) there is no doubt of that........." *Anugita*, Ch. XXIX. We have the reason stated. "The householder, and the Brahmacharian, the forester, and also the beggar, all these four orders are stated to have the order of the householder for their basis. Whatever system of rules is prescribed in this world, to follow it is good; this has been celebrated from ancient times."

[3] *Anugita*, Ch. XXXVI has: "Some men of dull understanding extol action. But as to the high-souled ancients they do not extol action". See the reasons given.

[4] *Santi Parva*, Chapter XXI, 3 (Dutt's Edn.).

a position to appraise correctly the relative values of the life of action and renunciation. "The path that lies to the south and leads to the regions of light is reserved for men devoted to action. These are acquired by persons subject to birth and death." That end, however, which persons who wishing to have salvation seek cannot be described. "Yoga is the best means for attaining to it."[1] The spirit and path of renunciation alone lead to Moksha. The life of action must be itself a life of austerities and penances leading to the cessation of all action whatever. Whenever renunciation is discouraged, it is not because life of domesticity is to be preferred. "When Renunciation is discouraged, it is not the spirit but the formality of it."[2] The truly emancipated person is he who has renounced the world and stands aloof from it unattached, having broken all his bonds.

Thus we are justified in holding that a hiatus is assumed in Hindu Thought between Karma and Jnana, between a life of action and faith, and the path of knowledge which alone can lead to final Emancipation. And because such a divorce is presupposed knowledge can never have reference to conduct. Indian philosophy has this element of value that it insists upon the truism that evil is due to Avidya, and so knowledge would dispel it.[3] But knowledge itself is not teleological, and so cannot find its expression in morality. In other words it is not knowledge that would lead to right action. If it were so it would be very near the Socratic idea implied in his famous paradox "knowledge is virtue." If evil is moral evil, the knowledge that it is evil would inspire man to strive for its elimination. And this moral striving will be a progressive fulfilment of virtue. In other words life would be

---

[1] *Santi Parva*, Chapter XIX, 14-15 (Dutt's Edn.).
[2] *Ibid.*, Sect. XVIII (P. C. Ray).
[3] Rashdall: *Theory of Good and Evil*, Vol. II, p. 253 ff.

"a real, and not a merely apparent, struggle" to diminish evil, to which our moral consciousness invites us. "The evil is a real evil, though an evil destined to be more and more diminished."[1]

The fundamental defect of the Indian view is that evil is looked upon, not as moral evil but as intellectual evil. So it is to be destroyed not by the practice of virtue, but by the acquisition of discriminating knowledge. And this knowledge tells us that in the ultimate there is no right or wrong, no good and evil. What we look upon as evil is mere appearance. The real universe is one in which nothing really happens. Evil is to be predicated only of this world of becoming. In that ultimate being which is a timeless and changeless state, action and inaction do not find place. It is a stage of Pure Inertia which transcends our Thought.

From the standpoint of Indian Thought it would, therefore, appear that Temporal Existence is a lapse from this ideal state. Life is verily a mistake. If there is a God, he must have willed this universe in a fit of absence of mind. This Life, Here and Now, being unsubstantial and illusory, can have no values which would determine its significance from the standpoint of moral effort. "For the philosophies in which that which becomes is mere appearance", observes Rashdall, "values too should be merely apparent and unreal."[2] In other words, the world of fact cannot be appraised by that of value.

And this unnatural divorce between the Here and Now, and the Hereafter, is inevitable when the idea is wrongly conceived, when the goal of man is placed so distant and beyond all reach, that even Thought cannot

[1] Aristotle was largely right when he said: "To the attainment of the virtues knowledge conduces little or nothing" (*Eth. Nic.* Ch. iv, 3) but most of our mistakes are due to lack of thought. What we should have is "moral thoughtfulness".

[2] *Theory of Good and Evil*, Vol. II, p. 353.

approach it. It is assumed by more than one of the philosophical systems of India that knowledge of the ultimate reality is not possible. God or the Absolute of metaphysical speculation is unknown and unknowable. He is Pure Self-consciousness. The faculty of Thought is powerless, or incompetent to know Reality. And yet it is equally asserted, inconsistent though it appears at the very face of it, that knowledge of the Atman will take us to emancipation. And Atman is Brahman ; *Tat Tvam Asi.* This doctrine of the emancipating knowledge of the Atman, Deussen praises as the decisive and striking expression of the "eternal philosophical truth." We are unable to appreciate the great scholar's admiration ; for the doctrine itself presents inconsistencies. In the first place, we fail to realise how mere theoretical knowledge could have such saving grace unless it expresses and justifies itself in a life of moral striving. Secondly, the quest after the monadic Atman has paralysed action resulting, as it did, in a contemplative life, meditation and resignation being the chief virtues to be practised.

The whole metaphysical formulation of Indian thought is fundamentally defective. God is not a distant, unknown and unknowable Reality, but One of Whose presence, every second of our lives, we have living witness. We have every means of knowing Him and focussing Him in our everyday life. He reveals Himself in many ways. Thought is not incompetent to know Him, though we admit it is not adequate. Our confusion is due to the confounding of the unknowable and the unfathomable. We might not reach to the very depths, but that does not mean we cannot also touch on the surface. Indeed every judgment we make is an affirmation of God and takes us nearer to Him. To reject Thought or Reason is to kick away the very ladder which will help us to climb to our ideal. The rejection of the faculty of Thought is itself an emphatic admission of the competency of Reason. We must use the faculty of Thought even to repudiate it. And when we say that God is not knowable through Thought or Reason we are already recognising the faculty of Thought in making this judgment.

Any metaphysical statement of the universe, moreover, must try to understand it in terms of a Moral Order. Our judgments are essentially moral judgments and moral judgments are judgments of Value. The ingredients of Existence must be sought for in Truth, Goodness and Beauty. We can have no ethics otherwise. And life itself is not to be understood as a vanity. It must possess a meaning; not merely a provisional one which is negated in the ultimate Reality, but something more profound which shall find its significance only in reference to that ultimate Reality. When we come to restate the metaphysical idea of Reality it must be such that the Here and the Hereafter are organically related. In fact there is no line dividing the two. What is conditioned and the unconditional are two aspects of Reality. Time and Eternity do not exclude each other. The Finite is not a negation of the Infinite. Because the embodiment is imperfect we cannot reject it as unrelated to the Perfect. The ultimate End, in other words, is the completest embodiment of all our ideals, spiritual, moral and social which we strive after in our life, Here and Now.

Fellowship with God could be, therefore, realised by living this Life, Here and Now. Service of Man is also the service of God. And so our ideal shall not take us away from this world of our Social Relationships. We cannot go in quest of God leaving aside His Manifestations. Release is a false, elusive idea; God himself is bound to us by inseparable ties. We shall be the more free the more we are bound. Our Freedom shall be our Bondage.

This means that our traditional outlook and attitude to life must be radically revised. We can only hope to exist by re-formulating the vision of the life we wish to live, Here and Now. The view that we shall plead for in the following pages shall insist upon the intrinsic value of this our worldly existence. The world of Fact has to be appraised by that of Values, not purely individual but by that of social values—values, moreover which are truly moral. Action would then be Right Social Action, not my action as an eccentric individual, trying to realise an individuality, unattached and isolated, but any action which aims at true individuality and personality, in trying to realise itself in the membership of the Great Co-operative Republic, in the Larger Life of Humanity.

The view that we shall insist upon shall, therefore, conceive of the Universe as a Spiritual Unity. "Reality," as Tagore says, "is the harmony which gives to the component parts of a thing the equilibrium of the whole."[1] And every part, being a lesser whole, is valuable from the spiritual point of view. And in this vast scheme of life no element can be dispensed with. And the Supreme Real, the Almighty God can be attained, in and through all the complex facts that go to make this our earthly existence. The world is not an evil and we ought not to turn away from it. Our life is a valuable trust and is invested with the highest potentialities. The more we contribute towards the larger life, the more we will be sharing it. Our individuality lies essentially in our realising it as an organic personality in the great spiritual World-Process called Life. Instead of trying to seek God, beyond our relationships of life, we need to focus Him in these very contacts of ours and sublimate them with an animating impulse that they may subserve a noble End. Our quest, therefore, shall be a co-operative quest. And we shall seek to obtain God's Love, by sharing it with each other ; for Fatherhood of God implies Brotherhood

---

[1] *Nationalism*, pp. 33-35.

of Man. The seed that shall leaven this Earth shall be the word of Christ :

"Thou shalt love the Lord thy God with all thy heart, and with all thy soul, and with all thy mind, and with all thy strength

"Thou shalt love thy neighbour as thyself."

And so the Reality of God, and the Value and Destiny of the Soul, shall be, as they were for Plato, primarily as regulative Ideas for the direction of our life Here and Now. Eternal Life or Immortality is not a state placed in a remote future, but an "all satisfying present experience of the love of God." The Kingdom of Heaven is not only at hand, but is already in the midst of us. We can no longer look upon the world as subjected to the power of evil, "if only we can think of God as our Father. And divine life ceases to be postponed to a future, either on earth or beyond the grave. It has indeed, a future, in the sense that the seed has a future in the plant that springs from it ; but the principle of that future is already here. The leaven is already working in the mass, "until the whole be leavened."[1] We ought not, therefore, to turn away from life ; and the pessimistic tendency can only be repelled "by the insight which detects 'a soul of goodness in things evil.' " We must, indeed, have Emerson's faith that "evil is good in the making." And "God is not a transcendent power who rules from a far-away heaven ; He is without as He is within...." He can be reached and realised by the participation in life, Here and Now, by the sharing of His Love with our fellow-creatures. Indeed that is the only way perhaps for living the True Life. "He that loveth not, knoweth not God ; for God is love...... If we love one another, God dwelleth in us, and his love is perfected in us."[2]

---

[1] Edward Caird: *The Evolution of Religion*, Vol. 2, p. 101.
[2] *The First Epistle General of John*, iv, 8-12.

This means that our religious ideal must be radically revised, and this we can only do by re-formulating our metaphysical conception of Reality. For in India "no religious movement has ever come into existence without developing as its support a philosophic content."[1] Perhaps this has resulted in placing philosophy in the place of religion. The reaction on ethics and politics can never be exaggerated. The tendency to over-rationalise submerged everything in an impersonal and non-moral world-view. There could not be an ethical conception of the universe. "It is beyond possibility of doubt that in India from the first philosophy is intellectual, not moral in interest and outlook."[2] The virtues that are to be developed, according to the different systems, are mostly negative in nature ; and that makes Hindu Ethics if not "anti-social",[3] at any rate unsocial or non-social. In other words, Indian thought seems to have no true Ethics which can regulate social morality and help to formulate the ideals of social progress. And true Ethics is impossible unless we recognise the worth of the individual and his destiny. Although in Indian thought the emphasis is on the autonomous Self, it is a Self which has no individuality, and, indeed, no content whatsoever, and of which nothing can be predicated. Consciousness, experience and knowledge of it are impossible ; for these presuppose duality—of the knower and the known, of the subject and the object. But when the Self is said to be beyond Thought. what is there to be perceived, experienced or known? Indeed, there is no longer even "Individuality". Everything is sucked up into the *Ekam Eva Advitiyam*. When Man, then, has no individuality, no life to

---

[1] Radhakrishnan: *Indian Philosophy*, Vol. I, p. 26.

[2] A. B. Keith: *Religion and Philosophy of the Veda*, p. 434.

[3] This expression of Principal McKenzie is taken strong objection to by Hopkins who has done nothing, however, to refute it.

live, can there be anything he has to fulfil in life? What basis can he have for existence? Must he not have an individuality, even if he is to transcend it ultimately? How is he to realise God, the Supreme Real, if he himself does not exist?

In the end we are led to a bottomless abyss of Nothingness. "Indian thought reaches not conclusions but—catastrophes." We see a regular progression of Thought linking up Yajnavalkya, Buddha, Nagarjuna and Sankara. The Brahman or Atman which exists in itself and by itself, above and beyond perception, experience and knowledge, unknown and unknowable, indeed may exist, or *may not exist*! For what can be predicated of that which transcends Thought! Thought involves relations; and relations diversity or difference. But Reality is Bare Identity. If, therefore, we cannot think of the Reality of God, how can we say: He is! Might not we conclude: there is no God and nothing exists!

When stated thus, it does not mean that we are ignorant of other strains of Indian Thought, notably that of Ramanuja and the Bhakti Schools. But after all, when everything is said, even Ramanuja's philosophy, though admitting unity in diversity, and the relational character of knowledge, and the reality of sentient existence, and hence the worth of man's individuality, fails to satisfy us, for in his thought, there is no place for Society. And unless we have an adequate conception of Human Values and Life we can have no recognition of Personality either. We should, moreover, recognise that of all the different types of thought, it is the Adwaita that has had a predominating influence on Indian ideals. And from the religion in which everything is God (Pantheism) or He alone exists (Monism) the step is easy which takes to the religion in which God is ignored, and nothing exists (Nihilism).

The position comes to this: We are to believe in the

idea of God which can have no religious content; or in the alternative, believe in a religion in which God is ignored, and may not even exist!

When the vital conception of religion are thus atrophied, the whole of life in its various aspects cannot fail to be affected. And the Indian Polity, which is the reflex of the ideals and thoughts of the people, the institutional response, the concretised embodiment of their ideas and aspirations, cannot but be influenced, through and through, by the religious ideal. Some of the root-ideas of the general systems of Hindu philosophy such as "the doctrine of the creation of the Social order, are embedded in the ideas and principles" of Hindu political thought.[1] A mere general treatment of religio-ethical or socio-religious concepts of the Hindus is not sufficient, as Ghoshal supposes, for the understanding of the Indian Polity. To imagine "that the study of statecraft and cognate topics branched off at an early period in the history of the race from the general stream of Vedic culture, forming an independent branch of knowledge which might be called a secular science", is just to think that the Hindu mind could conceive of the secular life as un-affected by the religious. We are emphatically of opinion that the Indian Polity was what it was because the ideas of the people at large were what they were. Modern writers, not having the patience to search into the metaphysical foundations of the Indian State are surprised, even feel shocked and scandalised when they come across Kautilyan maxims. They jump to the conclusion that for Kautilya there was a divorce between religion or morality and politics. This verdict, however, reveals an inability to understand underlying principles. Kautilya was the product, if we may

---

[1] Ghoshal: *Hindu Political Theories*, p. xi.

We wish Ghoshal had developed the theme in detail in his brilliant and scholarly treatise.

say so, of the whole theological and metaphysical thought of the times. His maxims were in general harmony with the content of the idea-systems of his age.[1] And far from experiencing and expressing any repugnance, later writers on the Polity reverently look back to him as authoritative. Further, if we carefully take in the ideas embedded in *Santi Parva*, and if we critically examine the social and political ethics of the community as revealed in the Vedic and Heroic Ages, since then, we will be driven irresistibly to the conclusion that Kautilya was not alien to the spirit and practice of the times. And to imagine a cleavage between Philosophy or Religion and Politics is to assert the amazing notion that the thoughts of people do not affect their institutions. Society, State, Religion, Philosophy and Ethics all act and react on each other to produce the complex fact that we seek to study in the pages that follow—the Indian Polity. Even as there is a progression of philosophical thought, there is also a regular progression of political thought, a stream that gathers volume as it irrigates the vast expanse of history. *Santi Parva* and the *Arthasastra* are but stages in the flow. We shall moreover find that Kautilya and the rest are really religious in outlook. They never sacrificed religion and morality to statecraft. Kautilya, above all, has inevitably to pay homage to the socio-religious ideal of Indian philosophy before he could proceed to a discussion of the principles of statecraft. And statecraft could not be otherwise than what it was with such a religious and metaphysical background as it had. If we would raise our political ideal to purer heights and revivify our whole Polity, we should primarily reformulate our religious and metaphysical formulations. Above all, we should revise our traditional attitude towards life. Let us first have the vision of life that we wish to have, and

[1] See Bandyopadhyaya: *Kautilya*, p. 47.

then, in its light, we could build up our institutional life. We examine our achievements in the past, therefore, to realise the effects our world-view had on the Polity. That would bring home the urgent necessity for re-visualising our ideals and values.

CHAPTER III

POLITICAL CONSTITUTION

"The Constitution is the soul of the state"
ISOCRATES

We have so far tried to establish the necessity for revising our traditional attitude to life. Thereby we do not in the least depreciate the achievements of our ancients. What they had realised was something very great—greater perhaps than what most of us even imagine. We are to-day dominated so much, to borrow a characteristic expression of Carlyle, by "Profit and Loss philosophy", that we are prone to pass over the creations of the human spirit. In a sense, the human mind could not have arrived at a more comprehensive coherence of the inner spirit than what our fathers had realised in their endeavours to perfect the life within. And some of the solutions they had found for the profound problems of life are still of living interest. The world would certainly be much the poorer for ignoring their findings.[1]

The achievements of the human spirit, taken by themselves, do not give us, however, any idea of the virtues, of the excellences required for working institutions of a civic or political nature. The old Indian life has indeed survived the shocks of all the foreign inroads, and India is even to-day what it has always been. The true India is not the India of the towns but of the villages. The soul of the people is revealed in the real life lived in the villages. And it would not be too much to assert that there the India of to-day is the "India of a thousand, or two

[1] See Max Muller: *India, what can it teach us?*, pp. 13-14.

thousand or three thousand years ago''.[1] There has been no perceptible change in the time-honoured instincts and methods of life of the millions of our people who are outspread in those unfrequented spots. From the cradle onwards the same dull routine of daily life, marked out by immemorial custom holds inexorable sway. Thus to a very great extent the characterisation of India as static is, perhaps, deserved. It may be, as Tagore puts it, "in the rythm of life, pauses there must be for the renewal of life''.[2] Only the pause in our case has been, unfortunately, unusually too long. This was a great forced necessity, however, and not something inherent, as some have supposed. It is not that the East is unchanging or that it cannot move ; but that movement itself was fraught with danger. In all early periods the first need is the evolution of what has been termed, "a cake of custom''. All life was to be brought under the binding force of a comprehensive rule. Men were to be taught to subordinate their selfish interests to the common object of the community. Chaotic forces and anarchic impulses were to be curbed and suppressed so that even "mere'' life would become possible. That is why Bagehot says : "later are the ages possible. First are the ages of servitude''.[3] It is indeed, difficult to evolve a common homogeneous mode of life. But what is more difficult still is to get out afterwards of such a fixed order. If the first step is cementing a "cake of custom,'' the next step is to break that very cake of custom. The principle of variation is the basis of progress. Dull uniformity must yield to the expression of a manifold, variegated existence. The caste-system, from this point of view, would seem to be a step in the right direction. The law of differentiation, be it racial, or religious or functional, we are at present not called upon to deter-

[1] Max Muller: *India, what can it teach us?*, p. 7.
[2] R. Tagore: *Nationalism* (Ind. Edn.), p. 51.
[3] Bagehot: *Physics and Politics*, p. 30.

mine, has richly moulded society into myriads of shades and colours thus rescuing it from the monotony of a single, dull background. While recognising the part this unique system had played in the march of progress,[1] we should definitely realise that it has actually hindered the third and the most important step from being taken. Though not the only contributing cause—for we shall see that other factors also were at work—nevertheless it has had a predominating influence in condemning our country to a stifling stagnation. This third step, to the principle of which we most often pay a passing homage without bestirring ourself to realise it in fact, is the evolving[2] of unity in diversity. It is just at this stage, when unity was to be realised in diversity, that the progress of India seems to have been "arrested." Her civilisation has, therefore, been characterised as "arrested civilisation". Great thinkers, like Bagehot, try to account for this peculiar phenomenon; and it would be unscientific to ignore their arguments. To our mind, however, the reason why India paused in her full tide of progress cannot be explained with a reference to "the peculiarity of arrested civilisation" to kill out varieties at birth, before such tendencies have had time to develop.[3] The tendency of our society to crush out divergences iof opinion and compel the individual members to conform to social usages and customs is a result and not the cause of "arrested" progress. Most European writers and some even of our own scholars confound the effect with the cause. The circumstances that have conspired to keep India at a standstill, ever looking

---

[1] We refer the reader to Radhakrishnan's *Hindu View of Life* for a very sympathetic treatment of the problem.

[2] We are afraid the word "evolve" is not a proper term to be used; we wish that it should only be understood in the popular sense only.

[3] See Bagehot: *Physics and Politics*, p. 54 ff. He also gives as other causes the influence of land and religion.

backwards and feeding upon her "Golden Age", it would appear from a deeper analysis, are reducible to two factors, neither of which could be ignored. Of these the more important is the metaphysical view of life[1] we have been discussing in the last chapter, which abstracted man into a world of phantasy and of imagination, abstracting him from the humanity around, from the manifold relationships of life, into the self-constituted dreamy universe where in fancied identity with an incomprehensible and unknowable Brahman, Atman or the Absolute, an illusory synthesis was sought. The other factor is to be found in the ever present danger from foreign invaders who, time and again, swept down from without and deluged the plains of Hindustan. The healthy conditions under which humanity is to march and advance in civilisation were thus absent. In the stress of war when the very existence was at stake it would be madness to think of change. Innovation would spell revolution and revolution certain and imminent disaster. Who would think of repairing their ships in the hurricane season and put out to sea! As well keep fast to the safe shore. The supreme necessity of the hour was self-preservation. Society cowered for safety. To conserve the already acquired elements of progress was the all-absorbing anxiety—not to advance, but to cry halt and prevent retrogression. High walls were built around to shut out the howling wind and the piercing showers. Caught in a whirlpool of anarchy, movement was instinct with danger. Immobility was therefore the refuge.

And all through the centuries the body-politic has remained rigid. A death-like langour seems to have spread over its limbs. Like the shadows in the famous "den" of Plato we move about; and even make virtue of necessity, by making our "stability" a matter for boasting.

[1] The result being the hold authority had on the individual. The End of the Indian Polity was stability, not progress.

How often do we not come across persons, well educated and capable of distinguishing semblance from reality, who proudly declaim the strength of our national institutions, that have withstood these thousand years the onslaughts, of pitiless Time, and of barbarous vandalism! Has not our hoary faith survived the aggressive proselytism of the innumerable heresies that beat against its stronghold in vain! Have the terrible political hurricanes that swept over the land, time and again, touched the vital breath of the recesses of the country's spirit! Little reck we of the vaunted glories of material power if only we are left undisturbed.

> "The East bowed low before the blast
> In patient, deep disdain;
> She let the legions thunder past,
> And plunged in thought again".[1]

And we are assured that this shall ever be thus! What has not changed these thousand years is not likely to change during the millenium to come.[2] Not that we do not grow or change, but that we cannot. Even the desire to change is not there; we only ask to be let alone. The famous reply of Diogenes to Alexander would, perhaps, best illustrate the Indian attitude. He cares not to question the powers that be, so long as he is left undisturbed. And it is therefore held that a paternal despotism is the only possible form suited to India.[3]

We do not wish to go into a detailed discussion over the

---

[1] cf. Matthew Arnold.

[2] cf. Vincent Smith on the caste system *Oxford History*, pp. 34-43.

[3] See Edwyn Bevan: *Indian Nationalism*, pp. 35-39.
Viscount Morley: *Indian Speeches*, p. 18.
Bryce: *Studies in History and Jurisprudence*, Vol. I, p. 27 ff.
Bagehot: *Physics and Politics*, p. 182.
Marvin: *India and the West*, pp. 69-70; 169.

controversy that has been raised over the fitness of the Indian to work free and representative institutions. We would only point out that it is impossible under any circumstance hereafter, to return to the old system of paternalism.[1] Now that the disintegrating force of education has been at work these many years, we will be deceiving ourselves if we think that despotism can subsist in the future. Within the last few years a new India is coming into existence and we hope, with the reformulation of our ideals and the re-visualising of the kind of life we would live, it is possible to transform even the life of the millions of our countrymen outspread in the distant villages. The days of autocracy are indeed over. And "India would be rendered ungovernable under any system which does not confer genuine political responsibility".[2]

The grounds for political allegiance are at root moral and do not rest on force. We shall see later that Indians gave in their submission to the former governments, not through compulsion, but due mostly to the belief that the rulers had the claim to govern by "Divine Right".[3] Now that the theocratic idea has lost its importance the necessity has arisen to redefine the grounds for political obligation. It would not do to unsympathetically remark, as Ramsay Muir does, that to the Indian, to obey the law has not yet become "a moral obligation, because he does not yet instinctively feel that the maintenance of the law is a common interest",[4] and that because the Indians have no respect for the "Reign of Law" they are not fit for self-government.[5] As Spinoza has said,

---

[1] See J. S. Hoyland's admirable book *The Case for India*.

[2] Lionel Curtis: *Letters to the People of India on Responsible Government*, pp. 16-17.

[3] We shall examine later on the various theories advanced.

[4] Ramsay Muir: *Nationalism and Internationalism*, p. 17.

[5] We would recommend to the cretic to refer to conditions nearer "home". Prof. Dicey, in his *Law of the constitution*

"in the best State the laws will be faithfully observed. For there can be no doubt that seditions, wars, and contempt for, or violation of, the laws should be imputed not so much to the wickedness of the subjects as to the bad constitution or organisation of the state".[1] We should think that the necessity to make examples daily of offenders against the laws is the inevitable consequence of the bad constitution of the State. Fear and force are bad motives to appeal to. People, compelled by fear, obey simply because they must; they can have no living interest in the concerns of the State. And if in such a State the people do not actually break out into rebellion, it is only because they are afraid to do so. This passive acquiescence how shall we term it,—a state of peace, or absence of war! Indeed the State whose peace depends on the inertness of its subjects may better be called a solitude than a State!

The State, therefore, has to fulfil certain conditions if it is to exist. And the laws of the state should be so framed that men render obedience urged by hope and love. "If any law is of such a character that a whole people could not possibly give its assent to it", writes Kant, "...then it is not just".[2] And if the laws are "the soul of the State", they must desire, in the words of Demosthenes, "what is just and honourable and useful".[3] Laws are the correctives of errors, but if they are evil, everything would go wrong. States which coerce men into

---

has, it appears to us, good reasons to deplore recent tendencies, for he notes a remarkable decline in the Englishman's respect for "Rule of Law". See "Introduction", p. xxxviii.

[1] *Tract, Pol.* V. 2—Quoted by Duff: *Spinoza's Political and Ethical Theory*, p. 298.

[2] *The Critical philosophy of Kant* by Edward Caird, Vol. II, p. 339.

[3] Demosthenes in Aristogeit—quoted by Dickinson: *The Greek view of life*, p. 73.

obedience are "states of discord".[1] That is why Plato insists that the laws of the State ought "to have the character of loving and wise parents, rather than of tyrants and masters".[2] They must be the concretised embodiments of noble aspirations ; the expression of the best life the people wish to lead with their help and under them. They must try to secure that best life for all and for each. Only when the State essays to fulfil these conditions can men be loyal to its laws. They can be made to observe them so long as, through such laws a righteous order is secured. Thus in the last resort only such laws can be considered just and efficient which render the enforcement of their own penalties unnecessary ; and which promote the moral and ethical ends of life.

The authority of the State lasts, therefore, only so long as it seeks to secure to its citizens their ideal of life. Thus the form the State assumes is not the result of an artificial creation. It is the spiritual framework which is the condition of the people's endeavour. The constitution is the institutional response to the thoughts and aspirations of the people. A good constitution is that which is rooted deeply in the affections of the people, which has penetrated into the very fibre of their existence. It should be the concretised symbol of the conception of life they wish to live.

And in this respect it is healthy to go back to the Greek idea of the constitution. The modern tendency to define the constitution with a reference to the form it assumes is unhappy. The numerical differentia, ignoring the qualitative and ethical factors, will give us no idea of the nature of the constitution. Austin may define the constitution as that which fixes the structure of the supreme government. And it is usually understood to mean

---

[1] Plato: *Laws*—Book VIII, p. 214.

[2] *Ibid*, Book IX, p. 241.

"an attempt to embody in a single authoritative document, or a small group of documents, the fundamental political institutions of the state".[1]

But a mere description of the form will tell us nothing about the spirit of the institution. We may with great artistic skill build up the skeleton from dismembered bones; but if the soul does not infuse it with its vital breath, the body will not move and pulsate. The State is not a machine but an organism and the constitution is its soul. It should embody its scheme of life, and must tend "consciously or not, to bring the lives of those living under it into harmony with its particular scheme". The constitution is thus an ethical and moral force. That is why both Plato and Aristotle attribute to it far-reaching influence either for good or evil. As Newman says,[2] their idea has this merit that it never loses sight, as modern enquiries do, of the full significance of the State and its organisation. Socrates had implied[3] that "constitutions must be distinguished, not by the number of the depositories of power, but by their attributes and by the character of their rule." Plato works out the same idea which was further developed still by Aristotle to whom the contrast between the holders of power is not a numerical but a qualitative contrast. He takes into consideration not only ethical but social factors as well. Thus the constitution determines the character and ethical level of the community. It expresses "the creed with regard to the life it should live". And the test of a good constitution lies in the nature of the life it secures to its citizens. And as Aristotle would have it, "the most desirable life" is the clue to its structure. We should aim not at the mere preser-

---

[1] See Marriott's *English Political Institutions*, Introductory pages.

[2] *Politics of Aristotle*, Vol. I, p. 211.

[3] *Ibid.*, p. 212.

vation and continuance of life but at the continuance of the best life.

We are aware that this insistance on the ethical, moral and social factors will strike as strange to most people, even perhaps in our own country. We have been so suffused with the numerical sense that it has come to mean an effort to recognise and consider questions of quality and value. Our absorbing anxiety is how to distribute seats and power to satisfy the clamouring claimants ; how to define in precise terms the responsibility of the executive and the powers of the legislatures. We are in great danger of losing sight of the whole, having entangled ourselves in a minute analysis and definition of the parts.[1] Nobody, so far, pauses for a moment to envisage the view of the life our polity is to secure for us. We fondly hope that any constitution will work so long as our attitude towards life is what it is. Events during the past few years have, however, pressed on us the conviction that the constitution is indeed an ethical and moral force, and so has a powerful influence for good or evil. Just to illustrate, we may refer to the demoralising and disastrous effects of the introduction of the communal principle into the form and spirit of our polity. So long, therefore, as our attitude towards life remains unchanged and so long as we try to import all the perfections of our social order into our Polity, the millenium will never dawn. It would be erecting our political edifice upon the quicksands of social defects and moral inertia. What is needed to-day is not a mere "relocation" of sovereignty. More urgent still is the re-interpretation of life, the life we wish to live and which the State is to insure for us. It is only then that we can formulate adequate grounds for political

[1] A careful study of the various constitutions suggested, not excluding the Nehru Report, will certainly elucidate our contention.

obligation. It is only then that we can create an enduring or stable constitution. As Epictetus has well put it,[1] it is not with brick and stone that the structure should be built but with the thoughts of men. The supreme requirement is that the constitution should be a true imitation of life. The form must reflect the spirit.

And the task of the political philosopher and legislator is by no means easy. Unless he is at once a combination of both he can in no way understand the problem before him. For we should recognise that the constitution cannot be fixed once for all, if the State is to be a living organism. It would require renewal with constant adjustments. That is why Plato insisted that kings should be philosophers and philosophers kings. A purely legal emphasis, in its very nature, may oftentimes, fail to reach the significance of an advance in public temper. To interpret the genius and soul of a people a prophet is needed. Philosophy must be pressed into the service of statecraft.

"It is an axiom that no political system can work which is not congruent with the social system of the country in which it is established," writes Ramsay Muir, "and the creation of a system congruent with Indian social conditions is a problem before which the boldest political speculator may well quail."[2] For unless the proper *ethos* is secured and maintained, the form of the State, whatever it may be, will have no chance of permanence. Wisdom must be implanted in States and ignorance expelled. Ignorance is ruin, and so the adequate working of the constitution presupposes people educated in and infused with its *ethos*. But of this later. What we are here endeavouring to point out is, as Montesquieu has well said, "the Constitution may happen to be free, and the subject not. The subject may be free, and not the Constitution". This necessarily

---

[1] Ch. VI, p. 116 *Epictetus* Trans. by G. T. W. Rolleston.

[2] *The Expansion of Europe*, p. 299.

implies that every constitution will not be suited to every people, unless its *ethos* is carefully fostered. Many factors have necessarily to be considered—the peculiar habits of the people, their customs and beliefs, their view of life and so on. It would be impossible to foster a plant, giving it the root of another plant. "It is like dressing our skeleton", as Tagore puts it, "with another man's skin, giving rise to eternal feuds between the skin and the bones at every moment". We should plant the roots by preparing a proper understanding and appreciation of the kind of life which we seek to have.

Now a serious difficulty which is concerned with the practicability of our ideal, presents itself. On the one hand we may be reminded that a constitution cannot be created by premeditated design. It must be the natural outcome of complex facts in the nature of the people themselves. On the other hand, "to find the best form of government; to persuade others that it is the best; and having done so, to stir them to insist on having it"[1] is the order of ideals in the minds of those who look upon the constitution as a problem to be worked out. But these two positions are not really irreconcilable, though a one-sided emphasis will certainly be erroneous. In the first place, as J. S. Mill points out, "political institutions are not trees which once planted" are ever growing while men "are sleeping". Again, to err being human, such institutions may be the outcome of faulty judgment, and conscious human agency may be set to work to mend or end them. Thus the one great fact of institutional life is the reality of interaction—of the constitution and community. The social or political constitution may predispose the people to adopt certain beliefs, customs and tastes; and these very beliefs, customs and habits may

[1] J. S. Mill: *Representative Government*, p. 175 (Everyman's).

give the constitution its peculiar temper and character. Thus, as De Tocquieville truly observes, "the whole art of the legislator is correctly to discern beforehand these natural inclinations of communities of men, in order to know whether they should be assisted or whether it may not be necessary to check them".[1] For we should recognise that in every community there are both centripetal and centrifugal forces at work, tendencies which bring men together in an organised community and tendencies that drag men apart. And, as Bryce truly says, "a political constitution or frame of government, as the complex totality of laws embodying the principles and rules whereby the community is organised, governed, and held together, is exposed to the action of both these forces".[2] The political philosopher has not merely to speculate on abstract theories ; he has also to study the particular phenomenon before him, appealing to its history. That is why at the very start of our inquiry we have insisted on the necessity of the historical method. History explains how the particular phenomenon has come to be what it is. It shows whether it is the result of tendencies still increasing or of tendencies already beginning to decline. To fulfil these requirements history as we have demonstrated, is not to be a mere record of political events, but must be the investigation of all the complex forces that affect the particular result we have before us. That is why we have asserted that the mission of history is to examine the content of life.

And the examination of the content of life that history unfolds acquaints us with the view of life that our fathers placed before themselves. For, let us reassert with all the emphasis that we can, that it is the metaphysical outlook, the attitude towards life which dominated their

---

[1] *Democracy in America*, Vol. II, p. 153.

[2] *Studies in History and Jurisprudence*, Vol. I, p. 217.

endeavour that permeated all their institutional accomplishments. To the extent that view was partial, to that extent the Polity they evolved was stamped with its imperfection.

The Problem of the Indian Polity is, as we envisage it, primarily to formulate the most desirable life to be lived. The traditional attitude towards life must be reinterpreted in idealistic terms so that it shall permeate our institutional life with a healthy influence, harmonising conflicting tendencies, so that the social and political organism shall pulsate with the true rhythm of a spiritual effort at the realisation of the most perfect and the beautiful ; that we can thereby concentrate and focus God in our everyday life ; that we may establish the Reign of Love ; and in loving each other shall realise ourselves in the love of Him whom we seek in our age-long quest, ever old and ever new.

We shall therefore examine our past achievements in the light of the attitude towards life and the Polity we evolved in response to it, so that we shall be in a position to reformulate our ideals and the vision of the most desirable life to be lived.

BOOK II

THE HINDU POLITY

"The subtle and profound spirit of India, which finds its fullest expression in the absolute idealism of the Vedanta of Sankara and the sceptical nihilism of Nagarjuna, is alien to the conception of man as a political organism, whose true end can be found only in and through membership of a social community."

A. BERRIEDALE KEITH

'When our new "national" school of writers on Hindu polity say that in ancient India there were republics, the king regarded himself as merely exercising a trust, a cabinet of ministers was held to be necessary or that the people enjoyed self-government,—they may be literally correct; but we feel that this is not the whole truth, that there are certain qualifications which have been withheld from us. In the mind of a twentieth century reader, the above statements imply the direct influence of the people on the foreign policy of the State, the responsibility of the executive to the governed, the reign of a law which emanates from a legislature representing the citizens,—in short the control of the administrative machinery not by one man's will but by the will of Society. And yet, every one of these latter connotations is untrue and should have been expressly contradicted by the writer in order to guard against our forming a misconception of ancient Indian Polity as it really was.'

JADUNATH SARKAR

CHAPTER IV

THE END OF THE STATE

"A crowned king should always rule with an eye towards Dharma."

KRISHNA DEVA RAYA

"Kings should always protect the four orders in the discharge of their duties. It is the eternal duty of kings to prevent a confusion of duties in respect of the different orders."

SANTI PARVA

"The observance of one's own duty leads one to Swarga and infiinite bliss (Anantya). When it is violated, the world would come to an end owing to confusion of castes and duties.

"He, the king, shall never allow people to swerve from their duties; for whoever upholds his own duty, ever adhering to the customs of the Aryas, and following to the rules of caste and divisions of religious life, will surely be happy both here and hereafter. For the world, when maintained in accordance with injunctions of the triple Vedas will surely progress but never perish."

KAUTILYA

According to Hindu ideas the End of the State is to maintain Dharma. It is Dharma that sustains the kingdom. If it increases the people also increase; if it decreases they suffer; if allowed to completely disappear we have no longer a State as such, but a condition of things best described as anarchy. Throughout the vicissitudes of Indian History the End of the State to keep intact the moral and social order has never been lost sight of. What does the term "Dharma", therefore, mean? What is its ethical content; and what is its influence on the Polity?

The term "Dharma" has well been called the blank cheque of Indian thought. It is very comprehensive[1] and

[1] See Jolly's Article on Dharma: *Ency. Rel. and Ethi.*

has baffled any single explanation. No word or words in the English language can express the whole of its meaning; and hence the difficulty of a proper exposition.[1] We shall therefore try to analyse its content, especially as it is manifested in its absolute and empirical aspects; and, perhaps, we could then try to relate the significance of the implications of the term to the Indian Polity.

Dharma, in its metaphysical aspect, refers to the Universe as a whole conceived as a system or order; it would then be the principle underlying such an order. Thinkers and sages from the earliest times have felt that the Universe is no brute collocation of facts, perpetually in conflict and shifting about; a ceaseless revolving of "unguided matter", to borrow the expression of William James, "vast drifting of the cosmic weather"; but is the expression of the Divine Mind; and that if we could reach to it we could then also realise that the Universe is objectified reason, and that God is not indifferent to what takes place either in Nature or in the Human World. From the conception of the Universe as a Natural Order we could approach it from the higher idea that it is a Moral Order too. We could then grasp the principles underlying the Moral Government and concentrate or concretise them in the synthesis of human aspiration. We would not then turn away, as Hume did, with the sceptical dissent that no inference could be drawn that "affects human life or can be the source of any action or forbearance." We could then refuse to accept as final Naturalistic and Epicurean explanations and escape from even the mere passivity of the Stoic.

In the physical world there rules a regular order; natural phenomena present a regularity which would compel the admission that a system prevails in spite of appearances. The behaviour of the Sun, the Moon, and the

[1] See Principal McKenzie's *Hindu Ethics*, pp. 38-39.

seasons seems to be guided by some intelligent principle. And the idea of a "Reign of Law", must slowly have dawned on the consciousness of mankind. Some such idea must have presented itself to the mental panorama of the Rig-Vedic seers when they tried to comprehend it by the term "Rta". The movements of nature are repeated in a regular order which led the Vedic sages to assert that phenomena are "obedient to the reign of Law Eternal." The idea is expressed in a hymn to the Dawn,[1] who keeps "Varuna's eternal Statute, who breaketh not the law or order, day by day coming to the place appointed". And this "Law Eternal", this "Holy Law", rules every other natural fact. "The flowing of the floods is Law."[2] Even the Sun is set according to Law.[3]

This Law or Rta, this Universal Principle of the physical order, is it inhering in things, or is it a power external to the world? This is the problem that still baffles mankind; and Science and Religion give different answers. And modern enquiries, assuming that the two are irreconcilable, reduce everything to a Positivist basis. This is the result of the long-drawn-out duel between what Kant distinguished as objective certitude, and subjective certitude—knowledge and faith. Our ancestors, however, recognised the Will of God or Gods in the working of the Universe where modern scientists see simply the play and interplay of the forces of Nature in a constant process of resolving and dissolving. They held that this physical order was upheld or maintained by some higher Powers, which are often personified into Gods like Agni, Varuna, Mitra and so on. Sometimes we have even Rta set up as a deity. But above all Varuna and Mitra are the "Lords of Rta". They watch ever and promote the Law.

---

[1] *Rig-Veda*: Bk. I, Hymn 123 (Griffith's).
[2] *Ibid.*, Bk. I, Hymn 105.
[3] *Ibid.*, Bk. I, Hymn 136.

The conception of the Universe as a Physical Order, we said, might lead to the idea of the Universe as a Moral Order, guiding our steps with unerring certainty to the Ultimate End or Cause, in the light of which we could understand the world as a great spiritual process. Thus we could have arrived at the idea of "Value" or "Worth" which Kant placed in the first rank in the formulation of his ethical ideals. Sentient Life would indeed be "a Divine Education" preparing man for the path of perpetual progress. The foundations of ethics could be established ultimately, not on external sanctions, depending on the ordinances of gods like Varuna or Mitra, but on internal sanctions, inhering in conscience, in the nature of Man as a Spiritual Being. This in turn would have inevitably led to the formulation of the ideals of true social morality, ideals striving after Ends, not placed in some Transcendental Good, but essentially deep-rooted in the essence of man as man, realisable in and through the manifold contacts of life.

We do find, of course, in the Rig-Veda the conception of Rta as a Moral Order. Perhaps both the meanings, Rta as Natural Order and Rta as Moral Order, are present side by side, though unconsciously.[2] We have also devout prayers addressed to Indra,[3] Mitra and Varuna,[4] which seem to have some ethical bearing. In the tenth book of the Rig-Veda we have a hymn addressed to Indra.

> "Oh Indra, lead us on the path of Rta, on the right path over all evils."

In the Seventh Book of the Rig-Veda we have a hymn addressed to Mitra, Varuna,

[1] See A. B. Keith: *Religion and Philosophy of the Veda*, Chapter 16.

[2] Max Muller: *Hibbert Lectures*, 1878, pp. 237-253.

[3] Hymn 133. We have followed Max Muller.

[4] Hymn 65 (Griffith's).

"Bonds of the sinner, they bear many nooses;
the wicked mortal hardly may escape them."
"Varuna, Mitra may your path of Order bear
us O'er trouble as a boat O'er waters.

But we after all feel that the religious impulse itself is devoid of moral feeling; and the motive to religious life and prayer is not in the teleological springs of Man's Will, but that motive exhausts itself in an inordinate greed for wealth and power, for victory over Dasyus, for the possession of slaves etc.; and the reward for observing the Law is the abundance of things yielding pleasure.[1]

"The winds waft sweets, the rivers pour sweets
for the man who keeps the Law.
So may be the plants be sweet for us."

The appeal, moreover, is to an external factor, some power outside of us whose behests we have to obey, and transgression of which would bring upon us punishments. Right and wrong, in other words, have no ethical meaning, but are so according as the Law is observed or neglected. Rta comes to be identified as accuracy in sacrifice and ritual. It is impossible to search for ethical ideas in the ceremonialism of the Brahmanas, and Law has already become sacerdotal. Principal McKenzie is perfectly right in saying[2] that Rta as "moral order" should not be understood as possessing the full connotation that the term has in modern speech. The "Moral Order" is something imposed on Man.[3] Hence the Prayer:

"Whatever law of thine, O God, O Varuna, as we are men,
Day after day we violate,
Give us not as a prey to death, to be destroyed by thee

[1] *Rig-Veda*, Book I, Hymn 90 (Griffith's).
[2] *Hindu Ethics*, p. 7.
[3] *Rig-Veda*, Book I, Hymn 25 (Griffith's).

In wrath,
To thy fierce anger when displeased."

Furthermore, the idea of Law as the Ordinance of a God, be he Varuna or Mitra or somebody else, might have led to the idea of a Divine Will regulating human affairs establishing a personal touch, suffused with true ethics, leading ultimately to a conception of the kind the Israelites had of Jehovah. But this evolution is necessarily precluded by the Polytheism which is the constant feature of Indian religion.[1] In the Rig-Veda, apart from the monotheistic idea in its germ in the conception of Prajapati, the very idea of Rta itself might have led to the culmination we so desire. Rta personified as a deity could have attained a pre-eminent rank in course of time over the other deities. We learn here and there that the very gods also are subject to Law; and their power and strength are due to Law.[2] In the first Book we have:

"Mitra and Varuna, through Law, lovers and cherishers of Laws,
Have ye obtained your mighty power."

But Rta, however, gradually sinks in rank, and subsequently everything is sucked up into the Impersonal World-view which begins to dominate Indian thought hereafter.

During the Upanishadic Age the term "Dharma" comes to be substituted for "Rta". We further see the close connection between the Absolute and Empirical views. On the one hand the conception of Law becomes

---

[1] The Vedic religion in its Brahmana period made some advance towards a chief God in Prajapati, the creator, and this tendency never led to Monotheism in India. On the other hand the Vedic religion developed the incipient identification of the Gods, with one another and with nature into the one pantheistic World—Soul of Vedanta System. Macdonell, *Comparative Religion*, 964.

[2] *Rig-Veda*, Book I, Hymn 2 (Griffith's).

more complex and abstract. It is declared that "the Law is what is called the true."[1] Truth and Law are terms which mean the same thing. A little further on in the *Brihad Upa.*, we get a reasoned formulation of the metaphysical basis of all things in this Universe. We learn that the Brahmana is that which is the shining immortal Person in the Law (dharma) which is the honey for all things.[2] On the other hand, metaphysical foundations are established for the authority of the Social Order, or Dharma in its practical aspect. Indeed the bases were already laid during the earlier times. J. N. C. Ganguly is of opinion that even before the Upanishadic Age "the foundations of Moral, Social and Political law was laid down for ever."[3] A Rig-Vedic seer sang "Of Rta, sure and firm-set are the bases," and as human laws reflect the laws of the Gods[4] we find attempts to justify existing human conditions by reference to their supposed originals in the society of Gods. We are told that "verily in the beginning this was Brahman, one only." But being one it was not strong enough. So it created Kshatra. The Kshatras among the Devas are Indra, Varuna, Soma, Rudra, Parjanya, Yama, Mritya, Isana. Still not feeling strong enough the Brahman created the Vis, the classes of Devas which in their different orders are called Vasus, Rudras, Adityas, Visve Devas, Maruts. Even then, not still feeling strong Brahman created the Sudra colour as Pushan. This earth is that Pushan. And still not feeling strong the Brahman created ***"THE MOST EXCELLENT LAW (DHARMA)."***

---

[1] *Brihad Upa.*, 1. 4. 14.— Prof. Ajit Kumar Sen is certainly right in ascertaining that the Upanishadic conception of Law is metaphysical rather than an ethical one; and so we are not to equate law and morality. See his chapter on "The Concept of Law", p. 112 in his *Studies in Hindu Political Thought.*

[2] *Brihad Upa.*, 2-5.

[3] Article in *Ind. Hist. Quarterly*, Vol. II, p. 575 ff and p. 809 ff.

[4] Hopkins: *Ethics of India*, p. 38.

This is the Order existing among the Devas ; and we also see the heirarchal idea justified. Though Kshatra power is glorified, and though Kshatra is given precedence on certain occasions yet the Brahman being his birth-place is the first in rank. And among the Devas the Brahman is Agni.

The Divine Order of Society has its counterpart here on earth. In the *Satapatha Brahmana* we are told how the Brahman and Kśhatriya take precedence over the others. "The Priesthood and the nobility are established upon the people."[1] The two castes (the Vaisya and Sudra) are enclosed on both sides by the priesthood and the nobility and are made submissive.[2] The Brahman and Kshatriya go behind the Vaisya and Sudra. ***THEY ALWAYS GO FIRST IN ORDER TO AVOID A CONFUSION BETWEEN GOOD AND BAD.*** In the *Brihadaranyaka Upanishad* we have a very important and interesting passage. It relates : "among the Devas that Brahman existed as Agni (fire) only, among men as Brahmana, as Kshatriya through the (divine) Kshatriya, as Vaisya through the (divine) Vaisya, as Sudra through the (divine) Sudra." Thus the four-fold classes of society are really a natural reflection of what subsists among the Gods. If the Divine Powers that be are themselves subject to this ordering of Dharma how can human beings doubt the wisdom of the classification into the four castes? The caste system is, indeed, taken for granted, as a Divine Creation.

The question may be asked, is this four-fold classification of society the embodiment of a Purpose which could be realised in and through it? Is the Empirical Order the means to any end? If the functional scheme regulating the different classes and orders is the response to any intel-

---

[1] XI Kanda 2 Adhyaya 7 Brahmana, 16.
[2] VI Kanda 4 Adhyaya 4 Brahmana, 13.

ligible principle which tries to economise human energy, and thus make life a great co-operative endeavour, then it is possible for us to determine the importance of each function and assign its rank in the scale of social values. This means the appraising of the world of fact by that of values or to use the Kantian phrase of the "Realm of Ends." It is necessary to point out that the metaphysical outlook underlying the whole "Dharma" in the *Abstract* is such that it precludes any effort so to sublimate human relationships, as to enable man to recognise that in and through them he could realise the Supreme Real. For the opposition between the Temporal and the Eternal, Matter and Spirit, Empirical and Absolute, our ancient sages tried to bridge over, not in reconciling both in a higher synthesis but by denying any reality whatever, or at the most admitting a provisional reality to the Temporal or Empirical. The highest truth is "Thou art That", and in the ultimate, the Atman is all these which we have accustomed ourselves to distinguish as wife, husband, sons, wealth, social classes, Devas and so on. As Yajnavalkya enunciates : "Whosoever looks for the Brahman-class elsewhere than in the Self, was abandoned by the Brahman-class, whosoever looks for the Kshatra-class elsewhere than in the Self, was abandoned by the Kshatra-class. Whosoever looks for the worlds elsewhere than in the Self, was abandoned by the worlds. Whosoever looks for the Devas elsewhere than in the Self, was abandoned by the Devas. Whosoever looks for creatures elsewhere than in the Self, was abandoned by the creatures. Whosoever looks for anything elsewhere than in the Self, was abandoned by everything. ***THIS BRAHMAN-CLASS, THIS KSHATRIA-CLASS, THESE WORLDS, THESE DEVAS, THESE CREATURES, THIS EVERYTHING, ALL IS THAT SELF."***

Thus, in the ultimate, we arrive at an identification of everything with Atman, Atman with Brahman, and

Brahman is all this, this Atman, this Dharma and so on.

Let us pass on to Buddhistic thought. We have seen that Keith's remark[1] that "Dharma enters Buddhist thought with an interesting history" is literally true. The extreme statements that Brahman is everything (Pantheism) and that Brahman alone exists (Monism) contain hidden pitfalls which we have considered in the last chapter. The Absolute which is unknown and unknowable indeed may even not exist. This is the inevitable catastrophe resulting from confounding what is *unfathomable* with the *unknowable*. We have also, therefore, noticed how an Absolute, or the Principle of Being, conceived in Monistic terms, step by step leads to Nihilism. The first leap into the void is Brahman, the second is Nirvana. The Buddhist, as we have seen, looks upon everything as "becoming in apparent Being". "The speculation of the Brahmans," writes Oldenberg, "apprehended being in all becoming, that of the Buddhist becoming in all apparent being. In the former case substance with causality, in the latter causality without substance."[2] There is no fixity anywhere. All is impermanance, suffering and change. The Brahman as the Absolute, could not therefore be looked upon as the Real. And without "Being" there can be no substance. If at all there could be anything absolute within the restrictions of Buddhist Metaphysics, it would be the Law of Causality. Buddhism recognises the working of the Law in Nature and uses the term *dhamma* to denote this. Decay and impermanence are predicated of all life; the law of destruction is universal; "whatever we see, whatever we hear, our senses as well as the objects which are presented to them, everything is drawn within the cycle of

[1] See his *Buddhist Philosophy*, pp. 68-74.

[2] *Buddha*, p. 251.

origination and decease; everything is only a Dhamma, a Samkhara, and all Dhammas, all Samkharas are transitory. Whence this cycle? No matter whence; it is there beyond ken. The existence of the conditional is accepted as a given fact; thought shrinks from going back to the unconditional."[1] The term, Dhamma thus, as we have seen above, applies to the chain of causation. The whole phenomena are "Dhamma"; the individual is himself a grouping of many elements, "Dhamma". Although separate they are members of a chain, linked together by causal laws. Man is a "living continuous complex, which does not remain quite the same for two consecutive moments, but which continues endless number of existences without becoming completely different from itself."[2] The idea of causation and the idea of transitoriness are thus merged into the idea of continuity. The path of salvation from this endless round is ruled by laws; "the aspirant who has entered on to the path to salvation is subject to the rule that he cannot fall away from the fulfilment of his purpose; the non-returner (anagami) to the rule that he cannot be born again in this world."[3] The Tathagatha shows the true path; he preaches the Dharma, and those who walk in his path reach the highest goal. This doctrine, he enunciates in a discourse called the "Dhamma-chakka-ppavatiana" or the "foundation of the kingdom of Righteousness."

We need not go further into details; it remains only to notice a curious development. In course of time Dhamma takes the place of Brahman; and sometimes even the expression Brahma-chakka is used. And just as "Brahman" is unknowable, Dhamma also is unknowable.[4]

---

[1] Oldenberg: *Buddha*, p. 270.

[2] Poussin: *The way to Nirvana*, p.52.

[3] Keith: *Buddhist Philosophy*, p. 70.

[4] "Slight as is normally the recognition in the Buddhist texts of the Brahman doctrine of their rivals, Guger has shown that

We shall not linger long over the subsequent history of the term Dharma. As it goes on gathering ethical and moral content in course of time, it came also to be identified with righteousness and religious merit. We have seen that the Sankhya is a system which denies the Absolute. Its Purusha are unattached tō Prakriti. According to this view, as much as to the Upanishadic and Vedantic views, there is ultimately no righteousness or unrighteousness. This same is true of the Buddhist and Nyaya-Vaisheshika schools. The Mimansakas look upon Dharma from the objective stand-point and so external. And especially the Purva Mimansakas lose themselves in ceremonialism which to them constitutes "Dharma"—Dharma in its empirical aspect, the whole social order in its varied relationships. As already pointed out, the Social Order is concretised Dharma. The various writers, whether legal codifiers or writers of treatises on statecraft, were under the belief that they were giving expression to Dharma; and so they wrote Dharma-Sastras, Sutras, Smritis etc. to enunciate what constituted Dharma. The Grihya Sutras and the Dharma Sutras tell us especially what a householder has to do. In the Dharma-Sastras, and Smritis, here and there, we can trace observations on politics in relation to Dharma; the Epics especially Mahabharata, are again a rich mine of literature on Dharma. And from all these various sources we have information regarding the different aspects of dharma, of castes and

---

the term Dhamma not rarely is used as a substitute in expressing the Buddhist ideal for the Brahman of the Upanishads, while the term Brahman itself is occasionally preserved. The famous phrase, "wheel of the Law (Dhamma-chakka)" is also paralleled by Brahma-chakka; the Dammayana by Brahmayana; the Tathagatha is not merely an incorporation of Dhamma but also the Brahma; the Dhamma even claims the worship which is the lot of the Brahman in the Upanishads." Keith: *Religion and Philosophy of the Veda*, p. 550.

orders, of the domain of law and usage, of observances with a view to acquire religious merit, and so on. We realise that Dharma includes almost everything, Philosophy, Religion, Ethics, Politics, Sociology, Economics, and so on.

We have already seen the metaphysical content of the term Dharma. In the last chapter we have discussed the social and ethical implications. If the Absolute is unknown and unknowable and in the last analysis a bare monistic monad, or if again, the Absolute is denied or ignored, what foundations for a true religious life can we have? If God is not knowable, surely His Will cannot be ascertained. We cannot, therefore, be wrong for not following what we do not know; ignorance is virtue. If again, I myself am God, surely I can do no wrong; merit and demerit cannot attach to any action of mine. Being God I am already perfect. Or, if the hypothesis of God is discarded, and the Universe is understood as coming together in the phenomenal sense of Purusha and Prakriti, then the Purusha being *independent beings, things-in-themselves* are unattached and unaffected. Further, if the Universe is mere grouping of Dharma, of which all that we can observe points to its transience and unsubstantiality, we can never reach to the sheet anchor which alone will be the intelligent background. Thus from whatever angle of view we try to take in the metaphysical statement of Indian thought, we are irresistibly drawn to the conclusion that it could not be the basis for a true life that can be lived, here and now.

Let us now see, if in the empirical view of Dharma, we get any better impression that could have served for the foundation of social philosophy. And here especially have we to go by the maxim that by the fruit we shall judge the tree. For a clear conception, therefore, we shall try to follow the various classifications of Dharma we have in the sacred and legal literatures.

Manu classifies Dharma generally into Varnashrama-dharma and Sadharanadharma ; Prasastapada into Sámanyadharmas and Visheshadharmas ; the Mimansakas into Laukika and Shastrika or Paramarthika. We have other laukika and shastrika or Paramarthika. We have other classifications also, that of the Ramanujists etc which we may not go into.[1] The most comprehensive classification, however, is that of the Mitakshara.[2] According to Vijnaneswara, (the writer of the Mitakshara) Dharma is of six kinds : Varna Dharma ; Ashrama Dharma ; Varnashrama Dharma ; Guna Dharma ; Nimitta Dharma ; Sadharana Dharma.

Of these, it will suffice for our purpose if we try to understand Varna Ashrama Dharma and Sadharana Dharma ; to the others we might give a passing reference.

Let us take Sadharana Dharma first. What is its import ? By Sadharana Dharma Vijnaneswara means the general duties of all men down to chandalas. Manu, however does not include the chandalas or the untouchables and he has one set of duties for the four castes, and another set to be observed by the dwijas or the twice-born alone. The Buddhist and Jain systems, too, have their schemes of duties which can be studied together in this connection :

To begin with Yajnavalkya.[3] He gives the following lists, one for all, and one for the twice-born :

The universal duties of all men are : Harmlessness ; Veracity ; Non-stealing ; Purity ; Controlling of the organs ; Liberality ; Self-Control ; Mercy ; Forgiveness ; and Vijnaneswara informs us that these are the means of the acquisitions of Dharma for all men beginning with the Brahmana and ending with the chandala.

---

[1] We refer the reader for further details to S. K. Maitra's admirable little book: *Ethics of the Hindus*, pp. 1-25.

[2] *Yajnavalkya Smriti*, pp. 4-5.

[3] *Ibid.*, tran. by Srisha Chandra Vidyarnava, pp. 236-237.

The universal duties for the Twice-born are :

"He should be wife-loving, pure, maintaining the dependent and be engaged in Sraddha, and the ceremonies and with the Mantra "Namah", he should perform the five sacrifices."

The following is the list of Sadharanadharma according to Manu.[1]

The general duties of the four castes are :

"Abstention from injuring (creatures) ; Veracity ; abstention from unlawfully appropriating (the goods of others), Purity, and control of the organs." (x. 63.)

The duties to be observed by twice-born, and common to the four Orders are known as the Ten-fold Law :

"Contentment, forgiveness, self-control, abstention from unrighteously appropriating anything, (obedience to the rules of) purification, coercion of the organs, wisdom, knowledge (of the supreme Soul), truthfulness and abstention from anger, (form) the ten-fold law." (VI, 92.)

The list according to Prasastapada is :[2] Moral Earnestness. Regard for the Spiritual (Dharma-Shradha, Dharma Manah Prasadah). Refraining from injury to living beings (Ahinsa) ; Seeking the good of creatures (Bhutahitatwa) ; Speaking the Truth (Satyavachana) ; Refraining from Theft (Asteya) ; Sexual Continence (Brahmacharya). Sincerity, Purity of Motive (Ampadha) ; Renouncing or restraining anger (Krodha Varjana) ; Ablution, personal clealiness (Abhisechana Snana) ; the eating of linseeds and other specified substances on special occasions for the object of suchi or purification of the body (Shuchidravyasevana) ; Devotion to the Deities recognised by the Vedas (Vishishta Devata-Bhakti) ; Fast-

[1] X, 63 and VI, 92.

[2] The present writer is very much indebted to S. K. Maitra, *Ethics of the Hindus*, for his material.

ing on specified occasion; Moral watchfulness (Apramade) i. e. the unfailing performance of the unconditional duties (nitya naimittikanam, Karmanam avashyainbhavena karanam).

Vasishta gives the following list:[1] Truthfulness; suppression of anger; liberality; abstention from injuring living beings; procreation of offspring.

Kautilya[2] gives the following list of general duties: Harmlessness, truthfulness, purity, freedom from spite, abstinence from cruelty and forgiveness.

The Epic[3] has a discourse on Dharma in general. Bhishma enumerates the duties of the four orders or castes: Suppression of wrath, truthfulness of speech, justice, forgiveness, begetting children upon one's own wives, purity of conduct, avoidance of quarrels, simplicity and maintenance of dependents.

We have already noted the rules to be observed according to the Yoga of Patanjali. They are universal in the sense that they are applicable to a man of any class, profession, place, etc. The Yama and the Niyama form the ethical training to prepare the man for the religious life.

Asoka, the great Emperor-Saint, proclaimed the moral principles of Dharma in his Edicts for the instruction of the common people. We shall not discuss if he was a Hindu or Buddhist, for reasons already noted elsewhere. We shall make a list of the negative and positive principles of his Dharma.[4]

Negative Principles: 1. Animals must not be killed. 2. Living beings must not be hurt. 3. Festival meetings

---

[1] S. B. E., Vol. XIV, part II, p. 26.

[2] Shamashastri, p. 7.

[3] Santi Parva: section IX.

[4] From the article of Rev. Heras on *Asoka Dharma and Religion*, reprinted from the *Quarterly Journal of the Mythic Society*, Bangalore, Vol. XVII, No. 4.

must not be held. 4. Social or superstitious ceremonies are not recommended.

Positive Principles: 1. Gentleness. 2. Liberality. 3. Proper behaviour towards relatives. 4. Obedience to elders. 5. Compassion. 6. Kindness. 7. Self-control. 8. Goodness. 9. Impartiality. 10. Purity.

The Sanatsujatiya has twelve defects which a man should avoid and twelve great observances. The defects are wrath, desire, avarice, delusion, craving, mercilessness, censoriousness, vanity, grief, attachment, envy and reviling others. The great observances are knowledge, truth, self-restraint, sacred learning, freedom from censoriousness, sacrifice, gift, courage and quiescence. (*Sanatsujatiya*, Ch. III.)

The duties of men according to Buddhism are, as we have noted, summarised in the Noble Eightfold Path, to wit: Right faith, right resolve, right speech, right action, right living, right effort, right thought, and right self-concentration.

According to the Jains[1] there are two lists, for monks and for laymen. There are Mahavrata to be observed by monks and Anuvrata by laymen. There are also rules of conduct imposed on the laymen, called Silavrata, which again is of two kinds, Gunavrata and Sikshavrata.

The five Vratas to be observed by Monks are: Not to kill, not to lie, not to steal, to abandon sexual intercourse, to renounce all interest in worldly things, especially to keep no property.

---

[1] See Jacobi's article in *Ency. Rel. and Eth.* The present writer has practically quoted verbatim from that article.

The Silavrata are :

Gunavrata	Digvirati : limitation of distance up to which a man will go in this or that direction.
	Anarthadanadavirati : or abstain from engaging in anything that does not strictly concern him.
	Upabhogaparibhogaparinama : or setting a measure to the food, drink and things a man enjoys, avoiding besides gross enjoyments.
Sikshavrata	Desavirata : reducing the area in which one will move.
	Samajika : the laymen should undertake to give up, at stated times, all sinful actions by sitting down motionless and meditating on holy things.
	Pausadhopavasa : or to live as a monk on the 8th, or 14th day of the lunar month at least once a month.
	Atithisamvibhaga : or literally to give a share to guests, but it is understood in a less literal sense viz. to provide the monks with what they want.

The references suffice for our purpose ; and they are sufficiently representative. We pass on to note the Varna and Ashrama Dharmas.

The Varna Dharma relates to the duties of the castes. The duties of the castes according to Manu are :[1]

---

[1] I, 87-91.

Duties of Brahmans : teaching and studying (the Vedas) ; sacrificing for their own benefit and for others giving and accepting of alms.

Duties of Kshatriyas : to protect the people, to bestow gifts, to offer sacrifices, to study (the Vedas), and to abstain from attaching himself to sensual pleasures.

Duties of Vaisyas : to tend cattle, to bestow gifts, to offer sacrifices, to study (the Vedas), to trade, to lend money, and to cultivate land.

Duties of Sudras : "One occupation only the Lord prescribed to the sudra, to serve meekly even these (other) three castes."

According to Prasastapada[1] the duties of the castes are :

(a) The duties common to the three castes of Brahmin, Kshatriya and Vaishya. These are :

Sacrificial ceremonies (Ijya yagadi). Acquisition of knowledge by study (Adhyayana). Charity (Dana).

(b) The duties obligatory on the Brahmin only. These are :

Acceptance of gifts (ratigraha). Teaching (Adyapana). Performance of ceremonial sacrifice (Yajana). The way or mode of life prescribed for a brahmin (Svavarnavihita Samskara).

(c) The duties obligatory on the Kshatriya only. These are :

Protecting people from external aggressions and internal disturbances, as well as governing them with a view to place prosperity (Prajapalana). Chastising the wicked (Asadhunigraha). Not retreating from battle (Yuddheshu Shivartana).

---

[1] S. K. Maitra: *Ethics of the Hindus*, pp. 12-13.

The way or mode of life prescribed for a Kshatra (Svakiya Samskara).

(d) The duties obligatory on the Vaisya only. These are :

Buying (kraya) i. e. procuring commodities from others after paying their proper price (mulyain dattva parasmat dravyagrahanam). Selling (vikraya), i. e. bartering away commodities to others after realising from them their legitimate price (mulyam adaya parasya svadravya danam). Agriculture (krishi). Breeding and rearing of cattle (pashupalana). The way or mode of life prescribed for a Vaisya (Svakiyasamskara).

(e) The duties obligatory on the Sudra only. These are :

Being subservient or in subjection to the other three castes (purva-varna-paratantra). Observing such rites as do not require the utterance of the sacred Mantras or incantation (Amantrika Kriya).

Vasishtha[1] thus describes the duties of the four castes :

Of the Brahmin : studying the Veda, teaching, sacrificing for himself, sacrificing for others, giving alms, and accepting gifts.

Of the Kshatriya : studying, sacrificing for himself, and bestowing gifts. His peculiar duty is to protect the people with his weapons.

Of the Vaisya : studying, sacrificing for himself, and bestowing gifts, and the peculiar duties are agriculture, trading, tending cattle, and lending money at interest.

Of the Sudra : To serve the superior castes.

Kamandaka[2] gives the following description of the duties of the different castes :

---

[1] II, 13-20.

[2] *Nitisara*, section II, 19-21.

> The holy acts of teaching, of conducting sacrifices on other's behalf, and of acepting alms from the pious, these have been enumerated by the sages for those belonging to the superior sect (Brahmana.)
> A king should live by his weapons and by protecting his subjects. The means of subsistence of a Vaisya are cattle-rearing, cultivation and trade. The duty of the Sudra is to serve the twice-born sects, one after the other.

The references given so far are exhaustive. We do not propose to give more, as the instances already cited show that there is no substantial difference of opinion regarding the nature of the duties of the four castes We shall, however, draw special attention to the classification given by Kautilya, as it throws light on some of the most important aspects of the Indian Polity. It would serve also to dispel the mistaken notions held regarding the influence of religion on the political ideas of Kautilya. Far from there being a divorce between religion and statecraft, we shall see that Kautilya, even in spite of his empirical bent of mind, is as sacerdotal in his general ideas as Manu or any other writer. And in this connection we may also draw attention to what *Santi Parva* has to say, though in brief.

Kautilya enunciates :[1]

"As the triple Vedas definitely determine the respective duties of the four castes and of the four orders of religious life, they are the most useful.

The duty of the Brahman is study, teaching, performance of sacrifice, officiating in other's sacrificial performance and the giving and receiving of gifts.

That of a Kshatriya is study, performance of sacrifice, giving gifts, military occupation and protection of life.

---

[1] *Arthasastra*: Shamasastry, p. 7.

That of a Vaisya is study, performance of sacrifice, giving gifts, agriculture, cattle breeding and trade.

That of a Sudra is the serving of twice-born (dvijati), agriculture, cattle breeding, and trade (varta), the profession of artisans and court bards (Karukusilavakarma).

According to *Santi Parva*,[1] the following are the duties of the castes :

Duties of Brahmans : Self-restraint ; study of the Vedas ; austerities, practice of charity ; performance of sacrifice.

Duties of Kshatriyas : A Kshatriya should give, not beg ; should himself perform sacrifice, but not officiate at the sacrifice of other's. He should never teach the Vedas, but study them with a Brahman preceptor. He should protect the people. Always exerting himself for the destruction of robbers and wicked people, he should put forth his prowess in battle—Establishing all his subjects in the observance of their respective duties, a king should cause all of them to do everything according to the dictates of righteousness.

Duties of Vaisyas : A Vaisya should make gifts, study the Vedas, perform sacrifices, and acquire wealth by fair means, protect and rear all domestic animals, and trade. A Vaisya should never desire that he should not tend cattle. If a Vaisya desires to tend cattle, no one else should be employed in that task.

Duties of Sudras :

"The creator intended the Sudra to become the servant of the other three orders. For this, the service of the three other classes is the duty of the Sudra. By such service of the other three, a Sudra may obtain great happiness. He should wait upon the other classes according to the order of seniority ;

[1] Section LX.

a Sudra should never amass wealth, lest by his wealth he makes the members of the three superior classes obedient to him. By this he would incur sin. With the king's permission, however, a Sudra, for performing religious acts, may earn wealth. It is said that the Sudras should certainly be maintained by the three other orders. Worn out umbrellas, turbans, beds and shoes and fans, should be given to the Sudra servants. Torn clothes which are no longer fit for wear should be given away by the regenerate classes to the Sudra. These are the latter's lawful acquisitions."

We shall now pass on to the Asrama Dharma or the Law of the Orders, the Brahmacharin, Grihasta, Vanaprasta and Parivrajaka.

Kautilya[1] describes the duties of the four orders thus :

"The duty of a householder is learning, livelihood by his own profession, marriage among his equals of different ancestral Rishis, intercourse with his wedded wife after her monthly ablution, gifts to Gods, ancestors, guests, and servants, and the eating of the remainder.

That of a student (Brahmacharin) is learning Vedas, fire-worship, ablution, living by begging, and devotion to his teacher even at the cost of his own life, or in the absence of his teacher to the teacher's son, or to an elder classmate.

That of a Vanaprastha (forest-recluse) is observance of chastity, sleeping on the bare ground, keeping twisted locks, wearing deer skin, fire worship, ablution, worship of Gods, ancestors, and guests and living upon foodstuffs procurable in forests.

That of an ascetic retired from the world (Parivrajaka) is complete control of the organs of sense, abstaining from

---

[1] *Arthasastra*, p. 8.

all kinds of work, disowning money, keeping from society, begging in many places, dwelling in forests, and purity, both internal and external."

Kamandaka[1] gives the following description.

"The duties of a Brahmacharin are to live in the family of his preceptor, to worship the sacred fires, to study the *Vedas* and their auxiliaries, to observe vows, to perform ablutions during the three periods of the day (in the morning, at noon, and in the evening), to beg and to live for life with his spiritual guide. In the absence of a preceptor, he should live with his (preceptor's) son or with one of his fellow Brahmacharin, or he may, if he likes adopt another mode of existence.

"During the whole period of his pupilage, he should wear a Mekhala along with his sacred thread, bear matted hair or a shaved beard, carry a *Danda*, and live with his Preceptor. Afterwards at his own will he may choose any other mode of life.

"The duties of a house-holder are to celebrate the *Agnihotra* sacrifice, to live by the profession prescribed (for his sect) and to avoid sexual intercourse during the Parvas.

"The duties, of those who have married and settled down, are to worship the Gods, the ancestral manes and the guests, to show mercy to the poor and the wretched, and to live according to the precepts of the *Srutis* and the *Smritis*.

"The duties of those who have resorted to the forest are to keep matted hair, to perform *Agnihotra* sacrifices, to sleep on bare earth, to wear black deer skin, to live in solitary places, to sustain themselves on water, suculent roots, *Nivara* crop, and fruits, to refuse to accept alms, to bathe thrice in the day, to observe vows, and to adore the Gods and the guests.

[1] Kamandakiya *Nitisara*, pp. 20-22.

"The duties of the wandering mendicants are : to renounce all actions, to live upon what is obtained by begging, to dwell under the shelter of a tree, to refuse smallest gifts, to do no harm to other created beings and to maintain an equality of attitude towards them, to be indifferent alike to friends and enemies, to be unmoved by joy or grief, to be purified in mind and in body, to curb the speech, to observe vows, to retract the senses from their objects, to keep the mind always collected, to be absorbed in contemplation and to purify their intentions."

According[1] to Prasastapada the duties of Asrama are :

Of the Brahmacharin :

Guru-shushrusha ; Indhana-aharana or collecting of fuels ; agnou homa or offering incense to the sacrificial fire ; and Bhaikshya.

Of the Krtadara grihastha, or married person living with his family :

Performing the five sacrificial ceremonies or Yajnas every morning and evening by means of one's own earnings. The Panchayajna are :

(1) Bhutayajna or sacrifice to bhutas or elements ;
(2) Manushyayajna or the serving and entertaining of guests ;
(3) Devayajna or the offering of incense to the sacred fire ;
(4) Pitryajna or paying respect to the dead through shraddas etc. ;
(5) Brahinayajna or the reading of the sacred texts, the Vedas.

Over and above these duties there is the duty to beget children by co-habitation with his wife in the proper season.

Of the Vanaprastha and Brahmachari Grahastha :

Valkaladidharana or wearing the bark of trees ;

---

[1] S. K. Maitra: *Ethics of the Hindus*, pp. 13-16.

Keshadidharana or letting the hair grow ; Vanasya phalamulasya bhojanam or living on the roots and the fruits of the jungle ; and Atitisesha bhojanam or dining on the surplus of the meal after entertainment of all the guests.

Of the Yati or the mendicant seer duties of self-restraint or Yamas ; harmlessness ; veracity ; refraining from theft ; sexual abstinence. Duties of self-realisation or Niyamas : cleanliness ; contentment ; arduous application and devotion ; reciting Vedic Texts ; meditation on the glories and the perfection of the Lord.

There is no necessity to give further references. We could refer the reader to Manu, Yajnavalkya, Vasishtha, Baudhayana, Apasthamba, Gautama and Brihaspati, and a host of other writers, but we desist from considerations of space and time.

The Guna-dharma and Nivritta-dharma need not detain us long. The first refers to the special duties such as, according to the explanation of Vijnaneswara (Mitakshara), "It is the highest duty of a king who has been duly annointed and the rest, according to scriptures, to protect the subjects, etc." The second refers to secondary duties such as "Penances which are occasioned by omitting to perform what is commanded or committing what is forbidden."

The Mimamsaka classification,[1] is into laukika and Paramarthika. The laukika or secular duties are empirical and rest on human sanction, whereas the shastrika or paramarthika, (i. e. scriptural) are non-empirical and rest on religious or divine sanction. The latter have greater validity since they do not rest on mere human experience. The scriptural duties, again, are either kamyakarmas, or Nityanaimittikakarmas. The former are conditional on

[1] What follows is a summary of S. K. Maitra's exposition.

subjective desire and so are valid only when desired for a particular end. The latter are not dependent upon any such subjective motive, and are either Nityakarmas or Naimittikakarmas, i. e. duties obligatory always or on special occasion. These scriptural duties are negative and positive, vidhis and nishedas (positive injunctions and prohibitions). What is most important, and must be borne in mind is that the Mimamsakas regard scriptural sanctions as of greater validity than human experience. Moral good, though viewed at from the criterion of pleasure and pain, does not depend upon empirical experience, but is non-empirical because revealed by the scriptures. What the scriptures enjoin is Dharma or Adharma, the object being the acquisition of merit, and freeing oneself from demerit. Dharma, therefore, has reference to sacrificial worship, to prescriptive observance. The regulations of the ritual are enjoined by the Veda. These injunctions are "Incitements to actions" but the actions the Mimamsa is interested in are the Vedic actions, all worldly actions being ruled out. And of the Vedic actions, those which relate to sacrifice are the most important. They are of three kinds, Yoga, Homa and Dana. Sacrifices again, are of three kinds, agnihotra, masagnihotra or of both. We shall serve no useful purpose in trying to unravel more details. Everything appears to be mechanical and artificial. The Mimamsa, however, is of the greatest importance to the Hindus, as it regulates the whole of their life even at the present day.

From a consideration of the Mimamsa conception of Dharma, we are naturally led to the Vedantist idea of Dharma. Sankara held that the observance of Dharma would lead man to the final stage when he gains saving knowledge; the performance of works being held indispensable for the purification of the mind. But Sankara is thus far in conformity with traditional notions as when he accepts that morality might be a matter of prescription.[1] The seekers after liberation according to him, must perform ritual works and other obligatory duties, i. e. Nitya-karmas, and not kamya karmas and then they become regenerated and pure, works proving useful as a means to the birth of the spiritual, regeneration of the mind. As he puts it : "Works are meant for the purification of the mind."[2] And he makes a distinction between the higher works and the lower, between works performed with desire, and those which are absolutely detached from any motives to the fruits thereof. And the four requirements laid down by him, for the Vedantist are (1) discerning between eternal and non-eternal substance, (2) renunciation of the enjoyment of reward here and in the other world, (3) the attainment of the six means—tranquillity, restraint, renunciation, resignation, concentration, belief, (4) the longing for liberation. This will suffice, as we have discussed more fully elsewhere.

Our discussion, so far, will enable us to realise that the conception of Dharma is not so simple as we are tempted to take it to be at first sight. Its scope cannot be defined within definite limits and we can only understand its comprehensiveness by a reference to almost every aspect of human life. The term itself may mean many things according as the sense in which it is used. It may mean support or stability. It may also mean the cause of stability, law or ordinance. It may again refer to the innate nature of a thing. Sometimes it may be taken to mean as referring to institutions and traditions

Dharma, as Law, may have reference either to the Sacred Law or Revelation, or to law or custom which

---

[1] "Reasoning which disregards the holy texts and rests on individual opinion only, has no proper foundation.—The true nature of the cause of the world cannot—even be thought of without the help of the holy texts". Quoted by Urquhart, *The Vedanta and Modern Thought*, p. 66.

[2] K. Sastri: *Advaita Philosophy*, p. 149.

regulates the life of the individual and the community, or again to the Life which is according to the Law. When understood in its connection with the other ends of life, Artha, Kama, and Moksha, Dharma may mean that which man must follow in his effort to seek final Liberation. Again, Dharma may mean religious merit which accrues to a man as the reward of his Karma.[1]

But although its scope is not so easy to determine, we are at any rate in a position to evaluate its precise nature. The clue to a proper understanding lies in the answer we receive to the question : "What is the End of Life and how is it to be attained?" Dharma, both in its absolute and empirical aspects is the ruling principle of life, the one aspect as the goal, the other as the means. The two aspects moreover are closely related in a peculiar sense ; in the ultimate there is no divorce between them. This relation, however, cannot be easily comprehended unless one is familiar with the fundamental characteristics of the Indian mind. Indeed it would be far more true to say that what is to be realised is the absence of any relation, for relation involves diversity, the Real being the absolute aspect of Dharma, its empirical aspect having only provisional reality and validity. Both the conceptions of Dharma as the Absolute Being immanent in the Empirical realising or fulfilling itself into a Universe, and of the Empirical reaching its completion in the Absolute through progressive achievement are perhaps foreign to the Indian mind. Deussen is perfectly right in saying that "Moral transformation remained foreign to Indian thought." The Transcendental Good is to be attained by passing beyond morality. Empirical Dharma does not complete itself in the Absolute Dharma. We have no idea of the moral

---

[1] Refer to Prof. V. G. Paranjpe's interesting article in the Fergusson College Magazine, on *Was there a Manava-dharma-Sutra?*

transformation of the imperfect to the perfect. The realm of morality or Empirical Dharma must, shall we say, annihilate itself to give way to the Absolute. If the ethico-spiritual ideal of deliverance or Moksha is to be achieved through the sharing of life and experience with others, fellow-seekers in the Great Quest, it would imply that the individual cannot isolate himself from the rest of the Universe. Ethics, instead of aiming at psychological preparedness by philosophical detachment, for the Final End, will be a continuous hungering after virtue and Righteousness, the Supreme End, in that case, not placed in some remote, unreachable far realm, but itself being the consummation of progressive fulfilment of our moral and social ideals. In other words, the End will be the complete embodiment of that Purpose of which we are the incomplete expressions so far ; the finite would then grow into the infinite, shorn of its limiting nature. This would be the true realisation of individuality. Our inner melody would then break out into the Song Eternal, having at last touched the key that would tune it with the Infinite. It would be the stage of the most perfect realisation of the Good, the Perfect and the Beautiful, of our social moral ideals ; not the stage when morality is transcended, but when morality fulfils itself.

This view involves the idea that the Supreme Good, which is our End, is itself also that which is morally the most perfect. The ideals of morality and our idea of the ultimate End cannot be isolated from each other. Every judgment we make of our Final aim must be a moral judgment and every effort towards it must be its ethical embodiment. The ideal moral judgment, moreover, "implies a conception of the ideal good for society as a whole."[1] We ought to aim, not only at perfection, for ourselves but for others as well. True moral life will, in other

[1] Rashdall: *The Theory of Good and Evil*, Vol. I, p. 96.

words, not merely aim at the individual's good, but would seek to promote the general good. No man can be a law unto himself. He must, in the words of Kant's categorical imperative, "act as a member of a kingdom of ends." He must so act that he would treat every human being as of equal intrinsic value; no one would realise his own good unless he would also seek to promote the good of others. Morality is essentially rooted in the idea of value, which would only find its meaning by breaking the confines of one's private seeking so that it shall be sublimated into a quest for the true social good. All particular ends or hypothetical imperatives, as Kant calls them, must be subordinated to the Supreme End which would seek to realise the Ideal Society. It would be nothing short of taking upon ourselves the burden of the Cross. It is only by losing our life that we shall find it.

Self-renunciation or self-sacrifice is, therefore, the first condition to self-realisation. Individuality can only be perfected by its projection into something beyond itself. A man is more of an individual the more he seeks to realise the ideal society. "The good, conceived as self-realisation," as James Seth truly observes, "is a social, not an egoistic good."[1]

Unfortunately, in the whole conception of Dharma, both as the good and the means to prepare oneself for the realisation of that good, we have no idea at all of this view. The aim of empirical Dharma is merely to help the individual to attain *Chitta-Suddhi* or self-purification, the inward expression of objective morality. We are of course not arguing against true inwardness. "Real justice", according to Plato, says Nettleship, "means not the mere doing of one's own business in the state, but such outward doing of one's own business as is an expression of a corresponding mode of action within the soul; if the out-

[1] *Essays in Ethics and Religion*, p. 168.

ward action is really just, it means that the soul is just within, that like a just state the whole soul and the several parts of it perform their proper functions in relation to one another." The principles of conduct must be deeply rooted in the facts of one's inner life. What we are emphatically protesting against is the cleavage that has been created between the inner life and the rest of existence. The doctrine of detachment is certainly anti-social in nature. The ideal of life must be sought for in life as a whole, in the duties of everyday life, in our family relationships, in our obligations as members of a commonwealth.

But this is impossible so long as life is looked upon as evil ; so long as freedom is understood to be the breaking away from the bonds of empirical existence, so long as we are supposed to be held in bondage. The release from bandha or bondage lies through the negation of experience and cessation of Karma. Freedom, therefore, cannot be anything positive, it is devoid of any content ; it is transcendental.

This is inevitable, as we have seen, when God is conceived of as He is in Indian Philosophy. He must be brought into positive organic relation with the world. It is only then that we can live this life, Here and Now, to the full. So long as we imagine that the Transcendental Good can be attained only through the severance of the ties that link us as members of this world, so long we look upon this world with extreme suspicion. We cannot but look upon wife, children and friends as distractions that tempt us away from the path that would lead to Moksha. How can we have real zest in life unless we place our trust in it !

In other words, Hindu ethics does not provide any place for society. That ethics is essentially individualistic, and so has no idea of social values. Personality is not conceived to be the flowering of the individual in his realising organic communion with Humanity and with God. It is on the other hand an elusive and hence impossible quest at trying to know the monadic Atman. In all the various descriptions of dharma, we do not get anywhere the conception of positive social service. This is impossible in an ethic which denies all value and reality to life. The Self alone is held to be true ; "everything else is of evil".[1] And so all endeavour is towards realising this Self. Ethical discipline has no reference to Social Ends, but only to *Chitha-suddhi* or purification of the mind. Almost all the duties that we have noted above aim at the attainment of the individual's perfection. In other words if the use of the expression be permitted, we might say that these duties are self-regarding. The individual is anxious for his own salvation, and, as Macdonell has truly observed, "there is consequently little scope for the development of other-regarding virtues."[2] The emphasis is on the self, on the individual attaining self-sufficiency and independence. The idea of self-autonomy, therefore, is the fundamental basis of Hindu ethics. "No man can help another in the attainment of his end ; just as he cannot reap what another has sown so also he cannot help another to his fruition."[3] This theory is the result of the doctrine of Karma that we have examined already. And the Law of karma is essentially individualistic.

And yet, in the whole scheme of life that Dharma rules there is no place really for the individual. The doctrine of self-realisation need not be necessarily individualistic. The more the man may realise his true individuality the more he denies himself and dedicates his life for the service of his brother and neighbour. This is the key note of the teachings of the great master minds of the west beginning

---

[1] *Brihad Upa., III, 5 Brahmana.*

[2] *Lectures on Comparative Religion*, p. 67.

[3] S. K. Maitra: *Ethics of the Hindus*, p. 9.

with Plato. In modern times we know how T. H. Green has made the Doctrine of Self-realisation the watchword of political and social reform. Ethics is essentially social ethics, and the individual can best realise himself in trying to apply his moral principles in the realm of social and political conduct, working in common with others towards the well-being of society.

The Doctrine of Self-Realisation is, however, understood in a very peculiar sense, in Hindu thought. A hiatus is provisionally assumed between the empirical self and Absolute Self. A divorce is effected between knowledge and faith, between *jnana* and *karma*. And whatever provisional value is allowed for ethical discipline, the final stage is not the completion or perfection of our moral or ethical life, but the transcendence of all our ideals of morality and life. So it is not the transformation of the empirical, by a gradual process of perfecting itself through the growth of righteousness and the elimination of evil, into the perfect Kingdom of Righteousness. It is on the other hand the attainment of knowledge of the identity of Atman and Brahman, of the Self which is the self of all ; "Everything else is of evil". This doctrine of salvation, as we have seen, is not really the perfection of individuality, but the negation of individuality. This end of life, examined critically fails, therefore, as the basis for the individual's real life. The non-empirical dharma is indeed emptied of all content whatsoever.

It remains to be seen if in the empirical existence, the individual counts for anything at all. The social order is held to be the concretised embodiment of Dharma. And Dharma is eternal. It is not a human achievement and so is not to be interfered with, in any way, by man who has simply to accept it as it is. We are told that the ordering of society is once for all fixed. What is divinely instituted shall not be touched by the sacrilegious hand of man. In other words, man has no choice in the ordering of society ;

he has to conform to it without criticism. His duties are the duties of the station into which he is born. His place in the social organism is clearly defined for him, but not by any human agency. It is the inexorable Law of Karma that has determined the particular form and nature of his birth. If he is fortunate in being born a Brahmin that is due to his good action in the past. If he is born a Sudra or a Chandala, it is so because of his evil action in a past life. He ought not to complain and struggle against destiny. If in the present life he scrupulously adheres to and performs the actions prescribed for him, he may hope to secure a better birth in the next life. He has no choice, therefore, to chose his own duties. The whole functional system of society or "Dharma" rests on prescription and authority—not human authority, but scriptural, and so divine. The individual is told what actions are right and wrong ; and penances are ordained for purification if there is any transgression. But why the actions are right or wrong is not open to discussion.[1] Indian Ethics does not concern itself with questions of value. Right and wrong are not moral estimates as we would understand them, in the modern sense. Right action refers only to prescriptive observance and rituality correctness.[2] We are mistaken if we read any social significance in the call to action wherever we find it in Hindu thought. *Karma Kanda* is devoid of true morality ; for the works enjoined are in fact often emphatically anti-social. And in all, the blight of passivity remains. Man must blindly follow even in matters that pertain to the ultimate end. It is held that autho-

---

[1] "How can those born in that order, who follow the practices of that order and that have their refuge in them, censure those duties? If indeed those duties be censurable, then why should not the supreme ordainer be blamed? *Santi Parva*, Ch. X, 19.

[2] "Whatever system of rules is prescribed in this world to follow it is good; this has been celebrated from ancient times".—*Anugita*, Ch. XXX.

rity must be self-valid ; and only the Vedas therefore are authoritative. In this scriptural authority there can be no place for the individual's conscience ; no true self-autonomy. We read of the famous reproof of Gargi by Yajnavalkya, when she tried to ask him questions about Brahman. "O Gargi, do not ask too much lest thy head should fall off. Thou askest too much about a deity about which we are not to ask too much."[1] Even Sankara insists upon scriptural authority, for, Dharma is for him a matter of prescription. The Vedas have been held to be infallible by almost every section of Orthodox Hindu thought. In other words the function of the scriptures is not to enlighten the individual's conscience, but to supersede it. Ethical conduct is not that which finds its sanction inhering in the man's conscience, but that which is guided by an external factor which he has to accept. Thus, we have mere rules and regulations instead of principles, a mechanical instead of a spiritual morality. We do not exaggerate in the least if we state that even in the empirical sense the individual is practically ignored His action is not the response to the promptings and dictates of his conscience, and he must subordinate his judgment, if he has any, to scriptural authority.[2] But what scriptural authority itself is, he has no direct means of knowing. It is the priest who interprets. In the last analysis, therefore, "Dharma" is practically reduced to sacerdotalism.

And sacerdotalism means, in fact, the spiritual and social superiority of the Brahman class. This is especially to be noted in the regulations of Varna Dharma. On a future occasion we shall discuss Varna Dharma

[1] *Brihad Upa.*, III, 6, 1.

[2] "When any doubt arises regarding what should be done, it should be settled by the injunctions of the scriptures which tend persons versed in Vedic scriptures or three of those who frequently recite them may declare". *Santi Parva*, Ch. XXXVII, 21.

from the point of view of social justice. Here we shall only remark that the hierarchal idea involved in Varna Dharma means the degradation of the lower castes, the members of which seem to be most reluctantly recognised as human beings at all. And when we have invidious distinctions between caste and caste, we can never have a social order which is the expression of spiritual harmony. It would indeed be ironical to characterise Varna Dharma as social, as some writers have done. In our view it is purely narrow and sectional.

And the idea of Varna has acted as a freezing influence on social virtues; it has dismembered society into innumerable little groups, divided by insurmountable barriers. Thus, Varna Dharma precludes the idea of a common life to be lived by humanity at large. To limit the ideal is to mutilate it.

The Sadharana Dharma, again, cannot be understood as being social in nature, simply because the duties are supposed to be universally applicable. It only means that these duties should be observed by all, irrespective of caste. They have no reference to man's relation, in a positive sense, to his neighbour, and so do not point to any ends realisable by him as the member of the human society.

We come to the crux of the problem when we try to understand the significance of Ashrama Dharma. The life of man is divided into four stages, that of the Brahmacharin, the Grihastha, the Vanaprastha and the Parivrajaka. Detailed regulations are laid down which determine and rule the kind of life to be lived in these four periods. The one peculiarity of this scheme which, in our opinion, vitiates the whole ordering of life as such, is that these four stages are not natural divisions of life, in the sense that each one stage prepares for and imperceptibly leads into the next. In fact we can see the hiatus separating one stage from the other. The discipline of the

Brahmacharya stage does not point to its own fulfilment in the stage that follows. In the Vanaprastha stage no part of the experience that the man acquires during the household stage has any significance. The homeless life can have no affinity with the home life. And it is only in the homeless condition that the limiting factors like caste etc. could be got over. And in this, as we had remarked elsewhere, the practice of Buddhism is also that of Hinduism (of course using the two terms in a very vague sense as exclusive of each other, for as we pointed out it is very difficult to prove that there were two different religions as such). Buddha says (*Cullavagga* of the *Vinaya-Pitaka*, IX, 1, 4 quoted by R. Fick) : "just as the great rivers, such as the Ganga, the Zamuna, the Aciravati, the Sarabhu and the Nahi, when they pour their waters into the great ocean, lose their names and origins and become the great ocean, precisely so, O monks do these four castes, the Kshatriya, the Brahmana, the Vaisya and the Sudra, when they pass according to the doctrines and prescriptions of those who have attained perfection, from home to homelessness lose their names and origins and take from here onward the name Samana attaching to the son of Sakya." Worldly ties are bonds (bandha) that condemn man to Going and Coming. We are, indeed, aware that most often the Grihastha life is spoken of as the most important. This should not mislead us to conclude that a life of domesticity is looked upon as valuable in itself ; or that man's End can be realisable in and through it. The importance attached to the household stage can be simply explained by a reference to other ideas that are inseparably associated with the Hindu mind. The most significant of these as we have seen is that which demands male offspring, a "Putra" to continue the domestic religion and offer libations to Gods, Rishis and Pitris. Once the continuity of the household worship is insured, then the Grihastha is enjoined to renounce the world and live as a hermit in the forest.[1] And this view of life is that which we meet with "not as an exception, not as a chance occurrence, of which we can speak as we do of an unusual, extraordinary thing. No, the practice seems to be as common with the king, with the householder, as it is with the pious Brahmana."[2] And the universality which attached to the phenomena of homeless asceticism is the fundamental characteristic of the culture of India. "Not only did the world-sick old people renounce the world but even kings who were in undisputed possession of sovereignty and in the fulness of their power; young princes preferred the severe life of the ascetic to the glitter of sovereign power; rich tradesmen gave away their riches and heads of families their wives and children in order to build a hut in the forests of the Himalaya and to live on roots and fruits or to eke out an existence by begging alms. The thought of the transitoriness of earthly goods, of the unworthiness of human existence, supplies generally the impulse to renounce the world."[3] This view, therefore, in our opinion is emphatically anti-social. In it we can never have an idea of positive social service. Such service is possible only when the reality of the social order and of its members is recognised; when there is also an adequate idea of human values. What is transitory, worthless and untrue can never inspire us to social action, if we also assume that its nature is eternally thus. The idea of fixity of society precludes any such inducement to work for its betterment. And if we take into account the doctrine of self-realisation that dominates Indian thought, we will note that the world of our relationships is a mere appearance, for where there is no duality, there is no "other" to think of. There are

[1] Refer *Apastamba*, II, 21, 1; *Manu*, VI, 37.

[2] Fick: *"Social Organisation in North-East India"*, p. 60.

[3] *Ibid.*, pp. 67-68.

no fellow-creatures, no humanity apart from the self. Social service, indeed, becomes a mockery, for there are no social Reality and social values. Man's true end is to realise his own self. Emancipation or Moksha is the attainment of his own salvation. This Doctrine of Liberation is essentially selfish, each to shift for himself. He need not think of others and work for them, for there are no "others" at all.

Thus we are driven to the conclusion that the whole of Dharma in its Varna, Asrama and Sadharana aspects, etc., is individualistic in its nature. But this, let it be noted, only in its empirical manifestation, as relating to the realm of works and moral conduct. Even here, however, it is individualistic in a peculiar sense; only so far as the Sadharana-marga is concerned. The individual himself, as we have seen, has no choice. In Varna, and to a less extent in Asrama aspects of the ordering of life, his place and duty are determined for him, and this factor which determines is Authority.

And if we try to grasp the significance of the value and destiny of the human soul, we will realise that Dharma, in its non-empirical aspect is essentially related to Dharma in its empirical manifestation. There is no individual and so no individuality to be merged in a Transcendental Absolute. The End is not the complete realisation of One's Personality in the communion with God. There is the hiatus between Karma and Jnana which can never be overcome. Karma which refers to the common life can never help the individual to the knowledge which takes him to the transcendental goal. There is no possible link between the realms of Action and Being, and so Ethics does not aim at the perfection of the Here and Now. There is no hope that this world can be turned to account, so long as its reality is not recognised. The function of the ethical scheme of Dharma is purely negative; it only prepares the individual through the discipline of *chitta-suddhi* to pass over to the stage where ethics has no further place. The Transcendental Good or Moksha is a negation of all experience and life ; it is the transcendence of empirical relationships, not their fulfilment in perfection and virtue. No merit or demerit acquired through the observance of Dharma can be carried over into the ultimate stage. Thus the Here and Now has no organic relation to the Hereafter. The life, Here and Now, has no meaning in reference to the Hereafter. All Dharma that relates to the Here and Now is only negative as it prepares only the psychological attitude for the ultimate where Dharma is itself transcended. There is no idea of a progressive fulfilment of the Spirit, through Love and Service, so that Life will be the consummation of the devout prayer "Thy kingdom come". Service of Man is not conceived of as at least a partial expression of the service or worship of God. This world through the realisation of moral ideals will not become the Kingdom of Righteousness and Love ; the perfection of our ideals of the Just, the Noble, and the Beautiful. Dharma, in other words, does not aim at a Divine Harmony which shall rule Life in all its parts. It is negative, inasmuch as it points to a discipline which seeks a way of escape from life altogether ; it is negative because in the ultimate it is not a fulfilment but a negation of itself.

In the last analysis we are forced to hold that the two aspects of Dharma, the Absolute and the Empirical cannot be divorced from each other though a hiatus is assumed between them. The idea that would give us the clue to link these two aspects is the motive to religious life. In the metaphysical aspect Dharma referred to the principle underlying the universe taken as a whole. "Dharma", says R. Tagore,[1] "Is the innermost nature,

[1] *Sadhana*, p. 74 (Indian Edition). It is in this sense that Montesquieu uses the term "Law". He says "Laws in their most

the essence, the implicit truth, of all things. Dharma is the ultimate purpose that is working in our self''. But we do not know how far Tagore is right here in interpreting for us the thought of our ancients. We would certainly agree with him when he says that ''the true striving, in the quest of truth, of Dharma consists not in the neglect of action but in the effort to attune it closer and closer to the eternal harmony.''[1] The ideal of Dharma, if it is to be of living interest to us, must be revisualised so that it shall serve for the formulation of true spiritual life ; then only can we identify it with the Goal of our Eternal Quest. But so long as we assume a hiatus between our End and our Life, so long as Dharma in its Empirical aspect would refer as it did to our fathers to the Marga or discipline necessary to prepare us for the Transcendental Goal, this Ultimate End is not a fulfilment of our life, but its transcendence. But of this End itself nothing positive can be known, because thought cannot reach it, we might almost say, is incapable of reaching it. No predication is possible. Ethical discipline has its significance, therefore, only so far as it prepares man for self-purification and philosophical detachment. The great service that Ethics should render is obligingly to decree its own disappearance in the end. And this peculiar view is due to the insistence of the doctrine of Karma which refuses to take any notice of vicarious punishment or suffering and insists that no other can help any one in the realisation of the spiritual life. But in both aspects of Dharma the individual has no real significance. The individual must have an individuality even if in the end he is to transcend it. The absolute conception of Dharma does not give us any war-

---

general signification, are the necessary relations arising from the nature of things''—*Spint of the Laws*: Bk. I.

[1] *Sadhana*, p. 128 (Indian Edition).

rant to hold that it is constituted of a Unity amid diversity. It is a bare identity in which individuality finds no place.

And even in the Empirical sphere, which at first sight appears to favour Self-autonomy, we indeed recognise that this Self-autonomy does not refer to the positive freedom of the individual, so that he has the choice and the will to live according to his ideals. Freedom, if it should have any social and moral bearing must involve the idea that the individual should have the permission and capacity, not only to work out his own selfish salvation, but the salvation of others as well by sharing their burden and experience. In other words, freedom can only be itself if it finds self-expression in positive social service. But these notions, as we have seen, are completely out of place so far as India is concerned. The individual who is supposed to be autonomous in a spiritual sense, is nevertheless to be led by an authority which is outside of himself. His place or station in life is definitely fixed for him by society. If he tries to abandon duties incumbent on him as a member of the particular Varna etc. into which he happens to be placed, then society in its coercive aspect, brings him round to a proper sense of his Dharma. Dharma, in other words, in the last analysis, is Swadharma.

And society, in its coercive aspect, is the State as represented by the king. The End of the state is to maintain Dharma,—the Absolute and the Empirical. As we have already said, the two senses of Dharma are closely connected. K. V. R. Aiyangar points out that "to make law in its wider sense, all its legislative authority had to be guided and controlled by the existence of law as an ideal."[1] And, as we have seen, in its empirical aspect the law as the ideal has reference to the preparedness of man for the final or non-empirical aspect which is the state of

[1] *Ancient Indian Polity*, p. 64.

emancipation or Moksha. Dharma is the means to the realisation of salvation, and as the ideal it is the supreme principle underlying the Universe. It is the operative criticism of all the institutions that form the Indian Polity. It is the sanction for and justification of the State. "The State upholds it for its nature which helps the State to realise some truth or part of it within its jurisdiction."[1] And there is a reciprocal relation that subsists between the State and Dharma. On the one hand, it is stated that it is Dharma that preserves the kingdom, while on the other hand the main justification and function of the king is the protection of Dharma. The institutions of the social order are the embodiments of Dharma, and the State being a centre of society is to preserve and advance the normative principles underlying the body-politic. The End of the State is to maintain and advance Dharma.

But this End of the State is, however, not a positive and active embodiment of a creative quest. It is merely negative. That is why its function is primarily what Green and Bosanquet speak of as the "hindrance of hindrances". It is to see that the individual is not molested in the observance of his Dharma. The State seeks to protect him in the performance of his duties. Or, as Dr. Bhandarkar puts it,[2] "the least that the king was expected to do" was "to grant Yoga Kshema". To express the idea in modern language, the State was to ensure security against external foes and internal dissensions. We shall see later how the State set to detect, pursue, and destroy all those who were a danger to its internal and external security. From this point of view the State does not rise much higher than the police conception. We do not suggest that this was the only End the Ancient Indian State subserved.

---

[1] J. N. C. Ganguly: *Art. in Indian Historical Quarterly*, Vol. II, p. 575, 1926.

[2] *Some Aspects of Ancient Hindu Polity*, p. 181.

It did much to promote culture. But we do maintain that whenever the Indian theorists themselves have sought to formulate grounds for political obligation they have always based the claims of the State to the allegiance of the people on the protection offered to them. This protection, moreover, has an end in view. It is not the mere security which is obtained by the maintenance of law and order. If it were so, we would be justified in characterising the Indian state as a Legal or "Police-State".[1] The protection has this end in view, that it seeks to further and promote Dharma. The Sentient Order, we have seen, is supposed to be the embodiment of Dharma. In other words, Dharma, or the eternal principle underlying the Universe, in its empirical manifestation, is the social order or structure that we have, known as the Varnashram. And these two concepts are "so closely related to each other that we cannot conceive of the one without the other".[2] And when we say that the End of the State is to maintain Dharma, we mean that the two aspects of Dharma, as the Norm and the social fact, would be mere empty concepts, so long as the Danda of the king does not help them to manifest themselves in this world of senses."[3]

But as we have said the End of the Indian State is negative. The State sought to remove obstacles in the way of Dharma. And the method it used in the prevention of wrong, and the enforcement of Dharma was Force, as represented by *Danda* or the "Rod of Chastisement." When we come to consider the grounds for political obligations, in a future chapter, we shall note that though the method used by the State was force, its basis, how-

---

[1] cf. P. Banerjea: *Public Adm. in Anc. Ind.*, pp. 39-40.

[2] Ajit Kumar Sen: *Studies in Hindu Political Thought*, p. 115.

[3] *Ibid.*, p. 115.

ever, was not force. Here we shall observe that the End of the State, that of affording protection by the removal of hindrances, need not necessarily be exclusively negative. "It is not possible to distinguish," as James Seth truly observes, "the removal of obstacles from the provision of opportunities, and the State may encourage as well as compel."[1] And the State could enable its members to live "a life perfect and complete in itself," as Aristotle visualised the End of the State, by providing opportunities, and, above all, by fostering the proper "ethos". This positive object would be achieved when the State tries to reflect in every aspect of institutional life, the spirit of the End which it seeks to serve. If, for instance, the End of the State is conceived to be "good life", as both Aristotle and Plato insist, and as also many modern political philosophers insist, it is possible, through a proper system of education, in the large sense that the Greeks used the term, to enable the citizens to attain to such a life. We are aware that we are here attributing to the State a moral influence which some of our modern thinkers are chary of admitting. In our opinion, we cannot relegate the State to a corner by looking upon it as merely one association among others. We shall return later to the consideration of the interesting problem raised here. At any rate, we are in a position definitely to assert that to the Indian, the State, as represented by the monarch was really a great influence. As we shall see presently, the king is looked upon as the maker of his age. This has important bearings on the concept of Dharma.

All this, however, is not due to any direct and positive contribution which the State makes towards the life of its citizens. The State, in Indian thought, is not the symbol of the idea of a co-operative endeavour, and its End is not the "Best Life" as we would understand it.

---

[1] *Essays in Ethics and Religion*, p. 172.

This is inevitable when certain fundamental ideas are assumed as they are in Indian Thought. The "Best Life" as the Supreme Good or End cannot be lived so long as there is no conception of human values, the intrinsic worth of personality, and above all, so long as the empirical life itself is brushed aside as an obstacle and a burden. As we have elsewhere said, in a view of life which insists that Existence is mere "Appearance", or "lapse" from an ideally perfect state, and so all endeavour should be directed towards recognising our mistaken interest in this world of relationships, and we should seek the way of escape from life altogether, in such a view the values themselves, if at all there is any idea of them are "appearance". Such an attitude can never lead to a life of service and co-operative endeavour. Service and co-operation are impossible when the reality of the Social Order and Human Relationships is itself not recognised. There can be no zest in living. The blighting thought recurs ever and again that this world is an inn. "Our union here with wives and kinsmen and well-wishers is like that of travellers at an inn in the road" ;[1] "a thousand sorts of relationships" are made, such as mother, father, son, wife, brother and friend, but the chilling doubt gnaws at our mind : "In truth, however, whose are they and whose are we?"[2] for, all the while the world is sinking in the deep ocean of Time and "Life and its surroundings are always revolving like a wheel and the companionship of those who are dear is only for the time being."[3] Consolation can only be gained by the realisation of the transitoriness of existence and the true nature of ourselves. Verily the Self is all this that, through ignorance, we have tried to differentiate as

---

[1] *Santi Parva*, Chapter XXVIII (Dutt's Edn.). cf. Omar Khayyam *Rubiyat*.
[2] *Ibid.*, Chapter XXVIII (Dutt's Edn.).
[3] *Ibid.*, Chapter XXVIII (Dutt's Edn.).

husband, wife, sons, creatures, etc. "When the Self has been seen, heard, perceived, and known, then all this is known."[1] But really, there is no knower and the object to be perceived. All our empirical predications are true only "when there is, as it were, duality." The Self, therefore, is not to be comprehended by the affirmative process of taking in every manifestation around us as revealing something of Reality. If it were so, we could at least look upon the world and Life as existing in God. The Universe is not beside or apart from God, but immanent in Him, partaking something of His Reality. Therefore, we would not turn away with a sigh of despair that life is transitory, unsubstantial and evil. If we find defects, they are remediable defects. In truth, we are eternally progressing towards perfection. "An imperfection which is not all imperfection, but which has perfection for its ideal," as Tagore profoundly observes, "must go through a perpetual realisation."[2] And so the direction of Humanity is towards the "Good". Life, therefore, is not evil. "Existence itself is here to prove that it cannot be an evil."[3] In our opinion, there is no absolute evil. If evil is absolute, indeed, it could not harm us at all. Evil is that which falls short of our ideal of Good. What is imperfect and finite in our nature and life, is what we look upon as evil. But imperfection is not the negation of perfection, but only a partial or incomplete embodiment of the Perfect. The finite is not the denial of the Infinite, but only its limitation. There is no hiatus, and the dividing line cannot be drawn, for no line can be distinguished. The Finite and the Imperfect imperceptibly grow and shade into the Infinite and the Perfect. And thus is the eternal life-process.

---

[1] *Brihad Upa.*, IV, 5, 6.
[2] *Sadhana*, p. 53 (Ind. Edn.).
[3] *Ibid.*, p. 53 (Ind. Edn.).

But this view that we are advocating implies the belief in the perfectability of this life, here and now, by seeking to concentrate God in our midst, in all our actions. Our home could be made His home, and our work could be transformed into His work. Our End is not a transcendental End, which can only be reached by abstraction from this our life of relationships into a dreamy universe of imagination, which is supposed to be behind and beyond all this "Appearance". "No, in the very heart of our activities, we are seeking for our End." "We are crying for the across even where we stand."[1] This shore and the other shore to which we wish to be carried across, are one and the same in God. "Here rolls the sea and even here lies the other shore waiting to be reached."[2]

This is not the traditional Indian view, though Tagore, in his book, tries to make it such. The quest after reality takes man away from life, it is held that through the transient the Immortal Seat cannot be gained. The Reality cannot even be comprehended. It can be described only by *Neti, Neti*. This is not childish petulance, as Tagore imagines ;[3] it is the reasoned conclusion of a subtle philosopher like Yajnavalkya, and many others besides. It is the metaphysical formulation of Reality as conceived apart from this our life and world. And the End therefore of all human effort is to realise the only reality in the Self, which is gained by turning the gaze inward. To look forward, or outward, is to "fall into the snare of widespread death".[4] *The doctrine of salvation is the emancipating knowledge of the Atman.*

But this Self is non-social. It is a monadic Being, a *thing-in-itself*. It exists in itself and by itself, and is un-

[1] *Sadhana*, p. 162 (Ind. Edn.).

[2] *Ibid.*, p. 164 (Ind. Edn.).

[3] "Like a child dissatisfied with its dolls, our heart cries, not this, not this"—*Ibid.*, p. 162.

[4] *Katha Upa.*, II, 4, 2.

attached and unaffected, like the drop of water on the lotus leaf. The doctrine of Self-realisation is not what it meant to T. H. Green for instance, the perfection of true individuality which is essentially social in its nature.[1] It cannot be "nourished and evoked by the varied play of relations and obligations in society, but lies in a sort of inner Self, to be cherished by enclosing it, as it were, in an impervious globe.[2] The Self is to be attained by with-

---

[1] Bosanquet's criticism of Mill. *Phil. Theory of the State*, p. 60 ff. The criticism is true not only of the empirical, but also of the Transcendental Self, as conceived by Hindu thinkers.

[2] For, to T. H. Green the Self is "not an abstract or empty Self. It is a self already affected in the most primitive forms of human life by manifold interests, among which are interests in other persons. These are not merely interests dependent on other persons for the means to their gratification, but interests in the good of those other persons, interests which cannot be satisfied without the consciousness that those other persons are satisfied. The man cannot contemplate himself in a better state, or on the way to the best, without contemplating others, not merely as a means to that better state, but as sharing it with him."

(*Prolegomena to Ethics*), pp. 236-237.

And Bradley truly observes that: "The 'individual' man, the man into whose essence his community with others does not enter, who does not include relation to others in his very being", is a fiction (p. 168). And he further says: "I am myself by sharing with others, by including in my essence relations to them, the relations of the social state. If I wish to realise my true being, I must therefore realise something beyond my being as a mere this or that; for my true being has in it a life which is not the life of any mere particular, and so must be called universal life", p. 173.

"In short, man is a social being; he is real only because he is social and can realise himself only because it is as social that he realises himself. The mere individual is a delusion of theory; and the attempt to realise it in practice is the starvation and mutilation of human nature, with total sterility or the production of monstrosities." (Ethical Studies.)

"Indeed it is probable that we become aware of ourselves only as we become aware of others. It is at least questionable whether there could be a self, that is a self-conscious self, except in a

drawing from outward senses and relationships, just as the tortoise draws in its limbs.

And the whole scheme of Dharma, as we have seen, lays its emphasis on Self-autonomy. In the duties to be

---

society. What we begin with must be a whole within which self and world, myself and otherself, become gradually discriminated. And as we develop, there is still a sense in which we are the whole within which we make the distinctions of subjects and objects of myself and otherself." H. J. Paton: *The Good Will*, p. 303.

Harold Laski, however, posits that the ultimate fact of human experience is that "each of us is ultimately different from our fellows". According to him the individual is real to himself "not by reason of the contacts he shares with others" but on account of the "one unique thing that separates him from the rest of society". "His true self is the self that is isolated from his fellows and contributes the fruit of isolated meditation to the common good which, collectively, they seek to bring into being". Laski does not, however, tell us how in isolation the "common good" can be brought into being. "Man is a one among many, obstinately refusing reduction to unity. His separateness, his isolation are indefeasible; indeed, they are so ultimate that they are the basis out of which his civic obligations are builded. He cannot abandon the consequences of his isolation which are, broadly speaking, that his experience is private and the will built out of that experience personal to himself. If he surrenders it to others, he surrenders his personality". (*Liberty in the Modern State*, pp. 20-31.) The view thus expressed by Laski contains a profound truth, for as Sir Henry Jones has truly said, "Privacy and exclusiveness are evident characteristics of personality". (*The Principles of Citizenship*, p. 58.) And as a person has an excluding personality 'Whatever forces, whether of the physical or of the human world, play around it and beat upon it, like the waves of the ocean on a rock-bound coast, the "self" is still a sacred realm whose very existence depends upon its security against intrusion.' (Pringle-Pattison, *Hegelianism and Personality*, pp. 216-18). But we may yet say that if a person "excludes", he cannot "isolate". If the self is "the most exclusive and impervious of all that we know", it is also "potentially the most comprehensive". It is always the centre, the owner, the user of a world; and he is the most fully and truly a person whose world is widest and richest". (Sir Henry Jones: *The Principles of Citizenship*,

performed and the virtues to be practised, there are no positive elements. There is no idea of co-operation, of the sharing of experience, so that life itself could become

---

p. 61.) Man, in other words, is measured by his world. His self is the centre, the focus, the life of a wider world. "The Self", as Bosanquet tells us, "is what it includes". (*The Principle of Individuality and Value*, p. 325.) We shall have to maintain, therefore, that "exclusion" or "privacy" is "a miserable half-truth". (Sir Henry Jones: *The Principles of Citizenship*, p. 65.) Everything depends on our view of personality, and we shall realise that the freedom of isolation is impotence and slavery. It is the suppression of personality. For, when we attempt to investigate the personality of the individual citizen, we find that its ingredient elements are due to the State and to its manifold institutions. Every shred and element of his personality are "derived from the State, in which he has been nurtured;" "he grows with his world, his mind fills and orders itself; and when he can separate himself from that world, and know himself apart from it, then by that time his self, the object of his self-consciousness, is penetrated, infected, characterised by the existence of others. Its content implies in every fibre relations of community. He learns, or already perhaps has learnt, to speak, and here he appropriates the common heritage of his race, the tongue that he makes his own is his country's language, it is (or it should be) the same that others speak, and it carries into his mind the ideas and sentiments of the race (over this I need not stay), and stamps them indelibly. He grows up in an atmosphere of example and general custom, his life widens out from little world to other and higher worlds, and he apprehends through successive stations the whole in which he lives, and in which he has lived. Is he now to try and develop his 'individuality', his self which is not the same as other selves? Where is it? What is it? Where can he find it? The soul within him is saturated, is filled, is qualified by, it has assimilated, has got its substance, has built itself up from, it *is* one and the same life with the universal life, and if he turns against this he turns against himself; if he thrust it from him, he tears his own vitals; if he attacks it, he sets his weapon against his own heart. He has found his life in the life of the whole, he lives that in himself, 'he is a pulse-beat of the whole system, and himself the whole system.' " Bradley: *Ethical Studies*, p. 172. See also Sir Henry Jones: *The Working Faith of the Social Reformer*, p. 48 ff.

a Corporate Quest. In the whole discipline which seeks to attain *Chitta-Suddhi* or "self-purification", what is aimed at is psychological aloofness. And so the ideal of Dharma is non-social, and hence, non-ethical. The absolute concept of Dharma is beyond right and wrong, good and evil. The empirical concept of Dharma is thoroughly saturated with the idea of self-sufficiency and so of self-autonomy. Though the ideal is the transcendence of individuality in the ultimate, or absolute state, some sort of individuality seems to be provisionally conceded in the empirical state; but an individuality which is thoroughly non-social, non-ethical and so non-moral. We have raised the question, elsewhere, of how it is impossible to conceive the merging of individuality into the state of Moksha or Nirvana, without first positing an individuality to be so absorbed. We do not exaggerate in the least if we say that the Indian ideal is the negation of individuality, and so of the intrinsic worth of Personality and Human Values. So, it is in a limited sense, as applying to sentient facts, that we say that the Indian conception of Dharma, and so of Life, is individualistic. Moreover, whenever we talk of Dharma what is really meant is "Swadharma". This view is bound to last so long as the Doctrine of Karma has its hold upon the consciousness of the people. And this doctrine of Karma (allied with that of Samsara) is closely connected with another idea which has no less influenced the life of our country, and which means again the denial of true individuality. And this is the presumption that the Social Order itself is unalterable. The individual who is supposed to be autonomous and "self-regarding", a being-in-himself, whose acts affect nobody but himself, and who cannot share in the experience of others, has nevertheless to conform to the duties of his station in life. The Indian society has always been "governed by strict traditional morality or caste-rules." The dire consequences of the infringement of these regulations would be the opening of the flood-gates of social chaos. The State has therefore to keep a constant vigil to see that nobody would be either lax or negligent of his Dharma.

But this concept of Dharma, individualistic in nature, and because of that, has a plural application. What is dharma to a particular Order or caste is not dharma to another. The State is to keep the various Orders, castes etc. in the performance of their particular dharma. The principle underlying the doctrine of Swadharma is that "man secures happiness in both the worlds by doing his own duty." If on the other hand, he were to give up his own duty and take up another's, his whole work is turned into adharma. We are not informed why a man cannot take to other forms of conduct except those prescribed, except if we should infer that one's duties are fixed for him by his birth and Karma. And it is dogmatically stated that "There is more happiness in doing one's own Law without excellence than in doing another's Law well. It is happier to die in one's own Law; another's Law brings dread."[1] The same idea is also expressed by Lord Krishna: "One's duty, though defective, is better than another's duty well performed."[2] It is therefore impossible to speak of Dharma as a universal ideal which seeks to embrace the whole of Hindu society, much less of mankind in general. We cannot share the view expressed by S. K. Maitra that the "special feature of the Hindu treatment is the recognition of a list of common or trans-communal duties" and that in them "we have therefore the foundation of a universal ethics of humanity."[3] Hence we cannot hold that "the idea of a common human life," as he puts it, is involved in the whole scheme of dharma.

---

[1] *Kaush Upa.*, iii, 3, 1.

[2] *Bhagavad-gita*, Chapter XVIII (p. 127 Telang's). See also *Santi Parva.*

[3] *Ethics of the Hindus*, p. 24.

As we have already pointed out there were a set of duties which had to be observed, and which were of universal application in the sense that even a chandala is expected to follow them. From this, however, we cannot deduce that the participation of a common life is implied. The very nature of Sadharana dharma, or the duties, which were of universal application, is that it aims at self-sufficiency. The virtues to be developed are not properly speaking social virtues which could be practised and attained by man only as a member of the human group. S. K. Maitra, however, gives us a correct view in his concluding observations when he admits that Hindu morality primarily aimed at self-autonomy. Even the communal duties have in fact this end of self-autonomy in view : they are debts to the community by the discharge of which the individual gradually qualifies for freedom and self-sufficiency."

Thus we are forced to hold that the Indian scheme of life could never lead to the idea of a common life for mankind as a whole. "Caste", as Beni Prasad observes, "does not admit that every individual is in his nature universal."[1] The functional theory of Dharma "strikes at the root of individuality, and amounts to a denial of personality." Human values are completely lost sight of.

We shall not be wrong therefore in asserting that the vast majority of the population that composed the State could have absolutely no interest in the End of the State. It would be cynical to maintain that the State for them is to maintain their Dharma. For their Dharma is to serve the higher orders, and so the End of the State would be the perpetuation of their servility and degradation.

The one obvious lesson of history is that "Classes excluded from a share in power have always been classes excluded from a share in benefits."[2] The more

---

[1] *Theory of Govt. in Anc. Ind.*, p. 7.

[2] *Laski Grammar of Politics*, p. 27.
See also p. 35 where he says: "The State is not ourselves

you limit the number of those upon whom the Social Good is conferred the greater will be the number of persons whose personality is suppressed, and who would therefore never find satisfaction in the working of the institutions of the Polity. They would never feel an organic interest in the State unless they could identify themselves with what it does.[1] The State must seek to give expression to their wants and aspirations, it must embody their ideals.

It is amazing to find, however, amongst some of our modern scholars a tendency to apotheosise everything of the past to such a ridiculous extent that we are at a loss how to take the volumes of verbiage they have brought out in a really serious manner. "India's constructive principle of social organisation", writes Dr. Radhakamal Mukerjee, "has been the co-operation of individuals in the group, as well as of individuals with the larger society and polity in and through the group life under a scheme of communal and personal values. And the concept of Varnashrama-dharma, the code of communal duties, however corrupted by close interests in the course of ages, has in its central idea proposed the subordination of exclusive group-interests to the organisation of the Dharma, or the ideal of man's full comprehensive life, satisfying personal as well as social, material and spiritual wants on the basis of a social federation securing to each group and its members their rights as well as their duties in a universally recognised order."[2] Dr. Radhakumud Muker-

---

save where we identify ourselves with what it does. It becomes ourselves as it seeks to give expression to our wants and desires. It exerts power over us that it may establish uniformities of behaviour which make possible the enrichment of our personality. It is the body of men directed towards bad end."

[1] We shall note the philosophical implications of this idea further on.

[2] *Democracies of the East*, p. 100 ff. The reader will note one striking peculiarity of the book. Statements are made regarding ancient India without any attempt being made to substantiate

ee is equally vague in expression and representation, for e maintains of ancient India that "the division of castes vas not quite rigid and was no bar to the free mobility of abour, both vertical and horizontal. Social divisions and conomic occupations were very far from coinciding...... Thus the recognition of the dignity of all labour was a evelling influence promoting a social equality and brotherhood which subdued the pride of caste."[1] There are other writers, notable amongst whom are Benoy Kumar Sarkar and Jayaswal, who seem to fall in with similar views that they seem to have almost formed a school of hought in itself,—perhaps the "national" school of writers alluded to by Jadunath Sarkar. It is very necessary to dispel some of the false impressions given by these scholars, if we would understand the real significance of our ancient Polity, the End it sought to attain, and its nature judged from its fruits. We have chosen the statements of Dr. Radhakamal Mukerjee and Dr. Radhakumud Mukerjee because they are sufficiently representative of the rest.

Dr. Radhakamal Mukerjee, it seems to us, is trying to identify what he wished the Polity to have been with what it actually was. Another statement of his might be considered along with the general characterisation noted above. He remarks : "The Asrama-Dharma or the Code of Individual Duty in India, associated with Varna-Dharma or the Communal Code, represented an eternal

---

them. If the author had given any references to his authorities we could have judged how far his interpretations are valid. We are perhaps, simply to take the statements as they are.

[1] *Local Govt. in Anc. Ind.*, p. 64 ff. Dr. Radkumud Mukerjee, unlike his brother, gives copious references to his authorities in substantiation of his statements. Unfortunately all his references are one-sided and wherever he gives evidence of the opposite findings, he is not critical and exhaustive enough.

code of duty of a universal character and sought to hinder the crystallisation of group feeling. In the Indian scheme no one group would enfold the individual, because of his multiple nature. The individual would enter into various group relations and use these for an expanding scale of communal and spiritual life."[1] Sober history will shrink back from such unscientific generalisations. The writer has not thought fit to tell us what he means by "an eternal code of duty of a universal character", in what specially the universality lies, and above all, how the individual could enter into varied "group relations" to use them for an expanding scale of spiritual life. He seems not to have understood the significance of the doctrines of Swadharma and Karma. Moreover, he does not know that the "close interests" that have corrupted the conception of Varnasrama Dharma, are not of modern origin. However further back we may try to trace the history of our social relations, close or exclusive interests seem to have always been there. These interests have been largely influenced by caste, and before the rise of caste proper, by that of race. Hence duties, even as early as the Vedic times, were already conceived in the exclusive spirit. They were "regarded as being owed to one's own people".[2] No duties were recognised towards the Non-Aryan Dasyus who were a "wicked and godless people." And the contempt which has always dominated the attitude of the higher castes towards the "despised castes", the Sudras and the untouchables, and the gross inequalities of the Law, will give the direct lie to the characterisation of Indian society, either ancient or modern, as a "Social Federation securing to each group and its members their rights as well as their duties." The writer, evidently, does not realise that the elementary requisite

[1] *Democracies of the East*, p. 101.

[2] Principal McKenzie: *Hindu Ethics*, p. 9.

of a federation is the relative equality of the component elements. Moreover, it is adding insult to injury to say that the millions, who formed the Sudra and the depressed castes, possessed rights which they could enforce and enjoy in a "universally recognised order." The writer, however, truly enough deplores that "in India the castes and their codes have become rigid, and the elaborate differentiation and seggregation have encouraged disruptive tendencies",[1] but he is not faithful to history when he thinks that this is so only of modern times, and that in the past "in India nothing was more characteristic than the inter-locking and overlapping of groups, the elastic and flexible interaction between the groups which made it possible for individuals to change constantly their relations, their groups, without destroying social cohesion."[2] This statement is a half-truth. The doctrine of Apad-dharma, which is valid during times of distress, does provide for change of professions; but this is subject to another powerful idea, that of caste hierarchy. Members belonging to the higher castes could take temporarily to the callings of the lower castes, and this indulgence is not applicable vice versa. "The more Brahmanical culture spread in the course of centuries", writes the great scholar, Richard Fick,[3] "the more did the priestly classes succeed in stamping their desired psysiognomy upon the Indian society through their religious and social influence. The superiority of the Brahman caste which came gradually into recognition and, at first, surely not without opposition, influenced to a great extent the further development of the social condition; it was essentially the prime cause of the various groups of the Indian society which had been formed on the lines of professions or

[1] *Democracies of the East*, p. 103.

[2] *Ibid.*, p. 102.

[3] *The Social Organisation in North-East India in Buddha's Time*, p. 31.

races, modelling themselves upon the Brahmanical caste and so becoming what the theory had already made them." Thus by the time we come to Buddhist times the organisation of society had already become rigid. The Buddhist writers, "never cared in the least to contradict the caste-theory as such and thereby introduce a better organisation of society." So even as early as Buddha's time, the castes were "an important factor in the social life." We have already said elsewhere that Buddha cannot be looked upon as a social reformer.[2] We have the concurrence of the eminent scholar Richard Fick who also says that we cannot look upon Buddha "as the destroyer of rigid limits fixed by orthodox practice...... The castes continued after the spread of the Buddhist doctrine quite as well as before ; the social organisation in India was not in the least altered by Buddha's presence."[3] The differences between the ancient caste-system and the modern castes should be sought for in the growth of organisation. But the essential elements of caste, such as "the customs relating to connubium, interdining and contact of impure persons," have always been present, and it is they which

---

[1] "No one is allowed to marry out of his own caste", writes Megasthenes (M'Crindle: *Ancient India*, p. 41) "or to exercise any calling or art except his own: for instance, a soldier cannot become a husbandman, or an artizan a philosopher". According to Strabo (M'Crindle: *Ancient India*, p. 86) "An exception is made in favour of the philosopher, who for his virtue is allowed this privilege", i. e. the privilege of exchanging profession or trade, and of following "more than one business." Arrian's explanation is different. The general permission given to the philosophers, or the sophists, as he calls them has no reference to privileges, but eligibility into that order. For he says that "it is permitted that the sophist only be from any caste." (M'Crindle: *Ancient India*, p. 218.) In other respects Arrian's description confirms the descriptions of others.

[2] "The Buddha, we may assume in point of fact, was not a social reformer"— Keith: *Buddhist Philosophy*, pp. 120-122.

[3] *Social Organisation*, p. 32.

"set up absolute barriers". Moreover the "confinement of every class within a wholly fixed profession", (valid except in times of distress) really isolated the castes from one another. And precise rules "govern the mutual relationship of the castes in its minutest detail and try to prevent their fusion."[1]

Dr. Radhakumud Mukerjee, we have just noted, talks of social equality and brotherhood as subsisting in ancient India. To refute his general statement is not a difficult task, as he himself seems to be painfully aware of the imperfections in his statement. That is why he goes on to note "certain notable exceptions to this principle of equality of social status." The language in which the Chandalas are described justifies the remark that we have made elsewhere, that the members of the lower castes are grudgingly recognised as human beings at all. For they are called "the lowest race that go upon two feet—meanest men on earth." Dr. Radhakumud Mukerjee admits, moreover, from the evidence he has, that "there is a substantial agreement" between Pali works and the Brahmanical law-books, "in respect of the trades or professions implying an inferior social status" ; and "the crafts and castes, trades and professions, on which the Hindu law-books impose a social stigma, are practically identical with those mentioned in the Buddhist books." Evidently he made an absent-minded statement when he claimed that "the recognition of the dignity of all labour was a levelling influence promoting a social equality and brotherhood which subdued the pride of caste"

To talk of "Social Federation" and "Social Equality" in reference to the Indian Polity may imply ignorance of the significance of the terms used. The whole scheme of Dharma, as we have seen,

---

[1] *Social Organ.*, Fick, p. 38.

is based upon distinctions between man and man, and, group and group. The Social Order is to be composed of privileged castes on the one hand, and the servile castes on the other. And as we have observed, the general nature of the life prescribed by the rules of Law is individualistic.

The beliefs and the attitude towards life that influenced those times, in short the whole conception of Dharma, have a great influence on the Polity, and in fact, determine its nature as such. The Indian State could never be the embodiment of a common End and a corporate Quest. The people under its jurisdiction were subjects and not citizens of a Commonwealth. The majority of them could never identify themselves with the State and its activities. The State, in other words, did not aim at establishing "uniformities of behaviour which make possible the enrichment of personality."[1]

This was the inevitable result of the individualistic outlook on life. But this, in itself, however, may not have brought about the particular shape and temper that the Indian Polity assumed and acquired. Individualism may insist upon minimum governmental or social interference i. e. *Laissez Faire*; but individuals themselves, because they are essentially human, cannot but come together in varied relationships; and this contact could evolve, in course of time a common life to be lived through common institutions. Students of Hellenic institutions, and especially of Athens, know the strongly individualistic tone they had. This is most to be seen in their religious ideas. Religion in Greece, as also in Rome, was largely domestic.[2] Fustel de Coulanges has clearly shown the fundamental agreement in the ideas of the Greeks, the Romans and the Hindus. The same customs and beliefs,

---

[1] Laski: *Grammar of Politics*, pp. 35-36.

[2] See Fustel de Coulanges: *The Ancient City*; Basu: *Indo-Aryan Polity*, Introduction—*Camb. Hist. of Ind.*, Vol. I, pp. 229-235.

as well as even superstitions, that existed in Ancient India, we find also in Greece and Rome. And yet there is a universe of difference in the subsequent history of these peoples. The Greeks and Romans evolved political institutions that have served as models all through the centuries ; and they have given us glimpses into the possibilities of human beings as institution-builders. The Hindus, on the other hand, have mostly been under the monarchical form of government, though other forms might not have been unknown. And they have never attempted the building up of political communities. We have no thinkers like Plato or Aristotle, giving us the philosophy of the State. Our writers are not concerned with political philosophy as such ; they have left behind treatises on administration and state-craft. And this fundamental difference in the development of the two great branches of the Aryan stock, the Eastern and Western, is above all due to the attitude to life which influenced the two peoples. The Eastern Aryan did not set any value on life here on earth ; he was intent on escaping from life altogether. The Western Aryan, and especially the Greek, had a keen sense of the joy of living, and life on earth to him was something worth living for, and so something worth striving after.[1] Perhaps environment has to answer for the difference to a certain extent. Dr. Prapullachandra Basu has tried to explain why the Indo-Aryan and the Graeco-Romans who started with the same ideas about religion, came to have different outlooks in course of time. "The vision of the Indian was bounded by the immortal rather than the mortal, by the infinite rather than finite."[2] The Indian spirit delighted to find its wings and soar aloft into the ethereal sky, and scorned to remain in this little nest, the world, of which worldly-minded people alone, caught

[1] See Prof. J. B. Bury's *History of Greece*, pp. 6-7.
[2] *Camb. Hist. of India*, Vol. I, p. 649.

in the wide-spread snares of death, get enamoured. The Indian turned away from life, and would not think it worth while to turn to account what the world has to give us. The idea of the City of God never presents itself to the Indian mind.

The transformation of the Indian outlook on life was due to many causes.[1] The Aryans, when they first came to India were a vigorous, optimistic people; and their early hymns, through every line, breathe hope and trust. Instead of spurning away life, prayers are addressed to the Gods for long life and worldly prosperity, for victory and possession: "Sight and life and joy do thou give us; long may we see the sun as it rises." But this healthy spirit gradually gave way until a radical change was effected. And "the inborn feelings of the Aryans" were destroyed "to make room for an altogether different conception of life and human destiny."[2] Whatever might have brought about this revolution, we are not wrong in asserting that the *Other worldly* spirit is never healthy if it abstracts man from life, here and now. And unless we have an adequate idea of human values and social values, we can never have real zest in life. So long as the thought persists that salvation can only be attained by following the path of no-return, so long as the world is looked upon as a penal colony, and existence a curse, so long man would not enter into the spirit of the Life, Here and Now. And therefore to interest oneself in any sphere of worldly activity would only mean the perpetuation of bondage. Political life and even ethical life cannot attract the mind of man who desires to transcend both. The individual would gain nothing by such distractions as

[1] The reader may consult writers like Oldenberg, Keith and Poussin who try to account for the change in the Indian outlook. Above all, Griswold's Art. on Indian Pessimism in *Ency. of Rel. and Eth.* will be found highly useful.

[2] Poussin: *The Way to Nirvana*, p. 16.

social relationships would present to him. He would direct all his endeavour at realising his true self. Brahmanical civilisation thus resulted in enhancing the individualistic tendency that was already present in the religious conceptions of the Aryans. Whereas in Greece and Rome, by the development of political institutions, scope was found for the growth of a corporate spirit and common life, in India the emphasis on spiritual life, determined as it is by the doctrines of Swadharma and Karma, precluded any such development of corporate life and spirit, and the whole life soon came to be dominated by Brahmanical culture and ideas. This is to be noted especially with regard to "Dharma" that we have been discussing all the while. And the Brahmanical ideas of a sacerdotal nature, that have had such a tremendous influence on the concept of Dharma, have increased instead of being diminished in influence, as Maine truly contends,[1] by the British dominion in India. Even after the terrific impact of the West on the East, which has thrown every idea of the Indian into the cauldron, to emerge therefrom in what particular form nobody is able to foretell, we have still the same influences persisting. Our modern thinkers only try to express them in the terminology of the West; but the ideas are still there. Indeed, they seem to be acquiring a new impetus and a new lease of life. Hence it is that we think no emphasis can be too strong in the note of warning that we would strike. If our country would live the best and complete life, rich and perfect in its content, these dangerous ideas must be discarded altogether. They are antisocial, and can never foster a corporate spirit.[2]

They did not, and could not have fostered a corpo-

[1] *Village Communities*, p. 20.

[2] "Men being made to preserve, to nourish, to clothe themselves, and do all the actions of society, religion ought not to give them too contemplative a life"—Montesquieu, Bk. XXIV, Ch. 11.

rate spirit in the past. Dr. Ramesh Chandra Majumdar is of opinion that "The spirit of co-operation was a marked feature in almost all fields of activity in ancient India and was manifest in social and religious as well as in political and economic life."[1] Everything depends on the right interpretation of the term "corporate." The mere coming together of individuals for purposes, economic or political or religious or social, cannot be regarded as a true manifestation of the corporate spirit. It is a fact of common experience that hundreds of pilgrims flock to the numerous sacred shrines of India every day. Shall we be justified, because of that, to maintain that every such gathering in a temple is a Congregation and represents the idea of a Church or Samaj? We may be referred to Buddhist gatherings, but we believe that it would be a grievous misjudging of the true Buddhist spirit to characterise them as "corporate". The same may be said of other institutions besides the purely religious. Men are men and they cannot help coming together and the constant intercourse of persons following similar professions, or brought together for some other reason, necessarily would develop in course of time a system of regulations and conventions that would seek to guide and determine mutual relations. This should not tempt us to jump to the conclusion that every institution, like the guilds for instance, was the embodiment of a "Corporate" ideal. Nothing can be said to be truly corporate in spirit unless there is implied the idea of sharing the experiences of a common life, and the idea of each particular member as contributing to the realisation of a common ideal, which could be attainable only in and through a partnership of endeavour. In other words a "Corporate spirit" can only be present when the coming together of individuals means, not that they come as units (a, b, c, d, and so on) but that they are related

---

[1] *Corporate Life in Anc. Ind.*,—Introduction.

to each other in a vital harmony that makes them members of a spiritual organism. And our main contention has been that nowhere in Indian speculation do we get an organic conception of life, Life, Here and Now, comprehended by a scheme of spiritual values. And the attitude to life, or, in other words, the philosophy of life that we have, receives an added emphasis by the Doctrine of the Atman and the value of ethical discipline that are essentially individualistic in nature. From such a background of Philosophy and Religion, no universal creed in its true spirit can ever emerge. Any religion to be truly Universal must be grounded upon the two fundamental ideas of the Fatherhood of God and the Brotherhood of Man. And there can never be a brotherhood unless it be that of a fellowship united by the ideals of a Common Life. The members of the Fraternity shall feel that, as children of a Common Father, they are equal in His eyes. God has no partiality. Once the idea that all men are equal in the eyes of God is accepted, it would act like a leaven, and permeate every aspect of a man's life. Ardent souls would never accept the inequalities of life as absolute, and would understand them, as in their nature they certainly are, merely as accidental. The Loving Father sends His rain for the good and the wicked ; and He would not condemn some of His children to servitude, destitution, and misery, and bless others with power, opulence and happiness. The barriers that divide man and man, class and class, caste and caste etc. are man-made barriers. The immense inheritance of God is despoiled by the ungrateful children who are forgetful of their common extraction. The tragedy of it is that it has never been in history that the meek inherit the Earth.

But if Universal Brotherhood has not yet been realised in human life, it could at least serve as an ideal towards which ardent souls would work incessantly. They would refuse to acquiesce in the present order of things.

All the inequalities and unrighteousness that prevail are due to remediable causes, and if actualities fall short of our ideals, man should try to transcend the limitations and work for the establishment of the Kingdom of Righteousness. The City of God may exist only in idea, having nothing corresponding to it on earth anywhere. But as Plato has said, in heaven "there is laid up a pattern of it... which he who desires may behold, and beholding may set his own house in order."[1] The question, therefore, is not whether a perfect polity did exist in fact. What is really important is that man "will live after the manner of that city, having nothing to do with any other." The ideal pattern will be the Law of Life.

The ideal itself, however, can never be a living force so long life is not interpreted in terms of Value. The actualities of life have been treated, in Indian thought, as bonds or fetters that tie man down to a world of appearances. Moreover they are the result of causes, the operation of which is beyond the control of man in the present. The past determined the present, and the Law of Karma must have its way. We can never turn our present life to better account by merging ourselves in the interests of this world. It is after all an inn. The world is not what it appears. Only the Gods are truth ; mankind and worldly life are false.[2] Man should seek eternal life, emancipation from the round of existences. If he should at all immerse himself in action, it should only be such action as would either prepare him for philosophical detachment, or insure a happy paradise in a future world. The performance of sacrifices and the observance of ritual would procure for man a higher state elsewhere. Moreover he has a debt to discharge as the member of his family ; he has to con-

---

[1] *Republic*: Bk. IX (p. 306, Jowett).

[2] See *Narada*, p. 93-94; cf. Hopkins: *Ethics of India*, p. 54.

stantly keep vigil by the domestic hearth, and offer libations to Gods, Rishis and Pitris.

The whole of the life of man was to be devoted to the requirements of religion. And the religious ideal, as we have seen, draws man away from the world of social relationships. The Best Life is not the life to be lived and realised Here and Now. It is a life which is alien to all our experience and can be attained only by the abandonment of the most exquisite of our social ties. It is a state when man is no longer affected by what happens around him, when he is free from all "pairs of opposites". And so the "Best Life" as the "Good" can never have a social significance. It is an egoistic conception of "Social Good", there is no idea of the place of man in Society. The good man is not he who seeks to identify his views with the point of view of the whole of which he is a member. He cannot therefore endeavour to realise the "Social Good", or the coherence of the whole. Where the reality of life itself is not recognised there can be no recognition also of a "goodness", which is the Universal coherence, the expression of the harmony of the Great Society of which we are members. The "Good" has reference to the isolated individual, to be attained by psychological detachment. The End is self-sufficiency and the individual's emancipation from *Samsara*. The ideal is not to live this life, but to escape from it altogether.

The attitude of religion towards the world of social institutions is therefore one of ascetic aloofness. Life is an evil ; and the world a penal colony. The good man can save himself by flight ; he should not be a victim to the temptations of life. He cannot turn to good account what the world has to give ; and so he must turn away from the squalid and gross realities of existence.

The Good Man is the Good Saint or Ascetic. He is freed from the mistaken interest in physical life. He is concerned only with the spiritual life. He must not be disturbed by mundane considerations. Others should look after his needs. Pious people who were not fortunate in being born among the higher castes, could, however, earn religious merit by the service they would render to such "guests" ; and may be they could thus insure for themselves a better birth in a future life. The Good Man is primarily he who had a good birth ; for as we have seen, it is birth that determines the "dharma" of the man. The "Good" life has obligatory significance only to the "Good Man", i. e. one who was born as a member of the higher castes. As we have already seen, according to the *Satapatha Brahmana*, the Brahmana and the Kshatriya are good, whereas the Vaisya and the Sudra are bad. The lower castes in that case must be conceived to be worse. The Brahmanas and Kshatriyas "always go first in order to avoid a confusion between the good and the bad".[1] If unfortunately there were to be a confusion of duties, if there were to be "Varna-Samskaram", then "the eternal rites of castes and rites of families are subverted".[2] Social dissolution would be the inevitable result. "The world would come to an end", says Kautilya, "owing to a confusion of castes and duties. Hence the king shall never allow people to swerve from their duties.[3] The State is to maintain Dharma. The whole of the functional scheme of Dharma is, thus, with a view to the maintenance of the Social Order intact ; some subserving the religious ideals, some others in protecting them, and the rest ministering to the wants of physical life. The castes that served as "means" or "instruments" should never be confused with the castes that were "ends". The End of the State had vital reference and meaning to particular elements or castes only. As we

---

[1] *Satapatha Brahmana.*

[2] *Bhagavad-gita*, Ch. I.

[3] Bk. I, Ch. III.

justly remarked, it would be cynical to maintain that to the lower castes and classes, the State is to maintain their "Dharma", for that would be the perpetuation of their subjection. Some castes were to minister to the wants of "mere life" while the higher castes, freed from the anxieties of life, should seek the "Best Life", if such a use of the phrase, with the limitation we have already noted, be here permitted. And the "Best Life" presupposes the necessity of leisure. Those who are engaged in religious performances and those who afford them protection, should be freed from the anxieties of daily life. The lower castes should cater to their physical needs. When certain classes (or castes) are leisured classes, the rest are the toiling masses.

And just as in Rome and Greece, in ancient India, too, the Polity rested, to a large extent, on a slave-owning basis.[1] Slavery, as an institution, existed beyond doubt in ancient India.[2] Those who refuse to admit that slavery existed in ancient India, cite Megasthenes as authoritative, forgetting that his statement has reference to a particular locality and not to the whole of India. Strabo quotes the evidence of Onesikritos which proves that the statement of Megasthenes, if true, could apply, and was

[1] The term "slavery" sounds obnoxious, and the kind of slavery that existed in America during the seventeenth and eighteenth centuries never perhaps existed in ancient India. And some of the excesses of Rome during the days of her degeneracy also were absent. But the kind of slavery that existed at Athens did certainly also exist in India.

[2] Prof. Banerjea: *Public Administration in Ancient India*, (pp. 25-27) says: "slavery, such as existed in olden times in other parts of the world, was unknown in India," but he admits that "there existed in Ancient India a class of persons who were not completely free. This class was known as the Dasas."

J. Jolly however emphatically maintains that "Slavery was a reguar institution in India up to its abolition by the British Government in 1860—Introduction to *The Arthasastra of Kautilya*, p. 39.

peculiar to "that part of the country over which Musikanos ruled."[1] There is no necessity, moreover, to take the evidence of Megasthenes as true; his mendacity is well-known; even the Greek writers, themselves, have questioned his veracity. Dr. Winternitz says that though Megasthenes emphatically states that there was no slavery in India, "both the Arthasastra and the Dharmasastras know different kinds of male and female slaves."[2] Dr. P. Basu recognises the existence of slavery "within the pale of Aryan polity".[3] Richard Fick,[4] the eminent German scholar, discusses the status of the slave in ancient India, and maintains that so far as "conduct and legal position" are concerned, in the Indian slave we have the "same categories and similar relations" as those we find in the slaves of Greece and Rome.[5] The various law-givers, like Apastamba, Gautama, Narada, Manu, Yajnavalkya, Brihaspati, etc. recognise the institution of slavery as a component element of the polity, and lay down regulation accordingly. We have innumerable references to slavery in the *Jatakas*, in *Viramitrodaya*, and above all in *Kautilya*.

And apart from the positive evidence of the law-books themselves, we have a priori reasons for holding that the Indian Polity must have rested on a basis of slavery and serfdom. We should further remember that there was a numerous element in the polity which was more degraded

---

[1] The kingdom of Musikanos lay in Sindhu, along the banks of the Indus.—See M'Crindle: *Ancient India.*

[2] *Some Problems of Indian Literature*, p. 101. See also *General Index*, S. B. E. cf. Jolly: *Arthasastra of Kautilya*, p. 39.

[3] *Indo-Aryan-Polity*, p. 48.

[4] *Social Organisation in Ancient India*, pp. 312-313.

[5] We would refer the reader to a very able article in the *Calcutta Review* of Aug. 1930 by Mr. Narayanchandra Banerjee on *Slavery in Ancient India*. He also discusses the reasons that led to enslavement.

in status than the slave. There were the despised castes who were "untouchables", and were "impure." The slaves, properly so called, were infinitely better in their condition, than these outcastes, who were grudgingly recognised as human beings at all. The slaves "lived together with the families to which they belonged, they lacked the local isolation and external combination of the despised castes."[1] The slaves of India never formed a caste. As Mr. N. Banerjee observes :[2] "Slavery was not restricted to any particular class of people, nor were slaves recruited from the lower castes. We have evidence showing that Brahmins, Kshattriyas, or men of high birth often became slaves." The despised castes, however, were those of the lowest castes, and they followed the despised professions. Their calling carried "impurity" with it. And according to the functional scheme of Dharma the despised professions were to be followed by the despised castes, and the nobler professions by the higher castes. Those who belonged to the highest castes, indeed had no profession at all, whatever the theory might say. They were the leisured classes. They were the "Ends", and the lower castes served as their "means" or instruments. The Brahmans generally enjoyed large grants of lands from the monarch. It is considered to be a pious act, conducive of religious merit, to bestow gifts on Brahmans. The Kshatriyas, themselves, had only military duties to perform. "Others make their arms and others supply them with horses, and they have others to attend on them in the camp, who take care of their horses, clean their arms, drive their elephants, prepare their chariots, and act as their charioteers. As long as they are required to fight they fight and when peace returns they abandon themselves to enjoyment,—the pay which they receive

[1] Richard Fick: *Social Org.*, pp. 312-313.
[2] *Art. in Calcutta Review*, Aug., 1930.

from the state being so liberal that they can with ease maintain themselves and others besides."[1] Whatever the Brahmanical theory was in itself, the Brahmans, as we know them in the various *jatakas* and other Pali works, were rich agriculturists and merchants. We have Brahman "gentleman farmers."[2] There were also Brahmans who followed diverse professions. We have indirect evidence of this in the qualifications required of Brahmana eligible to officiate in the Shraddha ceremony. Gautama goes to the extent of sanctioning both agriculture and trade as lawful professions for a Brahmana "provided he does not do the work himself".[3] The Vaisyas could look after agriculture but we have strong reasons to maintain that they were more of the nature of proprietors than of labourers themselves. The actual task of cultivation, tending cattle etc., must have been carried on by the Sudras and the lower castes, and by slaves. The state of society presented to us in the works of the Buddhist period warrants the conclusion that the Brahmans, Kshatriyas and Vaisyas belonged to the higher and the middle classes. The outdoor and indoor work was done by male and female slaves, and by people belonging to the lower castes. And these lower castes were prohibited by sacred precepts, custom and law, from acquiring any property. Of course there were exceptions to the rule, but the law was always in favour of the higher castes. We shall be discussing the problem in a future chapter. A Sudra, for instance, we are told, "should never amass wealth, lest by his wealth, he makes the numbers of the three superior classes obedient to him."[4] The lower classes, the Chandalas, were treated with contempt by the authors of

---

[1] M'Crindle: *Ancient India*, p. 217.
[2] See *Cambridge History of India*, Vol. I, p. 246.
[3] *Gautama*, p. 225.
[4] *Santi Parva*, Sect. LX (Ray's: pp. 193-196).

the law-books who attempted to "confirm them in their low position by legal prescriptions."[1]

The Hindu Social System, based on the scheme of "Dharma" may be described, as Beni Prasad has truthfully done, "as consisting of the privileged Dvijas on the one hand and a servile proletariat on the other.[2] The Polity that subsisted in Ancient India was pervaded by a close oligarchic spirit, accentuated by the theocratic presumptions of the highest castes. These castes perpetuated their own domination by the institutions of property and social privilege. As Richard Fick has observed : "The more Brahmanical culture spread in the course of centuries, the more did the priestly classes succeed in stamping their desired physiognomy upon the Indian society through their religious and social influence."[3] And the Indian State, whatever some of our modern scholars might say, was never freed from theological and metaphysical influence. The Indian Polity was always a Socio-religious State. We shall discuss the problem later. We shall only state here that the conception of Dharma had a profound influence on the Polity, and determine its spirit and nature. The State exists to maintain Dharma.

And the End of the State, as visualised by Hindu thinkers, would be far from the idea of Dharma, or justice, if we would understand the terms in their ethical and moral implications. "Dharma", as the End of the

---

[1] Fick: *Social Org.*, p. 318.

[2] *Theory of Govt. in Anc. Ind.*, p. 26.

Dr. Sen Gupta makes a searching analysis of the society in Ancient India and finds that the men were divided into the respectable and the servile. "And from the respectable classes again were isolated two privileged classes who enjoyed a special measure of pre-eminence in Society"; the class devoted to religious pursuits, and the military class "Excluding these privileged classes the people were divided into born masters and those born to serve." *Sources of Law and Society in Ancient India*, pp. 15-16.

[3] *Social Org.*, p. 10.

State, could have significance to the privileged few. Somadeva Suri, in his *Nitivakyamrita*,[1] indeed defines Dharma as that which promotes the greatest good of society. But the "greatest good of society," according to Hindu thinkers is not what we, in modern times, mean by the term "Social Good". The greatest good of society was to keep it intact, by maintaining the various orders and castes in the performance of their "Swadharma" thus averting social dissolution. And so "the greatest good of society," could be the greatest good only to particular classes or castes in it which are "ends". The other classes or castes were mere "means"; to them, "the greatest good of society" was the perpetuation of their own degradation. They were excluded from power, privilege, and property. They were in no position to acquire and forge the sanctions that would help them to free themselves, and ultimately to assert their equality with the rest. It was this fear, that given the opportunities, the lower classes would not be slow in making their influence felt, that dictated the spirit of the whole of the social legislation of the day.

Our plea is that the "Social Good" must have a wider reference than what it has in Indian thought; and that it must be conceived in terms of a more inclusive whole. The State must be a spiritual harmony and the expression of a universal coherence. Its members must feel that they are members of a common society, co-operating in a common activity and sharing in a common good. The Indian State and society, with the distinctions of caste and divisions of classes, can never visualise the idea of a common social good, so long as the barriers are allowed to remain. The functional basis of Dharma is not conducive to social harmony. The harmony that Hindu writers have thought of is a society in which each Order or Caste

---

[1] Chapter I.

was to perform its respective duties, but these duties, as we have already pointed out, set the seal of inferiority and servitude on a large proportion of the population. This is the inevitable result of the Varnashramic ideal. We can never maintain, as some of our modern writers try to do, that the Indian Polity was founded upon the true principles, of "Division of Labour" and "Social Harmony".

And if we would raise the question that Plato sought to answer: "where does justice (or Dharma) reside in the State?", we would not be surprised if we arrive at a finding opposed to the Platonic idea.[1] In the first place the functional scheme of Dharma is not based upon true principles of "Division of Labour". Justice, in its functional aspect, meant for Plato that a man should do the work of the station of life to which he was called by his capacities, and that each class should work at its appointed function, the principle behind this idea being that function, either that of the individual or of the class, must have reference not to the particular interest of the individual or class, but to the social whole to which the individual or class belongs. It is very important to note that differences in function arise from natural differences, of human capacity. The social whole is, however, the harmony of the economic, military, and philosophic classes that are its component parts. The economic class is not a whole, and cannot be treated as such. The military class, again, is not a whole, and the philosophic class much less. The function of each of these classes has primary reference to the good of the whole body politic, and in the effort to

[1] We have found it necessary to discuss this problem because many of our writers try to build upon wrong analogies. The Indian theory, Dr. Sen Gupta recognises, goes "further than Plato in conceiving with Aristotle that there were some men who were born to serve and others who were born to be served," and also in the exclusive attention given to the hereditary principle. *Sources of Law and Society in Anc. Ind.*, p. 17.

seek and attain the good of the whole, the good of the particular also is achieved. Each class, however, has to perform its special function, but this special function points to an end which is larger than the interest of the class, and involves the idea of co-operation aiming at universal coherence. The Indian scheme of Dharma is based on altogether different principles. Function has no reference either to capacity or specialization. Plato felt, for example, that the art of government should be entrusted to the experts who were given the education and training necessary. We would not call in the services of a carpenter to attend on a sick man, but of a man well-versed in medicine. Talents differ, but as the poet Emerson has said, "all is well and wisely put" in the Ideal State. But in the Indian conception of Dharma, function is not determined by natural differences, by the differences in talent. The man's duties in the station of life to which he belongs are determined by the accidents of birth. Certain qualities are supposed to inhere in the Soul, persisting through innumerable transmigrations: some subtle matter, called Karma, pursuing the Soul which it defiles and these determine the nature of the birth. Function is not fixed by the aptitude and capacity of the individual, but by the caste in which he is born, the assumption being that the very birth in that particular caste is due to differences in the qualities of the Soul. As Lord Krishna, in the Gita says: "The fourfold division of castes was created by me according to the apportionment of qualities and duties." The three qualities are Satwam, Rajas and Tamas, and everything that lives:

> "...... hath its being bound
> With these Qualities by Nature framed."

And, therefore, the work of Brahmanas, Kshatriyas, Vaisyas and Sudras,

> "Is fixed by reason of the Qualities
> Planted in each."

The individual must, therefore, conform to the Dharma of his caste. If he is unfortunate in being born a Sudra whose duty is to minister to the needs of the higher castes, he has no right to complain. If he happens to be a Chandala, he has only to curse his own fate. On no account may the castes which are "means" be confused with those which are "Ends". The rights and duties of the various castes, in other words, are not based upon co-operation and so can never result in functional harmony. There can be no co-operation if the lower castes have no share in it. Rights and duties are co-relative terms, and there can be no rights and duties in the social whole, unless there is a mutual recognition aiming at coherence. It is the place of the individual or caste in the co-operative whole which gives rise to specific rights and duties. And function must be grounded upon faith in the equal dignity and moral value of all labour, so that it does not involve inequalities in status. In other words, there must be full recognition of the idea of the unity of purpose of the Great Fellowship which we serve. This is possible only when we recognise that we are children of a Common Father. Rights exercised by any particular caste or class which find their satisfaction in its particular desires and interests are a blasphemy and a crime against God and Mankind. Man, who is made in the image of his Father, shall never be degraded into a "means", and the "End" of one man or caste shall have similar significance to the rest. We all seek Him, though in different ways. And nobody has the right to enslave another. There can be no natural slave whatever Aristotle or Manu would say. Every man has potentialities which would qualify him to seek and live the Best Life. None can be excluded in the participation of the Great Quest.

A Function must, therefore, be "an activity which embodies and expresses the idea of social purpose. The essence of it is that the agent does not perform it merely for personal gain or to gratify himself, but recognises that he is responsible for its discharge to some higher authority."[1] Society is not the mere collection of points, "each concentrating material in itself". "Society means a real unity of purpose",[2] and the individual persons are not *selves in themselves*, but find their true personality in merging themselves in that of others. The social good is the embodiment of the Social Purpose. The Good Man is not he who, according to Hindu thought, seeks self-sufficiency and "self realisation". We have already urged that the ideal of "Self realisation" could be given a larger and wider significance than that of the realisation of the isolated self. It is the realisation of the rational Self which is essentially a social Self, and can never be isolated from its relations with others. The individual must, indeed, be a coherent individual; and if self-sufficiency refers to the harmony of the inner life we can have no objection. That is what Plato meant when he said that justice in the individual is the harmony of the three parts of his soul, the appetitive, the spirited and the rational. But justice, to Plato, meant Social Justice. "The conception postulates a view of the individual as not an isolated self, but part of an order, intended not to pursue the pleasure of isolated self, but to fill an appointed place in that order."[3] The individual or the particular caste is no longer good merely as a coherent individual or caste. True individuality lies in sharing the larger life, and aiming at a wider co-operation than that of the individual or of caste. "I regard a man as good", says Paton, "not because he co-operates with me or with you considered as isolated individuals but because he co-operates with a whole of which you and he and I are organic parts......and I am not good as co-

---

[1] Tawney: *The Acquisitive Society*, p. 9.
[2] Muirhead and Heatherington: *Social Purpose*, p. 98.
[3] Barker: *Greek Political Theory*, p. 177.

operating with you who are just different from myself but I am good as co-operating with *us*, that is with a whole of which I am only a part. I cease to be merely myself, and become as it were the expression of both the will and the judgment of the whole society. If I were a perfectly good man in a perfectly good society I and all other men should attain to that level in all our thoughts and actions."[1] And so the Social Good is that which arises in our relations to others, who are not considered merely as "others", but as the members of the same society who co-operate with us in a common activity, and share in the Common Good. As Laski profoundly observes, social good is the "ordering of our personality that we are driven to search for things it is worth while to obtain that, thereby, we may enrich the great fellowship we serve."[2]

Social Good, therefore, must be the embodiment of Social Purpose, and that purpose can be concretised in institutional terms by the conception of function which has reference to Social Justice which conceives of "men united to each other, and of all mankind as united to God, by mutual obligations, arising from their relations to a common end." Function, therefore, is primarily ethical and spiritual as it was to Plato. The Principle of the Division of Labour was not an economic problem to him, but a moral one aiming at the spiritual well-being of the whole community. The Indian conception of "Division of Labour" is more akin to Medieval Christian theory than to Plato's. "Society, like the Human Body", it was held, "is an organism composed of different members. Each member has its own function, prayer, or defence, or merchandise, or tilling the soil. Each must receive the means suited to its station and must claim no more. Within

[1] *The Good Will*, p. 308.
[2] *Grammar of Politics*, p. 25.

classes there must be equality. Between classes there must be inequality ; for otherwise a class cannot perform its function, or—a strange thought to us—enjoy its rights." Social well-being exists, it was thought, in so far as each class performs its functions and enjoys the rights proportioned thereto. "The Church is divided in these three parts, preachers and defenders, and...labourers[1] ...And this view, as much as Aristotle's and Manu's involves the ordering of Society, with some classes as "means" and the others as "ends", and goes to the very foundations of ethics. The modern attack on the ethical formulation of function is misjudged and G. D. H. Cole[2] is mistaken in thinking that the ethical emphasis means the denial of personality. It is the emphasis on the economic aspect of life that is unhappy in its results. Man shall not live by bread alone ; but this is often overlooked and the attempt is made to interpret all life as a struggle to obtain the means of subsistence. "In sober truth" writes Huxley,[3] "to those who have made a study of the phenomena of life as they are exhibited by the higher forms of the animal world, the optimistic dogma, that this is the best of all possible worlds, will seem little better than a libel upon possibility." From the point of view of the moralist the animal world is on about the same level as a gladiator's show. The creatures are fairly well treated, and set to fight...whereby the strongest, the swiftest, and the cunningest live to fight another day." And the writer goes on to examine human phenomena very critically and sadly notes that even there, there is the internecine struggle for existence. There are the "deep-seated organic impulses" which impel him to the struggle.

---

[1] Tawney: *Religion and the Rise of Capitalism*, pp. 22-25.

[2] *Social Theory*, p. 48 ff.

[3] Evolution and Ethics: Essay on *The Struggle for Existence in Human Society*.

But this view of human life is inherently wrong, in-asmuch as it conceives of man on the natural level, and does not take cognisance of the supreme truth that he is a moral being striving after ends which the economic interpretation can never take in, in all their significance. And we hold that it is the introduction of economic passions into human struggles that accentuates class-spirit and class-war. Nobody was more alive to this danger than Plato himself when he talks of the State, divided against itself, the rich and the poor contending for mastery, as the State of discord. To him such a State was not a single State, but, in reality two states. He correctly diagonised the malady that was ruining the Greek Polity. If the feuds within the city were merely political, there would not have been such bitterness as we find ; it is the introduction of economic and social forces that has given Greek political strife its peculiar intensity.

And, in the modern world too, we notice this unfortunate tendency growing in intensity with the thickening of the class-struggle. We hold that this is inevitable so long as we look upon life as a mere struggle for existence. The economic interpretation of history, as we have already pointed out, is untenable from whatever point of view we may consider it. And its greatest defect is that it ignores the working of spiritual forces in human life. The result is that to-day we have "Stasis" on a world-wide scale. The causes of the evil have been discussed by Thucydides and his words have not yet lost their significance, for the causes are there "so long as the nature of mankind remains the same."[1] And the human society has become "divided into camps in which no man trusted his fellow." We can hope to exist only by re-defining to ourselves what our ideals should be ; and by correctly understanding the nature of our life, in and through which we have to

[1] *The Peloponnesian War* (Everyman's Edn.), pp. 223-226.

realise our ideals. We hold, therefore that the elimination of the ethical factor from function is dangerous to the organic welfare of society. Society is a spiritual organism, and all its parts are members, each of the other. If the Social Good and Supreme End have not equal significance to all, then social justice is injured and Humanity mutilated.

And the functional scheme of Dharma, with its ordering of the castes, is the denial of social justice, based on gross inequalities. In the first place there is no adequate idea of social justice, for, as we have seen, there is, indeed, no place for society in Indian thought. Secondly justice or Dharma can have no reference to the coherence of the whole of the community, but to the coherence of the parts, considered as isolated units. For, we have seen that Dharma, in the last analysis, is Swadharma. The End of the State is the expression of a selfish and thus a partial good. It does not seek the good of every element in it, but of particular elements which are "ends", the rest being mere "means."

So to raise the question again, "Where does Justice or Dharma reside in the State?", we would be forced to admit that, in the Indian Polity, it does not reside in the coherence of the whole, but in a part of it. The State enthrones in the seat of power, monopoly and prestige, the few who belonged to the higher castes ; and backs them up by force, by the rod of chastisement, represented by and vested in the person of the king. It would be wrong to characterise this condition of State and society as harmonious, for it is not harmony, but an unstable equilibrium which is maintained. Justice or Dharma is the interest of the strong ; or to express it in its converse, the necessity of the weak. In other words, Dharma is the child of fear. If the restraining force of the State were not there, if the king failed to wield the rod of chastisement, then we have a condition of affairs described as *Matsyanyaya*, the larger fish devouring the smaller. Dharma, in its manifestation in the State, is just government and administration of Law; and most often is the expression of retributive justice. We shall discuss this more fully in our chapter on Political Obligation. Here we shall only say that the conception of Dharma never rises to the moral grandeur of Plato's idea of Social Justice. Only some members of the Polity are enabled to live the "Best Life", while the rest are practically enslaved. Some castes are to follow the nobler functions while the lower castes are to follow the meaner though necessary functions. There is no recognition that the members of the lower castes, through a proper system of education and given equal opportunities, would be enabled to rise higher and be fitted to discharge the higher and nobler functions. Function is to be determined by birth, not by capacity. The quality of the lower castes is *Tamas*; and it is not possible so long as they belong to the lower castes to rise higher. It is never possible in the present birth. At best, by serving the higher castes, they could insure for better conditions in a future life, when the quality of the Soul would be *rajas* or *satwam*. Their Dharma is to serve the higher castes; and they are not capable, because of their birth, of the higher and the nobler functions, for lack of the necessary quality of the Soul. The Sudra, according to Manu, is a natural slave; "though emancipated by his master, is not released; since that is innate in him, who can free him from it?"[1] So the Sudra, or the member of the lower castes, is a "means" or instrument, to be pressed into the service of the higher castes. And so, we maintain, the Indian Polity is based, not on Social Justice, but on Social Injustice; some classes in it being "Ends", and the rest being "means".

We hold that the Ideal State, in which Social Justice

[1] *Manu*: VIII, 414.

is most completely realised, is that in which no individual or class is suppressed or degraded to the level of the mere "instrument", and no class or individual can be an end in itself. In other words every individual or class or caste shall at once be both end and means,[1] and function shall be related to the Social Harmony or Coherence, by a Partnership in the Virtue of the Larger Life. The idea must gain universal acceptance that we are children of a Common Father, and that barriers that divide man from man are artificial and unnatural, "the product of less gifted minds", as Prof. P. A. Wadia profoundly observes, "who fail to see the wood for the trees".

We shall, therefore, not be wrong in concluding that the End of the State, as visualised by Hindu thinkers, is imperfect and unjust. The State, that is the institutional response to this End, could not but be a despotic monarchy, restrained in its turn only by the attitude towards Life that we have described, and the theocratic influence of Brahmanism.

We shall now proceed to the study of the various aspects of the Hindu Polity, in the light of the End it proposed to realise through the State.

---

[1] See *Mackenzie's Ethics*, p. 336 ff.

CHAPTER V

THE SPHERE AND NATURE OF THE STATE

"Not only material security, but the perfection of human and social life, is what we aim at in that organised co-operation of many men's lives and works which is called the State. I fail to see good warrant of either reason or experience for limiting the corporate activity of a nation by hard and fast rules."

SIR FREDERICK POLLOCK

(*Hist. of Science and Politics*, p. 134.)

"Political theory would mark time by the perpetual swing of the pendulum between non-interference and paternalism."

(Hsiao: *Political Pluralism*, p. 46.)

"The State as a completed reality is the ethical whole and the actualisation of freedom."

(Hegel: *Philosophy of Right.*)

"The State or political community, which is the highest of all communities, and which embraces all the rest, aims, and in a greater degree than any other, at the highest good."

(*Aristotle.*)

The End of the State, as we have seen, is to maintain Dharma. The security and prosperity of the realm depends on the proper performance of Dharma. The different Orders and Castes were to be strictly confined to their appointed functions in life. "Kings should protect the four orders in the discharge of their duties. It is the eternal duty of the kings to prevent a confusion of duties in respect of the different orders."[1] When any caste has strayed from its path the king shall bring it back to the path of duty.[2] If a man neglects his duty and does that which is forbidden, if he violates the rules of his caste or

---

[1] *Santi Parva* (Ray's), Sect. LVII, p. 174.

[2] *Narada* (Jolly), p. 215. See also *Yajnavalkya*, I, 360-361. *Vasishtha*, XIX, 8. *Vishnu*, III, 37.

order, he shall be punished until he amends.[1] It is the duty of the monarch, therefore to lead back to the path of duty those who leave it.[2] Neglect of Swadharma is the most henious of crimes ; and there is no expiation for them that cast off the duties and practices of their order and caste.[3] Confusion of duties would endanger the stability of the State. If the restraining power of the State were not there to prevent the commingling of the castes owing to confusion of duties, then impiety would spread apace, and religion be undermined. The eternal rites of families would be neglected, and dire calamities would overwhelm the Polity in confusion worse confounded. The State would dissolve into mutually repellent atoms, and the strong would prey upon the weak after the manner of fishes in the water. The functional harmony of the Polity would be disturbed as the "means" would become the "ends" For "the hearts of men of all the orders, fall away from their respective duties. Sudras live by adopting lives of mendicancy, and Brahmanas live by serving others."[4] The lower Orders or castes would become bold and usurp the position of the higher. Dharma, therefore, in the last analysis, as we have seen, is Swadharma ; and nobody is to be permitted to follow any other's duty, however excellent. To regulate the life of man, so that there shall be no lapse, either in private or public, would involve extensive supervision and censorship. The king is credited, therefore, with extensive powers, even over the morals of his subjects. He could interfere in the most private of relationships.[5] There could have been no limit to State-Action, except such as was imposed on it by the attitude to life that we have discussed, and the nature of the

[1] *Apastamba* (Buhler), p. 238.
[2] *Gautama*, p. 231.
[3] *Santi Parva* (Ray's), Sect. XXXVII, p. 113.
[4] *Ibid.* (Dutt's), LXIX.
[5] *Narada*, p. 188.

End it sought to promote. We have seen that the phenomenon of homeless asceticism was universal in ancient India. We hear of numerous kings abdicating, and becoming ascetics, or Rajarshis.[1] The ideal king is he who lays down the sceptre of office in his old age, who "transmits his crown to his son, and betakes himself to the woods, there to live on the products of the wilderness and act according to the ordinances of the Vedas".[2] So long as he is the monarch of men, he has to uphold the "Swadharma" of the Orders and castes. We shall discuss this problem in greater detail when we consider the province of Law. And the injunction laid down in the various law-books that the king is to observe the particular laws of families, castes, orders etc. has been misconstrued by some writers on the ancient Indian Polity into implying that a strict policy of non-intervention was forced upon the monarch.[3] Nothing can be further from the truth. It only meant that Dharma was binding on the king as well ; and as Dharma is Swadharma, the duty of the king in maintaining Dharma is to keep the various orders and castes in the observance of their respective duties. The king could not ordinarily bring about a social change, involving a change of duties. Under exceptional circumstances as we shall see, he could do even that. But what we shall have to recognise is the fact, that even the function of the king which aims at the maintenance of the various orders and castes, or families etc., in the performance of their Swadharma involves, not non-interference, but on the other hand, active interference in almost every aspect of human life. In the earliest period of Indian history it might be true to maintain that the sphere of State-action was limited

[1] See Banerjea: *Public Administration in Ancient India*, p. 90.
[2] *Santi Parva* (Ray's), Sect. XXI.
[3] Dr. Radhakumud Mookerji, for instance maintains that "a policy of non-interference was recognised as the ideal policy of the State". *Local Govt. in Anc. Ind.*, p. 3.

to the irreducible minimum of providing internal and external security. But "as society became more complex with the progress of civilisation the sphere of state-activity tended gradually to extend, until about the sixth or fifth century A.D. it embraced almost the entire life of the people."[1]

The only limits to the power of the State, if at all they can be recognised as such, are influences of a theocratic or theological nature. The Indian Polity was never freed from theocratic conceptions. It is wrong to assert that the State was freed from religious influences, and made to rest purely on positive bases. We shall presently return to this problem. The only check on the power of the State is to be found in the attitude to Life that we have examined already. This world is looked upon as unsubstantial, and life as a condition of misery. Perhaps the king would be led to look upon his fellow-creatures, as Schopenhauer would have us look upon them, as "fellow-sufferers." And the thought of the transitoriness of earthly splendour, and the vanity of glory may serve to remind him that his sceptre and crown must one day tumble down into the dust, and nursing his cravings he would come to his death, for :

> "Brief is this life, all the sages have told us;
> Transient it is, and essentially changing."

And he may also, even as Asoka had realised, experience a violent reaction against the pleasures of life, and be led to long for the path that would take him across to the further shore ; so far as earthly ambition goes, it is never satiated :

> "The king having forcibly conquered the earth,
> To the shore of the ocean, holding the land

---

[1] Banerjea: *Pub. Adm. in Anc. Ind.*, p. 40.
See also Prof. Beni Prasad: *Theory of Govt. in Anc. India*, p. 35.

> This side of the Sea, may yet all unsatisfied
> Hanker after the further side also."

And in the various works that we now possess which paint for us the life of those early times, we do come across numerous princes who, having drunk the cup of life till satiety, having abandoned themselves to a life of licence and luxury, suddenly feel the touch of a new influence, awakened may be by some chance occurence, as the sight of a leper or a corpse, and feel irresistibly called upon to wander forth, abandoning home, into the homeless life :

> "Forsaking home, a homeless life to lead"

The unknown future, the call of the Hereafter, has always had a peculiar fascination for the Indian mind and prince and peasant alike sought the peace that could be only had in the forest home :

> "In such a spot,
> To breathe is to be purer........"[1]

The Indian spirit scorned to limit itself by the obligations of mundane existence, and sought its place with the placeless, by treading the track of the traceless. The home has no affinities with the hermit life, and "liberty of the soul" could be attained only by abstraction from the world. Few could reach to the spiritual vision of the great Kalidas who "on the foundation of the hermitage of recluses" has "built the home of the householder."[2] It was felt that only in the ultimate, when the lamp is blown out as it were, or when the individual drop is absorbed into the bosom of the vast ocean of the Infinite, could man be freed, in the absolute sense. If it is not possible in the brief span of a single life-time to achieve this deliverance, the man may, by meritorious deeds, insure for himself another birth under better or more favourable circum-

---

[1] Kalidasa: *Sakuntala*, Act I, Sc. I.
[2] *Ibid.*: *Tagore's Introductory Essay.*

stances. "Those whose conduct has been good", according to *Chandogya-Upanishad*, "will quickly attain some good birth, the birth of a Brahmana, or a Kshatriya, or a Vaisya."[1] For all favourable circumstances are reducible to the one fact of birth. And birth, as we have seen, is determined by the quality of the Soul. Sukracharya,[2] while restating the idea that we have noticed in the Gita, effects a direct relation between works and qualities of the soul or virtues, and human birth is the result of qualities like *Tamas*, *Sattva* and *Rajas*. And so, one who is born a Sudra, has not to complain but accept his present condition, as the outcome of his past, and should by meritorious deeds acquire the necessary quality to insure a birth in the higher castes. In a future life, if fortunate, he may be born a Vaisya or Kshatriya or Brahmana. The strict adherence to Swadharma, ("A man can't give up the trade he was born to, as the saying is, even though it has a bad name"—Kalidasa, *Sakuntala*, p. 112) would enable him to acquire religious merit which would stand him in good stead in a future birth. The Sudra should, therefore, willingly allow himself to be used as "means". "To serve the other (three) castes (is ordained) for the Sudra", says *Apastamba*, "The higher the caste (which he serves) the greater is the merit."[3] He should never assume a position equal to that of a member of the higher castes.[4] Had he not been of sinful nature would he have been a Sudra ![5] Lest he should be born in a worse caste in future, let him observe his Swadharma, for that is the only path consistent with safety. A Chandala, likewise shall follow what is prescribed for him. Indeed, he cannot be born

---

[1] *V. Prapathaka*, 10 Khanda, 7.

[2] *Sukraniti*, p. 8; 122-123.

[3] *Apastamba* (Buhler); p. 2.

[4] *Ibid.*, p. 165.

[5] See *Bhagavad-gita*, p. 85 (Telang's).
Anugita, Ch. IV.

again in a worse human condition, for he is the meanest of bipeds, scarce worth being noticed as human at all; he is "the refuse of society".[1] But what if he be born a hog, or a dog, or a vulture, for his negligence of Swadharma in this birth! Let all, therefore, follow their own Dharma, determined by their birth in the particular caste, if they aspire to enter the path that leads to final liberation. A Sudra must always seek to serve the higher castes, and a Chandala, who himself is the refuse of society, to serve it by removing its refuse, that is by performing the duties of scavenging, carrying of dead animals, etc. If the various orders and castes fall away from their duties, *Varna-sankaram* would result. Then Dharma becomes Adharma; and the social equilibrium is destroyed. The Polity moves from its hinges, and crashes down into the abyss of the original chaos.

The State, therefore, exists to uphold Dharma. It realises in its own nature aspects of it. It participates in or receives a share of virtue or vice that the people reap according as they perform or neglect Dharma. Gautama says that the king "obtains a share of the spiritual merit (gained by his subjects)".[2] The king, who represents the State, must therefore be vigorous in his duties, not only in the interests of the spiritual prospects of his people, but also if he is to consider the prospects of his own salvation; for he shares in the sins and virtues of his people. If even a single individual in his dominions be negligent in his Dharma, then that would react immediately on the harmony of the Polity. He who transgresses his limits is an "offender against social harmony."[3] If the king maintains the social order and sees that the various castes perform their appointed functions "the

---

[1] *Brihaspati* (Jolly), p. 359.
[2] P. 231.
[3] *Santi Parva*, Sect. XXXIII (Ray's).

result is the advent of a golden age."[1] "Without doubt all men succeed in acquiring the objects they desire and preserving those that have been acquired. All the vedic rites become productive of merit. All the seasons become delightful and free from evil...... Diseases disappear and all men become long-lived...... The Earth yields crops without being tilled and herbs and plants grow in luxuriance......"[2] The king, therefore, must "prevent a confusion of duties in respect of the different orders." Otherwise, dire consequences would follow.[3] If the king protects the castes and orders that follow religious observances, he is more than repaid by the resultant accumulation of merit. It is the duty of the king to protect the sacred groves, so that the dwellers in the hermitages suffer no disturbance in their rites. King Dushyanta, we are told by Kalidas,[4] proudly claims a lofty role as the descendant of Puru; he is conscious that he is charged :

> "......with the care and
> maintenance
> Of justice and religion;......"

And the castes and orders, engaged in religious observances, are exempt from taxation; and according to Sukracharya, they are to be maintained by stipends, gifts and honours.[5] They pay taxes of a higher kind by the rendering of spiritual services which the king values very highly. "These hermits", says Dushyanta, "by the fruits of their penances, pay me a very different kind of tribute, which I value more than baskets of gold and jewels."[6]

---

1 Beni Prasad: *Theory of Govt.*, p. 35.
2 *Santi Parva* (Dutt's), LXIX, 82 ff.
3 See *Narada*, p. 216.
Manu, VI, 20, 21, 24.
4 *Sakuntala*, Act I, Sc. I.
5 *Sukra-Niti*, p. 76.
6 *Sakuntala*, Act I, Sc. II.
cf. Santideva: *Siksha Samuccaya* (Ratnakuta).

The king, and that is the State, can thus by the protection afforded, and the restrictions imposed, increase the Dharma in the realm, or by the neglect of the exercise of his functions, the king might endanger the spiritual welfare of his state. "If a king acts heedlessly, a great evil becomes the consequence....... Unrighteousness increases, causing a confusion of castes. Cold sets in during the summer months, and disappears when its proper season comes. Drought and flood and pestilence afflict the people....... Ominous stars arise and awful comets appear on such occasions. Diverse other portents, indicating destruction of the kingdom, make their appearance...... The virginity of maidens is defloured...... All rights of property come to an end among men...... The four orders, the Vedas, and the duties in respect of the four modes of life, all become confused and weakened......"[1] And so the king who is righteous "is regarded as the creator", while he who is sinful "is regarded as the destroyer". He is, indeed, the maker of his age. "The Prince is the cause of time (the maker of his age)," says Sukracharya,[2] "and of the good and evil practices. By a terrible use of his engine of sovereignty, he should maintain the subjects each in his proper sphere." It is the king that is "the cause of the setting on foot of the customs, usages and movements", and hence he is the cause or maker of time ; the age or time is not the cause of usages etc.[3] Manu also makes a similar claim when he observes that "the various ways in which a king behaves (resemble) the Krita, Treta, Dvapara, and Kali ages ; hence the king is identified with the ages (of

---

[1] *Santi Parva*, XC and XCI (Dutt's).
[2] *Sukra-Niti*, p. 11.
[3] *Ibid.*, pp. 5-6.

the world).'"[1] So the respective ages are all dependent on the king, for he "constitutes the age."[2]

The king is the root of Dharma, and he maintains Dharma by affording protection to his subjects, primarily by seeking to prevent disturbances to the observances of religious rites. That is why special protection is always given to Brahmans and hermits. He should not show leniency to the lower orders, for they might overpower him, as they are selfish.[3]

And protection is afforded if the king employs the four means indicated by the sciences. Protection is "the very cheese of kingly duties."[4] For, "the protection the king grants to his subjects upholds the world."[5] And he protects as "a great deity in human form." "As lord of the land the king is a Zeus Agamemnon, a human divinity incorporating the essence of the deities Indra, Vayu, Yama, Varuna, Agni etc., that is of the gods who protect the world in the eight directions."[6]

And under the comprehensive head of Protection we shall have to bring "all the work of the ancient Indian State in the departments of what we should now call the Church, Education, Poor Relief...... the Police, Criminal and Civil Justice, Legislation, Medical relief, Public works, the Army and the Navy, and the consular and

---

[1] IX, 301.

[2] *Santi Parva*, XCI; see also LXIX.

[3] *Sukra-Niti*, p. 90.

[4] *Santi Parva*, Sect. LVIII (Ray's), 177.

[5] *Ibid.*, Sect. LVII (Ray's), p. 176.

The reward of a righteous king who affords protection is that he acquires "all those regions that are acquired by persons leading duly the Grahastya, the Brahmacharya, and the Vanaprastha modes of life." (*Santi Parva*, Sect. LXXI). And the king "earns merit that is a hundred times greater than what is earned by recluses in their asylums within the wood." (*Santi Parva*, Sect. LXVI).

[6] *Cambridge Modern History*, p. 288.

diplomatic service......"[1] Further, when we remember that the king "must not suffer sin to be perpetrated in his kingdom, but should cause virtue to be practised,"[2] it is clear that there can be no aspect, either private or public, too sacred, that it could not be interfered with by the State. An enumeration of the duties of the king would reveal how all-embracing the sphere of state-activity and influence was.[3] He was the executive head of the State, and "the centre of the State", as Kautilya[4] claims, for, in him is vested the supreme political power. He sustains the realms,[5] by providing security, internal and external. He is the Supreme Judge, and the final Court of Appeal. All officers of State were appointed by him, and were responsible to him. During later times, he could also legislate, as his Edicts have the force of Law. In war, he is the commander of the military forces. He is the guardian of the minors in his realm. "If there is a maiden who has nobody living to give away in marriage, she should have recourse to the king and marry with his permission."[6] The king moreover could punish persons who perform defective marriages. "The king himself shall impose a fine on him who gives a blemished damsel (to a suitor) without informing (him of the blemish)."[7] The king was the head of society and the protector of religion; "and in his executive capacity he guided, and to some

---

[1] *K. V. Rangaswamy Iyengar*, p. 67; see also p. 22.

[2] *Santi Parva*, Sect. XXIV (Ray's), p. 63.

[3] See Bandyopadhyaya: *Kautilya*, p. 59.

See p. 90 where he says: "the king was the centre of political life and the pivot of the whole constitution. All power remained concentrated in him and from him emanated authority which was delegated to the agents of administration". See also p. 111.

[4] *Arthasastra*, Bk. VIII, Ch. I.

[5] *Satapatha Brahmana*, IX, 4, 1, 3.

[6] *Narada* (Jolly), p. 169.

[7] *Manu*, VIII, 224; see also IX, 73. cf. *Yajnavalkya*, I, 66. *Vishnu*, V, 45, 47.

extent controlled, the religious and moral life of the people."[1] Sometimes he could effectively change the ordering of Dharma, in its functional aspect, though ordinarily he is enjoined not to interfere. "One should not do mean works," says Sukracharya, "and the king should not also order for such. But in the absence of one who is to do that work, the king's order should be obeyed. For even superior men have to do inferior works which become duties in time."[2]

The State, therefore, was of the autocratic type, and highly centralised. We do not suggest thereby that the Indian Polity always possessed this character. And, again monarchy, perhaps, was not the only form of government known in India. Prof. Rhys Davids speaks of republics "with either complete or modified independence," which existed "side by side with more or less powerful monarchies."[3] At the time of Alexander's invasion we hear of cities possessing a democratic form of government.[4] But the normal Polity, and that of which all Hindu theorists and statesmen concern themselves about, was the monarchical. Kautilya,[5] it is true, gives a passing reference to them, and he notices that the greatest defect of these states is what Thucydides has observed, internal faction, or *stasis*. But the prevailing system, even in the Vedic age, was the monarchical.[6] Further, it is a notorious fact that Greek writers on India cannot be trusted ; and whenever they speak of republics or democracies, we have not to understand by those terms the types of Polities in a developed form which they suggest. We fully agree with

---

[1] Banerjea: *Public Adm. in Anc. Ind.*, p. 79.

[2] *Sukra-Niti-Sara*, p. 87.

[3] *Buddhist India*, p. 2 ff.

[4] *Ancient India; Its Invasion by Alexander the Great*, p. 292 ff. See p. 81 for the aristocratic form of govt; see also p. 154.

[5] McCrindle: See *Camb. Hist.*, pp. 491-492.

[6] *Camb. Hist. of Ind.*, p. 491.

the cautious view of Richard Fick who considers that when Megasthenes speaks of free states it is hardly probable that republics are meant thereby. What the Greek messenger saw was that in the neighbourhood of great monarchies there were individual cities or small states maintaining their independence and so were autonomous. Prof. Rhys Davids probably refers to them. But that "the constitution of these small states was wholly different from that in the monarchies", Richard Fick is justified in refusing to accept. He says : "the difference consisted, in my opinion, only in the greater or less part which the remaining members of the royal families took in the government by the side of the king and by which they more or less limited his absolute power. A rajah stood even in Vesali and other free states at the head of the government, though he was only *primus inter pares*, who had precedence over his kinsmen in the Council."[1] We are perfectly justified in maintaining that the normal Polity is the monarchical, and that exceptions belong to obscure periods, sometimes marking a transitional period in the history of the particular state. At any rate the growth of the great kingdoms proved destructive to the other forms of political organisation in India.

By the time we come into the full light of the dawn of history we find the State already a centralised bureaucracy, the sphere of its action being as wide as human relationships. The only limitation, if it could be so called, was theocratic in nature ; and we have already noticed it. Prof. Bhandarkar is, in a sense, right when he observes that the Hindu state was limited in one sense and unlimited in another. The limitation he says, was sacerdotal or socio-religious. But "there was no visible assignable limit so far as the State aspired to be benevol[illegible] and

[1] Fick: *Social Org.*, pp. 137-138.
See also Oldenberg: *Buddha*, p. 101.

helpful to the people, intellectually, economically, and socialistically."[1]

A brief review of the history of the evolution of the Indian Polity would make our point much clearer. Much is not known of the Polity that existed before the coming of the Aryans. Mr. Hewitt[2] refuses to admit that the Aryans "exterminated and drove out their predecessors, and forcibly assumed the government of the country" and "based their social polity on Aryan precedents." He has tried to prove, therefore, "the great share taken by other races besides the Aryans in the formation of the Hindu religion, Hindu government and Hindu social customs." It is quite possible that the conquered races might have largely influenced the civilisation of the Aryan conquerors. It has happened in the case of other peoples elsewhere in history. One thing, however, has never happened. The conquering people never took in the political ideas of the subjugated population, and have everywhere tried to impose on the conquered their own form of government whatever that might be. It is perhaps safe to recognise that so far as the political institutions were concerned the Aryans did build upon Aryan precedents only, and did not borrow the ideas either of the Kolarians or of the Dravidians.

The Kolarians were settled in village-communities, "each with its dependent hamlets as newer clearances by fresh groups of settlers were made. Each parent village was governed by its headman, now called the Munda, chosen from among the first settlers, and frequently though by no means always, the office was continued from father to son. Over the village, united under the same priest a common chief (now called Manki) was chosen. He presided at the assemblies of the representatives of

[1] *Aspects of Ancient Hindu Polity*, p. 194.

[2] See his two articles in the *Journal of the Royal Asiatic Society*, 1888 and 1889.

the union, formed generally of the village headmen and the leading cultivators, though all had a right to attend. These unions of villages must have been called by some name like Pirs or Parhas, the present name, and it was in this way in the districts first organised under the Kolarian rule that the divisions now known as Pergunnahs were formed."

The Dravidians believed firmly in the "necessity of a strong central government to maintain law and order." When they therefore, assumed the government of the country formerly inhabited by the Kolarians, they "retained the village communities established by their predecessors, but reformed the village system. They made each separate village, and each province formed a union of villages, more dependent on the central authority than they were under the Kolarian form of government." The tendency towards centralisation is also to be noted in the South of India. A recent writer[1] on Dravidian India observes that "in the ancient Dravidian village there was developed a compact tribal organisation under more or less centralised government." And the elective system that was prevalent among the Kolarians gave place to the system of nomination from the central body.[2] All public offices, "beginning with headships of villages," were thus filled by nominees appointed by the State. The result of the changes effected was towards greater efficiency. We know how stubborn the resistance was which the Āryans encountered, and how they had to fight their way through, inch by inch. The Dravidians were indeed wealthy and powerful and were not the barbarians that many who read the descriptions of the Dasyus in the Vedas would take them to be. They had a highly efficient organisation and possessed cities and forts.

---

[1] T. R. Shesha Iyengar: *Dravidian India*, p. 175.
[2] Hewitt.

With the coming of the Aryans the tendency towards centralisation becomes more marked. The ordinary form of government in Vedic times is the monarchical. The king is the leader of the people. There were other elements present in the Polity, elements common to all the peoples of the Aryan stock. But the regal power began to grow and consolidate itself from the very beginning. It was the continuous state of war that helped this strengthening of the monarchical element. In their victorious advance, the Aryans had to fight for every inch of ground with the original settlers, who, as we have seen, were themselves highly civilised and efficient. This resulted "almost necessarily in strengthening the monarchic element of the constitution."[1] Dr. Basu is perfectly right in observing that "the king was indeed a prominent person with regal paraphernalia and not merely the first of men."[2]

The Aryans were also living in villages, some of them small and some big. "The village does not appear to have been a unit for legal purposes in early days and it can hardly be said to have been a political unit."[3] But the states being small, "there was hardly any distinction between the Central and the Local Government."[4] All the people, however, were alike "politically subject to the king." Even as early as the *Atharwaveda*,[5] the king is referred to as having a share in the village. The gramani or village chief may have been either selected or appointed by the king.

It is difficult to decide how far the monarch was limited in his powers. Shama Sastry goes to the extent of observing that the king was at the mercy of the People's

[1] *Vedic Index*, Vol. II, pp. 210-216.
[2] *Indo-Aryan Polity*, p. 72; see also p. 62 ff.
[3] *Vedic Index*, Vol. I, p. 246 ff.
[4] Banerjea: *Public Adm.*, p. 289.
[5] IV, 22, 2.

Assembly.[1] Narendranath Law also maintains that there are clear signs that the power of the monarch was curbed by the existence of the assembly."[2] Everything depends on the nature of the People's Assembly. Most probably the work transacted by the People's Assembly might have been mainly religious and social. How far the meetings of the People's Assembly were for political purposes is first to be determined before we could claim that the People's Assembly could curb the power of the monarch. If we could argue from historical analogies, we have not sufficient warrant to assume that the king was at the mercy of the Assembly. He no doubt attended the meetings of both the Sabha and the Samiti, and his prosperity rested on maintaining harmonious relations with them. But we cannot speak of constitutional checks or limitations to the power of the monarch. If the king is elected by the Assembly, then perhaps the body which appoints the monarch may be said to have control over him. But the election of the monarch is still a moot point. The position of a war lord, we might assume, depends on the choice of the mass of the fighting men; the bravest and the strongest might be elected to lead the forces. But when the war lord has succeeded in establishing himself as king, more or less on a permanent basis, the monarchy assumes more and more a hereditary character, and even if the principle of election is still continued, it is merely a formality which has long lost its true significance. A state of continuous war and the settlement in an alien territory surrounded by hostile peoples, tend to concentrate power in the hands of the Executive. The saying is too true that war begat the king.[3] And his power practi-

---

[1] *Evolution of Indian Polity*, p. 87.

[2] *Ancient Indian Polity*, p. 11.

[3] The poet Cowper tries to trace the origin of kingship to war; to the necessity felt for a leader.

cally becomes supreme. The regal power is insecure only in the hands of an incompetent weakling. If the king happens to be a strong man he exercises extensive powers, not only in war, but in peace as well. He is moreover the Supreme Judge; and so is himself not under the jurisdiction of any other institution. "Himself immune from punishment (a-dandya) he wields the rod of punishment (Danda)."[1]

During the Epic Age, "kingship is practically universal; and it is only individual passages which contemplate the existence of states without a king, of states where people are miserable indeed."[2] The king and the royal family are all important. If at all the king's power is in any way limited, it was by that of his brothers and ministers, as Prof. Hopkins points out. But this limitation is properly speaking no limitation at all; for there was no constitutional machinery that could be brought into operation to make this limitation real or effective in any sense. Prof. Hopkins is wrong in maintaining that "the epic king is no autocrat."[3] The various didactic injunctions that we have in the Epics belong to a later age. "In the Heroic Age", as Prof. Siddhanta points out, "the king would probably not be bound by any such rules; and provided he kept his retainers pleased there seems to have been little he could not do."[4] And to decide whether the

---

"..........................At length
One eminent above the rest, for strength,
For stratagem, or courage, or for all,
Was chosen leader. Him they served in way
And him in peace for sake of warlike deeds
Reverenced no less ....
Thus kings were first invented."

The Winter Morning's Walk.

[1] *Vedic Index*, Vol. II, p. 213.
[2] Prof. Siddhanta: *The Heroic Age of India*, p. 176.
[3] *Cambridge History of India*, p. 271.
[4] *Heroic Age of India*, p. 178.

king was an autocrat or otherwise, it is very necessary to determine what his relations with the Assembly were. The Samiti, we are told, practically "disappears as an effective part of government."[1] And the Sabha could not have been democratic as Prof. Jayaswal would like to make it out. If the Sabha exercised political powers as such, we might go a certain distance to meet the views of those scholars who want to make out that there were democratic assemblies in ancient India. The supreme question to be decided is how far the functions exercised by the Assembly were of a political nature. And even if political, what influence could the Assembly wield on the monarch? We shall have to recognise that the privilege to give advice, when consulted, is not the same thing as the right to enforce the adherence to the advice so given. The king might have felt it advisable to seek and ascertain the opinion of the people, but he was certainly not bound to follow it. Above all, we shall have to note that the questions so referred to were certainly not political, for the Assembly long ceased to have political influence, if ever we could hold that it effectively exercised it. Prof. Hopkins rightly points out that "the Sabha or assembly is here simply a military body for consultation. Both priests and people are silent in the face of force."[2] Thus we find Prof. Hopkins singularly contradicting himself, for when he says that the Assembly had no political power, he cannot maintain that the king was no autocrat. If the brothers of the king or his ministers could upbraid or reprove him, it does not follow that they were effective limits to his autocracy. The king was not obliged to follow their advice, and there was no machinery provided for in the Constitution which could be brought into operation as against the king, if he chose to reject the counsel of his

[1] *Vedic Index*, Vol. 2, p. 431.
[2] *Cambridge History of India*, p. 271.

brothers or ministers. There was indeed a council known as the "Rajasamiti," but its members seem to have been mainly priests. We are further told that the ministers were to be Brahmans. But at critical moments we find the king seeking the counsel not of this "Rajasamiti", but of his relatives and generals. And in times of emergency, as for instance in the case of the minority of the king, it is not the "Rajasamiti" that is seen to function, but, some individual generally entrusted with the duties of the king. Moreover the "Rajasamiti" was merely consultative in character. "The Prince goes to the council to listen to its deliberations, but if he has made up his mind already the council has no influence with him."[1] And even in his international dealings or relationships the king is not bound to follow anybody's advice. It was his personal influence, we might almost say, personal interest, that decides.

The village seems to have been brought more under the control of the central government than formerly. The discourse of Bhisma on the means of the consolidation of the state may be taken to be typically representative of actual conditions. It also illustrates the policy of the kings towards local institutions. Bhisma is reported to have said: "I shall tell thee how a kingdom may be consolidated and how also it may be protected. A headman should be selected for each village. Over ten villages (or ten headmen) there should be one superintendent. Over two such superintendents there should be one officer (having the control, therefore, of twenty villages). Above the latter should be appointed persons under each of whom should be a century of villages; and above the last kind of officers should be appointed men each of whom should have a thousand villages under his control. The head-man should ascertain the characteristics of every

[1] *Heroic Age of India*, p. 184.

person in the village and all the faults also that need correction. He should report everything to the officer (who is above him and is) in charge of ten villages. The latter, again, should report the same to the officer (who is above him and is) in charge of twenty villages. The latter, in his turn, should report the conduct of all the persons within his dominions to the officer (who is above him and is) in charge of a hundred villages......... Some virtuous minister, with watchfulness, should exercise supervision over the administrative affairs and mutual relations of those officers. In every town again, there should be an officer for attending to every matter relating to his jurisdiction. Like some planet of dreadful form moving above all the asterisms below, the officer (with plenary powers) mentioned last should move and act above all the officers subordinate to him. Such an officer should ascertain the conduct of those under him through spies."[1] There are many interesting facts that the passage reveals ; and we see the state setting up a huge machine of inquisition into operation in its capacity as the moral guardian of the people and the protector of Dharma. We shall have occasion to discuss the institution of Espionage later on. Here we wish to point out that all the essentials of the Kautiliyan State were already formulated in the Epic Age, by the sages and statesmen of the time. The *Arthasastra* does not point to any new departure ; but seeks to systematise with an added emphasis the political ideas already prevalent. In a sense the *Arthasastra* is the epitome of the tendencies of political thought of all the former epochs. Its supreme contribution is to make theory correspond to the actual practice of the age, and reject all other cross-currents of thought that had obtained provisional validity under particular circumstances of place and time.

---

[1] *Santi Parva*, Sect. LXXXVII (Ray's, p. 280 ff).

Before we pass on to the next period we would therefore sum up the nature of the Polity during Epic times, in the words of Prof. Siddhanta that : "The most prominent factor of the heroic state was the king, and next to him his personal retinue. The generous king had always a faithful comitatus, and within his kingdom his powers were practically unlimited."

By the time we come into the full light of the dawn of history we find the State already a centralised bureaucracy, the sphere of its action being as wide as human relationships. The process of centralisation was carried almost to perfection, especially under the Mauryan monarchs ; and the imperial idea gains definite ascendancy. "Alexander's invasion made manifest the weakness of a system of small independent States", and so "the people probably welcomed, or at least submitted to, Chandragupta's attempt to establish a centralised imperial government."[1] Justin observes, indeed, that Chandragupta "changed the name of freedom to that of bondage, for he himself oppressed with servitude the very people he had rescued from foreign dominion."[2] Though we do not have from him positive evidence regarding the nature of this oppression, we can very well infer from the information we have from other sources that this has reference to the fundamental nature of Hindu monarchy itself.[3] The advance of the imperial idea, moreover, has always meant the submergence of all institutions inimical to its principle. The history of the world, everywhere, illustrates the truth of our statement. And India is no exception : and the "establishment of an imperial rule meant the sweeping away of all the free institutions of the country."[4] And

---

[1] Banerjea: *Public Adm.*, p. 47.
[2] Justin: (*McCrindle*).
[3] *Camb. Hist. of India*, p. 473.
[4] Banerjea: *Public Adm.*, p. 47.
Bandyopadhyaya: *Kautilya*, p. 64.

with the extension of kingly power, such institutions as were of popular origin tend to be superceded by institutions strictly subordinate to the monarch. "The growth of the king's authority led to the substitution of the Great Council (Raja-Sabha, Raja-Samiti) and the Privy Council (Mantri-parishat) of the king for the ancient meetings of the folk."[1] And this tendency is also to be noticed in another direction. The village is brought under the immediate control of the Central Government. Local administration is very closely linked to the Central, and this is achieved by a very complex administrative machinery. The account given by Megasthenes of the various officials of the State "points to a highly organised bureaucracy."[2] All power is concentrated in the hands of the king ; he is the key-stone of the Polity. The evidence of other Greek writers also points to the fact that the king was practically an autocrat. He controls the whole administration.[3] The civil administration of Chandragupta will enable us to realise the true nature of the system of his government. It was "based upon the personal autocracy of the sovereign."[4] A strong hand was required to keep the vast empire won by him : and weakness would not do. The administrative machinery was efficiently organised. "The Central Government, by means of local officers, exercised strict control and maintained close supervision over all classes and castes of the population."[5] All evidence that we possess points clearly to the royal absolutism of the period. This is especially true of Asoka's rule. Dr. Bhandarkar observes that the subjects were at the mercy of the king who was thus "no better than a despot."[6]

---

[1] Banerjea: *Public Adm.*, p. 97.
[2] *Camb. Hist. of India*, p. 417.
[3] *Ibid.*, p. 491.
[4] V. A. Smith: *Early History of India*, pp. 126-127.
[5] *Ibid.*, p. 133.
[6] *Asoka*, p. 63.

The evidence of the Law Books[1] and the *Jatakas*[2] is conclusive again, and the king appears throughout as an absolute ruler. The system of administration is that of a centralised bureaucracy. The village is brought directly under the personal supervision of the king or of his officers, and free institutions are things of the past.

We shall thus realise that the descriptions of the Hindu Polity in the works of modern writers are profoundly misleading. The patriotic scholarship of the modern renaissance tries to make out that the ancient Indian State was a constitutional monarchy, and was strictly limited in its activities. It is even held that the village-communities were "little republics" framed on a popular or democratic basis.[3] It is absolutely unscientific to apply modern politi-

[1] See Prof. Gadgil's Essay on *The Village in Sanskrit Literature.*

[2] Fick: *Social Org.*

[3] See Giddings: *Studies in the Theory of Human Society*, pp. 71-72.

Benoy Kumar Sarkar maintains that since Mauryan times these "village sva-rajes, those primary units of self-rule" have been reduced, "to an atrophied state". *The Political Institutions and Theories of the Hindus*, p. 58.

Considerations of space have prevented us to go into more details regarding the village communities of Ancient India. Dr. Radhakumud Mookerji has written a whole book on *Local Government in Ancient India*, as we are able to judge, on very scanty evidence; and his book is full of sweeping generalisations from which every sober historian must shrink back. At best, he can point to the evidence of the Uttaramallur inscriptions. It is impossible to draw any general conclusions from them for they refer to the peculiar case of a Brahmin colony. Further the inferences that Dr. Mookerji draws from the evidence do in fact, in no way follow from the nature and details of the evidence itself.

If the reader is anxious to study village conditions in India in more detail, we give below the references which will perhaps be of use to him.

Refer Banerjea: *Public Adm.*, pp. 47; 49-52; 97; 128-129.

R. Mookerji: *Local Govt.*, Introduction, pp. 8-11.

cal phraseology without an adequate understanding of the nature of the Hindu State. We do not certainly maintain that the king was necessarily always an arbitrary tyrant. But to characterise the basis of his power as constitutional

---

For a discussion of Village Government:—
Refer: Banerjea: *Public Adm.*, pp. 283-298.
Apastamba, pp. 161-163.
Narada, pp. 155-164.
Manu, VIII, 259, 260, 263, 265.
Yajnavalkya, II, 150, 151, 153.
Viramitrodaya, pp. 456, 460.
Were Village Communities Universal?
Refer: Matthai: *Village Government in Br. India*, pp. 8-9.
Mayne: *Hindu Law*.
(See Webb's Preface to Matthai's book for some interesting problems.)
System of land holding in Village Communities: Matthai: *Vill. Com.*, pp. 9-10.
Origin of Village Communities: Matthai: *Vill. Com.*, pp. 10-14.
Officers etc. of Village Communities: Matthai: *Vill. Com.*, pp. 14-18.
Village Panchayats: Matthai: *Vill. Com.*, pp. 18-21.
Sphere of the State: Local and Central Govts.: Matthai: *Vill. Com.*, pp. 32-33.
Maine: *Village Communities*:—
pp. 12-13 Indian Village Communities not a dead institution.
66-68 Law in the Village Community.
109- Ownership of Land.
111-113 Customs of repartition of Land.
112-113 Private property and the causes for the break up of the Village Community.
113-128 What is a Village?
113-114 Secrecy of Family Life. cf. *Greece and Rome*.
116-117 Legislation in Ancient Vill. Community,
122-125 The Village Council.
159-160 Self-sufficiency of the Village.
166-168 Exclusiveness of Village Communities.
R. Mookerji: *Local Government in Ancient India*:
p. VIII, Marquis Crew on *Self-Govt. and India*; cf. S. Webb, xxiii-xxiv, Marquis Crew on the *Indian Theory*.

would imply ignorance of the terminology employed. There never has been any constitutional tradition, much less any constitutional machinery to control or restrain the king. The checks and balances, so freely spoken about, exist only in the imagination of our modern writers. The king was an autocrat, his power being tempered only by the attitude to life that we have explained. We shall presently discuss the theocratic nature of the Polity. Through the varnish which the didactic portions of the Law Books and the *Jatakas* try to give to the picture of monarchy, its true colour, however, often reveals itself, and we have generally "the picture of the old unrestrained king", who "lets himself be guided by nothing except his own, often extremely selfish desires".[1] If the king follows the general moral duties prescribed, this "necessarily takes much from his character as an absolute despot." But unfortunately we see in him very often "an unrestrained tyrant guided by his own whims and caprices."[2] There was no element in the constitution that could limit his power. The ministers or, Ministerial Body were purely of an advisory character.[3] The people had no

p. 2—Sir G. Birdwood on *Indian Village Community*.
2-3 Sir C. Metcalfe on *Indian Vill. Com.*

Mookerji maintains that local institutions became affiliated to the State under certain agreements, pp. 5-7.
pp. 7-10 The Ancient Empires of India.
124-125 Legislation and Local Assemblies.
157-212 Administrative machinery.
Beni Prasad: *Theory of Govt.*, pp. 14; 50.
Radhakamal Mukerji: *Democracies of the East*, p. 197 ff.

[1] Fick: *Social Org.*, p. 100 ff.

[2] *Ibid.*, p. 101 ff.

[3] According to Kautilya also the "ministers were all royal servants, selected and appointed by the kings and holding office during "royal pleasure"…….they were more of courtiers seeking royal favour, than the custodians of the public right, maintained by the support of the people". And so the Council of Advisers

participation in the administration of the State and so there could never be a "limitation of kingly power through the will of the people." If the king were wise and virtuous his rule would be a benevolent or paternal despotism. If he were wicked, the only recourse left to the people would be to desert their homes and take refuge in the jungles,[1] or rise in armed insurrection.[2] The distinction may well be expressed as Montesquieu does, Monarchy as that in which a single person governs by fixed and established laws, a despotic government that in which a single person directs everything by his own will and caprice.[3] The king was expected to govern according to sacred injunctions, and the precepts of the *Dharmasastras*. There was no constitutional machinery provided for to control the king in case he violated these maxims, and chose to rule according to his own will and caprice.[4]

We thus realise that it is unscientific to describe the nature of the ancient Indian Polity in the language of modern political phraseology. Dr. Radhakamal Mukerjee maintains that the Ancient Indian Polity was a Communal Federal Democracy. Narendranath Law and Banerjea and most others try to make out that it was a Constitutional Monarchy.[5] Dr. Radhakumud Mookerji emphatically asserts the federal nature of the Polity, and seems to prove that associated life in ancient India developed

---

or the Ministers was nothing more than an advisory body.—Bandyopadhyaya: *Kautilya*, p. 129.

[1] For example as in *Kusa Jataka*, V, 520.

[2] Some modern writers have chosen to call this "The Right to Revolt". See Ghoshal: *Hindu Political Theories*, pp. 198-200.

[3] *Spirit of the Laws*, Bk. II.

[4] See Bandyopadhyaya: *Kautilya*, p. 80 ff.

[5] See Bandyopadhyaya: *Kautilya*, pp. 127-129 where he very rightly rejects the assumption that there was constitutional government in the past. Jayaswal seeks to prove that the king was constitutionally a servant; indeed, a salaried servant of State, See *Hindu Polity*, Part II, Ch. XXXV.

on a democratic basis to fulfil the ends of national life. All these characterisations are profoundly misleading and are misconceived. The Ancient Indian State was an Absolute Monarchy, limited in one sense, but unlimited in another. Autocracy was always tempered by reverence for scriptural authority. Moreover, the attitude to life, pointing as it does to the vanity of existence and vain-gloriousness of regal splendour, acted as a constant check on the conduct of the king. But all this was not through any positive institution that sought to limit the authority of the ruler ; the check on his autocracy was more through the effect of "suggestion" of spiritual penalties. Sometimes, however, the king might not formally participate in the administration. He might leave the actual Government to the responsibility of any near relative, or relatives, or to some able minister, or ministers. In that case, the administration assumes an oligarchical character. Moreover, with the increase of territory, State organisation would become highly complex, making it impossible for any single person to direct efficiently the administration of the country. The king may delegate his powers to his ministers, thus securing the necessary division of labour.[1] But all this does not at all prove that the king is less the head of the State. He is ever the final source of authority, and ultimate repository of State-Sovereignty.

Another tendency in a certain section of our writers on the ancient Indian Polity deserves our consideration at this stage. Attempts are made to interpret the Indian State in terms of Pluralism.[2] It is one thing to characterise

---

[1] Kautilya says: "Sovereignty (rajatwa) is possible only with assistance. A single wheel can never more." The King "shal employ ministers and hear their opinion", Bk. I, Ch. VII, p. 14.

[2] "The Pluralist doctrine holds" writes Coker, "that the other associations arise naturally and spontaneously and that their essential functions in society are independent of state determination". (*Dunning's*, p. 89.) Dr. Hsiao has examined the pluralistic

the State "as it ought to be", and quite a different thing, however, to apply that principle of characterisation to any actual State, either in the present or of the past. If it is absolutely necessary for us to understand the nature of our ancient Polity in terms of Monism or Pluralism, we can only say that the State was neither pluralistic, nor barely monistic. It was, however, certainly unitary, and never federal. The local groups, it is true, were not products of decentralisation. Nor was the State the product of federation. Dr. Radhakumud Mookerji makes the fantastic assertion that the Mauryan Empire "aimed at an elastic system of federalism or confederation"[1] and makes a still more astounding assertion by maintaining that the ancient Indian institutions "became affiliated to the State under certain agreements."[2] The State does not, we admit, crush out the individuality of these local institutions, but this does not mean that these local groups had political significance as such, as against the State. The tendency, as we have observed, is towards a rigid centralisation so far as the political aspect of the State is concerned. If the various institutions within the State were allowed to live their independent life it is so because of the very ideal of Dharma which the State sought to maintain and realise. We shall discuss this question more fully when we determine the Province of Law. If it is inevitable that we should use the terms Monism and Pluralism, we would prefer to describe the ancient Indian State as

---

theory exhaustively, and declares: "Whatever may be the avenue of approach—whether it be through law and legal theory, through the problem of representative Government, or, lastly, through economic and social organisation—the final outcome of the pluralistic argument is, in every instance, not multiplicity as such (as we naturally expect) but some unity that transcends and points beyond mere multiplicity." (*Political Pluralism*), p. 127.

[1] See his *Local Govt. in Anc. Ind.*, pp. 7-10.

[2] *Ibid.*, pp. 5-7.

Monistic,[1] the principle of interpretation being furnished in that case by the very nature of the End the State sought to attain. Dharma is, as we have seen, in the last analysis, Swadharma and is determined by various factors, the most important being the Law of Karma. Inasmuch as the basis of Dharma itself is thus individualistic, it has a plural application. This has, perhaps, misled our scholars in hastily concluding that the ancient Indian State was pluralistic. "Briefly stated, the Indian theory favours neither anarchy nor the unqualified pluralism of discrete and isolated groups without reference to any nexus or solidarity as provided by the State, by Dharma, or otherwise."[2] In practice, the Indian State has always been an absolute autocracy, with a complicated system of administration under the direct or ultimate control of the central government.

We might, therefore, say that the basis of the State, is monistic, but expresses itself in its outward manifestation as pluralistic. Or, to be more accurate, we could express it by saying that the Indian State was a unity in diversity. This we shall realise more clearly if we try to understand the relations between the State and the other institutions.

We had observed that the primary duty of the king was to afford protection that thereby Dharma could be upheld. The subject was to be protected in the observance of his Dharma. He should suffer no disturbance or molestation while engaged in his duties. The function of the State thus seems to have a negative aspect, inasmuch as it is to remove obstacles or the hindrance of hindrances. But more is involved in the End of the Indian State than is discernible at the first glance. The State was not only

[1] Dr. Kung Chuan Hsiao says that a monarchy is necessarily a monistic state: *Political Pluralism*, p. 3.

[2] Introduction to *Local Govt. in Anc. Ind.* by R. Mookerji, pp. xxiii-xxiv.

to afford protection, but was also to keep the various orders and castes etc. in the due performance of their Swadharma and to prevent any allegiance. Nobody was to be allowed to take to the Dharma which was not his "Swadharma". The State was to prevent a confusion of duties. This would be impossible unless the State, in some way, entered into the life of each individual, group, order or caste. Even the adjustment of mutual relationships would not be possible unless the State is capable of entering into the spirit of the relationship itself. The State cannot be an "alien" factor, trying to adjust mutual relations from outside. It is only by imagining a world of things-in-themselves, of society, of church, of family, of guild etc. as isolated units that we might maintain that the state is a contrivance to decide mutual relations. We do not solve but add another complication by assuming, as Laski does, that Society is federal in its nature.[1] The state is held to be either a federation of social groups, religious, vocational etc., or that it is a community of communities, whose chief function is to keep the "ring." And so the function of the State is to restrict itself to the safeguarding of the rights of each component group or community. If society is federal we ask, what is that principle which links together the various elements in the Federation?[2] Is that principle inhering in the elements or external, and so imposed from without? What is external or "without", in the absolute sense? How can it bring together the separate elements in a federal union? If the principle of linkage is apart from the links, then, evidently

---

[1] There is a kind of Federalism in which there is no absolute division of power etc. which we are not discussing at present. Miss Follett calls it the true Federalism.

[2] Dr. Hsiao, in his *Political Pluralism*, says that Federalism and Monism are not incompatible, p. 7. He further says (p. 6) that "the idea of a legal sovereignty seems, nevertheless, to be present in a federal state.

there is no chain as a consistent whole. Moreover, to our consciousness, it is never presented, as if there were atomic elements called links existing as isolated units which were then brought together as the copula does a train. Our unit of experience is already a series. We do not think of the links and then of the linkage. A thing, in other words, can never be separated from its relations. Indeed it is not even comprehended but for its relations. The existence of no object is possible for knowledge unless we understand it in its relationships with other objects. A thing which exists in itself and by itself is a metaphysical absurdity.

And if we accept that no object could be known except through its relations ; or in other words, if our knowledge is relational, it is plain that no object which does not enter into relation with another object can even be known to that object. If we could make the bold assertion, we could postulate that no object is absolutely outside of any other object. There is something which is common to both which makes mutual cognisance possible ; and this something must in some way be inherent.

If the reluctance is to regard the State as that third something, the right attitude is to try to discover any higher factor than the State. Most Pluralists point to the idea that the Will of the State, is not all-inclusive : for Social Purposes are widely divergent. Our answer, then, is that the Pluralist has anyhow to search after an all-inclusive factor. There must be some institution whose purpose must be, according to them, the co-ordination of the groups. And this institution, we say, ought to have legal pre-eminence. Its decisions must be binding ; otherwise co-ordination is impossible. The idea of "negotiation" that Laski insists is very clumsy. If a stage is reached when a deadlock becomes inevitable unless things are allowed to drift into atomic chaos, some exercise of compelling force must be conceived if society is to cohere.

The Monist is not wrong when he refers to the State as possessing legal pre-eminence. The modern Idealist would go further and think of the State, not only as a legal institution, but also as ethical and moral. What we wish to point out here is that the function of co-ordination itself points to the necessary existence of an agent which would be monistic in nature. There must be in society a unitary or monistic principle which brings about a Unity of Purpose. Society cannot be simply regarded as a federation without first stating the principle that brings together the federal units, and without deciding the worth or value of that principle in relation to the life of the whole. This view that we insist would emphasise that society is a spiritual organism. We would not be satisfied with any other idea that seeks to explain the nature of our life. It must be understood in organic terms. Even to think of Society as an aggregate, as some modern philosophers do, will not satisfy us adequately. And so to postulate a Pluralistic Universe is to attempt the impossible task of describing a circle without the centre.

It is a paradox, therefore, which can never stand the light of reason to maintain that the State can restrict itself to "keeping the ring", and interfere only as an external factor. Even the adjustment of mutual relations presupposes the capacity of the State actively to enter into the life of each of the institutions between which the adjustment is to be effected. Without understanding the principle that is the basis of the particular association, how is it possible, we ask, to determine its relations with other institutions and adjust accordingly?

And, again, if the State were to keep the various component elements, be they individuals, castes, orders, or vocational groups, in the proper performance of their Swadharma, how could it be possible unless, somehow, the State could judge and determine what that "Swadharma" involved. Merely as an external factor, the State could never so regulate the life of the various Orders and Castes. The State must itself be the all comprehensive expression of the life of Society at large, if it is to function at all.

The State was the centre of Society in ancient India.[1] The king was the key-stone of the social arch. The king was not only the head of the State but also of Society.[2] It is a profound misunderstanding of the true significance of the Indian monarchy to maintain that "India presents the rare and remarkable phenomenon of the State and the Society co-existing apart from, and in some degree of independence of, each other, as distinct and separate units or entities, as independent centres of national, popular and collective life and activity".[3] A truer conception of the Indian Polity, it seems to us, is that maintained by Prof. Beni Prasad who realises that there is no clear distinction between Society and the State. The Polity is "all one whole. The same organisation is at once religious, political, economic and military. It is generally viewed in a comprehensive manner." This is due, as he rightly points out, to the fact that "the habit of looking at it primarily from the political angle of vision is not cultivated." That is why "of the social order and of Government as the agency of its enforcement the Hindu thinkers have a clear view, but the very insistence on these two concepts prevented them from formulating the idea of the State as distinct from either. Society was organised preeminently as society; Government was a part of that

---

[1] J. N. C. Ganguli's Article, p. 819, Vol. II, 1926. (*The Indian Historical Quarterly.*)

[2] R. Mookerji maintains however that "in ancient India the king was head of the State, but not of Society." (*Local Government*, pp. 3-19.)

Prof. P. Banerjee clearly admits that, in a sense, the king was head of the State. *Public Adm.*, p. 79.

[3] R. Mookerji: *Local Government*, pp. 3-19.

organisation, like the spiritual hierarchy, like the industrial and commercial mechanism." That is why, perhaps, "the conception of the State does not emerge very clearly." Prof. Beni Prasad,[1] however, does not go far enough but equates the State and Government, and since the Government was generally monarchical the king is the State. Government refers to the structure and working of the State, and the king was no doubt the head of the Government. But he was also something more than that. He was the protector or sustainer of "Dharma", which in its empirical aspect is the concretised Social Order. So, it was he who set the perspective of all the other institutions within Society. The End of the State, which was to maintain Dharma, that is Swadharma, would be impossible unless the king could so keep the various orders and castes, and institutions, respectively, to the performance of their duties. This function of the king, if it were not vitiated by the fundamental defect of the philosophy of life, characterised as it was, by the individualistic doctrine of Karma, could have in course of time so affected the life of Society that the State would have become a great co-operative whole, within which the different institutions would have lived and perfected their existence. Each social institution by virtue of its internal co-operative impetus would have inevitably demanded a wider scope, pointing to a co-operative whole, beyond itself. In other words the State could have become the Society of Societies ; co-operation within a particular society widening into the Co-operative Partnership of the Great Society in which each seeks and finds its membership. This involves, as we have seen, the idea of functional harmony, a true co-operative spirit, having its mainspring deeply rooted in the faith that we are members of each other.

If the State is, therefore, to set the perspective of all the

[1] *Theory of Government*, pp. 8-9.

other associations within it, the welter of particular purposes must be converted so that they shall make for a coherent whole. If each association seeks exclusively the good of its members, instead of aiming at complementing its efforts with the efforts of other institutions so that the general well-being of society is attained thereby, such institution, so far as its internal coherence is concerned might be general in its nature, but certainly isolated, and as such, particular, with reference to society as a whole. It is manifest, as G. D. H. Cole[1] also admits that "very many associations, in seeking a partial good for their own members, are acting anti-socially and impairing the coherence of society as a whole." So Social Purposes must be "placed in coherent relationships." This involves, not merely co-ordination, but the entering into the very spirit and life of the associations whose relationships ought to be so co-ordinated. All particular purposes must find their ultimate sanction and meaning in an all comprehensive Divine Purpose, which they partially embody. It is that purpose that must correlate the rights and duties in each association and between associations.

It is that purpose, again, that confers justification on the State, "as it is", to the extent it is fulfilled, and condemns the State to the extent it is not fulfilled. The State, in other words, is a moral institution, and must find its meaning in embodying the Divine Purpose. We shall return to the consideration of this vital question in our chapter on Political Obligations. What we wish to state here is that it is a partial way of looking at things if we say that the State is not ourselves with what it does and that it becomes ourselves "as it seeks to give expression to our wants and desires."[2] For, as we conceive it, there is really no antagonism between our wants and de-

---

[1] *Social Theory*, p. 53.

[2] Laski: *Grammar of Politics*, p. 35.

sires, and the fulfilment of the State. The individual, in the first place, is not merely finite.[1] Finitude which has for its End Infinity, must go through an eternal process of reaching out into the Universal Beyond. And, moreover, humanity is not a mere aggregate and no single man, however eccentric, can wholly stand outside it. And any judgment that he passes on it is, at any rate, at least a partial judgment of himself. The State is thus, "the universal in which each of us, as particulars, finds our meaning." The State itself might be, and certainly from our point of view is, particular in respect to the purpose it seeks all through the ages, as its End. We do not deny the value of the pragmatic method; and the State, "as it is", is to be judged in reference to its concrete achievements and failures. But what we wish to point out is that the very criterion of judgment points to the State which is the ideal, or the State, "as it ought to be." Moral adequacy is not the view-point merely of the individual who is finite; for the nature of the individual himself is essentially universal. The conflict is not between the individual and the State or between the State and Society. It surely arises, we admit, if they are viewed at as particulars, and when the individual could isolate himself from his herd, and is standing, "outside it and passing judgment upon its actions." In a spiritual organism no single member could so try to be an individual-in-himself. The true conflict is between the Real and the Actual, and not between the Real and the Ideal.

And not only that. It is the ideal that confers validity

---

[1] "Any adequate theory of Social Organisation must always begin by recognising that the individual is finite. If he is a member of the herd, he is also outside it and passing judgment upon its actions." *Ibid.*, *Laski Grammar*, p. 29.

upon the actual.[1] The State, "as it is", is to be judged in terms of the State, "as it ought to be". Particular achievements and failures might be submitted to the pragmatic test; but a judgment which is ostensibly from the point of view, as is claimed to be, of the individual who is finite can never be morally adequate to determine the rightness of not only the State as the ideal, but we venture to add, also of the "State, as it is".

To return, therefore, to our consideration of the State in its relation to society, or the other associations within it, our criterion is not to judge the State from the standpoint of view of the individual, or any particular group. There are no individuals by themselves whom we could regard as units in an aggregate. There are no groups, again, which can be abstracted from the Reality which is the whole and treated as such. The new individualism lays emphasis on groups considered as units. The individualists to-day are corporate individualists. The new individualism rests on the antithesis between the group and the State. The interest is centred in the groups, vocational or regional as the case may be; and the State itself is treated with scant courtesy. Modern writers, under the influence of this new individualism try to apply their conclusions in judging the nature of the Ancient Indian State. They maintain that the various institutions in society were either apart from the State or were independent, autono-

[1] "The ideal", says Sir Henry Jones, "is the truth of the real. The real has not realised itself until it is the incarnation of the ideal; for until that time its potentialities are *only* potentialities, latent forces indwelling but imprisoned, straining towards light and liberty." (*The Principles of Citizenship*, p. 75.) He further on says, "the ideal that is *only* ideal is empty; and the real that is not disturbed by an ideal which is its own and its inmost secret and substance, is inert, with the inertness and helplessness of death. Ideal and real cannot be held apart. They are related to one another as the life of the living is to its outward structure". (p. 76.)

mous units. This misconception, as we pointed out, is due to the character of Dharma itself. Dharma is Swadharma and the State should maintain it. The King had to see that the various castes, orders, and other institutions were duly engaged in the performance of their Swadharma. In exceptional cases the King could even interfere with the scheme of Dharma itself, and compel, as the necessity demands, a reshuffling of duties. All these point, not to the limitation of the King's sphere of action, but to the peculiar character of that action itself. If there were certain regions into which the King is not to enter, it is not that he is theoretically prohibited from doing so, but that the nature of the State itself is such that it does not necessitate interference except in exceptional cases. The relation between Dharma and the State is a reciprocal relation. If Dharma maintains the realm, the King, however, is to protect it. Law, therefore, depends as much on the King as he on it. Not that the King was above the law; but the law that has validity with respect to him, and as against him, is not the law that he applies or administers. We shall consider again this aspect more fully. What we wish to point out is that the King is not under the obligation of the ordinary law which he administers. In that limited sense we might say that he was above the Law.[1] This is especially visible with

[1] In other words, we cannot maintain the supremacy of Law over the State, if by Law we mean something positive which modern jurists have made familiar. Law in the modern sense, is that which is made or decreed by the State. It is the creation of the political power of the State and as such must be held to be below the State. But there is another sense of the term "Law" which we cannot ignore; and in all ancient theories, it was used in this wider sense. The Aristotlean conception of Law has its affinities with the Indian conception of Dharma, for to Aristotle, Law was "the system of rational order co-extensive and identical with the human reason". It is, as Dr. Hsiao says, the objective manifestation of moral rule in the social realm; or as the Indian

regard to Varna-dharma. Rules of pollution do not apply to him. He may touch an "untouchable" and still remain pure. The King himself may be a member of the lower castes as often he has been in history, but yet he is to be venerated as god on earth. In fact the King, once he becomes the ruler, is above caste. He also is above ordinary codes. He can do no wrong; in other words, he himself is immune from punishment; otherwise he cannot wield the rod of punishment.

So whenever we notice the obligation of the King to maintain the various laws of families, guilds, tribes, peoples, castes, orders etc., this does not point to a limitation of the sphere of the State, but as we have already pointed out to the nature of law itself. The Province of Law can only be understood, as we shall presently see, with reference to the Doctrine of Swadharma. Historically considered, it might also be possible that the State, a late product, when it comes to be super-imposed on the other associations, could not but accept them as they were. Fustel de Coulanges has shown how this had taken place in Greece and Rome.[1] And we have no reasons to hold that things were different in Ancient India.[2] But

---

thinkers have envisaged, the principle underlying the Social Order. And if Law is understood in this sense, "since the State as actual political power is never near the level of perfection, it is obvious that the State should acknowledge its inferiority to the ideal of law". Dr. Hsiao: *Political Pluralism*, p. 10.

[1] The Ancient City.

[2] Dr. Hsiao examines the argument that since society is an organisation of a multiplicity of interests and purposes there must also be a multiplicity of legal systems in order to give full expression to them. He refuses to see how the argument could lead to Pluralism. He says: "for no matter how far we decentralise our social organisation, no matter into how many departments we divide our social life, and no matter, consequently, how many centres of law-making we establish, so long as we uphold social solidarity as the all competent principle of Political organisation,

once the State is so established, it tends by its inherent logical necessity to become the Society of societies. "The other forms of community which precede and are independent of the formation of the State do not continue to exist outside it; nor yet are they superceded by it. They are carried into it. They become its organic members, supporting its life and in turn maintained by it in a new harmony with each other."[1] And the first manifestation of the State in its political aspect is thus the integrating cf the diverse principles of the different institutions in society, and the subordinating of all such societies in the organic union of the wider, comprehensive whole.

The king is the key-stone of the whole edifice and he is himself the supreme manifestation of the principle of integration.[2] As the protector of Dharma, he is the principle which is the "operative criticism" running through the numerous institutions of the social order. In him, as we have seen, are vested all the powers which are the essential attributes of sovereignty. By the time the functions of the State are most completely developed, especially on the judicial side, we find the King attaining

all these pluralities must finally be ordered and unified by this principle into an Absolute system." *Political Pluralism*, pp. 19-20.

We may note here the theory of legal personality of Dr. Gierke and Maitland. According to them the state and other groups are species of one genus. But the problem is whether the corporation which is considered as a person is "merely a collection of isolated individuals or whether it is an organismic entity, possessing a real will of its own." If we accept Dr. Gierke's view that the corporation by virtue of its distinct purpose, possesses "a group will"; distinct from the private wills of its members, must we not, asks Dr. Hsiao, by the same line of reasoning, attribute also a real will to the State, and conceive the State as an organic unity, namely, as a "real person"?

(*Political Pluralism*, pp. 35-36.)

[1] T. H. Green: *Political Obligation*, p. 146.

[2] See Sen Gupta's *Sources of Law and Society*, Part I.

to a position of pre-eminence commanding the obedience of people to an unusual degree. "To such a man all power in the society would naturally tend to gravitate."[1] We have every reason to think that the law-givers like Manu, Narada and Yajnavalkya were only registering accomplished facts, so that their theories were not divergent from the practice of their times. And in them "we find the kingship in the zenith of power. The autonomous village and minor societies appear to have considerably dwindled in authority and in Yajnavalkya are clearly supervised by leaders appointed by the King; judicial power of the King original and appellate has grown to enormous proportions and popular tribunals are reduced to a position of inferiority, exercising their functions by sufferance and subject to correction by the King. All the power that there is in the State centres round the King and the old societies retained a part of their own authority by a sort of delegation."[2]

Another important characteristic of the Indian State which has been variously interpreted remains to be noticed. We have seen that "the more Brahmanical culture spread in the course of centuries, the more did the priestly classes succeed in stamping their desired physiognomy upon the Indian society through their religious and social influence." And so far as social organisation was concerned, it was thoroughly saturated with theocratic ideas. But does this mean that the State as represented by the King was only "an appendage of the priests?" So far as we are able to judge, the State never became subordinate to the priestly organisation; and the Brahmans were always dependent on the King. Only in this sense however, is it true to maintain that politics were free from theological influences. But the State itself was

---

[1] Sen Gupta: *Sources of Law and Society*, Part I, p. 23.

[2] *Ibid.*, p. 24.

in a sense theocratic. It was the highest expression of the regulative principle of the social order. To imagine that it was not the reflection of "the theological and metaphysical environments" and could be absolutely unaffected by the ideas of the people is to suppose that the State can exist in vacuum.[1] It would signify that the End of Life, and the philosophical conception of the universe as conceived by Hindu thinkers could have no bearings at all on the Polity, and that the State was alien to the conditions of the Society of the times. The necessity, therefore, so to relate the political life to other aspects of social existence, has however led most of our writers to the expression of very peculiar and inconsistent statements. Dr. Bhandarkar admits that the Hindu State of Kautilya was based on religious foundation and that its social arrangement was looked upon as coming down from the Veda and so the Vedic character of the State reduced it to "something like a socio-religious state."[2] Prof. Banerjea states that the State never became a theocracy in the proper sense of the term ; but admits that the King was the protector, though not the head of religion ; and in his executive capacity he guided and to some extent controlled, the religious and moral life of the people. We need, therefore, to understand the Indian Polity more clearly ; for "it is not possible, judging from the religious bent of the ancient Hindus, that their political thoughts, aspirations, and activities, should have remained in absolute isolation from religion."[3] The clue to the

[1] Dr. Bhandarkar maintains that: "It is no longer correct to affirm that the Indians never freed their politics from the theological and metaphysical environments." *Some Aspects of Anc. Hindu Polity*, p. 3. The opinion of Dr. Bhandarkar is also emphasised by almost every writer on India.

[2] See Bandyopadhyaya: *Kautilya*, pp. 39; 46; especially p. 68 where he says that "Kautilya was a believer in the older sacerdotal theory of Dharma and its excellence over the body-politic".

[3] N. Law: *Aspects of Anc. Ind. Polity*, p. 142.

proper interpretation of the nature of the Indian State lies in the End it sought to achieve. "The State", as N. Law points out, "under the direction of the sovereign, leads the people under its protection to the final goal of human existence—emancipation—furnishing at the same time means therefor."[1] And so even the State, far from being freed from theological and metaphysical influences, itself subserves the spiritual purpose of man The monarch, indeed, looks upon the spiritual interests of his people as far soperior to their material interests.[2] Religious ideas "coloured the whole system from the State-ideal to the innermost strata".[3] And to suppose, therefore, that the Ancient State rested purely on positive bases is to misjudge the most essential of the characteristics of the Polity. "In regard to oriental monarchies we have to realise", writes Benoy Kumar Sarkar, "first, that Hindu states were thoroughly secular. In India paradoxical as it may seem to pre-conceived notions, religion is never known to have dominated political history or philosophy". (*The Political Institutions and Theories of the Hindus*, pp. 13-14). The State, we admit, was not theocratic in the sense that it was merely an "apendage of the priests." But it was certainly theocratic in the highest sense, for, without it, the conditions of the spiritual life could never be secured. That is why, as we shall presently see, the very conception of sovereignty was spiritualised. Though in a certain sense, there existed no State-religion in India,[4] religion, in its largest significance was certainly the very core of the Polity. Royal patronage was extended to all religious sects and faiths. The monarch himself was the supreme representative of the Divine. In him were synthesised the various prin-

[1] *Aspects of Anc. Ind. Polity*, p. 145.
[2] N. Law: *Ibid.*, p. 143.
[3] *Ibid.*, p. 151.
[4] Max Muller: *Six Systems*, p. 34.

ciples of social life. Though in origin kingship was to some extent military in character, it possessed always a religious significance. In all early polities the King was not only the war-chief but the High Priest as well. In India a priestly class begins to develop independently and we have traces of conflict between the secular and temporal elements, between Brahmins and Kshatriyas. The episode of Parasurama seems to indicate the temporary triumph of the priestly power ; but, whatever that might be, the necessity for an understanding seems to have been very early recognised. A sort of *entente cordiale* is established which was never seriously disturbed during all the centuries. We might even say that the priestly element became stronger from its being subordinated to the State ; for under its protection and patronage it was afforded the opportunity to permeate every aspect of life. When the necessity to be the representative of the military principle exclusively, gradually passed away, the monarch himself, in the capacity of the protector and sustainer of Dharma, became the expression of "the integration of the religious and military principles in a manner which gave to the military principle itself a secondary position.[1] The King was "a joint offshoot of the military and the religious principles."[2] He is, though not the head, at least the protector of religion. Religion was not conceived to be a human product, and the State, as represented by the King, is itself to accept it on authority. The State itself is under the spirit which rules the other institutions in society ; but being the centre of all life, and the condition of the life of the component institutions, and being entrusted with the maintenance of the Social Order, the State has supervisory, censorial watch and ward power over all. The position of the great Emperor Asoka to-

[1] Sen Gupta: ***Sources of Law and Society*, p. 20.**

[2] ***Ibid.***

wards religion or Dharma will enable us to realise the relation that subsisted between Religion and the State. The institution of "Dharma-mahamatras" was "in accordance with Hindu notions";[1] the primary purpose of the institution of "espionage", according to *Santi Parva*, "as we have already noticed, was to keep watch over the proper adherence to Dharma. The example of Asoka was "readily imitated in later times by rulers of various religions,"[2] by Harsha, by Kumarapala, and by rulers even in modern times. The State enforced very strictly the observance of Dharma and severely punished offenders against religion. The toleration,[3] that is so much talked about, never did really exist, if by toleration we understand the liberty of the individual to follow the dictates of his own conscience. Toleration had reference to the doctrine of "Swadharma". If the State allowed the different sects to subsist and even sometimes extended patronage to all, this in no way signifies that the principle of toleration was the guiding factor. The key to a proper understanding lies in trying to find out how far an individual, as such, could follow freely, not only in the mere expression of opinion, but in the translation of such opinion into the practice of every-day life, the dictates of his conscience. Indian toleration went only so far as the expression of opinion was concerned. A man may profess any principle; only he must never attempt to translate it into practice. "The conscientious objector was not permitted to allege his conscience as a justification for acts disapproved on principle by the government. Men might believe what they liked, but must do as they were told".

[1] V. A. Smith: *Early Hist. of Ind.*, p. 181.

[2] *Ibid.*, pp. 181-182.

[3] See the very sympathetic article on *Persecution* (Indian) by A. S. Geden in the *Ency. Rel. and Ethi.*, Vol. 9.

[4] V. A. Smith: *Early History of India*, p. 179.

Having thus decided the sphere of state-action, it remains for us to determine what the nature of the State is. We are inclined to hold that the State does not essay to secure the Good or Virtuous life for each and all of its members by any direct contribution of a positive nature. If Dharma were not Swadharma, the State could have employed itself in such an ordering of socity that the Good as the End would be the social or corporate embodiment of the aspiration of the community. The doctrines of Karma and of Swadharma preclude any such activity on the part of the State. As we have already observed the very idea of Dharma does not involve the idea of justice or righteousness in its moral significance; or that of justice or righteousness in its social implications. The truly ethical or moral must be essentially social as well. The good must be social, or no good at all. The non-social is also non-ethical and non-moral. If social justice is mutilated, Dharma cannot have reference to the coherence or excellence of the whole community, but to parts of it considered as "ends".[1] And if we further remember that Dharma as the concretised Social Order is held to be fixed, and incapable of modifications by any human agency, we shall realise that social justice or Dharma in the true ethical or moral significance, as we would understand it, can never be realised through the Hindu State. The Varnashrama Dharma being eternal must be accepted by the State. The function of the State is to keep the Social Order intact, a Social Order, the philosophy of which does not admit modification. What is, is conceived to be, is as it ought to be. "The aim of the

[1] *Santi Parva*, 16-19; 23.

"......the ultimate goal of social justice is the well-being of all the people."

"......equal justice can be given to all members of a society only if the end that society, pursues is such that it can be shared."—Pipkin: *The Idea of Social Justice*, pp. 551-559.

ancient Indian State was less to introduce an improved *Social* order", says Rangaswamy Iyengar, "than to act in conformity with the established *moral* order of the *Universe*."[1] And so "the root principle of our ancient Polity was that every function of the State had to be conditioned by and to be subordinated to the need to preserve both society and the State."[2] The End of the State is Stability, and not Progress.

The primary emphasis is thus laid in the necessity to maintain Law and Order. The State is to a large extent a "Police State"; meaning by "Police" not the mere organisation of the coercive power, but the enforcement of justice, in its legal aspects. Justice is judicial in nature; and the State as maintaining Dharma, primarily concerns itself with the organisation and the administration of justice. The king is the Dandadhara, or he who holds the sceptre of justice. The Rod of Chastisement is the emblem of sovereignty.

Our discussion has led us to conclude that in ancient India there was practically no limit to state-action and that the State was an autocracy, limited not by any positive factors, but by its very nature and End. If the End of the State, the maintenance of Dharma, had reference to the coherence and excellence of the whole Polity, we would certainly have accepted the facts of the Ancient Indian Polity as of supreme value for us even at the present day. There cannot be, we hold, any limit to the sphere of the State, if the State is an institutional response to the organised ideals and aspirations of the whole community, and also of the complex facts of human life. But the Hindu State was only a partial response. Its End had reference to particular elements in it only; and so the unlimited sphere of state-action, so long as that action is

---

[1] p. 72 ff.

[2] p. 73.

not the expression of the Corporate Will, is an unmitigated tyranny to the "despised", "depressed", and "dispossessed". The lower castes were, indeed, those on whom the burden or weight of the State most lay.

And inasmuchas the Social Order was supposed to be eternal and the individual was required to regulate his life according to scriptural injunctions, the maintenance of Dharma has in course of centuries resulted in the sterility of the Indian genius and the stagnation of the springs of life. Only that State, therefore, which is a true reflex of the complex of human life, is entitled to the exercise of power ; only that society, which is based on organic or natural principles can ever hope to live. The great problem is how to reconcile Order and Progress in a higher synthesis. There can be no unlimited rights to power, if its exercise does not seek to attain a progressive fulfilment of the Divine Purpose. The sphere of state-action can be allowed to be unlimited only when the Nature of the State is such that it shall be determined by the aims it subserves. And these aims must seek to embrace every element of the Polity, and be essentially formulated on the idea which Kant so profoundly insists, of the sacredness of Humanity in each individual. The Purpose of the State must seek to reflect the holiness of the Purpose of each individual. Mere particular interests may be chaotic, but if purposive could be raised from their mere welter into a larger coherence which shall stamp its perfection on the Nature of the Polity.

CHAPTER VI

THE CONCEPTION OF SOVEREIGNTY

'The truth is that when pluralism sets out to prove that there is no ultimate authority in society and that there should not be such authority it proposes a task which cannot be accomplished. For an ultimate sovereignty there must be, whether we find it in "natural law" "in reason", in "social solidarity", or in the individual's "sense of right". Furthermore, as soon as we admit the existence of an ultimate power, we must provide a definite channel for its expression—we must establish in other words, a "determined person", as the jurists say, through whom the voice of the common good is heard.'

(Dr. Hsiao: *Political Pluralism*, p. 139.)

"The Self properly understood is itself the sovereign."

Anugita.

We have discussed the end of the Ancient Indian State and determined the sphere of State-action. The maintenance of Dharma, as we have seen, involved extensive powers concentrated in the hands of the King. He could enforce obedience and visit wrong doers with the penalties of the law. Protection could only be afforded if the State was credited with the necessary coercive power to punish offenders against the harmony of the polity. Dharma could be maintained by a proper wielding of Danda. Artharakshana implied dushta-sikshana. Kautilya, therefore, regarded the King as the sole repository of coercive power.[1] His commands were respected because he had the power to compel obedience ; otherwise he could never be regarded as sovereign. We do not imply that the mere possession of supreme physical force constitutes his sovereignty. It is sufficient for us to note that obedience to his commands is habitually rendered by the mass of men. The power exercised by the King might have had various

[1] See Bandyopadhyaya: *Kautilya*, pp. 44-59.

sanctions, and physical force might have been only one such. The acquiescense of the people might be also due to the force of custom and habit, or to the strength of religious sentiment. The significant fact is that obedience does exist. The commands of the King were authoritative. He was the determinate superior capable of expressing the highest commands of the State. Against his pronouncements there was no appeal in the legal sense.

There have been attempts by certain modern writers to establish the limited nature of the monarchy in ancient India. With the growing acceptance of the doctrines of political pluralism, the tendency to press too much into the facts of the ancient polity is becoming more pronounced. We know how "the idea of a command seems too frequently to have carried with it to the minds of many thinkers the notion that a law must somehow be an arbitrary expression of the sovereign's unmotivated or purely selfish 'will' or caprice,—that it must be evolved in his inner consciousness out of nothing, and without any regard for the customary or ideal notions of right and wrong which men ordinarily consult in determining their conduct."[1] We would be perfectly justified in rejecting the idea if this be the meaning that is to be given to the word "command". Laws, as the sovereign's "commands", are not certainly his arbitrary creations, but are themselves the crystallised embodiments of the prevailing opinions of morality and righteousness.

We are also aware that, as Bryce has pointed out, there is an instinctive opposition to power which is based upon mere force and people naturally refuse to submit to it.[2] Arbitrary exercise of power ultimately invites resistance and the dread of revolution acts as a potential check. As we shall presently see, the exercise of sovereign power is

[1] John Dickinson: Article on *A Working Theory of Sovereignty. Pol. Science Quar.*, Vol. XLIII.

[2] *Studies in History and Jurisprudence*, Vol. II, p. 516.

always under certain limitations. But this does not detract anything from the essence of sovereignty. The relevant question with which we are concerned is that in every political society there is always a sovereign person or group competent to enforce its decisions. Under modern conditions, we do recognise that it is no easy task to seek to discover the real rulers in the State. This is due not to the non-existence of any ultimate authority as such, but to the complex conditions that defy analysis. Even Austin himself "fully recognises the existence of communities, or aggregates of men, in which no dissection could disclose a person or a group answering to his definition of a sovereign."[1]

This does not imply that there is no sovereign. As Sir Henry Maine asserts, this person may be discovered certainly as the centre of gravity in a mass of matter.[2] We are also aware that a purely legal emphasis might not take cognisance of the political aspect of Sovereignty, the power behind the legal sovereign before which the legal sovereign must bow in deference. This power might be the potential battle in the people at large, or it might be operative through the constitutional arrangements of the polity where they exist. As Ritchie has well put it, the problem of good government is the problem of effecting a proper relation between the legal sovereign and the political sovereign. Only in such a state where this harmony exists can there be peace.[3] But such reciprocity can only be secured in a pure democracy where the expressed will of the people through the electorate is law itself. But this is so because the power of the people is expressed

[1] Maine: *Early History of Institutions*, p. 377. (1893)

[2] *Ibid.*, p. 349.

[3] "The will of the legal sovereign is or should be the authorised embodiment or manifestation of the will of the political sovereign."

McKechnie: *The State and the Individual*, p. 131.

through legally constituted channels and made ultimately to prevail. Sovereignty, in that case, may rest with the "general will" as Rousseau would have it, or even "in the working of the system of institutions as a whole."[1]

We are also aware that the legal theory of sovereignty might be worthless considered from the moral point of view; its legal right to prevail does not constitute its moral sanction to exist, as Laski has well pointed out. It is true again, that certain forces always do exert a sinister influence on the sovereign who yields himself to exploitation, and it is the imperative necessity of our life to insist, along with Laski, that the policy of the State "is only sovereign where it is serving the Sovereign purpose" which is the "unique realisation of the common good."[2] The determinate person or group, considered as legal sovereign, might become oppressive in the exercise of power; for "in sober fact", says Laski, "government is exerted in the interest of those who control its exercise." Disobedience would then become a moral duty and revolution the safety valve that could operate in the last resort. The legal sovereign, for the time being in power, would be set aside and a new sovereign set up who thereafter is looked upon as the ultimate legal authority. Through revolution a re-location of legal sovereignty takes place. Legal sovereignty, as such, however, is never dispensed with and cannot be dispensed with. Revolutions is only an extra-legal remedy and can only be applied as an extreme necessity; it cannot be regarded as a normal weapon. Revolution implies a lapse to anarchy. Juristic sovereignty is "an essential lever of progress."[3]

In every State, therefore, there exists "some organ whose authority is unlimited."[4] That organ in the ancient

---

[1] *Philosophical Theory of the State*, p. XXIX.
[2] *Authority in the Modern State*, pp. 40-41.
[3] John Dickinson: *Article in Political Science Quarterly*, p. 34.
[4] Laski: *Foundations of Sovereignty*, pp. 236-237.

Indian Society was the King. He was the condition of the permanence of political society. The sovereignty which resided with him was passed on in perpetuity automatically to a new recipient on his demise. There was no period when sovereignty could be said to have been in abeyance. Sovereign authority, that is to say, was constantly and continuously operative. There was no interregnum on the death of a King, for, according to the well established practice, the eldest son succeeded to the throne. Primogeniture was the recognised principle. Only on exceptional occasions was the right of the eldest son set aside. Sometimes, it might be that a King, feeling his end approaching, might nominate his successor. Or he might even abdicate and pass on to his nominee his sovereign authority in his own life time. If in either case the choice happened to fall on any other except his eldest son, the people at large might have the feeling that the procedure was unusual, but nobody would think of questioning the competency of the King to dispose of the succession as he pleased. Sovereignty would devolve on the nominee as a right. The subsequent act of coronation may be considered necessary to confer dignity and sanctity on the person who occupied the throne. But it did not confer any legal right which the prince did not possess already. The act of coronation was a ceremonial function registering the fact of the accession and might imply the official commencement of the new reign. But what is very important to notice is the fact that the new King does not become legally sovereign because he is crowned; he is crowned because he is the legal sovereign. For, if we hold that the coronation ceremony alone confers the right to rule, then we shall have to seek for that person or institution that determines the ceremonial and performs it and then recognise that person or institution as the ultimate legal sovereign. The prince himself would not in that case be considered to be sovereign until he is appointed as such by the act of coronation. And we know that the ceremony itself is of a religious character to be performed by Brahmins according to the Scriptures. If we look upon the coronation as conferring legal sovereignty, then we would be inevitably led to the conclusion that those who determined the ceremonial and performed it were legally sovereign in the ultimate sense, the crown being at their disposal. We are reminded of the famous struggle between the Empire and the Papacy during the Middle Ages. This is not the place to discuss the strength of their rival claims, but it is sufficient to point out that a recognition of ecclesiastical pretensions over the disposal of the crown would certainly lead us to the inevitable acceptance of ecclesiastical supremacy. Evidently both the temporal and spiritual powers cannot be regarded to be legally sovereign at one and the same time, for dual sovereignty leads to perpetual conflict; for it would have meant establishing an *imperium in imperio*. In the end one of the two must prevail. We cannot, moreover, regard the spiritual authority as sovereign even until the act of coronation and that the Prince becomes sovereign ever thereafter, the spiritual authority having surrendered power once and for all. For sovereignty is inalienable. As a matter of fact, there was no occasion for a conflict to arise between Church and State in the ancient Indian Society; there was an *entente cordiale* between the two. We may even regard the King as representing in himself the principles of both as he was himself looked upon and as a sort of a divinity. A sacred halo surrounded the occupant of the throne. The King did not, therefore, become sovereign because supreme power was conferred on him by the coronation ceremony. The oaths and pledges taken on that occasion are of a formal character and should not be interpreted too literally. The new King begins to reign from the moment that the old King ceased to reign. The King, that is to say, according to the Indian conception, never dies. That is the implication of the principle of hereditary succession. In ancient times, we rarely have fratricidal wars of succession in this country. The crown was not looked upon as the prize of the fittest that survived. On the demise of a King the Polity was not dissolved into the original chaos to be rescued only by the strong hand that succeeds in suppressing or destroying all competitors in the field. The incidents that have stained the annals of Islamaic polity were due to the uncertainty in the Law of Succession. Every son of a King in the Muslim State was looked upon as equally entitled to succeed; primogeniture was not a sacred thing. A successful prince usually waded through a welter of blood to reach to the throne. Once finally seated, moreover, he would take every precaution to see that his reign would not be disturbed thereafter by wars of disputed succession, by removing by every possible means all claimants in the field out of his path. The usual method would be to blind all princes royal. We rarely hear of such things in the Hindu State. The sovereignty of the King was the guarantee of the continuity of civil society, and it was never in abeyance. In the exceptional cases when a King is reported to be deposed or expelled what we really have is a revolution. There was no constitutional machinery provided for, as we have seen, in the ancient Indian State to operate against a tyrannical monarch. If the ministers successfully conspired against him and removed him from power, or if the people expelled him by force they were really effecting a revolution. Our modern writers are not very careful in drawing distinctions and hence many false notions are given wide currency. What is significant, however, for our present purpose is that legal sovereignty as such was never dispensed with. Whatever might be the weapon adopted to get rid of a reigning King, every possible haste was taken to see that a new sovereign is installed in his place. If this is effected by the mantriparishad, or the samiti, that body acted only in an extra-legal capacity. To express it in technical language the mantri-parishad or the samiti is the *de facto* sovereign. It might set up a new King who in course of time may be recognised as lawful.[1] By the acquiescence of the people, the new King may come to be regarded as the legal sovereign in the State. And this legal sovereign is not himself limited by any positive provisions or constitutional devices. His sovereignty, so long as he could effectively exercise his power, was unlimited and absolute.

This sovereignty, moreover, was exclusively in the King. He did not share it with any other person or institution in the State. The Pluralistic theory completely fails in affording us any clue to the proper interpretation of our ancient Polity. We are not for the present concerned with the moral aspect of the question. We shall discuss that in our chapter on Political Obligation. Our attempt here is only to understand the nature of state-sovereignty in our ancient polity. Prof. Beni Prasad maintains[2] that "the monistic theory of sovereignty as applied to the state or government, fails completely ; only a pluralistic theory can grasp the Indian phenomena". According to him "the State was only one of the groups to which the individual belonged". Dr. Radhakamal Mukherjee also expresses a similar view when he says that "the merest knowledge of Oriental history would prove inadequate the unity or absoluteness of the State predicated by Hobbes, Austin, or Hegel", for the "State is by nature and history plura-

---

[1] The Glorious Revolution of 1688 illustrates our contention. The *de jure* sovereign James II was set aside by the Convention Parliament which was the *de facto* sovereign for the time being. The Crown was offered by the Convention Parliament to William and Mary who became legally sovereign in course of time by the acquiescence of the people. What was really effected was a revolution in spite of the disguise of constitutional procedure.

[2] *Theory of Government in Ancient India*, p. 9.

listic".[1] It would appear that these writers have imperfectly grasped the facts of our ancient Polity in their enthusiasm to read their modern theories into it. They are perhaps following the trend of Laski's thought, for we know that Laski insists that the State is merely a co-ordinating body and that it is only "one among many forms of human association".[2] According to him there is "no thought of unity"[3] in the allegiance of the individual. The ancient Indian State was not merely one association among other institutions. As we have already seen, it was the supreme institution of institutions which set the perspective of the rest. Prof. Beni Prasad is not right and he is following the trend of the thought of Laski, perhaps, if we might add, a little imperfectly. To Laski, our allegiance itself is as a fact, not unified, whereas Prof. Beni Prasad can conceive of a simple loyalty "to society as a whole". As we have already discussed, there was no antithesis between society and the State in ancient India ; and if the State be the key-stone of the social arch, the centre of the Polity, there seems to be no difficulty in trying to accept the Monist's contention. The perplexity is due to a misunderstanding of the Monist's position. So far as the life of our ancients is concerned, we might recognise that it was enclosed within what may be termed concentric circles of loyalty. The State, as represented by the King, claimed the highest allegiance of the people. There was no clash of loyalties and the State had not to compete with other groups in the claim it made on the allegiance of its members. The King, who represented the State, was something like a Zeus Agamennon ; he was verily a god in human shape than whom there was no other god on earth ; *Na Vishnu Prithvipathi*. The individual

[1] *Democracies of the East*, p. 24.
[2] *Grammar of Politics*, p. 69.
[3] *Problem of Sovereignty*, p. 11.

gave his loyalty at once to all the groups to which he belonged; but it was a loyalty which was widening in its scope, until it found its highest empirical expression in its relation to the State.

The fatal confusion in the analysis of most of our modern writers is due to the misunderstanding of the nature of society itself. "It is integral to the proper understanding of any given society", says Laski, "that it should be regarded as essentially federal in its nature."[1] If that were so, are the federal units be they individuals or groups connected with one another by relations which possess continuity? Do they remain as separate and persistent objects, existing side by side, in space and time? To our mind it appears that to interpret society as in its nature federal, is too mechanical to serve for an adequate understanding. A federation rests on the idea that the component elements or groups are brought together in some sort of union, but from which the conception of unity is excluded. The idea of unity, especially in its reference to human beings who are in nature spiritual, involves the interpretation of each individual in relation to a comprehensive whole, the awareness of which relation to the larger purpose of the Universal constitutes the meaning of every such particular or individual. This is possible as we have seen, because every individual is in his nature himself Universal. The difficulty can only be bridged over when we cease to think in special terms of the co-existence of objects, individuals or groups in society. No individual or group in society is wholly outside any other individual or group. Society is a spiritual organism of which the members seek and find meaning and purpose only in relation to it as a whole. The Unity to which they belong is larger than that of the group, be it family or guild, caste or order, with which, in the more immediate con-

[1] *Grammar of Politics*, p. 59.

tacts of life, they appear to be more intimately connected. The group itself, though general in reference to its members is particular in reference to the larger system to which it belongs. Facts or actualities may seem to belie the truth implied in our statement; but as we hold, the world of facts must be appraised in terms of value. Then certainly, all physical conceptions of social life would be proved fallacious; and the real character of the federal theory is revealed in all its implications.

The mere presence of various associations side by side, therefore, does not warrant us to maintain that they are brought together on a federal basis, the State being the factor that functions in the co-ordinating process. The State does not merely, as MacIver supposes, regulate "the outstanding external relations of men in society".[1] It is very difficult to determine what the external relations are and what the internal. No man can live a double life, the one abstracted from the other. The process of coordination or mutual adjustment really implies much more than what appears on the surface. The State purely as an external factor can never fulfil the function.

And if the State cannot function merely as an external or alien factor, it must enter actively into the life of every individual or group within it.[2] The State is not simply one association or group among other groups. The pluralists' revolt is the reaction against the State as wrongly understood. "The State" writes Laski, "like man, ceases to be human when it is exalted into Godhead. We dare not so exalt it lest we be imprisoned by the errors of the past. For it is ours to hand down undimmed the torch of cons-

---

[1] *The Modern State*, p. 5.

[2] "The mutual implication of state and citizen has the unity and intensity of a single life." Sir Henry Jones: *Principles of Citizenship*, p. 90. See also his *The Working Faith of the Social Reformer*, p. 100 ff., and p. 272.

cious life".[1] And the modern era that has seen the pluralist's attack also is the witness to the exaltation of the State to a degree never attained to before in the history of man. We do not refer to the theoretical exposition of ideas, but the State as it has actually become. Hitherto we had the Divine Right of kings ; now we have the Divine Right of the State. That proud title was "transferred from the person to the incarnate State. The mystic name that had exalted the obvious reality of the King now crowned a being as mystic as itself, the omnipotent majesty of the State."[2] The pluralist is perfectly justified in his attack, so far as it is directed against the external ideas of thinkers like Trietske ; and we are one with him there. But the Monist's position need not necessarily be identified with the extremism of Trietske. Monistic explanations of Society and State, we admit, are inadequate, if for no other reason but that they are at least too simple. We recognise that the problem is very complex but the right approach is to recognise unity in diversity.

Again, we admit that it is dangerous to attribute omnipotence to the State as it is. We are one with the pluralist in this respect. Our allegiance to the State is not to "what is", but to "what ought to be". Even the consciousness of other groups than the State need not mislead us into false interpretations. Our allegiance is a unified allegiance, if for no other reason, but that our personality, and indeed, even our consciousness, themselves are unified. We have no divisions of loyalty attached to parts of our personality which in turn are related to different groups in Society or State. We live and function with our whole personality and in any given moment of experience, our consciousness is a unity which can form an intelligent system which harmonises in itself the component, diverse

---

[1] *Problem of Sovereignty*, p. 210.

[2] Mac Iver: *The Modern State*, p. 9.

elements. To divide our allegiance is to dismember our personality and abstract parts of it and constitute them as separate and persistent entities co-existing in space.

The pluralistic theory, therefore, completely fails in affording us the clue to the proper understanding of our ancient Polity. "In the Monistic theory of the State," complains Laski,[1] "there seems no guarantee that man will have any being at all. His personality, for him the most real of all things, is sacrificed to an idol which the merest knowledge of history would prove to have feet of clay." The Pluralist is very solicitious for the freedom of man in vocational aspects of group life. And his resentment of the State is due to the fact that he supposes that it encroaches upon spheres not legitimately its own. What we would like to point out is that the State cannot be relegated to a corner like this. "The true state must gather up every interest within itself. It must take over many loyalties and find how it can make them one."[2] The relegated to a corner like this. "The true State must try to get the whole of man. It must be the symbol of his "multiple self", his "multiple self brought to significance, to self-realisation". "If you leave me with my plural selves," says Follett, "you leave me in desolate places, my soul craving its meaning, its home. The home of my soul is in the State." And so the ideal State demands the whole of man. It is only the State, not the actual State, but the ideal unified or unifying State that can contain the whole of man. His undivided allegiance is to the State. His allegiance itself is a unity ; a spontaneous unity, "the instinctive self-unifying" of his "multiple interests."

The State, therefore, does not compete with other groups. The loyalty to the State is a unified and not a competing loyalty. The State is the whole which is inclusive of all.

---

[1] *Problem of Sovereignty*, p. 24.

[2] Follett: *The New State*, p. 312.

Dr. Mukerjee's conclusion is unfortunately the result of an inadequate knowledge of Oriental history and he questions the validity of postulating state-sovereignty with regard to the political associations of the East. The merest knowledge of Oriental history whether of Turkey, or of Egypt, or of Persia or of India etc., would immediately bring home the supreme fact that the Sultan of Egypt, the Porte of Turkey, the Emperor of India, Hindu or Muslim, were all of them practically despotic and truly exercised sovereign powers. Even in the strictly legal sense, we might say that the monarch was sovereign in ancient India. We do not mean necessarily that he was the supreme law-making institution. Both Yajnavalkya and Manu, indeed, recognised the legislative activity of the King. The King's edicts have the force of law. But we shall have to note that there were other sources of law, like the sacred scriptures, custom and usage; and perhaps "the idea of the King's legislative powers did not take root in ancient Indian Polity".[1] This does not suggest any limitation to sovereignty, but only affords another illustration of the peculiar way in which that sovereignty expresses itself, having always reference to the cardinal idea of the Polity, that of Swadharma. The Province of Law is to be understood in reference to this doctrine of Swadharma. If the various groups, sacred or vocational had the authority to legislative for themselves, their legislation was purely of the nature of subordinate legislation, and so, non-sovereign in character. Before legal or judicial powers were concentrated in the hands of the Monarch, some sort of gentile arbitration must have existed. There were a number of groups in society antecedent to the emergence of the State in its completely developed shape. These groups mostly based upon religion and kinship, the gens and clans that we come across

[1] Sen Gupta: *Sources of Law and Society*, p. 81.

as existing in all the different branches of the Aryan stock, must each have had a body of rules enforcible by an authority vested in a person or body of persons more or less definite in character. The State, in the early days would never have thought of interfering in the private concerns of these groups even if we suppose it had the strength to do so. The State finds already a vast body of law existing in society and for a long time to come, suffers the relative independence of the groups as such. But the very necessity which called for the State, also makes for the concentration of all power in its hands. consequent on the integration of the commonwealth. The State, which in the primitive times of stress and strife, was the expression of the military principle, in course of time, becomes more significant. Called into existence for the sake of mere life, it continued to exist for the sake of good life. In saying this, we are not trying to trace the historical origin and development of the State. Indeed it is impossible to point to any period in time when any people could have existed without any political organisation as such. We are only trying along with Plato and Aristotle, to maintain that the State is a natural institution and so can never be explained away by trying to make it rest upon convention or contract. That is why we find it easy to reconcile the fact of the emergence of the State with the existence of various other interests within it. The State, in its developed form, whatever it might have been in very early days, is more than the expression of the military principle. That is why we said, on a former occasion, that though the State is a manifestation of force, its basis, however, is not force. In other words, though state-sovereignty manifests itself as force or coercive authority, its nature itself is grounded upon a moral foundation.

This is specially the case so far as the ancient Indian Polity is concerned. The conception of sovereignty, though wedded as it is to the idea of "Danda" or the

Rod of Chastisement, finds its true essence in something far deeper and vital than the principle of force. With the integrating of the various elements of the Polity, the military principle which had done much in effecting it is itself ultimately subordinated to a higher principle which is in a sense, we might say, a synthesis of the military and the religious. If the religious principle itself had triumphed in the sense that the classes in the Polity which represented it gained a predominance over the rest, then we would have had a pure theocracy or rule of the priestly or Brahmanic classes. The idea of the State that we receive from the *Smritis* especially would lead us to judge, indeed, that the religious principle did triumph over all other interests. And "it would be no exaggeration to say that all through its history Hindu society was wholly dominated by the religious idea".[1] But if the religious or theological principles triumphed, this was however due to the *Entente cordiale* effected with the military principle as represented by the Kshatriya caste. The King, who represented the military principle, came to be looked upon in course of time as the protector of Religion and Dharma. With the gradual recognition of this idea, the military aspect of the monarch tends to be thrown into the shade, and his position comes to be securely founded, not upon force, but upon moral grounds. We shall discuss this more fully in our chapter on Political Obligation. It is thus in the person of the monarch that the religious and the military principles are brought together in a higher synthesis; and the State is therefore the combined product of the religious and military aspects of the ancient Indian society and life.

This is clearly visualised in the End the State sought to attain. The End of the State is Dharma. In its absolute aspect Dharma refers to the principle underlying this

[1] **Sen Gupta: *Sources of Law and Society*, p. 26.**

universe. In other words it is the Supreme Reality, often equated with Brahman. The realisation of Dharma in the absolute is the achievement of Moksha or Deliverance. The ideal of the State is "the attainment of the *summum bonum* 'Moksha' " and the State is the machinery for the collective attainment of salvation (moksha) by the people under its care".[1] This salvation, however, as we have seen is not a concern which pointed to a corporate striving. The Law of Karma precluded any such ideal. Salvation could only be achieved by strict adherence to Swadharma. And this conformity to Swadharma, or regulating the social order was to be rigidly enforced by the King. And the King in functioning as the sustainer of Dharma is thus the sovereign in the truest sense of the term, and in this sense, he is the determinate superior in whom the principle of authority is vested. The outward manifestation of his sovereignty is symbolised in "Danda" or the Rod of Chastisement; and the underlying essence of sovereignty has reference to the achievement of Moksha by every individual within the State.

In the absolute sense every individual is sovereign in himself. According to Indian Metaphysics we have seen how the self is conceived of as unattached and unaffected, almost a thing-in-itself. Nobody can help in the fruition of another's spiritual life; each should reap or consume his own Karma. That is why the *Anugita* says that "the Self properly understood is itself the sovereign."

In the Empirical Life, the individual has to undergo the discipline which prepares him for that ultimate sovereignty realisable in the Self. The preparation is mainly to enable him to attain philosophical aloofness through psychological detachment. The individual has thus to pass through ethical discipline regulated by Swadharma. And it is here that the conception of state-sovereignty emerges

---

[1] N. Law: *Ancient Ind. Polity*, p. 144.

into man's life, in its empirical aspect, and has to be regulated and supervised by the State. It is the protection afforded by the King that sustains the realm and keeps every one in the proper performance of his duties, thus preventing varna-sankaram. The function of protection involves the right to force; and the State is, thus, sovereign. Otherwise it cannot function at all.

And, as we had said, even in the strictly legal sense the State, as represented by the King, was sovereign. We have gradually traced the disappearance of the autonomous villages and minor societies in ancient India before the advance of the regal power. This is specially clear in the development of the judicial aspect of the monarchy. All the power in the Polity tends to gravitate into the hands of the King. His judicial power, original as well as appellate, grows into enormous proportions; and popular tribunals and minor societies function "by sufferance and subject to correction by the King." Such tribunals and minor groups have only a permissive status, and their legislation, is what in strict law is known as subordinate legislation. They are non-sovereign legislative bodies, wherever they possess the right to enforce by the exercise of authority rules and regulations on their members. In the empirical sense the State as represented by the King is the supreme sovereign and we shall not be wrong if we locate sovereignty in the determinate person who is the King who is the head of the State.

Sovereignty in the absolute sense, however, lies in the Self, not in the Empirical Self, but the Self which is identical with the Absolute or the Supreme Real. We should incessantly remind ourselves of this idea of identity which is behind much of Indian speculation. In the ultimate, there is no duality as it were; and so there is no real antagonism between the Empirical and the Absolute, Appearance and Reality. The conception of state-sovereignty or the empirical sovereignty is only an appear ance, if we could use the expression, of the Absolute sovereignty which is to be "in the working of the system of institutions as a whole".[1] In other words the Absolute sovereign is Dharma, which is conceived of, therefore, as the King of Kings. Dharma is the operative criticism that runs through society as a whole ; it is the principle of Life and Universe. The State, or the empirical sovereign is itself subject to Dharma which is the Absolute sovereign. Dharma, at one end is equated with the Self, and at the other with Brahman, if we could thus for purposes of explanation describe it in spatial terms. In the Ultimate, therefore, all is harmonised in Dharma.

As we are more concerned for the present with the study of the State we shall try to understand more of its sovereignty, or sovereignty in the empirical sense. We have already said that the King was in a sense above the law and could do no wrong. He is above the law which he administers, and himself immune from punishment he wields the Rod of Chastisement. The law he is subject to is not, therefore, the empirical law which itself depends on him for its enforcement. We have thus seen that laws regarding caste, for example, have no binding on him. But the King is subject to a higher law, and thus he is, in a sense not above law. The sovereign of the King is Dharma ; or to use a theological expression, God's Law. The penalties for transgression imposed on him are spiritual and not constitutional in nature ; we have seen that there was no constitutional machinery that could be brought into operation as against him. To express our idea in the language of Bracton : "The King is below no man, but he is below God and the law ; law makes the King ; the King is bound to obey the law, though if he break it, his punishment must be left to God".[2] Only we

---

[1] Bosanquett's phrase is, in this sense, profoundly true.
[2] Maitland: *Const. Hist.*, p. 101.

should remember that the idea of law must be clearly grasped; to the men of ancient India it was much more than legal; it was essentially moral or religious in its nature.

The Indian monarch is practically a despot, and his rule is autocratic. There is no constitutional check on his sovereignty. He is practically absolute as against all within the State. By all this, we do not mean that his omnipotence was unlimited. We only do maintain, and that with all the emphasis that we can, that there were no constitutional limitations to his sovereign power. There were the limitations always acting as checks on his power, limitations that are always present, though implicity, wherever absolute power is exercised. Such limitations as Prof. Dicey[1] has shown, are external and internal; and they are true also of the ancient Indian State. "The external limit to the real power of a sovereign consists in the possibility of certainty that his subjects, or a large number of them, will disobey or resist his laws.[2] The internal limit to the exercise of sovereignty arises from the nature of the sovereign power itself. Even a despot exercises his powers in accordance with his character, which is itself moulded by the circumstances under which he lives including under the head the moral feelings of the time and the society to which he belongs." But the existence of these limitations is not inconsistent with the exercise of sovereign powers by the Indian King. His commands were always authoritative; and his edicts, as we said, had the force of law.

---

[1] *Law of the Constitution*, p. 74 ff. cf. also Laski: *Grammar of Politics*, p. 52.

[2] With no writer of the Monistic school has sovereignty meant omnipotence. "For no holder of the doctrine of sovereignty has maintained that the state's actual power was not limited by the possibilities of effective disobedience". F. W. Coker: *A History of Pol. Theories, Recent Times*, Dunning, p. 83.

Can we say the same thing of the sovereignty of the Indian State in its external or foreign relationships? Everything depends upon the principles of international law prevalent in those days. At the outset, we may accept that there was a considerably large body of moral rules having reference to the regulation of inter-state relationships in ancient India. Most of the rules lay down in minute details what the conduct of warfare must be. Some of them tell us how diplomatic negotiations ought to be conducted. Others, again describe the nature of treaties and their maintenance. All these rules, however, are pious maxims that were more observed in their breach. Pious resolutions are not by themselves effective in maintaining international peace. The prime necessity and the first step towards the establishment of a perpetual peace, is the erection of an International Court of Arbitration with requisite sanctions. No such institution was either established or even contemplated in ancient India. No wonder, because even at the present day we have not reasons to congratulate ourself that we have reached our goal. The so called "League of Nations" is in practice a "League of Brigands," and its existence spells ruin and death to the small states and unnumbered peoples battling for their very existence. Our international relationships are still not above the ethics of the footpad. In ancient India, too, the relations were not generally remarkable for morality. Kautilyan maxims were not merely professed but widely acted upon. We have no reason, as we have pointed out elsewhere, to think that Kautilya's treatise is removed from the practice of his times. In fact, as we have noted, his principles are the logical development out of the ideas already widely current in Indian political thought. The general impression we get from the perusal of the *Arthasastra* and other political treatises is that mutual suspicion characterised the dealings between the States. Perhaps the very existence of the numerous States acted as a serious check on the autocracy of the various monarchs. The subjects of a tyrannical King, being discontented, would always welcome the enemy as a deliverer. In this sense we might say a serious limitation acts upon State sovereignty in its external aspect. But it is not inconsistent with sovereignty itself. And, moreover, the limitation itself is of uncertain nature. If the King happened to be strong, instead of drawing back from venturesome undertakings, he might take the aggressive with all hope of success.

And here we come to the most characteristic ideal of Hindu Polity, which has some affinities to similar ideas and aspirations of Europe, in the Middle Ages—the ideal of *Ekchatrapathi* or Universal Sovereignty.—India has ever been, except during rare intervals, a mere geographical expression, dismembered into a congeries of petty kingdoms and principalities, mutually repellant, ever engaged in fratricidal strife. This, more than anything else, left her a prey to the onslaughts of her invaders. The necessity for some sort of political unity was pressed upon the imagination of every thinker and upon the counsels of every monarch. It is only after the advent of the British that the age-long dream has come to be fulfilled. And to-day the whole of the country has been brought under the sovereignty of a single suzerain. Many a time before in the history of this land attempts were seriously made to reduce the whole country under the sway of one sceptre, sometimes with success, though that too often partial. For a time under the hegemony of a dominant race or ruler, the centrifugal tendencies could be held in check ; but with the relaxation of the grip that held them together the country would again be cut asunder into the atomic condition. It is only at the present day that the process of fusing together the multiple races that inhabit this vast sub-continent into a nation is proceeding apace. Various factors are conducive to this result which we may not examine at present. What we wish to point out is that simply because earlier attempts at unity were not crowned with permanent success we should not be tempted into false judgments regarding the policy and aspirations of our monarchs in the past. For example the two parts of India, the North and the South, have been held by all historians to be irreconcilable under a single sceptre; and in support the familiar Deccan proverb is quoted that "Delhi is distant". Further the differences of race, culture, and habits and customs are emphasised to prove the inevitability of the failure of all attempts at integrating the diverse elements into a commonwealth. And to-day we acquiesce in British domination and even find justifications for such acquiescence. Is it the purpose of political philosophy to register accomplished facts? There can be no more an immoral bent of mind than the sanctifying of success.

What we would urge is the sympathetic valuation of our ancient ideals. The conception of Universal sovereignty was the ideal constantly present before the imaginative aspirations of poets, statesmen and Kings.[1] The whole realm should be brought under the shade of a single umbrella. The *Ekachatrapathi* was the sole guarantee for peace. So long as the country was parcelled out among numberless kings there was ever present the danger of war. But if it could be brought under a single sway, the condition of continuous warfare would cease as incentives to war would no longer exist. Indeed, it was not merely

---

[1] See V. A. Smith: *Oxford History of India*, pp. IX-X.

In Kalidasa's *Sakuntala*, the hermits bless the King, p. 8.

"Heaven bless you with a son, whose happy realm shall be all the earth between the bordering seas!

The blessing of Rishi Kanva is typical and in almost every ancient book you come across a similar benediction. Kanva blesses Sakuntala:

"'And may the son you bear as kingly be
As Puru, and reign over all the earth."

the sovereignty of India that was visualised in the conception of *Ekachatrapathi*. The ancient Indians never thought in terms of India alone. When they wrote sacred books on Dharma such Dharma was not the Indian Dharma but "Manava Dharma" When they dreamt of Universal sway, that was to extend to the limits of the world. Hyperbolic as these aspirations would appear, we shall realise that there is nothing strange about them, if we remind ourselves of similar dreams of some of the greatest poets and philosophers in the West. The great Dante was himself convinced about the necessity of Universal Monarchy.[1] To-day after the abortive attempts at a League of Nations, philosophers like L. T. Hobhouse, have come to realise the necessity of a World-State. In other words, thinkers all the world over are coming to recognise the need for a new movement in political ideas. A time there was when the Nation-State seemed to be the apotheosis of political aspiration. Ever since the force was released in the Titanic erruptions of 1789-1815 it has been spreading like a leaven and has been pressing for recognition. Almost every war fought since the Congress of Vienna is ostensibly for the cause of nationalism, and the Treaty that has brought to an end the recent Great War is frankly based upon the Principle of Nationality. The fond hope is that if the world would be reshuffled and planned consciously according to the demands of nationalism then every State being co-extensive with the nation, would be

[1] "The foundation of a universal empire under Alexander the Great gave temporary rest to nations heretofore incessantly at war...... The idea of a universal empire became the Greek ideal of a perpetual peace...... Such an empire was in the language of the Stoics, a world-state in which all men had rights of citizenship in which all other nations were absorbed".—Kant: *Perpetual Peace*, p. 32. "We shall not find at any time except under the divine monarch Augustus, when a perfect monarchy existed that the world was everywhere quiet"—Dante: *De Monarchia*, Book I, 54.

contented. Thus there would be an end to war. All mankind would be brought into a Federation, the Nation-States being the component units, each contributing something to the life of Humanity. Unfortunately, however, the national idea has brought us no nearer peace and in fact, has been highly prejudicial in its results. Nationalism has been the one force that has always made for war ; in its accentuated form it has everywhere manifested itself in the imperialistic garb. Nationalism, as we hold[1] is a narrow and separatist force, and since its inception we have the modern phenomenon of the world organised in competing units, units which are terrible machines of power, huge brutes, with souls dead. The venom of it lies in that so far as Europe at least is concerned, the spirit of the Nation, disruptive as it is, has succeeded in masking its true nature behind the movements of unification, of Italy, of Germany and so on. These movements, when successful, really became the expressions of the centrifugal tendencies, let loose by the dragon of nationalism, whose seeds have been sown so widely that the reaping has been no ordinary affair. The result is that to-day we have in Europe the dreadful spectacle of a number of Nation-States, armed to the teeth, facing each other as blood-hounds ready for mutual slaughter. The world-position is instinct with disaster ; it is ominous to peace. The danger specially lies in the overgrown strength of a few great powers who on one wrong move show their teeth to tear at each other.

The impending cataclysm has roused the fears of some of our finest thinkers to-day ; and an approach to the problem is now sought from a different angle. "In a creative civilisation," says Laski, "what is important is

---

[1] Miss Follett and others whom we shall notice at a later stage try to give a new meaning and significance to nationalism, and they maintain that nationalism can be a basis for Internationalism.

not the historical accident of separate States, but the scientific fact of world interdependence. The real unit of allegiance is the world. The real obligation of obedience is to the total interest of our fellowmen.[1] An Internationalism which has its basis in the existing Nation-States can never make for world peace. It is increasingly felt that no Nation-State ought to be sovereign in its external relationships. And if the concept of sovereignty is understood as implying the irresponsibility of the Nation-State to any authority outside of itself, then such sovereignty will be dangerous and ought to be limited. It is impossible, as Kant has clearly demonstrated, to secure perpetual peace between independent nations. Even the existence of certain maxims recognised as International Law is not sufficient to ensure peace. The different nations or States observe international obligations only so long as it is not their interest to repudiate them. The enforcement of International Law can never be possible so long as there are independent nations or States. "There is" says Professor Ritchie,[2] "only one way in which war between independent nations can be prevented; and that is by the nations ceasing to be independent". In a World-State, as Laski also insists,[3] "there is no room for separate sovereignties". Men must cease to think in terms of nationalism; and the whole of mankind must be knit together through fraternal bonds to constitute the Great Society.[4]

This is no impossible dream, no mere speculative Utopia. What ought to be, as we firmly believe, can also be realised. Already the idea of humanity, in the abstract, has appealed itself to the imagination of every forward

[1] *Grammar of Politics*, p. 64.

[2] *Studies in Political and Social Ethics*, p. 169.

[3] *Grammar of Politics*, p. 66.

[4] Long ago, Cicero had visualised the idea of the World-State. He said: "Particular states are only members of a whole governed by reason."—*De Legibris*, I, 1.

thinker, though the political organisation of this ideal, or in other words, the translation of the conception into institutional terms, has not yet been actualised. The World-State is no mere dream, "an illusion of sentimental hope". As Profs. Dewey and Tufts put it : "it is a very slight step to take forward compared with that which has substituted the authority of national States for the conflict of isolated clans and local communities ; or with that which has substituted a publicly administered justice for the regime of private war and retaliation."[1] If the intercourse between the different peoples be vitalised by the conception that they are all children of a Common Father, all obstacles in the way of establishing the Fraternity of Man could be swept aside with extreme ease.

To come back to the study of our ancient ideals, we said that the conception of Universal Sovereignty was constantly set before the ideal monarch.[2] The danger of divided and competing sovereignties seems to have been realised by every political moralist and statesman. Every individual State, as represented by its King, in practice was a sovereign State. It was not subject to any authority outside of itself. The enforcement of International Law was not organised with adequate sanctions. Kings waged war with each other as their sweet will and pleasure in-

---

[1] *Ethics*, p. 482.

[2] J. Jolly writes: (Introduction to *the Arthasastra of Kautilya*, p. 3) that in ancient India "every King would try to become the lord of a circle of states, and there was no check on him. The war of all against all which is the natural consequence of this condition of things, can only be brought to a successful close by a conqueror obtaining the universal empire of the world and enjoying the earth unopposed. A temporary termination of hostilities may be effected by the vanquished King concluding peace with the vanquisher, on condition of paying him a large sum of money, or ceding a part of his territory, or the whole of his territory except the capital and of giving him hostages of high rank."

duced them. Treaties between the various States were concluded according as the interests of the Kings demanded such alliances. Unless the land was brought under the sway of a single powerful monarch, it was cut up into innumerable kingdoms. The relations between these kingdoms, as we said, were not regulated by any recognised code of ethics. Wherever pious maxims are enunciated, no machinery was provided for to ensure the adherence that would alone bring about peace. "In inter-state relationship, displomacy knew no morality. Neither provoked aggression, nor the violation of the neutrality of other States, caused any surprise."[1] This condition of uncertainty in inter-state relationships was not peculiar to India only. "The ancient world is a world of perpetual war in which defeat means annihilation".[2] There was no friendly neighbour ; beyond the boundaries of the territory of every people "lay the land of a deadly foe". Even among the cultured Greeks the outsider was regarded as an enemy. Among the Romans it was worse, for Rome "was bound by ties of kingship to no other State. She was, in other words, free from a sense of obligation to other races." In ancient India, too, every kingdom was practically free from any sense of obligation to other kingdoms and the neighbour was always regarded as an enemy. This is laid down in the Doctrine of the Mandala ; and the doctrine, in spite of its being run to death by the ingenuity of scholars, contained the rough indication of the course of inter-state diplomacy.[3] The doctrine may be expressed in the language of Abul Fazal which is very moderate, and which perhaps reflects the ideas of Hindus even of his day. According to the doctrine the King "should consider a prince whose territories are coterminous with his own,

---

[1] Beni Prasad: *Theory of Govt. in Anc. Ind.*, p. 145.

[2] Miss M. Campbell Smith: Introduction to *Perpetual Peace* Kant, p. 6 ff.

[3] See Beni Prasad: *Theory of Govt.*, pp. 144-145.

as his enemy though he be profuse in demonstrations of friendship. With one whose country is situated next beyond, he should form an alliance. With a third more remote, he should avoid all intercourse whether hostile or friendly.[1] And the uncertainty of the times forced upon every King the imperious necessity of being prepared for war. Each King strained his every nerve to keep ready the fighting forces of his kingdom; and to insure against surprise, he always had a regular standing army, mostly of mercenary soldiers. "In fact", writes Megasthenes,[2] no one vested with kingly power ever keeps on foot a military force without a very great number of elephants and foot and cavalry". The size of the armaments maintained by the various Kings is staggering.[3] We are led to the sad conclusion that under the then existing circumstances perpetual peace could never be possible in ancient India. The new malady that Montesquieu spoke of[4] was not quite new; for it had attacked the Ancient Indian Polity; sapped its strength, and bled it white until it lay prostrate at the feet of every vigorous foreigner who swooped down upon the unhappy land through the gateways of the North-west.

The spectacle of ancient India that is presented to us especially during the periods of interval when the strong

---

[1] Abul Fazal's *Ain-i-Akbari*, trans. by Farrett, III, 259-261.

[2] *Ancient India*: (M'Crindle), pp. 160-161.

[3] For more details, read M'Crindle; and Prof. P. Banerjea's *Public Adm.*, Ch. XV.

[4] "A new distemper has spread itself over Europe; it has infected our princes and induces them to keep up an exorbitant number of troops. It has its redoublings, and of necessity becomes contagious. For as soon as one prince augments what he calls his troops, the rest of course do the same; so that nothing is gained thereby but the public ruin. Each monarch keeps as many armies on foot as if his people were in danger of being exterminated: and they give the name of Peace to this general effort of all against all." *Spirit of Laws*, XIII, Chapter 17.

arm of a central power is withdrawn, is sorry indeed. The dangers of a divided Polity always pressed upon statesmen and thinkers alike the imperious necessity of political unity. "A strong power was expressly enjoined to embark on a career of conquest, subdue State after State, and stand forth as the one all-embracing sovereign.[1] The actual State was a sovereign State ; the ideal State was to absorb separate sovereignties into an all comprehensive whole. Indian political thought, it is said, takes cognisance of varying degrees of sovereignty and there are numerous institutions or ceremonies which are related to them. The universal sovereign, after his "Digvijaya" formally proclaims himself by the performance of "Asvamedha".

We are not directly concerned here with the description of these various institutions connected with the idea of sovereignty. We shall only remember that though the actual State was sovereign as against other States, the ideal State was to absorb these independent States into a single polity, unified under a single sceptre. Dr. Radhakamal Mukherji[2] is clearly wrong in stating that "the Sarvabhauma, or the super-state of Indian history and tradition is not incompatible with a multiplicity of independent and semi-independent worlds, each true to its orbit and its own sun," if by this he is referring to the ideal as such. His description, however, is true of the actual State, that "India presented the picture of a congeries of independent and semi-independent peoples and states, a veritable "pluralistic universe".

We shall not also enter into a detailed examination of the various attempts at unity that history records. The physical manifestation of the aspiration took the form of the striving to reach to natural frontiers on all sides. The antagonism between the North and the South has to-day

---

1. Beni Prasad: *Theory of Govt.*, p. 145.
2 *Democracies of the East*, p. 25.

been dissolved in the political unification of the whole realm achieved during the last one hundred and fifty years. It has not yet been easy to reach to the natural frontier in the North-West of India. Only once in the history of India she had reached to her scientific limts on all sides. All through the ages she has been sighing in vain to find her geographical completion. Let us bear this in mind when trying to understand and determine our foreign policy. The key-note of India's foreign policy to-day lies in the Afghan regions; and that explains the enormous amount of money lavished on the army annually, in spite of the fact that the country is nominally at peace. It is the necessity to possess the key of the gates of the Hindu Kush, that has dictated the policy of aggression as well as defence, of every sovereign power in India. We should remember that every time the paramount power in India lost its hold over the North-West frontier, the flood-gates of invasion were opened to deluge the country with the it again to the fundamental idea of the Indian Polity, of the Mughals becomes intelligible, only when we relate it again to the fundamental idea of the Indian polity, the attainment of political unity which would be the guarantee of internal and external security. The spiritual aspect of the aspiration of achieving unity has not yet been solved. India is a home of many cultures, presenting diverse stages of civilisation. The problem is, how to evolve unity out of diversity and develop a homogeneous civilisation. This has been the despair of many a great reformer and the justification of many an apologist of imperialism. But the problem, though difficult of solution, is simple enough if we view it from the correct angle. A conflict of cultures is the indispensable condition of progress. In the absence of struggle each individual culture would stereotype itself and stagnate. Our ideal is not dead uniformity which would be insufferable boredom—not monotony but harmony. The fact that India is full of many cultures is really a very hopeful sign; out of the clash a richer culture, in itself the assimilation of the best of each individual culture, will ultimately evolve.

In this sense India is a world in epitome, and the Indian problem is really the world problem. In solving it, we shall be solving spontaneously the larger problem as well.

In the past India tried to solve the problem by trying to actualise the conception of the universal sovereign. This ideal was something which mediaeval Christendom well-nigh accomplished. The ideal of Christianity is that of the complete brotherhood of all men as children of a Common Father. The aim of the mediaeval Church was that of a world-empire, cemented together by a universal religion. But for the unhappy conflict between the Papacy and the Empire, the ideal of the Christian Commonwealth would have been largely realised. Moreover the Church allied itself with temporal interests and often itself led movements opposed to the true spirit of the teachings of Christ. Christianity became militant during the Crusades and sanctioned the spirit of war. It is a tragedy that the history of Europe has come nearer to the realisation of perpetual war than to the attainment of peace. In India, too, the spiritual interests of the State have often been a serious obstacle in the way of unification. Before the Mahommedans came it was not very difficult to reduce the whole of the country under one sovereign. The End of the State, to preserve Dharma, could have been better attained by gathering up all the Hindus under a single protecting wing. With the advent of the Mussalmans the country is permanently divided into two irreconcilable parts. It has been given to few to rise to the comprehension of the true ideal for India. Of monarchs, Asoka before and Akbar after the Islamic conquest could envisage the true end of this country's destiny. The universal State is not to be the achievement of arms, and should not rest on force. It should be organised for peace and not for war.[1] The bases of the World-State must be grounded on Religion. The different races must be fused together, and all distinctions of colour, creed, caste and stock which divide man from man must be swept away. How the Universal State could be achieved through peaceful conquest the great Mauryan monarch has shown.[2] And how the different cultures could be fused into one all-embracing civilisation the great Akbar has clearly demonstrated. His "Din Ilahi" is no mere dream; it is no monstrous freak of vanity as Prof. V. A. Smith imagines. Akbar was a philosopher-king, and his noble ideal was to bring about a peaceful revolution, by putting an end to the conflict of creeds through the spread of his "Divine Faith," and by social intercourse through inter-marriages, to sweep away once for all social barriers in the way of a universal amalgamation. Would to God, he had succeeded in this noble mission! We can never console ourselves for the passing away of the great vision before it could be caught in the concrete embodiment of a lasting institution!

Our examination of the ancient Indian Polity has so far revealed to us that the conception of sovereignty was its very core. This sovereignty was vested generally in the person of the King who represented the State. Internally the King was the supreme power in his land. Externally he was independent of other kings. This was true of actual India. Sovereignty was always vested in a determi-

---

[1] Christ says that those who use the sword shall perish by the sword.

[2] cf. the conversions of Charlemaigne; also *Koran*, Ch. 47: When ye encounter the unbelievers strike off their heads, until ye have made a great slaughter among them......verily if God pleased he could take vengeance on them without your assistance; but he commandeth you to fight his battles".

"The Lord *is* a man of war"—Moses: *Exodus*, XV, 3.

nate person or body of persons, so far as its empirical aspect is concerned. Sovereignty was itself composed of various elements.[1] This would show that even in theory our ancients recognised that the conception was not simple but highly complex.

The Ideal India, as we said, has no boundaries. It is co-extensive with the world. Our sages spoke of "Manava Dharma" or duties of Man ; our statesmen and monarchs dreamed of Universal Empire. Sovereignty, in the ideal sense, in its empirical significance, would mean the World-State. In its absolute significance, it has reference to the Self of Man, and Dharma as Sovereign. The Self is Brahman which is again Dharma. So, Universal Sovereignty is not antagonistic to Individual Sovereignty.

The Indian conception of Sovereignty, we believe, is still of supreme value and significance to the world. In it we might find the only solution for the world problem at the present day. Only, and this we cannot sufficiently emphasise, Sovereignty should not be understood in physical or spatial terms. Universal Sovereignty, in the sense of One-Man Rule is an anachronism. The career of Napoleon is proof of this. And again Sovereignty, as understood to be the principle of coercion or force is repugnant to our moral sense ; for our allegiance should not rest on force but on will. Lastly, Sovereignty, as traditionally explained is fallacious and we may agree with Laski,[2] that "it would be of lasting benefit to political science if the whole concept of sovereignty were surrendered." To speak of Sovereignty, either in the legal or political sense, as supreme over every other element

[1] (1) The King or Swamin, (2) The Amatya, (3) Territory, (4) Fort, (5) Treasury, (6) Army and (7) Ally.

See *Kautilya*, Bk. VI, Ch. I. But here the term is used in a general sense, and should not be confounded with the concept of sovereignty.

[2] *Grammar of Politics*, pp. 44-45.

within the State and independent of any external authority, is only possible on the assumption that independent Nation-states are inevitable. But this still reveals our inherent weakness, that we think of the State in physical i. e. geographical or spatial terms,[1] that we conceive the different States as existing side by side, their distinctive territories marked off by respective boundaries. The State, however, is an Idea; it is objectified Reason; the embodiment of our aspiration. In it our Soul seeks its true home. The State, for us, is a spiritual reality. And State-sovereignty inheres in the genuine whole, which is coterminous with the world. Sovereignty is a moral or spiritual principle; it is the expression of Will—not any particular Will, but the Common Will[2] which is the harmony of the Real.[3] It will be directed to the guiding of the human

---

[1] Miss Follett, whose book is pregnant with suggestions asks us to think of sovereignty (1) as *looking in* as authority over its own members, as the independence which is the result of the complete interdependence of those members; and (2) to this of this independence as *looking out* to other independences to form through a larger interdependence the larger says: "Interdependence is the keynote of the relations of nations as it is the keynote of the relations of individuals within a nation." *The New State*, pp. 350-51.

[2] "If we start from a conception of the fundamental unity of the human personality, and seek to transfer that conception to the state, we shall attain a view of the state as unity pervaded throughout by reason—as one in virtue of a Reason which animates each and every member and comes to light not in the minds of a chosen few, but in the Will of the whole community. We shall conceive the state as a single personality, and we shall ascribe sovereignty in the manner of Rousseau, to the general will of the whole personality." Ernest Barker: *Greek Political Theory*, p. 174.

[3] Miss Follett tells us the true conception of sovereignty based on consent. She writes: "Power is generated within the true group not by one or several assuming authority and the others 'consenting', but solely by the process of intermingling". (*The New State*, p. 303.)

mind to the Holy Quest, the expression of the highest Religion which points to the ultimate End and Destiny of Mankind.

Universal Sovereignty would then result in the establishment of perpetual Peace. In the sense of the "Reign of Love", it shall be the fulfilment of the devout prayer : "Thy Kingdom Come!"

CHAPTER VII

CITIZENSHIP IN THE STATE

"We must not think that anyone of the citizens belongs to himself, but that they all belong to the State."

ARISTOTLE

"To be a citizen is to merge one's being in that of others."

HETHERINGTON AND MUIRHEAD

"Those who cherish a part of the citizens and neglect another part introduce the most ruinous of all civic ills, sedition and discord."

CICERO

"It has been here insisted that no man can be a good citizen unless he personally interests himself in the affairs of the State."

LASKI

We have so far discussed the fundamental ideas on which the Hindu State rested. We shall now proceed to examine if in this economy of life there could be any conception of citizenship.

In the ideal State the good man is also the good citizen. This was Aristotle's conception and his was essentially an ethical ideal. The antithesis between the individual and society or the State is dissolved in a higher unity in which the personality of the individual is neither absorbed nor suppressed, but realised in its completeness. The individual is driven, by his nature as a human being, to strive after ends in the realisation of which he would be sharing his own life with others. To Plato and Aristotle there was no cleavage between private and public interests, and so "the interest of the State is nothing but that of its citizens. And conversely there is no part which really has a separate interest;"[1] the individual is not sacrificed to the State,

---

[1] A. C. Bradley: *Aristotle's conception of the State, Hellenica*, 1880, p. 209.

he finds his true meaning and significance in the participation of its life. In the ideal State of Plato the citizen is the State in miniature, and the State the citizen writ large. The individual would seek the realisation of his Self in going beyond his narrow existence into the vast expanse of the Great Society of which he is a member. He would be more of the individual, the more he seeks to serve the Great Fellowship. This is so because in his own nature he is universal. His personality expresses itself, not in eccentric behaviour, but essentially in the enriching of his representative character. He cannot, even if he would, isolate himself from his fellow creatures. 'The "individual" man, the man into whose essence his community with others does not enter, who does not include relation to others in his very being' as Bradley rightly observes,[1] is a fiction. The individual can never be self-centred; he is not a centration of power in an isolated point. He touches others as Nettleship says, at innumerable points. Society is not a mere collection of points "each concentrating material in itself". Society and the State, as we have seen, do mean a real unity of purpose. In the various relationships of lover and beloved, husband and wife, parent and child, brother and sister, master and friend, we have the manifold expressions of a purpose which impels the individual to seek for his meaning in an existence which is beyond his mere self. Citizenship is the expansion of the individual in the life of his community by such an ordering of his will and personality that he would seek to merge himself with the rest. By enriching the community of which he is a member, he spontaneously realises his true self.

In such a view citizenship is inseparably bound up with the idea of a common Purpose or End. The individual

---

[1] *Ethical Studies*, p. 168.

[2] Muirhead and Hetherington: *Social Purpose*, p. 98.

would feel that he is fulfilling, either directly or indirectly objects that have a common significance for all. The true citizen is he who seeks to share with others, to identify himself with others, who by fulfilling the duties of his station in life is contributing to the Social or Common Good. Such an identification is possible because, as we conceive it, the individual and the State are not mutually exclusive conceptions; the existence of the one implies the reality of the other. There is no individual Self exclusive of other selves, and there is no State or society which is not a unity or a community of Selves. In other words, the State is not a heap or a machine. "It is the objective mind which is subjective and self-conscious in its citizens it feels and knows itself in the heart of each".[1] The State is not alien to the nature of the individual; it is the whole in which he, as a particular, finds his position, and meaning. Just as the individual, in himself, is a coherence, the State is the universal coherence. The relationship between the individual and the State is not to be understood in physical or spatial terms. If purposive they are mutually inclusive. It is not fanciful to consider that the particular is in the Universal and the Universal is in the particular if only we cease to think of their relation in spatial terms. That is how Plato was able to realise that the individual was the State in epitome. We do not see any strangeness about this conception. We shall only remember that Plato was writing of the Ideal State; and his idea is not to be applied to any Actual State. The conflict, let us assure ourselves is not between the Real and the Ideal, but between the Ideal and the Actual. Our new Realists are not very particular of recognising this vital truth. In the Real or Ideal State the citizen is identical with the State; his will is the will of the State; his life that of the State. His duties would contribute to

[1] Bradley: *Ethical Studies*, p. 184.

the harmony of the whole ; and find their fulfilment in realising the coherence of the social system. In other words, the duties of the individual would be constituted on a functional basis, contributing to the health of the spiritual organism of which he is a member. Bradley, in his brilliant essay on *My Station and Its Duties*, has clearly interpreted the true bases for an intelligent citizenship. In the ideal State, both individuals and classes do exist ; their existence is in harmony or consistency with the larger unity. For individuals or classes are not ends in themselves ; they are at once ends and means as well.

In the Actual State, however, individuals and classes refuse to be fused together, and persist as separate parts. Indeed, as Urwick has rightly put it,[1] "each of us is now an exemplar to more people than we dream of ; each is, in a sort, an ambassador of his class wherever he goes". And in a Society in which Social relations are determined not only by the general factor of wealth that we have in almost every society, but also by the fact of birth in a particular caste, Urwick's statement takes on a sinister significance and its bearings on the life of the whole Polity can never be exaggerated. We shall presently consider this problem. What we would wish to emphasise is that all labels that divide man and man are injurious and must be destroyed. Every individual is of equal spiritual value ; no part or element in the State should be degraded to the position of an instrument or mere means. The State should seek to promote the Common Good, and embody a common Purpose. This End could be realised in a true functional Society, when the station in life of each citizen is determined according to capacity, and not the accident of birth. In the ideal State each citizen could give himself up to the service of the State. He

[1] *The Social Good*, p. 46.

would feel himself at one with its life; he would realise the unity which is the basis of harmony.

It is clear that citizenship as we would understand the term, could not have existed in the ancient Indian Polity. The great drawback of the State in Ancient India was that the rights of man as man were not fully recognised. "Individuals had rights and duties not as component parts of the body politic but as members of estates or classes in society."[1] The State was not a universal coherence; Dharma in the State aimed at the perfection of only parts of it considered as ends, the other parts only serving as means. Dharma, i. e. Swadharma, is determined by the accident of birth, on supposed merits and demerits pursuing man with inexorable necessity as the result of Karma, through the endless round of births. The station in life and its duties are dictated by the fact of birth in the particular caste. Citizenship, if at all we could use that term in reference to the ancient Indian Polity, was seriously affected by the caste-system. "From the commencement of the Brahmanic Period until recently, the position of a man in relation to society, and his duties both private and public, always depended more upon the importance of his class, than upon his individual capacity and character".[2]

If citizenship involves, therefore, the constant participation in creating and re-creating in institutional terms the common purpose that ought to animate with a living energy it means, as it meant to Aristotle,[3] the sharing in the function of governance; the citizens of the State should have a common care for its safety. There must be a common denomination in citizenship. This conception of citizenship could never arise in the ancient Indian State. The End of the State would preclude any such fulfilment.

[1] Banerjea: *Pub. Adm.*, p. 41.

[2] *Ibid.*, p. 20.

[3] Pol. iii, Cap. i ff.

The End of the State, as we have seen, was not to enable man to realise himself at his best, to enlist his service in the realisation of the Social or Common Good ; to enrich his personality, that thereby he would stamp on human endeavour the seal of an ever increasing purpose, the partial realisation of which gives him glimpses of the "Holy Grail", he is in quest of, thus urging him on and on with insatiate idealism. The End of the State was only to maintain an enforced equilibrium, not based on social harmony, but on the suppression of the personality of the vast majority for the maintenance of the privileged few. The intrinsic worth of personality was not recognised. There was no idea of personality which would blossom into its completeness, in the exercise of the functions of citizenship. So long as the idea of the Individual continues to be what it is in Indian thought, there cannot be any conception of personality at all. There cannot be as is assumed in the Atman doctrine a personality which is mere individual personality. "It is only in social life that a person realises his real nature",[1] says Haldane ; and according to him "the existence of the world is bound up with our own individual existence ; and the individual is what he is through his relations to others. "His personality was no *tabula rasa* at birth ;" other persons "are not outside his own spiritual life, but within it." And so the individual should realise himself in the participation of life which has social significance. The man must seek "objects which, when realised, are permanent contributions to a social good which thus satisfies a permanent self".[2] The doctrine of self-realisation can be thus understood as Green did, in the "permanent contribution to an abiding social good" of a self objectifying personality.

The principle of the Social Order, again, in India, does

[1] J. S. Haldane: *Mechanism, Life and Personality*, p. 29.
[2] T. H. Greene: *Prolegomena to Ethics*, p. XXIX.

not admit that given opportunities, the possibilities of a person would flower and blossom out irrespective of caste, and that every person has potentialities of equal development. These potentialities, it was conceived, were determined and fixed by the accumulated Karma of past births, and so it would be futile to battle against one's ordained station in life. The whole of social life was bound down by the caste theory of functions or Varna-dharma, which in itself was determined by the Law of Karma. Varna-dharma has in view the organisation of Society, in which each caste was to perform its own Swadharma, and so is strongly individualistic in nature. The Law of Karma emphasises the individual self; the doctrine of Swadharma, as regulating the life of the group, or Varna, is again particular in character, being only another kind of individualism. Varna-dharma aims at keeping each caste in the performance of its function. Thus, both in its individual and group aspects, Varna-dharma is merely particular and separatist.

Thus, from whatever angle of view we try to take in the Indian idea of human values and the Indian conception of Personality, we are forced to conclude that where values are not recognised, and personality denied, the individual as such could not have lived a significant life which he could share with others. "Caste does not", says Beni Prasad,[1] "admit that every individual is in his nature universal and that he has the right to select his own function". And accordng to the metaphysical tenets of Indian thought, the Self is to be realised, not in a life of partnership, but through renunciation. The Indian attitude to life, therefore, could never give rise to an adequate conception of citizenship.[2] The End of the State, instead

[1] *Theory of Government*, p. 7.

[2] Sir Henry Jones truly observes: "Except within Society as members of it and therefore as members of each other, men have no rights nor any consequence any duties. And, if they are mem-

of uniting all men in the common purpose set the stamp of inferiority on the vast majority of the population, condemned to be the "means" or instruments to the realisation of the good life of the superior castes considered as "ends". Invidious distinctions were thus made between man and man, caste and caste, class and class and so on. Human relationships were vitiated by gross inequalities.[1]

---

bers of Society and of one another, they are more than exclusive individuals, or in other words, their nature is universal.

Principles of Citizenship, Ch. vi, p. 141.

[1] We give a few references which are not perhaps very exhaustive but would give at least an adequate idea.

Inequalities in the Law of Interest:—
Banerjea: *Public Adm.*, p. 274.
Inequalities in the Law of Murder:—
Apastamba, pp. 78-79.
Gautama, pp. 280-286.
Cambridge History of India, p. 124.
Inequalities in the relationships of man and woman:—
Apastamba, p. 89.
Inequalities in the Law of Adultery:—
Gautama, pp. 280-286—*Narada*, p. 177 (see references).
Manu, VIII, 374-385.—*Yajnavalkya*, II, 286-8.
Vishnu, V, 40-41.—*Gautama*, XII, 2-3.—*Baudhayana*, II, 352.
Manu, VIII, 366-367.
Inequalities in the Law of Social Status:—
Apastamba, p. 165.
Gautama, pp. 208-209.
Inequalities in the Law of Hospitality:—
Gautama, pp. 198-205.
Inequalities in the Penal Code (regarding Sudras):—
Gautama, pp. 236-237.
Inequalities of Laws regulating Education:—
Apastamba, pp. 34-35.
Gautama, p. 258.
Inequalities in the Law of Inheritance:—
Gautama, pp. 299-307.
Cambridge History of India, p. 134.
Inequalities in the Law of Evidence:—
Narada, pp. 87-89.

Where equality of opportunities and status is denied, we cannot have citizenship. By equality we do not mean dead-level uniformity. As Leslie Stephen has put it,[1] every human being should be "so placed as to be capable of preparing himself for any other position, and should then go to the work for which he is best fitted." Every man's position should be determined, "because the qualities which determine a man's position would be the qualities for which he deserves the position, desert in this sense being measurable by fitness." In other words a man's position in life must be determined on a functional basis. And what is true of an individual is also true of a class or caste. "The only sufficient reason for classes is the efficient discharge of social functions." A class must be, "an organ for the discharge of certain functions," and each man in the body politic must be "able to fit himself for that class." This view of a functional society is, however, impossible when the determining factor is not fitness, but caste, and the supposed influence of Karma. We should further remember that some castes are looked upon as higher and others lower. The facilities and opportunities the members of the higher castes possess, are never and can never be possessed by those of the lower. And so equality can never mean "the demand for a fair start" in the Indian Polity. For one reason or another the vast majority of the population could not participate in a Common Life and exercise the rights of citizenship. The State could not therefore be a true partnership. It could never be

Inequalities in the Law of Assault and Defamation:—
Viramitrodaya, p. 472.
Narada, pp. 209-212.
Manu, VIII, pp. 267-269; 274; 270-284.
Yajnavalkya, II, 204.
Brihaspati, pp. 355-356.
(Appointment of Chief Judge—*Narada*, p. 250.)

[1] *Social Rights and Duties*, p. 204.
Discuss the question from the standpoint of Social Justice.

"a partnership in all science; a partnership in all art; a partnership in every virtue and in all perfection".[1] The political ideal of partnership was alien to the Indian mind. The participation of the benefits conferred by the State was not universal; whole classes and castes were excluded from the sharing of the Good Life. We are of opinion, along with Plato, that, "that State is in the highest condition in which the greatest number of the people apply the words "mine" and "not mine" to the same objects.[2] In other words all must share in the life of the community; otherwise there can be no society, "Call ye that a Society", exclaims Carlyle,[3] "where there is no longer any social idea extant; not so much the idea of a common home......" A State is according to us, the idea of the Family extended; and all the members must feel that they belong to a Fraternity. We believe in Plato's ideal of communism. It is a sublime conception in spite of the ridicule showered on it by critics from Aristotle onwards. The State, in ancient India, could not be the expression of the aspirations of the majority of the individuals included in it. This is because there was no society as a coherent whole; indeed, there was not one society but many societies. Citizenship could not have a political significance; it was the membership of the particular class or caste that gave the individual his legal and social privileges and duties. The State would primarily appear to the individual as an institution that provides him security within and without, that assures to him the conditions which hinder the hindrance to Swadharma. It is only in the ideal State of Plato and to a large extent in the actual Greek city-State that there was no social relation which was not also a political one. In ancient Greece all life was

---

1 *Reflections on the Revolution in France*, Burke.
2 *Republic*, V, 462.
3 *Sartor Resartus*, Bk. III, Ch. V.

focussed at a single point ; and that point was the city. The very intensity of the town life made possible the emergence of citizenship, due to the development of civic sense. It was not difficult, after the Greeks gained political consciousness, for them to evolve free institutions. Perhaps the size of the Greeks State had much to contribute towards the evolution of citizenship. We know what limits Aristotle has set to his ideal State. The citizens of his State must be able to assemble in one place. "Just as a boat can no more be two furlongs long than a span long", he says, "so a State can no more consist of one hundred thousand than of ten citizens." His citizens must know each other ; "if just legal decisions are to be given, and if office is to be apportioned to men according to merit, it is necessary for citizens to have a knowledge of each other's characters, since where this is not the case things must needs go wrong with the appointment of officials and the administration of law." The requirements of Aristotle could be satisfied by a State of a very limited size, and the Greek city-State was such a one. The citizens could flock to the meetings of the assembly and express their opinion directly on men and measures. In larger States, like the ancient monarchies and empires, or the modern Nation-states, this is impossible, except it be by the indirect method of representation. The idea of representation is comparatively modern, and in our modern State, the few do the work of the many. The majority of the citizens to-day have neither the leisure nor the knowledge necessary to participate directly in political affairs ; and they are content to leave the actual administration and its direction to the responsibility of their representatives. In the Greek State, and especially in Athens, the citizens could participate directly in the political life of the State. Pericles could well claim, with justifiable pride that the Athenian constitution could be called a democracy because its working was in the hands not of the few, but of the many.[1] The direct participation in politics is not possible in a large State to the extent it is in the City-State. And in the days when representation was practically unknown there could be no democracy in large States. By whatever name we call them, the large States of the ancient world were despotisms. The factors that determined the spirit of the City-State were wholly different from those which determined the spirit of the large States of Ancient times, and especially of the vast kingdoms and empires that India has known. In the City-State the relations of man with man became the determining factor in the moulding of character. In India man's contact with nature determined his character, "against the eternal background of the earth the cardinal events of life, birth, marriage, and death, gain a profound significance".[2] The mystery of life, the inscrutability of natural forces, unknown and unknowable, the inevitability of change and the sense of destiny all mark a deep impression on man's imagination; and leave him awe-struck, helpless, pessimistic and often passive. A peculiar sense of resignation influences his attitude to the changing fortunes of life, and he is impelled by the bent of his nature to seek peace in renunciation. The Indian could never therefore turn with real zest to the participation of political or civic life.[3] The Indian attitude to life is especially adapted to the needs of despotism, and the State could not but be autocratic. In a large State, in which the principle of representation could not be applied, despotism could be the only form of government. "No form of government," says V. A. Smith,[4] "except the autocratic was recognised as suitable to Indian conditions". And if we further take

[1] *Funeral Speech*, Thucydides.

[2] Mac Iver: *The Modern State*, p. 72.

[3] See Muirhead and Hetherington: *Social Purpose*, Chapter I for the implications of Civic Society.

[4] *Indian Constitutional Reform*, p. 19.

into account the pessimistic temper of the Indian thinkers themselves, we shall not wonder that in all their enunciations they favour absolutism. Perhaps pessimism and absolutism go together. In India, there could only be the King on the one hand and his "subjects" on the other. There could be no citizenship in the ordering of the State. In the Ideal State the citizens in their collective capacity are the rulers and in their individual capacity are subjects; but where participation in governance by the citizens is not possible, then the individuals are not properly speaking citizens but subjects; and the ruler is not also himself a citizen, but the owner of the State.

"Just as the State is not merely a community in territory or in the legal protection of person and property, so a citizen does not mean," writes Bradley, "one who resides in a certain city and can be sued in its law-courts. These are not functions of the State and do not involve participation in its end. If the citizen is to be really a part of the State he must live its life; and that in the concrete means that he must govern. Thus citizenship may be defined as "ruling and being ruled," and a citizen as one who shares or has the right to share, in government, deliberative, executive and judicial. In so doing he uses not only the virtues of obedience, not only the common moral virtues, but also the excellences of moral wisdom and command".[1] Thus conceived the good citizen is indeed, the good man if citizenship could have reference to the complete man and to complete life. In the Ideal State, where social, religious and political interests are harmonised, the individual acts as a whole individual; and the good he strives after is not the good of his individual self, but that which has reference to a wider and more inclusive whole. The man lives as a whole personality; he is not every time a separate individual as he turns to

[1] *Aristotle's Conception of the State*, Hellenica, p. 213.

the various aspects of life ; he cannot so speak of bits of the man as isolable. And so the good of the man is the good of the whole man, who again is a member of the Society consisting of whole men, and the good of the individual is the coherence which could be realised in the universal coherence. And the good of the individual has its influence on the State. If it is limited the State also is limited. If the good of the man is not all-inclusive, if it seeks an end which is not a sharing with others, the State also would not be all-inclusive. Its end, considered as the good, has reference, not to the coherence of the whole, but to some parts of it. We might say, that the man himself is the foundation of the State and citizenship ; and the factors that influence in moulding the good man also would frame the good State. The highest Good is at once the good of the State and the good of the individual ; there is a close interdependence between the two. As Bosanquet rightly remarks, the State is the condition of organised good life for its members. And so there is the closest of moral bonds between the citizen and the State.

"This highest good assumes a State," writes Pipkin, "that is positively concerned with justice for each individual and for all groups within its jurisdiction".[1] And in a State in which the principle of justice is strictly limited, in which there is no conception of Social Justice which refers to the coherence of the whole, then those excluded from the application of the principle are necessarily also those who are denied the opportunities to develop those virtues which would enable them to be good men and good citizens. The ordering of the ancient Indian State was a violation of Social Justice, because it was vitiated by gross inequalities. Even the written law of the realm,

---

1 *The Idea of Social Justice*, p. 547.

as recorded in the various codes could not make for the rule of fair play. The poet Euripides could say :

> "With written laws, the humblest in the State
> Is sure of equal justice with the great,"

if the same law with equal significance applied to all irrespective of distinctions. But in Ancient India, the law was not the same for all. It was influenced by the Caste-system. The higher castes were someties exempt from any punishment whatever if they committed offences ; and, in all events, the punishment when inflicted was never severe. But the lower the caste of the offender, the greater was the severity of the punishment. So the law of the realm was vitiated by inequalities.

Moreover the members of the State had not all of them an equal status. The Caste-system it was which determined the status of the individual. It is only the members of the higher castes that had any recognised status. The lower castes had no status at all ; and especially the members of the lowest classes were scarce treated as human beings. The members of the higher castes were born high because of the merit they had acquired in their former existence. The lower castes are so because of their past.

Curiously enough the members of the fairer sex have also always been held to be of sinful birth. Women are always coupled with Vaisyas, Sudras etc., who are by nature sinful.[1] The status of the individual was thus decided by the caste into which he happens to be born. The institution of caste, whatever its origin, whether religious or economic, determined the relations of men in society. The lower castes suffered most in the ordering of society. "In the eyes of the aristocratic Argeus, the lower castes such as the Chandalas, are impure. Their very sight causes pollution ; consequently they must be excluded from

[1] *Anugita*, Ch. IV.

the general society and must live in a special village of their own outside cf the town and earn a living by means of lower occupations".[1] We do not propose to go into the details of the evidence[2] we have before us, for the space

---

[1] Richard Fick: *Social Org.*, p. 50; see also his chapter on the Despised Castes.

[2] The references given here will enable the reader to understand the position of Sudras and the lower classes in Society. The institution of caste—clearly recognised in the period of the *Atharva Veda*—caste in *Rig Veda*. In the later *Samhitas* and particularly in the *Brahmanas*, we find references to some classes called the outcastes, who could not be touched etc., the Chandala and Paulkasa—only the term Vrishala in the *Rig Veda*.

Basu: *Indo Aryan Polity*, p. 52 ff.

Jatakas, II, 83 ff; III, 233; IV, 200, 376, 388, 390-2; IV, 144.

Cambridge History of India, pp. 260-261.

Shama Sastry: *Evolution of Indian Polity*, p. 25.

On the Rise of Caste, pp. 40-41.

See Hopkins: *Ethics of India*, pp. 59-60.

Vedic Index, Vol. I, p. 253 for Chandala Caste,

Ibid., p. 281 for Jati,

Ibid., pp. 347-349 for Dasyus,

Ibid., p. 386 for Dvija,

Ibid., pp. 453-454 for Nisada or Untouchables,

Ibid., pp. 466-468 Panca-Janah.

Ibid., Vol. II, p. 8 for Origin of Caste,

Ibid., p. 8 for Pulinda or Outcaste Tribes,

Ibid., p. 13 for Purta or Reward of Priests,

Ibid., p. 25 Pamiji-Stha, a functional Caste,

Ibid., p. 27—Paulkasa, a low caste (functional), Chandala.

Ibid., p. 74 ff. for Caste,

Ibid., p. 111 for Bheda,

Ibid., p. 170 for Mutiba,

Ibid., p. 181 for Mleccha,

Ibid., pp. 246-271 for Varma,

Ibid., pp. 342-344 Vratyas or Outcastes.

Ibid., pp. 388-392 for Sudra.

Richard Fick: *Social Organisation*, p. 50. "In the eyes of the aristocratic Aryans, the lower castes such as the Chandalas, are impure. Their very sight causes pollution; consequently, they must be excluded from the general societv and must live in a

at our disposal will not permit. What we would point out is that the Sudras and the lower castes suffered under serious disabilities, legal as well as social, that it would have been impossible for them, under any circumstance, to exercise the rights of citizenship. The right to exercise the powers of citizenship must have depended upon the power to enforce the recognition of such rights. The ancient Hindu Polity was such that this power of enforcing the rights could not be exercised by the people at large.

We have just said that the status of women in society was such that they could never have exercised the rights and privileges of citizenship. They were always considered to be dependent.[1] They were hemmed in by restraints on all sides.[2]

---

special village of their own outside of the town and earn a living by means of lower occupations." See his Chapter on the Despised Castes.

Ghoshal: *Hindu Political Theories*, pp. 28-30.

Anugita, Ch. IV.

See especially Elphinstone's *History of India*, pp. 14-21.

Banerjea: *Public Adm. in Ancient India*, pp. 20-21.

Exclusive of the lower caste etc., from the administration of Justice, see Banerjea: *Public Adm.*, p. 160.

For the civilisation of Pre-Aryan Time, see Banerjea: *Public Adm.*, p. 215.

See, S. K. Maitra: *The Ethics of the Hindus*, p. 18 and quote from legal books etc., to refute the statement of S. K. Maitra *Apastamba*, p. 2.

Apastamba, pp. 34-35; Sudras and Chandalas and Educaiton; *Gautama*, p. 258.

Apastamba, p. 165 for status of Sudras.

Gautama, pp. 229-231—also pp. 236-237.

Ibid., p. 277 for the definition of Outcastes;

Ibid., pp. 280-286;

Narada, p. 33.

Law of Evidence, Narada, pp. 245-246;

Brihaspati, p. 356; also p. 359.

[1] See *Manu*, IX, 2, 3.

[2] The following references will introduce the reader to some of the most important facts concerning women in India:

This degradation of the women was a general characteristic of all early societies; and even at the present day, the movement for emancipation has gained some success only in a few countries. The causes of the inferiority of the fairer sex which are of a general nature were operative in India as elsewhere. As Bagehot has pointed out

---

Banerjea: *Public Adm.*, p. 58;
Apastamba, pp. 88, 89, 158-159, 164; II, 10, 27, 3;
Gautama, pp. 194-195; 198-205; 267-269; XVIII, 22, XVIII, 1;
Narada, pp. 36-37; 49; 50-51; 89-92; 169-173, 176; 181-183; 183-184; 184; 184-185; 196-197.
Vishnu, XXIV, 38-39; XXIV, 41; XXV, 12, 13; XXV, 2.
Manu, V, 151, IX, 4, 93, IX, 89-81, IX, 3, V, 148, IX, 94, IX, 22; II, 213-214; IX, 14-18, IX, 10, 11, V, 147-156, IX, 48-51.
Yajnavalkya, I, 63, 64, I, 73, I, 85.
Parasa, VII, 6.
Samvarta, V, 66.
Vasishtha, XVII, 69-71; V, 1, 2. XVII, 2.
Baudhayana, IV, 1, 13; II, 3, 44, 45.
Brihaspati, pp. 307; 366-367; 367-369; 375-385.
Bhasa: *Pratima Nataka*, Act. I, p. 5, Act. I, pp. 13, 15.
Kalidasa: *Malavikagnimitra*, p. 78.
Sakuntala, pp. 54, 84, 89, 101.
Bhavabhuti: *Malati Madhava*, p. 23.
Cambridge History of India, pp. 88, 134-135; 292-294; 414-415; 481.
Kautilya, pp. 193-201.
Anugita, Ch. IV.
Santi Parva, Sect. XXIX.
Vedic Index, Vol. I, pp. 30; 274, 275; 395-396; 474-489, 284, 285, 537.
Vol. II, 114-115; 485-48.
Taittviiyaka Upanishad, I, Valli, 11 Anwaka, 1-2.
Pandita Ramabai: *The High Caste Hindu Woman*, Ch. VI, pp. 94-106.
Rig Veda, IV, 55.
A. B. Keith: *The Sankhya System*, p. 113.
Mrs. Rhys Davids: *Theragatha*, Nos. 98, 137, 99, 267-269, 453-458, 738.

"the non-combatant population is sure to fare ill during the ages of combat".[1] Moreover the religious necessity of having a "putra" or male offspring who would continue the domestic worship and offer libations to gods, Rishis and Pitris always tended to discount the value of begetting female children. To some extent also, the economic dependence on others counted in determining the status of the woman. The modern suffragist movement has gathered irresistible strength only when the woman has acquired the necessary power to depend on her own efforts for a living. Whatever the cause, the woman in Ancient India, as elsewhere, was in the position of inferiority, and so could not exercise the rights and privileges of citizenship.[2]

We are often told, however, that the woman in Ancient India occupied a position of enviable felicity, and that it is only in comparatively modern times that she has been degraded to a low position in society. The evidence that we have before us does not allow us to entertain enthusiastic imaginations of this nature about our past.[3] To point to the instances of a few great women is not proof of the general condition of the times. We have to look to the spirit of the law of times; the various regulations in the

[1] *Physics and Politics*, p. 79.

[2] cf. *Ancient Greece* (Herodotus).

[3] Max Muller in his *History of Sanskrit Literature* (pp. 14-15) writing on the position of women in Ancient India says that "cases like that of Maitreyi were exceptions, not the rule".

Manu expressly lays down (Bk. IX, 18) that "women have no right to read the texts of the Veda". Megasthenes gives the reason for the reluctance to allow women to study. He says that "the Indians did not communicate their metaphysical doctrines to women, thinking that if their wives understood these doctrines and learned to be indifferent to pleasure and pain, and to consider life and death to be the same, they would no longer continue to be the slaves of others; or if they failed to understand them, they would be talkative, and communicate their knowledge to those who had no right to it".

Dharmasastras, the references to the nature of women in literature; and from all these various sources we know that the woman in ancient society was certainly in a lower position than she is in to-day. And as we said, the stray instances of heroic queens that we have need not modify the general characterisation that we make here. A female on the throne is not unusual and so need not mislead us in our estimate of the position of woman in general. Even Montesquieu says, "it is contrary to reason and nature that women should reign in families, as was customary among the Egyptians, but not that they govern an empire".[1]

We might thus say that the ordering of Society in Ancient India was such that there could never emerge the conception of citizenship which would satisfy the End of the Ideal State and which would conform to the principle of true Social Justice. The rights of individuals in the State were not determined by reference to the coherence of the whole. "Right is," says Bradley,[2] "generally, the expression of the universal". A right thing to do is that in which the universal is realised and an individual has a right which is the expression of law. But, thus understood, the idea of right is essentially moral and "the emphasis is on the universal". When we speak of a right

---

Bhagavad-gita (Telang's Trans., p. 85) assumes that women are of sinful birth.

In the *Siksha-Samuccaya* (p. 83) we have: "The Bodhisatva in presence of his wife must realise three thoughts. And what are the three? She is my companion for passion and dalliance but not for the next world, my companion at meat and drink but not for the fruition of the maturing of my acts. She is the companion of my pleasure, not of my pain.—Three other thoughts are that a wife must be regarded as an obstacle to virtue to meditate and to wisdom. And yet three more: She is like a thief, a murderer, or a guardian of hell.

[1] *Spirit of Laws*, Bk. VIII, Ch. 17.

[2] *Ethical Studies*, p. 207.

we usually speak of it as that which could be enforced and that which is recognised by law. But here we are not concerned with the legal conception of right. If right be the creation of the State, as Bentham insists, then "there can be no right which is not constituted by law".[1] A legal right as Professor Holland defines,[2] is "a capacity residing in one man of controlling with the assent and assistance of the State, the actions of others." But a legal right need not be a creation of the State. Only the law courts must recognise it. The State may be at the back of the decisions of the law courts and may help in enforcing them. The rights that could be enforced in the courts of the realm in Ancient India, were, as we have seen, not universal in nature; they could not be enjoyed by every individual irrespective of caste and birth. Gross inequalities subsisted, and "in these we are struck with the prodigious elevation and sanctity of the Brahmins and the studied degradation of the lowest class".[3] The Sudras and the lower classes who were practically slaves had the same position in society, as the Helots had in Sparta and the serfs or the villeins had in the Middle Ages. The legal rights of the lower castes were practically non-existent; the law was on the side of the Brahmins and the higher castes. The lower castes had not even so much as the right to live as the right to serve. And so the conception of Rights, considered in the legal sense, the vast majority of the people could never actualise in their lives.

Can we at least say that the idea of right as moral was visualised as something universal, in the sense that what is wrong or right to one is necessarily also wrong or right to another? Or, to use an expression which has been almost universally misunderstood. Can we say that there was any conception of "Natural Rights", which the

[1] Bosanquet: *Philosophical Theory of the State*, p. 66.
[2] *Jurisprudence*, (Ed. II), pp. 61-62.
[3] *The History of India* by Elphinstone, pp. 14-21.

people should enjoy? Not rights which a man is supposed to have enjoyed in a condition of Nature, but rights which can never be independent of social relations. We mean rights which inhere in the nature of man as a social being, without the exercise of which he can never realise the complete spiritual potentialities in him. If the Society adhered to a common religious belief regulated by common moral ideas, then it would not be difficult to conceive of moral rights or duties which could be exercised or enforced by the force of the Public Opinion of Society. But such moral rights and duties are equally binding, with equal significance on all the members that compose the body-politic. And again, natural rights, in the sense we use the expression when we speak of the Right to Freedom, ought to be, in a society in which coherence rules, the possession of all, even of the slaves or serfs in the State. According to our ideal "we are entitled to say that the slave has a right to citizenship, to a recognised equality of freedom with any and every one with whom he has to do, and that in refusing him not only citizenship, but the means of training his capability of citizenship, the State is violating a right founded"[1] on a common human consciousness which is evinced by his relations with others. In the Ancient Indian State the conception of moral or natural right as a universal, could never have existed, because, for one thing, man himself was not recognised in his nature as universal, and secondly because a right in itself was not universal. The Doctrine of Swadharma lays emphasis on particular rights and duties applicable to particular castes and orders. Rights and duties which are mutually correlated must themselves be related to a functional scheme aiming at universal coherence. In other words the Life-scheme must be purposive; and Purpose or End, or Good, must be Common or Social; otherwise

[1] T. H. Green: *Political Obligation*, p. 145.

it cannot be Purpose, or End, or Good. And "where there is no recognition of a common good, there can be no right," as T. H. Green rightly asserts,[1] "in any other sense than power". In Ancient India the few who constituted the higher castes regarded their own right as independent of its correlation to duty ; and hence the right of the higher castes was so because they had the power to enforce it. The lower castes, if we might so express, had mere duties without corresponding rights. If "Rights and duties are sides of a single whole," and if there cannot be mere rights or mere duties or mere particular rights and duties as such, then the Good must be the practical identity of both. "Rights and duties are elements in the good ; they must go together". There must be perfect reciprocity. The right of the slave must be the right also of the citizen ; the duty of the Sudra or the Chandala must also be the duty of the Brahmin or the Kshatriya. Otherwise we have mere particular rights and duties, not correlated to the whole Polity. We can, in that case, never have Society or State which can be regarded as a System. We have merely a human aggregate. This is the difference that we have already pointed out, between the Ideal and the Actual. It may be that our Ideal may not square with facts ; It is in the Ideal State that we can have the perfect realisation of our complete Life and Personality ; because we have the conditions of perfect freedom. But in the Actual State in which the majority of the persons are practically slaves, such as the Ancient Indian State was, "it would have been a mockery to speak of the State as a realisation of freedom.[2] The inequalities that we have noted in our ancient Polity are not compatible with free-

[1] *Political Obligation*, p. 64.

[2] The opinion is that of T. H. Green, whose ardent disciple the present writer aspires to be.

dom;[1] and so long as such inequalities persist, there can never be the conception of citizenship either.

True citizenship can only develop when equality of civil and political rights is adequately established. We should even say that citizenship is impossible under any system in which economic inequalities are so glaring that life becomes impossible to the millions who constitute society. To live well, people must live at all. Good Life is impossible without first securing the conditions of mere life. And "every society," as Mr. Asquith has said, is judged, "according to the material and moral minima which it prescribes to its members".[2] No citizenship is worth having if wealth accumulates in the hands of the few, and the many decay, and await a lingering end. If one set of men are secured in the power of getting and keeping the means of realising their will, says T. H. Green,[3] in such a way that the others are practically denied the power, then it may truly be said that "property is theft". In a sense his statement that "the original landlords have been conquerors[4] is perfectly true, if it is applied to Ancient India. The Aryan conquerors became the owners of the soil; and the lower castes, the Sudras and the despised castes were left the meaner avocations or occupations to provide them with livelihood which was very precarious indeed. In other words, the Right to Live was not universally recognised; and the so-called untouchables, as we have seen, were scarce recognised at all

[1] The Social Philosophy of the Hindus does not admit of the Principles of Equality. "One should not desire equality with gods, cows and Brahmans", says Sukracharya (*Nitisara*, p. 119). "This is very harmful and destructive to the whole family, and so, one should always worship, respect and serve these. It is not known how much of the spirit divine is implanted in each".

[2] Quoted by Newman *Citizenship and the Survival of Civilisation*, p. 80.

[3] *Political Obligation*, p. 220.

[4] *Ibid.*, p. 226.

as human beings; they are bipeds in human shape. The social legislation of the times was exclusively in the interests of the higher castes; and the aim was to prevent the lower castes, by the acquisition of material wealth, to become the equals of the higher.

Considered from whatever point of view, we might emphatically assert that the conception of citizenship could never emerge out of the conditions prevalent in our ancient Polity. We are aware that what we might describe as "neighbourliness" was always a feature of our social relationships. But anything that seeks to cohere Society in a more organic sense might not have existed.

True citizenship, we hold, can only refer to the human being as a member of Society. He can realise his true self only as a member of his group. By abstracting himself from social relationships, by isolating himself from human realities he becomes more and more eccentric and morbid. Eccentricity, as we have said, can never make for the realisation of true individuality. Self-suppression and self-isolation can never help one to self-realisation. The Indian ideal, we therefore hold, needs a radical revision. The truth must universally be admitted that "the citizen who stands alone to-day is lost. It is as part of a group that he secures the power to fulfil himself".[1]

Further citizenship must involve, either directly or indirectly, the participation of the governance of the State. And the power exercised by the State, being in its nature fiduciary, must be subject to the scrutiny of and control by the citizens. "Those are always most truly citizens," as Laski observes, "who insist upon bringing back our rulers to a realisation of the conditions upon which their power is held.[2]

---

[1] Laski: *Dangers of Obedience*, p. 59 (Chapter on the Recovery of Citizenship).

[2] *Ibid.*, p. 9.

And lastly "The end of citizenship, and of all the institutions which it creates, is the development of individuality."[1] But the development of individuality is impossible so long as there is no adequate conception of the individual and what constitute his individuality. And we hold that citizenship essentially lies in the activity of man which seeks to enrich personality in the contribution to the life of the Great Fellowship of which all are participants. In other words, it is a partnership from which none can be excluded.

In the ultimate, therefore, citizenship cannot be limited.[2] If it should have any meaning, it should not refer to this and that particular group but to the group which constitutes Humanity. It is not fanciful to conceive the world as the unit of our allegiance. The national or the territorial State can never be an end in itself. We have to visualise Mankind as a whole; and the individual is, in that sense, the Citizen of the World. The ruling factors in world relationships shall be that of solidarity and interdependence. The World-State is to be regarded as one Family, just as Aristotle considered that the Family was the basis of the State. The world has shrunk in size and our relationships are cosmopolitan. Citizenship must be an all-inclusive partnership; and "consists in harmonising diverse but consistent loyalties and patriotisms in one living common interest, integrated and conjunct, which makes human life purposive, instead of being undirected or misdirected".[3]

In other words, there cannot be an adequate idea of citizenship unless we re-visualise the Common End that "life must subserve." Our "Dharma," must be restated

---

[1] Hetherington: *Social Purpose*, p. 210.

[2] Exclusion or limitation means slavery: cf. Laski: *Liberty in the Modern State*, p. 38.

[3] Newman: *Citizenship and Survival of Civilisation*, p. 44.

so that it shall be an all-inclusive Purpose, seeking to lay the foundation for the True Polity which is co-extensive with our moral aspiration as children of a Common Father to constitute ourselves into a Universal Fraternity.

CHAPTER VIII

GROUNDS OF POLITICAL OBLIGATION

"To ask why I am to submit to the power of the State is to ask why I am to allow my life to be regulated by that complex of institutions without which I literally should not have a life to call my own, nor should be able to ask for a justification of what I am called on to do."

T. H. GREEN

"If the purpose of the State be understood, as clearly as is possible at the time, and all existing power be directed towards the realisation of this highest conception, then is the Government right and good, whether it be in the hands of all, or in the hands of a few individuals, or finally in those of a single individual: it being understood, in this last case, that this single individual chooses his assistants according to his own judgment, who remain subject and responsible to him."

J. G. FICHTE

"The State as it was and is finds the roots of allegiance in all the complex facts of human nature; and a theory of obedience would have to weight them differently for each epoch in the history of the State if it were to approximate to the truth."

LASKI

We have said that force was not the basis of the State. We have to consider the grounds for political obligation in some other principle which would appeal to our reason. Institutions, we said, are embodied ideas, concretised purposes. The problem to be considered is how our purpose expresses itself in the life and ordering of the State. It has been observed that most of the life the ordinary people live is of a private nature.[1] They seem to be hardly

[1] Conditions in ancient Greece, especially in Athens, were essentially different from conditions that prevail in modern times. The Greek citizen had every opportunity to contribute his instructed judgment to the public good. The Athenian at any rate did not feel the cleavage between public and private life. In fact most of his life was of a public nature. He spent all his day in the market-place; and he was always in touch with the affairs

conscious of obligations of a political nature arising out of their relations with the State. To Aristotle, man is a political animal. And in the conditions that subsisted in the city-States of ancient Hellas the truth of his statement was largely realised. Can we say the same thing of Ancient India? Was the obedience that people rendered to the State merely from inertia?

Senart has frankly denied the idea of the State to Ancient India, and so he does not admit any beginnings of State-consciousness. He maintains that there was no foundation of a genuine political power in Ancient India, and so no political condition was evolved. "There was no vestige of a State."[1] Everything depends, however, on what we mean by the State. If we do not confound it with the form it assumes,[2] and try to grasp it as the idea which it is, it is certainly possible yet to use the term State in describing the political aspect of our ancient Polity.

In all discussions of the grounds of political obligation the distinction between the State and the Government seems to be generally overlooked. There appears to be an attempt to equate the two, and in condemning the acts of Government, the State also along with it is thrown overboard. Allegiance to the State as Idea is really different from obligation considered necessary to the particular repository of political authority which is the Government.

---

of his city. Laski is right in his characterisation of the nature of the life of modern man. "Our scale of life, and our method of responding to its wants have made him a private person to whom politics is a matter of episodic and tangential interest".

Dangers of Obedience, p. 65.

[1] *Caste in India*, p. 212.

[2] Those who take this ground argue on empiric grounds. Willoughby truly says, "We cannot refuse the designation of State to a society of men, if politically organised even though it be in the nomadic stage"—*The nature of the State*, p. 27.

The famous sociologist, Giddings says, "the State as idea, is disembodied and irresponsible."[1] But we never say, the Government, as it is, is to be held irresponsible. In all the criticisms of the State it is generally the particular person or body of persons through which its power is exercised that is vehemently attacked. It is forgotten that no idealist would try to justify the *Status quo*. His contention is that the actual achievements of the State must be judged with reference to an ideal standard, the idea of the State as the pattern, and that the State which is, is an imperfect embodiment of the idea of the Ideal State. But imperfection, as we hold, is not the negation of perfection, but only its limitation. And it is an imperfection too that gradually grows into perfection. The empirical criterion is apt to be fallacious, therefore, in our attempt to determine grounds for political obligation. We do admit, of course, that the Actual State is finite and that its power is always fiduciary,[2] and its rights are conditional. Our judgment of the State is with reference to the Purpose or End it seeks to achieve for its members. And people render obedience to the commands of the State, because they feel that the State is the condition of the fulfilment of their own purpose and life. The various institutions of Society subsist under the protecting wing of the State. "It is the structure which gives life and meaning to them all." "It includes the entire hierarchy of institutions by which life is determined, from the family to the trade, and from the trade to the church and the University. The State, it might be said, is thus conceived

---

[1] *The Responsible State*, pp. 15-16.

[2] cf. Laski: *Authority in the Modern State*, p. 46 where Laski says: "Power is held not for evil but for good, and deflection from the path of right purpose ought to involve the withdrawal of authority for its exercise."

as the operative criticism of all institutions......"[1] The obedience rendered to the commands of the State should therefore be explained by a reference to some other principle than force, though force may be said to inhere, in a sense, in the very nature of the State.[2]

The Ancient Indian State, at any rate, was an embodiment of Power.[3] The monarch is its sole repository. He wields "Danda" or the Rod of Chastisement. The organisation of justice and its administration constantly reminds the people, however distantly removed from the centre of Government, of a power standing above them, surrounding them and protecting them. The fact which is of

[1] These statements of Bosanquet (*Phil. Theory of the State*, p. 140) are perfectly true if applied to the Ancient State of India. And we have seen also that it is absurd to maintain that the State and the Society were aloof from each other in Ancient India. The Pluralist and the Pragmatist contend that the Idealist makes a confusion between State and Society. Hobhouse, for instance, complains: "to confuse the State with society and political with moral obligation is the central fallacy of the metaphysical theory of the State"....... (*The Metaphysical Theory of the State*, p. 77). As we have have insisted so often, it is impossible for us to exclude moral and ethical considerations from our study. We are afraid that the Pluralist and the Pragmatist, on the other hand, make a serious confusion between the State and Government. Otherwise Hobhouse would not say that "by the State we ordinarily mean either the Government or, perhaps a little more accurately the organisation which is at the back of law and Government"...... (*The Meta. Theory*, p. 75) and Laski would not maintain that the individual could stand outside and pass judgments on the actions of the State.

[2] For, as Fichte has said, the State "must be one of constraint." Those who feel no desire and so feel reluctant to regulate their life according to the purpose of the larger whole to which they belong must be made to do so by the action of the State. See *The Popular Works of J. G. Fichte*, Vol. II, p. 149 ff.

[3] "Power is means," says MacIver, "and we cannot think at all without relating means to ends." (*The Modern State*, p. 426.) This means that the State can never be merely a Power System.

supreme significance in our present consideration is that the people do accept—acquiese in, if we will—the decisions of the ruler. It may be that they are not conscious every second of the fact. In civilised societies generally obedience is rendered by the people at large almost quite unconsciously. This is so because, "in the course of countless ages the stern discharge of their chief duty by States," as Maine has explained, "has created habits and sentiments which save the necessity for penal interference because nearly everybody shares them."[1] And simply because the people do not appear to be conscious of political relations, we should not be led to the conclusion that the people were unrelated to the State, or that the State was to them no vital concern. After all, our consciousness itself admits of degree—of our awareness, more or less. In any given moment in experience some particular object may be present to our consciousness ; and we may appear to contemplate it exclusively. If by this we assume that our mind is blank for the time being to other impressions, we would be sadly mistaken in our idea of consciousness itself. In fact we are able to recall and sometimes to anticipate more or less permanent objects present to our consciousness. If the individual therefore lives and acts as if he does not know even of the existence of the State this should not lead us to the conclusion that to him the State does not exist. It is exactly here that Pluralistic writers on the Ancient Indian Polity have failed to interpret things in their real significance. They speak as if the individual was conscious of his membership of regional, religious and

[1] *Popular Government*, p. 63. And without habitual obedience to the laws of the realm civil society would become impossible. Even those who insist on the rights of the conscientious subject to disobey are careful to point out that "a right to disobedience... is...reasonably to be exercised only at the margins of political conduct. No community could hope to fulfil its purpose if rebellion became a settled habit of the population." *A Grammar of Politics*, p. 62.

vocational groups, like the village, caste and guild; but that he did not care to know who ruled over the State. And yet facts do not seem to bear out their contention. The character of the ruler immediately reflected itself in the nature of his rule and made directly either for the happiness or misery of each people. We come across numerous descriptions of unrighteous rule and the lot of the subjects who would fly into the jungles and there "live like beasts with their wives and children." The character of the State, i.e. of the nature of the rule of the monarch, was indeed of such a vital concern that, as we have seen, theorists went so far as to say that the King is the maker of his age.

The fact cannot be denied, therefore, that the State did enter into the life of each person within it; and what the State was could not be a matter of indifference to its members. Even if the State primarily revealed itself to them in its coercive aspect, we have still to explain why the people gave in their submission. We have observed that there is always a potential limit to sovereignty which could operate as a check—the resistance of the subjects. Was revolution considered legitimate by the ancient Indians?[1] If in every case of oppression the people did not revolt against their King, when they had the strength to do so, what was that factor which restrained them? What, in short, are the grounds for political allegiance?

The position of the monarch in Ancient India, let us first remind ourself was despotic, but not generally tyrannical. His autocratic nature lies in this that he is not himself under any constitutional limitations. But the sovereign power of the King was itself a reflex of Dharma considered as Absolute Sovereign. The End of the State was to maintain Dharma, and in its own nature, it realised aspects

---

[1] cf. Benoy Kumar Sarkar: *The Political Institutions and Theories of the Hindus*, p. 179 ff.

See also D. R. Bhandarkar's works.

of it. Power is always a trust, even when it appears to be most arbitrarily exercised; if abused it always invites resistance. The ancient State was not a State by courtesy; but because it rested on intelligent foundations. To understand the basis of political obligation it is necessary to realise that the individual obeys the State because he feels that it embodies, however imperfectly, a purpose which can be vitally related to his own life. Let us, in the first instance, examine the various theories put forward at one time or another, to justify the claims of the State on the individual; in the end, perhaps, we shall be in a better position to formulate the causes of the obedience rendered by the people to the decisions of the State.

We shall first of all try to explore the theories which seek to justify the sovereignty of the State, which try to establish the legitimacy of the rule of the monarch. And then we shall proceed to a deeper analysis of the facts of human nature itself which make man submissive to the power of the State.

A State is considered legitimate, either by its own right, because it rests on a divine sanction; or because its power is based upon an explicit covenant. The necessity of the State is recognised in both the conceptions. Only, the one idea places the State far above the scrutiny of man, and in that sense superhuman; while the other idea makes the State the creature of man and hence artificial and conventional. From both the conceptions the idea that the State is a natural institution, the expression of the facts inherent in the being of man as man is practically absent, that what confers legitimacy to the acts of the State is that what it does is the expression of our purpose, however imperfectly it might be.

We shall first examine the theory that regards the basis of the State as contractual.[1] We are not here con-

[1] See for the Social Contract Theory, *Vayu Purana*, Ch. 49; *Matsya Purana*, Ch. 122; *Raghyu Vamsa*, 1, 2; *Santi Parva*,

cerned with the question of origins, for we are seeking adequate grounds for political allegiance. The Social Contract theory interests us only so far as it tells us why we have to obey the State. According to this theory the sovereign power, once created, is legitimate thereafter. The covenant itself may be revokable or irrevokable, or renewable from time to time. With the details of the theory we are not concerned, if for no other reason but for the simple fact that no Indian thinker tries to stretch the idea to its logical implications. In the speculations of Hindu theorists the contract conception is very shadowy, and indeed, it is highly questionable how far they really imply a positive covenant as such.[1] In the stories we have in the *Santi Parva* and *Kautilya*, the tales are inserted simply to point to a moral; no historic explanation of the emergence of political society is even indirectly implied. And the moral points to kingship as a divine creation, and certainly not contractual in the sense of a human creation. In the stories of the Buddhist scriptures, again, no definite theory of origin is meant though the rise of kingship seems to be based upon popular agreement. In that sense monarchy may appear to be conventional, but the Buddhist thinkers stopped with this; they do not try to deduce from this fact any principles of relationship between the King and his subjects. What differentiates the Buddhist versions from the Hindu is that the former seem to attribute a purely secular origin to kingship. Especially Asvagosha tries to maintain that kingship has its origin in consent.

The idea of a contract wherever we have it in Indian literature is not a theory of political obligation as such;

---

pp. 216-18, 218-223. For the origin of the State read the story in *Digha Nikaya* which is called *Aggammasuttaita*, Rhys Davids: *Sacred Books of the Buddhists*, Vol. IV, p. 77 ff.

[1] Benoy Kumar Sarkar seems to have taken the contractual idea quite seriously in his discussions of the nature of the ancient Hindu State.

it does not seek to define the relationship between the King and the people, as for instance, under what terms the King holds and exercises power, and under what circumstances the people could revoke the covenant made with the King, on the ground that the conditions of the agreement were not observed. The value of the theories involving the so called contractual origin of Government lies in this that the consequences of the absence of Government seem to have been very clearly understood. Whether any actual State of Nature was believed in to have existed in the remote past is not relevant to our discussion, as also the belief in a Golden Age. Descriptions in the various sacred and legal books certainly do point to a period in the distant past when the condition of the world was one of heavenly felicity, when gods freely moved in the company of mortals, when super-men, rishis and yogis could fly about in ethereal regions because of their divine powers. The glowing picture of this Golden Age does not, however, correspond to the descriptions of the State of Nature in Indian Literature. The State of Nature was not the reign of God that Pope[1] thought it was ; it was a state of war which Hobbes has described. This fiction of the State of Nature was not invented by Hobbes ; for Plato and Cicero had long before him tried to examine it. The poetical fiction of the Golden Age, as Hume rightly points out, is "of a piece with the philosophical fiction of the State of Nature."[2] Both are highly fanciful and have no basis in history if we would understand the State of Nature as a condition of war "rather as a logical statement of what *would* be the condition of man apart from civil society".[3] We would not confound ourselves in trying to find historic foundations for the

[1] *Essay on Man*, III, 147 ff.

[2] *Inquiry concerning the Principles of Morals*, Sect. III, part I.

[3] Bluntschli : *Theory of the State*, p. 284.

theory and the theory of Contract which explains how the State came into existence will cease to have reference to any actual document of its kind. Rousseau,[1] who was in many respects more profound in his analysis than the others rightly speaks of a State of Nature "which no longer exists, which perhaps never has existed;" and to him the Social Contract was tacitly implied in every actual society. The articles of the contract "are the same everywhere and are everywhere tacitly admitted and recognised even though they may never have found formal expression". Or as Hume[2] said, the contract "was not written on parchment, nor yet on leaves or barks of trees...... we trace it in the nature of man." And the force or coercive power of the State is based upon the consent of the people, upon "their sense of the advantages resulting from peace and order". And so, if we would try to understand the significance of the Social Contract theory that we have in the thought of our ancients, we shall have to take it as only as referring to the elements to be found in human nature. The contract emphasises the fact of consent either explicitly or implicitly given; if it is attempted to give it a legal or constitutional significance, as defining the relations between the King and the subjects determined according to the provisions of a covenant, then the contract idea has no basis either in reason or in fact.

One important truth lies beneath the discussions of the State of Nature and Contract. And that is the necessity of the State without which there could never be either civil or political society. Indeed life itself would be impossible. The State of Nature has been characteristically described as *Matsyanyaya*; and the distinguishing characteristic of it is the absence of the Reign of Law. If there were a society of gods or god-like men, then, indeed, there would not be

1 *Contrat Social*, I, vi.

2 *Of the Original Contract.*

any necessity for a compelling power. "When mortals were bent on doing their duty alone and habitually veracious there existed neither law suits, nor hatred, nor selfishness", writes Narada.[1]

"In former ages men were strictly virtuous and devoid of mischievous propensities", says Brihaspati.[2] Now that avarice and malice have taken possession of them, and now that the practice of duty has died out among mankind, "lawsuits have been introduced and the King has been appointed to decide law-suits because he has authority to punish."[3] And it is because man is not by nature virtuous that coercive power is found to be necessary to keep him in check. In the estimate of human nature, the Indian view approximates to that of Hobbes and provision for security must be made, "not by compacts, but by punishments."[4] And so the basis of the Indian State does not rest on contract; and as we said, the contract idea and that of the State of Nature are incidentally brought in to point to a moral. This is especially clear if we try to see what the story of the contract in itself is. In all the tales, except those to be found in Buddhist scriptures, the idea of contract is very shadowy, and that too, it is not primarily between men and men. The creation of the King himself is a divine act. After the King is ordained by Brahmà, the people enter into a compact with him. This compact itself is not an elaborate formulation of the rights and duties of the citizens. What is important, for our purpose to note, is that the King is not created by the people but by God. There is a very interesting story recorded in the *Santi Parva* of how men, "in days of old, in consequence of anarchy met with destruction devouring one another like stronger fishes devouring the weaker one

[1] P. 5 (Jolly).
[2] P. 277 (Jolly).
[3] *Narada*, p. 5.
[4] Hobbes: *On Dominion*, Ch. VI, 4.

in the water." A few amongst them met and made certain compacts to live together. After sometime, they realised that they were still going to destruction; and so they proceeded to the Grandsire saying, "Without a King, O Divine Lord, we are going to destruction. Appoint someone as our King. All of us shall worship him and he shall protect us"! The Grandsire, thus appealed to, asked Manu to be King, who however was unwilling. His scruples were overcome only when the people bound themselves by a compact, to obey him. They promised him: "For the increase of thy treasury, we will give thee a fiftieth part of our animals and precious metals, and a tenth part of our grain! When our maidens also become desirous of wedding, we shall when the question of dowry comes up, give thee the most beautiful ones among them. Those amongst men who will become the foremost of all in the use of weapons and in riding animals and other vehicles, shall proceed behind thee like the deities behind Indra! With great prowess thou wilt be our King and protect us happily, like Kubera."[1] Here we see that it is God that ordained Manu to be King, and the people bind themselves by a covenant to obey the King. The compact, therefore, is extremely one-sided. And so, we are perfectly right in concluding that the Indian speculators have not sought to maintain that the State is contractual;[2] the legitimacy of the rule of the King is not therefore to be decided by a reference to the terms of an explicit covenant, which confers upon him sovereignty.

The other theory which seeks to establish the legiti-

---

[1] Vol. I, Sect. LXVII, pp. 216-218 (P. C. Ray).

[2] We do not therefore agree with Prof. Pramathanath Banerjea's "sweeping" generalisation, as Ghoshal has rightly criticised; "Whatever might be the character of the monarchy on the surface, there is no doubt that at bottom the relations between the ruler and the ruled were contractual."

Pub. Adm., p. 72.

macy of the sovereign is that of the Divine Right. In India especially the belief in incarnation is very widely held, and, as N. Law has pointed out, "the divinity of the King is but one of its manifestation."[1] It has been said that "every King in India is regarded as little short of a present god."[2] A religious glamour hangs over the King's person as being not only representative of the old gods but as being also a part of Vishnu (when Vishnu was a form of the All-Soul).[3] According to Manu the King is the incarnation of the eight guardian deities, Indra, Wind, Yama, Sun, Fire, Varuna, Moon and Kubera ; for he has been formed of the particles of these gods. And so Manu maintained that "even an infant King must not be despised, (from an idea) that he is a (mere) mortal ; for he is a great deity in human form."[4] Sukracharya also repeats the statement of Manu and says that the King is, therefore, "the lord of both the immovable and movable worlds."[5] It has been suggested that the King was not a devata but only "a nara-devata."[6] But gods and Kings however are considered to be alike.[7] The King is "really a portion of Vishnu on earth."[8] The divinity of the King is recognised by almost every Indian writer and the Divine Right Theory appears in one form or another from almost the earliest times. We have it in the *Atharva-Veda*,[9] and also in the *Satapatha Brahmana*.[10] The facts of governance and obedience are general in every organised society. The many are content to be

---

[1] *Anc. Ind. Polity*, p. 116.
[2] N. Law: *Anc. Ind. Polity*, p. 116.
[3] Hopkins: *Ethics of India*, p. 107.
[4] VII, 4-8.
[5] *Nitisara*, pp. 12-13.
[6] Banerjea: *Public Adm. in Anc. Ind.*, p. 71.
[7] Hopkins: *Ethics of India*, p. 107.
[8] *Santi Parva*, pp. 179-191, Vol. I, Sect. LIX.
[9] III, 3; III, 4; IV, 22.
[10] V, 1, 5, 14.

ruled by the few, and in early times by a single person. The actual work of administration, in every State, is carried on by a small minority. Political thinkers, during all the ages, have sought to explain why the majority of men submit to the rule of their governors. Some have sought grounds for allegiance in the consent of the governed. Others have held that the causes of obligation inhere in the facts of human nature. A simple mode of explaining, which ultimately became the justification as well, was by a reference to the divine origin of the monarch's power. The ruler is the Lord of creatures; "hence while being one, he rules over many."[1] "Established by the gods, no one transcends him."[2] And so "no one should disregard the King by taking him for a man, for he is really a high divinity in human form". The basis of his power is divine; he has "purchased his subjects through (the practice of) austerities."[3] Even though he be worthless, he must be constantly "worshipped by his subjects" and "his bidding must be obeyed."[4] The right of the King to rule is thus based on divine sanction and his legitimacy rests on religious grounds.

The grounds of obligation are thus explained by the theory of kingship based on Divine Right.[5] Some

---

[1] *Satapatha Brahmana*, V, 1, 5, 14.

[2] *Santi Parva*, Vol. I, Sect. LIX, p. 179-191.

[3] *Narada*, p. 217. See also *Ghoshal*: H. P. T., pp. 214-216.

[4] *Ibid.*, p. 217. cf. *Sukra-Niti*, Ch. I, 30-34.

[5] Prof. Benoy Kumar Sarkar makes the astounding statement that "Hindu thought does not seem to have ever recognised any 'divine right' of kings......" and yet he makes bold to say that the secular idea of monarchy,—for according to him the State is purely secular—is not however inconsistent with the conception of the ruler as a "God in human form" (p. 179). We are afraid that the learned writer is himself consistently inconsistent. He himself postulates the close connection between Dharma and State; "No State, no Dharma" (p. 206) and discusses the bearings of Dharma as Swadharma and Varnashrama on the State

scholars have attempted to read close analogies between the Hindu theory and the theories expounded in the West. There is one important distinction which, however, we must notice. The Hindu writers assert that the King has the right to rule, not simply because he is the agent of the divine will, but that because he himself is a god. He is a sacred object and is in no way inferior to a deity.[1] The doctrine of the Divine Right of the monarch[2] was the novel dogma of Martin Luther as against that of Papal infallibility. But this theory, however, was not a theory of hereditary right[3] and the King himself was not deified. According to our writers the King is pre-ordained ruler ; and this ordinance is divine. It is determined by merit acquired in former births ; and so the monarch is not subject to the power or scrutiny of man. His fitness to rule, the righteousness or otherwise of his administration are irrelevant questions. The legitimacy of the sovereign cannot be questioned, because his ordination is not by any human power. And more than that, he is himself a god. The question is asked, "Why is the King, the ruler

---

(p. 211-214). He admits that "the violation of Swadharma and of Varnashrama brings back the "the State nature", and the State automatically ceases to exist (p. 214). And yet we are asked to think along with him that "Varnashrama, though obviously a socio-pedagogic and ethnico-economic term, is thus fundamentally political concept" (p. 214).

Jayaswal also seeks to prove that the King's status was human and contractual and so the Divine Right Theory could not find its soil in Hindu India. He maintains that "the Hindu theory of kingship was not permitted to degenerate into a divine imposture and profane autocracy."

Hindu Polity, Part II, Ch. XXVI A.

[1] *Narada*, p. 217.

[2] Jean Bodin was perhaps the first great thinker to write of the absolute power of the monarch.

[3] Students of English Constitutional History know how dearly the Stuarts had to pay for attempting to interpret and enunciate the Doctrine of Divine Right as that of hereditary right as well.

of men, a God?" and the familiar answer is always given that he consists of the elements of divinity. "The King assumes five different forms according to five different occasions. He becomes Agni, Aditya, Mrityu, Vaisravana and Yama."[1] This deification of the monarch by Hindu writers, some modern scholars suggest,[2] is due to the anxiety to make up for the deficiency of birth, especially when the King happens to be low-born. And this divinisation of royalty rendered monarchy still more despotic so that the theory was not only to explain, but also to justify the right of the King.

The Divine Right Theory, by itself, however, cannot explain why the majority of men suffer themselves to be governed by the monarch. It does, indeed, seek to establish the legitimacy of the sovereign, the principle of his ordinance being beyond the scrutiny of man. The subject has to render obedience because such obedience to the King is an essential article of his Dharma. What we have to account for is the fact that not only the unlettered, but also the most profound of our writers uphold the divinity of the King, even when they are keenly, and sometimes painfully, conscious of the defects of the sovereign. The constant exhortation is that even a worthless King is to be worshipped. "What other cause is there," it is asked, "in consequence of which the multitude live in obedience to one, save the divinity of the monarch?"[3] But more than the divinity of the King it is the recognition of the necessity of governance, and the apprehension of the results that would follow if there were no King at all, that is the real basis for obligation. As we have often repeated the key to the proper understanding of any problem referring to the Indian Polity is to relate it to the fundamental conception of Swadharma. "Without the

[1] *Santi Parva*, Vol. I, Sect. LXVIII, pp. 218-223.
[2] See Shama Sastry: *Evolution of Indian Polity*, pp. 146-147.
[3] *Santi Parva*, Vol. I, Sect. LIX, pp. 179-191.

governor, the subjects do not keep to their own spheres."[1] The governor is accordingly exalted to pre-eminence so that he could have such a hold on the popular mind as to command their loyalty. The doctrine of the Divine Right of Kings is a monistic doctrine through and through. "In it," says Hsiao,[2] "we find a typical monistic theory realised in the extreme form of the monistic State, in which all political authority is concentrated in one ruler, one government, and one system of law."

We have so far discussed the theories of Social Contract and Divine Right; and have come to the conclusion that the Social Contract theory could not establish the legitimacy of the monarch, firstly because the theory itself in Indian speculation is vague and dim, and secondly because it is extremely one-sided; thus, in no way can we maintain that the State in Ancient India was contractual. The Divine Right Theory is far more important as an explanation of the legitimacy of the Sovereign; in fact, even where the contractual theory is described, the actual origin of kingship is always, in Hindu thought, attributed to a divine creation.

But as a theory seeking to explain the grounds of political allegiance, the Divine Right Theory is only partially valid, the Social Contract Theory being out of the question; for it does not stand the test either of reason or of fact. No partial explanation would therefore suffice; and the grounds for obligation must be sought for in the complex facts of human nature. Neither force nor consent could be the basis of political relationship. The grounds for political obligation could ultimately be based upon purpose. The individual obeyed the commands of the State, because he believed that the purpose of the State was somehow an expression of his own purpose; that the State embodied his own purpose, however imperfectly.

[1] Sukracharya: *Nitisara*, p. 11.
[2] *Political Pluralism*, p. 3.

But before we discuss this aspect of the problem, let us examine some of the other theories to be found in the literature of our ancients which account for the obedience rendered to the commands of the State.

"The man", said Bhisma, "that bends his head to a powerful person really bends his head to Indra." Men should therefore bend before those who are powerful. The King is the wielder of Danda and "all men should humble themselves before the King."[1] He is the supreme coercive Power in the community. As representative of the State he is the embodiment of Force. He must be obeyed because he has the power to compel such obedience. He could inflict punishment on those who infringed the regulations and laws of the State.

So stated, the theory may be misconstrued as referring, not to the principle of obedience and the basis of power, but to the nature and end of the State; that the State is, as maintained by the Sophist in Plato's *Republic* the interest of the strong. "Indeed this mobile and immobile world is our object of enjoyment," says the *Santi Parva*, "for the person that is strong."[2] The theory of Force, however, cannot serve as the basis of political obligation. No State, however arbitrary, can drive its subjects, against their will, like dumb cattle. Tyranny always invites resistance, and Force, regulated and applied unintelligently, reacts with unerring certainty on those who exercise it. We have yet to determine, therefore, why the subjects of the monarch submit to his authority, and allow themselves to be coerced. Even Treitschke who asserted that "the State is Power," and that "the highest moral duty of the State is to care for Power," yet admits that "the final object of the State's existence is not physical might; it embodies might only in order that it may protect

[1] *Santi Parva*, Vol. I, Sect. X, p. 23.

[2] *Ibid.*

[3] *Treitschke*, p. 40.

and develop the nobler aspects of mankind. The unadulterated doctrine of Might is Right is absolutely senseless and is immoral because it cannot justify itself." The acquiescence of the many to the rule of the few or the one cannot be explained merely by the Force Theory.

The theory of consent, we have already disposed of as being inadequate if it is to be interpreted in legal terms as implying the contractual basis of the State. Could we, however, take it in a more general sense? As power may be taken to be fiduciary in its nature, could we assume that the people tacitly consented to its investment in the person of the monarch, because the recipient exercised it in the general interests of the Community? Absence of resistance, or passive acquiescence might be taken as an indication of consent, though not explicitly given. If the exercise of the Power is in the interest of the governed, they generally do not resent; and thus they might submit to political authority. Any theory, however, that rests merely on "interests" and does not refer to wider things that matter will fall short of the truth, especially in its application to a country like India. And popular acquiescence might not after all be merely passive; and might involve the exercise of choice, however unconsciously. We have, therefore, to search for the grounds of political obligation in a principle which would try to include every possible fact that enters into the human nature. No single explanation would suffice. The phenomenon of rule and subjection is complex, and a theory of allegiance must try to unify the ingredients that enter into the fact of obligation.

The various theories so far examined contain some element of truth though each of them taken singly will not be able to serve as the explanation. The Monarch in Ancient India was the embodiment and sole repository of power. But power, in itself could never be the basis of the State. When concentrated in the hands of a single man, it enables him to assume the pretensions of abso tism. But absolutism however naked, always seeks mask its real nature by an appeal to some other princi which, while making power more absolute, throws a ha of justification on it. And this is the theory of Divi Right. But this again, in itself, is wholly inadequate serve as an explanation of political allegiance. The Ki exercises power in the exercise of functions of protecti and justice. Power is always a means to an end. But t doctrine of Divine Right, referring as it does to the sour and basis of Power, seems to exalt the instrument abo the function and results in a confusion between means a ends. The doctrine can easily be "perverted into t principle that the sovereign is above the State. So degenerates into a power doctrine and the State is del vered to its master. The true logic of association is thereb defeated, and its purpose dimmed."[1]..... The theologia might say, as did Bossuet, that "God has given to ever people its ruler." But divine appointment to rule must b evidenced in the nature of the rule itself and the characte of the sovereign. Indeed, in the various Law-books an treatises on State-craft we do have exhortations to th monarch to act always with an eye on Dharma. And th education of the ruler is so prescribed,[2] that if effectivel imparted in every case, the monarch would approximate indeed, to Plato's ideal of Philosopher King. And if powe is exercised by and is vested in a monarch of high charac ter and learning he has certainly the right to deman respect, if not obedience, from his subjects. In other word the man "who, by his wisdom and probity, is best quali fied to direct a certain social force has ethically the bes

---

[1] MacIver: *The Modern State*, p. 432.

[2] See for instance, Kautilya: *Arthasastra*, Bk. I, Chapters V, VI and VII.

ht to be intrusted with its control. In this sense there is Divine Right' of rulership.''[1]

But in an ordering of the State based upon hereditary :cession it is impossible to procure a continuous line of e and virtuous monarchs. And thus the "Divine ght'' to rule in practice very often becomes the Divine ght to rule arbitrarily and wickedly. Crowned monarchs gulate their conduct by the Machiavellian maxim: Right and wrong have nothing to do with the Govern- nt. The Kautilyan monarch answers exactly to the 'rince'', of Machiavelli.

We are convinced that a theory of political obligation ist also be a moral one as well. It must be based upon cardinal principle that the individual is capable of ualising an ideal of perfection for himself and feels the oral obligation, moreover, to strive after its fulfilment. other words, any theory seeking to explain or guide stitutional behaviour must be grounded upon the con- ptions of the moral freedom and the moral personality man. Hence we have also rejected the utility theory, mere interest will never satisfy our sense of adequacy.

Ultimately the individual renders obedience to the com- ands of the State because he feels that the State some- w is the condition of his moral or spiritual realisation d that it embodies several interests, and that its purpose the wider expression of his own purpose.[2] In short the ate is the condition of his very life and assures to him e realisation of his ideals and aspirations.

Above all, any theory of obligation that does not pri-

---

[1] Willoughby: *Social Justice*, p. 22.

[2] Laski says: "The only ground upon which the individual can ve or be asked his support for the State is from the conviction at what it is aiming at is, in each particular action, good...... deserves his allegiance, it should receive it only where it com- ands his conscience. Its purpose is at each stage subject to amination." See *Authority in the Modern State*, p. 46.

marily rest on the root conception of Dharma will not answer our purpose at all. The End of the State was to maintain and promote Dharma. It justifies itself to the extent it fulfils this End and stands condemned to the extent it hinders the realisation of this End. And whatever might be the immediate factor compelling the obedience of the subject, the true principle of allegiance must have reference to the End which the State sought to attain. The preservation of Dharma or the social order in tact was not merely the aim of the State ; it was also the condition presupposed for every individual member of the Social Order to live his own life. His Swadharma must be guaranteed to him. If there were any lapse anywhere in the kingdom that would immediately react upon the general harmony and with the confusion of duties that sets in, he would find himself unable to perform his duties. And the individual, ultimately, obeyed the commands of the State because the State was the guarantee of his Dharma.

Considered, therefore, from the standpoint of the End the coercive aspect of the Indian State becomes perfectly intelligible. Beholding the might of the monarch the inhabitants of the earth become "inspired with fear and set their hearts upon their respective duties."[1] Men are constrained to be virtuous only when placed constantly under necessity, for, their natural propensities are wicked. And so, as Manu asserts, the world is kept in order by punishment, "for a guiltless man is hard to find."[2] The function of punishment is thus to maintain the Social Order, for "Punishment alone governs all created beings". And for "the grand security of public order", Manu, "personifies the abstract principle and invests it with the highest attributes of sanctity and power, for it is "the surety for the four orders' obedience to the law".

---

[1] *Santi Parva*, Vol. I, Sect. LXVII, p. 215.

[2] VII, 22. See also Benoy Kumar Sarkar's exposition of the Doctrine of Danda, *Political Institutions*, p. 197 ff.

For, Manu writes: "For the (King's) sake the law formerly created his own son, Punishment, the protector of all creatures, (an incarnation of) the law, formed of Brahman's glory".[1] And if we further remember that the administration of justice is the most important aspect of all early polities, we will be enabled to explain why at all people reconciled themselves to the abridgement of their individual freedom. Though not in an explicit compact the "natural" liberty of each should be surrendered and placed in the custody of the community if liberty, worth its name, could be enjoyed. Force is ultimately justified if its exercise is conducive to freedom. Law and Order are necessary conditions under which we could have freedom and progress. That is why Treitschke, the greatest exponent of Force in modern times says: "Political liberty is politically limited liberty."[2] The consequences of *Matsyanyaya* would follow, as Kautilya warns, if no punishment is applied at all.

Stated thus the theory of Punishment, or Danda, seems to be the justification of Power and not a principle of political obligation which could be based on reason. After all the individual acquiesces in the curtailment of his natural liberty because he must. If it be possible he would rather live an unrestricted free life. He is not, however, a Robinson Crusoe on a desert island. And the liberty to unlimited action of his companions may actually mean such a serious encroachment upon his own that his life would indeed be unbearable and every second he lives in terror of his fellow creatures. Such a State is not Civil Society, but assuredly the State of Nature so vividly painted for us by Hobbes. Whether it has any basis in History or not, it has, as we have seen, its own moral to teach. And so to prevent social cataclysm, the State is invested with

---

[1] Ghoshal: *H. P. T.*, pp. 150-151.

[2] *Treitschke*, p. 19.

authority to impose the penalties of Law. Government means the curtailment of the individual's natural liberty; but it must be suffered patiently, for though an evil, it is as Spencer admits a necessary evil. Thus the conception of force, if true, is very crude and at best only negative in its significance.

To appeal to the instinct of fear to enforce obedience is dangerous and as the explanation of the grounds of political allegiance it would be highly unsatisfactory.[1] But in this theory of Force enunciated by the Hindu thinkers there is involved another idea which, if emphasised properly, will lead us to the discovery of the true principle of obligation. If people render obedience because they are coerced into acquiescence, such people will have no right to freedom in any sense. They are base and slavish by nature. It is hard, however, to find any people so degraded as to love their own fetters. It is not because of the force exhibited by the State that people render obedience. At any given moment the penalties of disobedience might restrain the individual and make him conform to the law of the Realm. But it is the realisation perhaps unconsciously and vaguely by the individual, but nevertheless very real, of the truth not merely of the necessity of the State, but somehow of the idea that the purpose of the State is not foreign to his own, that the same Dharma that he adheres to is realised while being preserved and promoted in the very State itself. Unless this identity is

[1] It would indeed mean that men "acknowledge only one right and that is the right of might" (Benoy Kumar Sarkar: *Political Institutions*, p. 200). Does this mean the identification of might with right? And that "the only right that people can claim is to be governed justly". As Carlyle would insist, rights are "correctly articulated mights", and so "strength we may say is justice itself". But Carlyle himself is very careful for he adds the important provision that right and might are identical in the long run, for might cannot succeed for a long time unless it is right also in the end. It succeeds when you "give it time".

held somehow, though we might not explicitly explain how the State will always be alien to the individual. And merely as an external factor, as we have seen, the State would never even fulfil the elementary function of the "hindrance of hindrances", and the adjustment of relations between the various institutions" of the Polity. The State as merely an external factor does not enter into the life of each institution and indeed of each individual. And if in the theory of force or punishment we find its justification that it is for the sake of Dharma or the Social Order, then the principle of allegiance is not force, but the principle of Dharma itself. The people rendered obedience to the commands of the monarch because the monarch by the protection he afforded sustained the Realm by the maintenance of Dharma.

This does not mean that other grounds of allegiance were not present. As we said a complex phenomenon must be explained by a complex cause. The consideration of the material benefits conferred by the State might be a powerful influence making for obedience. But at best it cannot be a rational ground in itself. It could only tell us why the people reconciled themselves to the fact of restraint. Almost every explanation of ours must, therefore, be traced back to the root idea of Dharma ; the State must be upheld because it is the condition of the proper performance of Dharma. The gifts or libations offered to Gods, Rishis, and Pitris will only bear fruit if the King is obeyed and respected.[1] The relation between Dharma and the State is reciprocal. If the King promotes Dharma, Dharma, however, sustains him. The life of the whole Polity depends on the King as he is the centre or the key-stone of the Social Arch. "Who is there that will not

---

[1] *Santi Parva*, Vol. I, Sect. LXV, p. 210.

worship him in whose existence the people exist and in whose destruction the people are destroyed."[1]

Every Indian thinker is, therefore, agreed as to the necessity of monarchy.[2] The grounds for political obligation must be explained, as we said, with a reference to the End the State was to seek and promote. It is Dharma that affords us the clue to the understanding of the problem. Dharma as the End of life can never be realised unless Dharma in the empirical life is rigidly enforced. The Social Order, i. e. Varnashrama, with its scheme of duties was to be correctly maintained. The individual was to be kept in due performance of his Swadharma. Otherwise, as we have observed, dire consequences would result. If the State failed to provide the security necessary for the maintenance of the Social Order, then Dharma would become Adharma ; for with the confusion of duties Swadharma becomes impossible. The State is a necessary institution if the individual should live according to his own scheme of life. Ultimately, therefore, the individual rendered obedience to the commands of the State because he felt that the State was the condition of his very life, and that the Purpose of the State was vitally related to his own Purpose. The state was embodied Dharma, it realised in itself aspects of Dharma. It was, certainly, particular and so imperfect, if we consider it in its relation to the absolute idea of Dharma as such. But it was itself universal in its relation to the individual members who composed it. As the embodiment of the Social Order every individual finds his due place in its scheme. And not only

[1] *Santi Parva*, Vol. I, Sect. LXVIII, pp. 218-223.

[2] See *Aitereya-Brahmana*, I, 14.

Taittiriya-Brahmana, I, 5, 9.

Bhasa in his *Pratimanataka* (Act 3, p. 36) describes the condition of subjects without a King; and in *Vasavadatta* Act VI, p. 72 he dilates on kingly dignity.

Kalidasa tells us in *Malavikagnimitra* what constitutes the strength of the King, p. 7.

that, he has no life which he can call his own outside of it. He finds his true meaning in the fulfilment of the duties of his station in life ; as a man, he is himself only as a member of the Varnashram. The rights he could claim and exercise belong to him as a member of his particular caste. A casteless man, a man excommunicated for any reason has no right at all. He is excluded from the participation of social benefits. Even the village barber and washerman would refuse to serve him. Terrible penalties are imposed on him ; he would be taken back into the fold only after the performance of due prayaschitta or penance. So much so, even at the present day it is not surprising to find even our best educated men quailing before the threat of social ostracism. As we have observed elsewhere, Hindu toleration referred only to the expression of opinion, and had no reference to conduct. A man is free to profess anything he likes ; only he must not attempt to translate his ideas into the practice of everyday life. To our shame, we know how we tolerate social slavery and moral interia, for we dare not risk expulsion from caste. Those for instance who are loudest to-day in demanding political liberty are most often those who would never extend social and religious liberty to the oppressed slaves who form a millions of the lower strata of this country. For, as long as even a single human being is looked upon as "untouchable" nay, even, "unapproachable" "unobservable," and "unthinkable,"[1] the passion for the so-called political liberty is only a masked hypocracy.

We now come to the crux of the Problem. When we said before that the individual rendered obedience to the State because he felt, somehow, that the purpose of the State was an expression of his own purpose we had in

[1] Especially in the South of India, a Brahmin is supposed not even to think of the so-called Pariah when he is having his meals. He, therefore, alludes to the Pariah as "chepparanivadu" i.e. one whose name should not be uttered; the "unspeakable".

view only those elements of the Polity, whose purpose was in a sense identical with the purpose of the State. For this purpose of the State never had a same significance to each and every individual within the State, "where there some individuals either not taken into account at all in the common purpose or not taken into account with all their powers while the rest were included—then the former," as Fichte rightly points out,[1] "would enjoy all the advantages of the union without bearing all the attendant *burdens*, and there would thus be inequality. Only when all without exception are taken into account, is equality the result". But equality would never result so long as the purpose of the State is to realise Dharma, i. e. Swadharma.

By no logic could we assert that the lower orders and castes obeyed the commands of the State willingly because to them the State was the condition of their life. Their Swadharma was to be slaves. It would be adding insult to injury therefore, if we cynically maintain that so-called "untouchables" members of the lowest and despised castes, saw the fulfilment—of their own purpose in the achievement of the State. If we restrict the membership of the Indian Polity to those who belonged to the higher castes and look upon the despised castes as "aliens" within the realm, the theory of Swadharma would be adequate as an explanation of political obligation. The Sudras and the lower castes were something like the Helots of Sparta and the villeins of the Middle Ages.[2] And as we have already observed the whole of the social legislation of the times resulted in the prodigious elevation and sanctity of the Brahmans and the studied degradation of the lowest class." For as Sukracharya states : "If to people below the rank of Brahmans the

---

[1] *The Popular Works*, p. 15.

[2] See Elphinstone: *History of India*, pp. 14-21.

King should behave with lenience these lower orders would overpower him just as the elephant-catchers master elephants."[1] The lower castes must be kept permanently in a position of economic dependence. The economic regulations to be enforced by the King were such as to make it impossible for the lower classes to assert themselves. For instance Sukracharya lays down that the "wages of Sudras is to be just enough for food and raiment" ; and he gives the reason that "the wealth which is stolen by the Brahman leads to good life hereafter, and the wealth that is given to the Sudra leads only to hell."[2]

Every individual belonging to the higher castes would cheerfully obey the State, because such allegiance was itself the guarantee of the privileges and benefits he enjoyed. The maintenance of Swadharma would mean for him an assurance that he could enjoy his rights freely ; the strong arm of the State would be there to help him against those who would encroach upon his rights. Such an encroachment, let us remind ourselves, was only possible by the re-shuffling of the social order ; or, at the least by the recognition of the claim of every individual, whatever his caste might be, to qualify himself for any profession to which he would be called by his capacities. In that case, confusion of duties arises from "Varnasankaram" and the "means" become "ends" ; as the *Satapatha Brahmana* would have it, there would be a confusion between the "good" and the "bad". Sudras and the lower orders would become bold and usurp the functions of the Brahmans and the other "twice-born", while the higher castes would be compelled to take to "impure" occupations. And, therefore, members belonging to the "twice-born" castes would always look up to the State as the sole condition of their own lives ; and would never feel any hesitancy to appeal to the restraining

---

1 *Nitisara*, p. 90.

2 *Ibid.*, pp. 98-100.

power of the monarch to keep down the lower orders in a State of abject servility. That is why the coercive aspect of the State is not only not looked upon with suspicion by the various writers of the codes of Law ; but what is more significant "Danda" or punishment itself, as we have seen, is personified and deified. The King, who is the "Dandadhara", or the wielder of the Rod of Chastisement is thus credited with such extensive and arbitrary powers that we have no hesitation to describe the Indian Monarchy as a veritable Leviathan.

The grounds for political obligation must, therefore, be reformulated so that Dharma shall be the principle that makes for universal coherence and the State, which is concretised. Dharma shall be, in all the senses of the idea, an all-inclusive partnership. In such a State, the anti-thesis between the individual and the State is dissolved in a higher synthesis, for there shall be no rulers on the one hand, and subjects on the other. The members of the State, in their individual capacity shall be citizens, and in their collective capacity the rulers. To express it, in other words they shall be at once citizens and rulers ; "means" and "ends."[1]

The grounds of political obligation must therefore ultimately be based upon the "End" or Purpose of the State, an "End" or Purpose which shall be common and social. Provided the End of the State is rightly visualised and provided also the State seeks to direct the life of the community in such a way that the "lowliest" and the "least" of its citizens is not excluded from the partnership of the Quest of the Larger Life, such a State can always lay claim to the highest allegiance of the citizen. No element in the State should feel that its purpose is external to it. The State shall do "unto the last" as it would do for its noblest and best.

---

[1] We shall return to this problem in our concluding chapter.

CHAPTER IX

EDUCATION AND THE STATE

"Knowledge is Brahman."

AITAREYA-ARANYAKA

"It is idle to make institutions without making the qualities by which they must be worked."

LESLIE STEPHEN

"To say that education is a social function, securing direction and development in the immature through their participation in the life of the group to which they belong, is to say in effect that education will vary with the quality of life which prevails in a group."

JOHN DEWEY

"Then let us not leave the meaning of education ambiguous or ill-defined. At present, when we speak in terms of praise or blame about the bringing up of each person, we call one man educated and another uneducated, although the uneducated man may be sometimes very well educated for the calling of a retail trader, or of a captain of a ship, and the like. For we are not speaking of education in this narrower sense, but that of other education in virtue from youth upwards, which makes a man eagerly pursue the ideal perfection of citizenship, and teaches him how rightly to rule and how to obey. This is the only education which, upon our view deserves the name; that other sort of training, which aims at the acquisition of wealth, or bodily strength, or mere cleverness apart from intelligence and justice, is mean and illiberal, and is not worthy to be called education at all."

PLATO

We have seen that the End of the State was to maintain and promote Dharma. The various orders and castes were to be protected in the performance of their Dharma. Strict adherence to Dharma insures the attainment of Moksha, the supreme goal of human endeavour. In other words the End of the State was to promote Dharma and that of man was to realise Dharma. The whole of life was to be dedicated to the fulfilment of this ideal. If education is the preparation for life, our ancients seem to have grasped this truth though in a characteristic sense.

For, it was not a preparation for life, Here and Now, but for the Future Life of the Hereafter. The other worldly ideal is impressed on the individual even from childhood. Education that was considered worth acquiring was knowledge of the Atman ; and the details of the educational curriculum referred to the study of the scriptures and the daily discipline. The importance of training from childhood seems to have been understood for the excellence to be perfected in the grown up man, must be implanted in him, even when a child.

The actual period of studentship seems to have been twelve years,[1] though some enthusiastic students might extend the duration of their studies to over thirty-six years, or even to forty-eight years.[2] We have the evidence of Megasthenes[3] who speaks of the Indian student spending thirty-seven years in studying. Sometimes we have one's studies spread over his whole life ; and in a way he can be said to be a student throughout life, though according to the strict Ashramic theory only the first stage in life is that of studentship. Ordinarily four stages are prescribed for man, Brahmacharya (Studentship), Grihasthya (Householder), Vanaprastha (Forest hermit) and Parivrajaka (Mendicant or Ascetic). It is very difficult to determine the time of the origin of this scheme. We see traces of it in the *Upanishads* and even in *Atharvaveda* and the *Satapatha Brahmana*.[4] Es-

---

[1] *Chand Upa.*, iv, 10, 1; vi, 1, 2.

[2] *Gautama*, ii, 45-47; *Apas.*, 1, 2, 12-16 of *Manu*, iii, 1. "For each of the three or four Vedas a study of twelve years is held to be necessary, so that just the maximum length of the period of study comes to be forty-eight years, while the minimum shall amount to twelve years."

J. Jolly: *Hindu Law and Custom*, p. 321.

[3] *Fragment*, 41.

[4] *Atharvaveda*, VII, 74, 1.
Satapatha Brah., XI, 3, 3.
Narendra Nath Law, pp. 1-2; 20.

pecially in the *Chandogya Upanishad* and the *Brihadarunyaka Upanishad*, we decidedly get the impression that the last Ashrama, that of the Ascetic is the best of all. Certain religious duties were to be fulfilled in the earlier stages which have reference to the debt to be discharged by every individual, the threefold debt owed to Gods, Rishis, and Pritris. After the birth of a Putra who could continue the religious duties, the Grihastha could generally pass on to the next stage. The insistence on family life that we get in some of our law books is not due to the recognition of the intrinsic value of the householder's life as such, but to the necessity of the domestic worship being continued uninterruptedly. At any rate this stage cannot be the end, for the Supreme End cannot be realised through it. It is not by living life, but by turning away from life that Moksha is to be achieved. The individual is to seek release of deliverance from the bonds of Sentient existence. Worldly fetters were to be broken and all desire for empirical life to be extinguished. Man cannot, and dare not, linger long in the second stage (Ashrama) lest he be entangled in the snare of worldly relationships, of widespread death and delusion. He must pass on to the Vanprastha stage treading the path of renunciation, and ultimately enter the last of his Ashramas here on earth, that of the Parivrajaka.

Detailed regulations are laid down which govern the conduct of the individual in the four stages of life.[1] During the period of Brahmacharya, the boy was to stay with his guru, and place himself completely under his guidance. "Even at the first dawn of day the student has to announce

[1] See Alberuni's *India*, Ch. LXIII (p. 130 ff.). Alberuni describes generally actually existing conditions. And we find that the theory as expounded by the various law givers corresponded, more or less, to the practice of the times. We would also refer to Richard Fick's *Social Organisation in North-East India in Buddhist Times*, for a general description of social conditions.

himself to his teacher and respectfully clasp his feet after saying his morning prayer ; he cannot sit beside him, cannot first speak to him, cannot seat himself in a careless posture in his presence, cannot pronounce his name without an honorific predicate, cannot dispute with him or scoff at him, must follow him at his work, etc. He must show respect even to the wife and the son of the teacher, yet he must be reserved in his conduct towards a young wife of the teacher...... To observe chastity is one of the principle duties of the Brahmacharin and moreover he cannot dance, sing, gamble and cannot anoint himself and cannot eat flesh, honey or spices, he cannot injure a living being and cannot lie slander or quarrel, etc....... Everyday he has to go out for alms and collect faggots for the sacred fire which is entrusted to his care ; he must however hand over the food he collects by begging to his teacher and shall receive of it only what the teacher leaves for him. Further he shall also regularly say the morning and evening prayers, sacrifice to the gods, sleep on earth and rise before sunrise. When instructions for study are given he must listen attentively ; if he is inattentive or disobedient the teacher may chastise him but not too harshly. At the end of the period of his study he shall make a present to the teacher as his resources permit and return to the house of his parents."[1]

After the completion of his studies the Brahmacharin becomes a Snataka and is allowed to marry ; and live for a while as a Grihastha. This stage too, "is covered with a thick net of religious duties."[2] The next stage of life is that of the Vanprastha during which the seeker of Moksha has to undergo severe mortifications which end at the complete destruction of all attachments and desires.

---

[1] J. Jolly: *Hindu Law and Custom*, pp. 321-322. See for further details.

[2] See J. Jolly: *Hindu Law and Custom*, p. 322 ff.

The Vanprasthas, "shall clothe themselves in barks of trees or skin, let their nails and hair grow, live on fruits, plants, roots of the forest, morning and evening offer sacrifice in the Sramanaka fire kindles on special ceremonies, generally perform the Mahayajnas as before, observe chastity, bathe three times a day and sleep on earth...... As special mortifications they shall expose themselves in summer to the heat of the sun enhanced by four fires, in the rainy season sleep on earth, in winter wear wet clothes, roll about on earth,—stand all day long on the toes or sit down or stand up alternately, stand with hands stretched upwards or with a stick raised high, shall gaze steadfastly at the sun or keep the face turned to the earth, remain under water for a long time, would not speak, fast for a whole month[1] etc......" The last stage of life, as already pointed out, is that of the ascetic, who is variously known as Bikshu, Yati, Sanyasin, Parivrajaka, and Pravrajita. The mendicant has nothing which he can call his own ; for he has severed all ties— and left behind all attachments. He has no home and no property. He "shall roam about as a beggar, shall stay nowhere for a long time, sleep on earth, wear a loin cloth as his only dress, shave his head bald, hold in his hand three staffs intertwined with each other and a beggar's bowl and a water pot, eat only what is given to him voluntarily, yet never any meat or sweets. He shall enter a village only to beg, but only in the evening when the time of taking the meals is past ; he can beg for alms only in seven houses, but shall not be depressed if he gets nothing, nor exult if he gets something. On the whole an unruffled temper and philosophical equanimity are the main things for the *Yati*. He shall wish neither for death nor for a long life and shall not even trouble himself to see whether somebody is hacking off his hand with an axe

[1] J. Jolly: *Hindu Law and Custom*, pp. 324-325.

or is sprinkling sandal powder on him. He should meditate over the short duration of life, the impurity of the body, transitoriness of beauty, tortures of hell, infirmities of old age and diseases, separation from the beloved, co-existence with the enemies and the endless transmigrations of the soul. Thus gradually shaking off all mundane propensities, roaming about alone, speaking to none, he is finally dissolved in the Universal Soul."[1]

This is the regulation of life according to ashrama-dharma; and when the scheme is fully developed we see that "the whole of life was looked upon as an education for the life beyond."[2] This Ashrama scheme emphasises the most fundamental of the characteristics of Indian education, that its end was to seek final liberation or release, and as a preparation for the ultimate it is not merely a system for the imparting of learning, but is in itself a whole discipline.

But it is a discipline of a peculiar kind. No part of it has reference to the virtues to be acquired for the duties of citizenship. The one absorbing anxiety is to obtain knowledge, the discriminating knowledge with the attainment of which man's mistaken interest in life is abandoned. Knowledge is Brahman; with its possession Avidya is dispelled. Man may indeed continue to live on, but he has no further interest in life. He has become Jivan-mukta.

Thus, the knowledge which our ancients wanted to acquire was not purely of an academic nature; it had a definite aim. It was felt that that knowledge only was worth acquiring which would enable man to obtain salvation. Consequently, the instruction that would enable a man to discharge his practical duties, especially in his vocational spheres of life, was despised. The more the

---

[1] J. Jolly: *Hindu Law and Custom*, pp. 325-326.
[2] Keay: *Ancient Indian Education*, p. 26.

other worldly spirit gained its hold upon the Brahmanical schools the more it made them "out of touch with the ordinary life of the world". And in the course of time, it came to be more and more held that the proper atmosphere for learning or discipline could not be secured amidst the distractions of human habitations. The forest Sanctuary came to be the ideal. The spiritual aspirant always felt that "Ekagratha" i.e. concentration is impossible except in the woods. There was no hope that "even in a palace, life could be lived well."[1] To the inmate of the hermitage the palace, "with its idle throngs, that come and go, loiter and pass and smile," is, "like a house devoured by fire". He looks upon the town folks, "lost in their pleasures, as a man, clean from his ablution looks on one that's smeared with dirt ; as one that's free looks on a menacled and fettered slave."[2] Ill bodes, therefore, the company of many people, for "dizzy the mind becomes", and hard is it, therefore, to obtain clarity of mind. In the silence of the forest home by the direct communion with nature, the Indian's outlook on life was impressed with its spiritual temper. Surrounded by the trees that seemed to kiss the towering clouds roaming about the silent forest, haunted by black-faced apes, and the spotted dear, straying by the tinkling streamlets, resting besides crystal springs, sleeping beneath the spreading, verdant growth, bright blossoms dropping as it were from the starry heavens, ever and anon, the refugee who went forth from home into the homeless life was soon deeply filled with "the forest sense of things". And there sequestered from the world, the dweller of the hermitage came to realise the need for detachment from all worldly relationships ; for,

---

[1] *Mareus Aurelius.*
[2] Kalidasa: *Sakuntala*, p. 93.

"Ne'er will the man with eyes
to see abide
Where aught may hinder
In the quest supreme."[1]

Never, in the history of the world did any people follow more consistently, consciously and single mindedly an ideal which they place before themselves as the End of life, than our ancients who considered no sacrifice too dear, no privation too severe, and penance too hard in their effort to gain the knowledge which would emancipate them from the fellows of this life, of Going and Coming. If at all we have to think of any parallel, we are reminded of another people, almost the contemporaries of our ancients, who with wholly different ideal and outlook on life, in the secluded valley of the Eurotas, where until the time of Epaminondes no invader ever dared to set his foot, gave themselves to the perfection of a single virtue to the exclusion of the rest, and considered no sacrifice too great in the pursuit of their ideal. It was a whole nation, in time of peace, drilled into a camp. The Spartan, as much as the ancient Indian, has shown to the world what a people might do and become in a passionate endeavour to realise the end it placed before itself.

And yet, when all is said, we feel that both the Indian and the Spartan aimed at the perfection of a part at the risk of mutilating the whole. Plato, who found so much to admire in Sparta, yet sadly noted that what was aimed at was not the development of an all round virtue, a coherence that shall rule all the parts, but only the perfection of that quality which is called forth in time of war; and that the excess of discipline and the vigour of the military exercises and the barrack room life had crushed out of the Spartan everything that was human, and had given to his character a coarseness and a brutality that always

[1] *Theragatha*, No. 106.

made him hateful to the other Hellenes. And the Indian ideal, as we have so often remarked before, abstracted man from this world of our social relationships into a dreamy universe of imagination, where in fancied identity with the Brahman, the *Summum Bonum* of life was sought. The fantastic self-mortifications considered necessary for spiritual discipline more often resulted in self-repression than in self-realisation. The Indian came into the world a stranger, and remained so until the day of his dissolution. His education was a preparation for the Hereafter, not for the Here and Now.

We do not suggest, however, that the education which would serve the interests of this world, though despised, was in any way neglected. We are told that there were thirty-two sciences and sixty-four arts. Alberuni, after enumerating the various branches of learning, says that the Hindus, "have a nearly boundless literature."[1] And the proficiency acquired by our ancients in the various branches of knowledge was very high. The many works of art that have remained to this day are eloquent witness to their creative instinct.

When everything is said, however, the knowledge acquired by the study of the sciences and the arts was considered necessarily lower than the knowledge of the Atman. When, indeed, is the knowledge, if by it the eternal is not obtained. The higher knowledge is the knowledge of the Self, which could be obtained by meditation and Yoga. The indriyas or the senses must be subdued and desire extinguished. The discipline of the students must aim at preparing him for the final stage. We very often find instances of people who passed on to the last stage, that of the Parivrajaka or the ascetic, straight from the student life.

---

[1] Alberuni's: *India*, p. 159.

Thus we find that the education of ancient India had two aspects, the higher and the lower. The higher education was the acquisition of the emancipating knowledge of the Atman. The lower knowledge had reference to the activities of man in his life, Here and Now; and this was specialised by the special classes in society. The caste system, in this respect, was an admirable institution. "It has brought about a vast system of vocational training which was made possible by the fact that a boy's future career was determined from his very birth, for upon his birth depended both his duties and Privileges in life."[1] Much has been said, however, about the caste system as the embodiment of the principle of "Division of Labour", that the time has come, we believe, to point out the evil effects of the system as an educational contrivance on the character of the Polity in general. First of all, as we have so often insisted, the scheme of life, according to Varna-Dharma, that is caste, is not based on the principle of the "Division of Labour". It is not the apportioning a function according to natural capacities and talents. The occupation a man could adopt was not a matter of choice. He could not take to the occupation of any other caste except that of the caste in which he was born. In times of distress a member of the higher caste could take to the profession properly belonging to a lower caste. But a member of a lower caste could, on no account take to the profession of a higher. Dire consequences would otherwise follow. We have a story related in the *Ramayana* of a Chandala (i. e. an Untouchable) who began to practice religious worship and austerities. This immediately reflected on the general harmony of the Polity. The child of a Brahmin died while the father was still alive. The weeping father brought the child to the King Rama and complained that the death was due to

[1] Keay: *Ancient Indian Education*, p. 180.

"something rotten in the State of the country."[1] Then Rama made enquiries, and subsequently heard of the Chandala who was practising austerities on the banks of the Ganges. He rode up to him, and killed him on the spot, saying : "That is it ! I kill thee on account of a good action which thou art not allowed to do." When the King returned home he found the Brahman's child restored to life. We have another story, that of Ekalavya in the *Mahabharata*, who had to cut off his thumb for daring to learn archery which was prohibited to his caste.

In the second place the distinction between the two kinds of knowledge, the spiritual and the material is vicious, the one considered as higher and the other as lower. Those who are engaged in the acquisition of the higher knowledge must be freed from the distractions and anxieties of life. The daily necessities must be guaranteed to them. Leisure in indespensable for a life of contemplation and yoga, and so they cannot themselves toil ; others must labour and toil to keep them going. Hence is the sharp distinction between the education for a life of leisure, and education for a life of labour ; the one considered as higher and the other as lower.

The caste-system is, therefore, the division of society into those who are to labour for a living and those who are relieved from this necessity—those who have ample opportunities of leisure, and those condemned to toil—the higher castes and the lower castes. This cleavage, as we have seen, roughly corresponded with the classes in society which were free, and those which were servile ; those which were, "ends", and those which were "instruments" bound to the service of ends external to themselves.

This distinction between "ends" and "means" as the basis of permanent division of society, is purely relating

[1] See Alberuni : *India*, Ch. LXIV, p. 137.

to the academic sphere, might not have been injurious in its effect on the general character of the Polity. But, as we have seen, it is itself the basis of rights and duties which exalt some and degrade others. There is an unnatural divorce between leisure and labour ; for leisure is not the reward for services rendered.

Hence we maintain that the caste system is a gross perversion of the principle of the "Division of Labour" and if we try to understand the educational system of ancient India in its two aspects, the spiritual and vocational, we will realise that the former laid to the path of freedom, and the latter to servility. In empirical life, this distinction roughly corresponded to the division of society into the free and the unfree. And it has the same significance if we relate it to the Transcendental Life. The one kind of education leads to final release ; the other to bondage to the Cycle of Going and Coming.

Could we grasp the immense effects this educational scheme had on the Polity? In the educational system there were some influences which educate the few into masters, other influences which educate the majority into slaves. Educational values, in other words, were not held to be common. The educational system of ancient India was adopted to the society of the times. It tended to perpetuate caste-mentality and thus to prevent social endosmosis. It admirably suited the character of the State, as we shall presently see. We shall here only note the effects on education itself. Culture became sterile, for education became stereotyped. It "turned back to feed on itself." As diffused through the channel of the caste-system, it assumed "the narrowest form of vocational training that the world has seen."[1] Originality was stifled and stagnation was the result.

This danger is, in a way, inherent in any system of

---

[1] Keay: *Ancient Indian Education*, p. 58 ff.

vocational training. What is generally aimed at is efficiency. This efficiency, it is hoped, is secured by "Division of Labour." But if the principle of the division of labour is not in essence the principle of coherence and of co-operation, it condemns the toiling masses to the membership of classes which are placed in a social status of permanent disadvantage. Their labour points to "ends" external to themselves. In other words, they serve a purpose which can never be related to their own lives. In the ultimate, therefore, the labourer is divorced from the meaning and significance of his labour. And moreover, if the product of labour is not the expression of the creative instinct of man, but is a mechanised output, it is something in which the personality of the human being does not enter. We are apt to think that these observations are true only of the machine-ridden age of the modern industrial era. And many have sung the praises of domestic economy, and the virtues it fostered that our criticism may sound strange. It is not machinery in itself that mechanises labour ; but the purpose which labour is held to subserve. If any human being or class is set to a task, the purpose of which cannot be vitally related to the particular person or class, the product is mechanical. Machinery in itself is not bad ; it is to be judged in terms of the end it seeks to serve. If it is to economise human energy so that it could be released to express itself in creative efforts of the Higher Life, we see nothing in it to condemn. To-day production is with a view to profit, and the human being is reduced to the level of the machine which he tends. This is why the age which has witnessed the discovery and introduction of labour-saving machinery is nevertheless the age in which labour is not saved, but crushed by the grinding wheel of a soul-less system. It was expected "that labour-saving inventions would lighten the toil and improve the condition of the labourer ; that the enormous increase in the power of producing wealth would make real poverty a thing of the past."[1] But "disappointment has followed disappointment", and "discovery upon discovery, and invention after invention, have neither lessened the toil of those who most need respite, nor brought plenty to the poor." This is so because the gains of increased productive power are not general. "It simply widens the gulf between Dives and Lazarus, and makes the struggle for existence more intense". The lower classes are excluded from the sharing of the results of material progress. The result is that "an immense wedge was being forced, not underneath society, but through society. Those who are above the point of separation are elevated, but those who are below are crushed down." And "amid the greatest accumulations of wealth, men die of starvation, and puny infants suckle dry breasts; while everywhere the greed of gain, the worship of wealth, shows the force of the fear of want." The remedy for the remediable but inevitable evils of our industrial age is not, however, rushing back to "barbarism" but in a more intelligent organisation of human life on principles of justice which shall make for universal coherence. The action of justice, as Ruskin says, must "diminish the power of wealth, in the hands of one individual, over masses of men, and to distribute it through a chain of men." The problem is essentially[2] a problem of distributive justice,[3] and not that of the opposition between domestic and factory economy. The evils that face us are not absolutely new; they are only aggravated by the present industrial system. We find them even in earlier times, though not in their accentuated stage. They are bound to be, and to last as long as society is not the reflex of true principles of justice, or to use the Indian term that has become familiar to us by this time,

[1] Henry George: *Progress and Poverty*, p. 7 ff.
[2] *Unto This Last*, p. 95.
[3] See Willoughby: *Social Justice*, Chapters V, VI and VII.

of Dharma. So long as Dharma is Swadharma the discrepancies are bound to continue.

And this idea of Swadharma as expressing itself through the caste system in vocational or occupational activities could not, and cannot, but result in exclusive interests which impede the social harmony. And an educational system that allots particular vocations to particular castes, the principle being not of aptitude or capacity but that of hereditary right to that particular profession might make for efficiency, technically so considered, but is highly harmful, nay even poisonous, in its general results on the character of the Polity as a whole. In the first place, any kind of vocational training based on the hereditary principle tends to stereotype intellect and ultimately to dwarf it. Every individual member of the community must be "capable of making an intelligent decision as to the way of life he will pursue".[1] He must be free to choose the work for which he is fitted. And this means that no one should be tied down to the training of a definite calling until he is in a position to intelligently exercise his choice. In early life the education of a boy must necessarily be of a very general nature. The purpose of education must be such as to enable the child to think for itself so that in time, it will slowly become conscious of its relation to the most vital concerns of life. In the early years especially, whatever tends to throw the child's habits into a particular groove to the exclusion of other aspects must carefully be avoided. The mind gets narrow owing to over-specialisation. It is impossible for a boy to tell with any certainty what his "bent" is until he has some idea of the many ways of life that are open to him, and the demands and satisfactions of each. It is, therefore, to the advantage of the community to keep its human resources as mobile as possible—i.e. not prematurely to specialise

[1] Hetherington: *Social Purpose*, p. 211.

them, as is done when we take a boy from school at twelve or thirteen and allow him to enter whatever occupation, chance or necessity may dictate."[1] The argument holds good more forcibly when even this limited choice, if we could so put it, is denied in a hereditary ordering of society. Individuals are born to a particular profession impelled thereto by past Karma ; for let us remind ourself that it is caste that determines profession.

In the second place any system of vocational training, in the emphasis it lays on specialised technique, gives a one-sided development of intellect, and ultimately machinises the whole life of the individual. It results in "the impress of intellectual habits into the validity of which the student has not been taught to examine." The mind gets accustomed to conventional details of the particular vocation, and rarely gets beyond at all. In other words the student becomes dull to the impulse of originality which alone is conducive to progress, for his mind is not receptive to novelty. His habits of mind are adapted to the needs of tradition and authority.

And above all, any system of vocational training, however useful in itself, may be too dearly paid for. Efficiency might be acquired "at the expense of more ultimate things." And especially when a particular profession is primarily a calling for the earning of livelihood it is degrading in its effects on a man's character. He values his profession for its cash value alone ; not as an avenue through which his personality is enriched by giving a free play to his creative genius.

From whatever point of view we might consider the problem, the vocational training imparted by the educational system, however useful or efficient it might have been in the technical sense, it was not conducive to the spiritual health of the society as a whole. Function must

[1] *Ibid.*, pp. 211-212, footnote.

be related to the coherence of the whole; otherwise we tend to perfect parts at the risk of mutilating the whole. And especially when the life of these "parts" is determined, as it is in ancient India, by Varna-Dharma, it results in some of them being raised to a prodigious degree above the rest, while others are being brushed aside with studied contempt. We need only refer to the so-called despised professions, considered intrinsically impure, to understand the nature of vocational training as determined by the principle of Swadharma. There are influences that train some into masters, others into slaves; some to noble professions, the rest to the despised.

Thus we have no hesitation in asserting that the educational system of ancient times was imperfect and unsound. It perpetuated class divisions and caste distinctions, and prevented the organic unity of society from being realised. And the distinction between the noble professions and the ignoble was broadly identical with the distinction between the free and the unfree. Such an unnatural differentiation, so disadvantageous to the majority, would have broken down inevitably, under the stress of competition, given conditions wherein the individual's choice could play a decisive part in the selection of career, but for the exaggerated recognition given to the principle of heredity. This principle of heredity is further buttressed on the doctrine of Karma. The caste of the individual is supposed to be determined by his accumulated Karma of the past. Caste, again, decided profession. And the education system that rested on the caste system was always in the interests of the higher castes which were "ends"; and it condemned the lower castes to perpetual degradation, for they were after all mere "instruments".

In other words, the educational system fostered the ethos of the society determined by the principle of swadharma, and tended to prevent the rise of divergences from the very birth. We cannot imagine the waste in human energy and intellect involved in this system. Whole classes were excluded from the learning that would enlighten intelligence and endow the mind with the capacities in the exercise of which freedom could ultimately emerge. At the present day, when social barriers are fast breaking down, it has been found possible for a few members of the lowest class the so-called untouchables to get themselves educated ; we mean educated, not according to the dictates of Swadharma, but under modern conditions of freedom. And we know how capable and useful they have proved themselves to be. It is monstrous to lay down as a general principle that persons born in a low caste are incapable of higher duties of life. At any rate, such a statement should never be valid unless proved by experience. And our reason tells us that there is nothing in caste itself to arbitrarily determine the vocation of any particular member of society.

We rightly condemn, therefore, the vocational system of education of Ancient India. And our criterion of judgment is not efficiency ; it is not material success ; it is not even the principle of utility. Perhaps from the standpoint of efficiency, material success and utility the results of vocational training by special classes in the community cannot be ignored. The numerous industries and arts that subsisted in India are witness to the high level of general culture reached by our ancients.

But, when all is said, vocational training is not the primary end of education. "Its aim must be to make a child at home in the worlds of Nature and of man, to train his will and feeling as well as his intelligence, to give him some appreciation of the value of life, and to train him in the endurance necessary for their pursuit."[1] And in any system of education, however technical it might be, there must be some place for subjects of a liberal

[1] Hetherington: *Social Purpose*, p. 212.

character that are based on an adequate conception of human values. For "life is always more than occupation." And no education should be confined wholly to the development of a single excellence. Indeed, it is very difficult to conceive of vocational education as an end in itself. And in the training imparted to the student a larger element which tends to expand his mind and enlarge his vision must be introduced. "A man is likely to be a more resourceful engineer or accountant if his mind has been trained in other studies than those that bear directly on his profession." And any scheme of instruction that tends to run in an exclusive groove stands therefore self-condemned.

We are ultimately driven to the conclusion that the vocational education of ancient India was imperfect, from whatever points of view we might consider it. Let us see if the so-called higher education was any better. For the primary function of education and any university system is to develop and foster such virtues which would make possible the realisation of freedom in the highest sense—freedom which can never be divorced from personality. A university is a communion of minds, a fellowship of spirits. The contact of individuals must make for the enrichment of personality, and this would be by the sharing of the things of the higher life. Educational ideals, that is to say, must be grounded upon moral and spiritual values. And as we have so often insisted, nothing can be truly moral or spiritual unless it is social as well. The true test of the adequacy of our ancient system of education is to ask how far it advanced the spirit of service and co-operation. And here we are left in no uncertainty. Where there is no recognition of social values, where the reality of the social order, indeed, is not recognised, we could never have any conception of service or co-operation. Thus there was no education that would prepare the individual to the exercise of the duties of citizenship. We shall return presently to this problem. At present we shall consider if the educational ideal was sound at least in its spiritual purpose.

The higher kind of knowledge was to lead one to emancipation. Avidya or ignorance was to be expelled, and knowledge or vidya implanted. Wisdom is impossible until the fetters that tie down the intellect of man are broken. Thought must become free. Our analysis of the conditions prevalent in Ancient India has convinced us that such freedom could never exist. We do not know much of the Universities that subsisted in ancient times, at Taxila, Nawadwip and other places. They were the resorts of scholars from far and wider, and served as beacon-lights of learning all through the ages. Our observations here are more directed to the educational institutions diffused through the length and breadth of the land. The minute regulations laid down in the various law books defining the relations between the Guru and the student tell us much of the spirit of educational life of those days. The one thing that immediately strikes one is that the idea of authority is fundamental.[1] "Brahmanical education, as well as other forms of education in India, looked for its ideal to the past rather than to the future."[2] The student has to accept everything on trust. Habits of implicit obedience are ingrained in him by the discipline of the Brahmacharya Ashram.

On all sides restraints are imposed which obstruct action and thought. The educational system, in the higher aspect also, leaves, "the interest of intellectual habits into the validity of which the student has not been taught to examine." The bold questioning spirit which was productive of the *Upanishads* and the other Philosophical treatises was a thing of the past. Indeed, even in the

[1] See Principal McKenzie's: *Hindu Ethics*, p. 48 ff.
[2] Keay: *Ancient Indian Education*, p. 176.

Upanishads we have no genuine spirit of doubt; they are dogmatic through and through. Truth worth knowing, of the universe and life, must be through the path of doubt. "The student", as Laski truly says, "cannot know until he has learned to doubt." The pathway to Truth is "a training in the habit of scepticism." And this is exactly what the student in Ancient India could not do. Tradition and Authority were fundamental. The numerous rules and regulations "entrap both teacher and student into the service of habit, which irritate and inhabit the emergence of intellectual freedom."

Both Guru and Sishya, teacher and student, were thus moulded in a definite type and both of them are infused with a particular ethos that was specially suited to the end the ancient Polity was to subserve. We have thought for to point this out because much has been said about the ancient system of education in its gurukula aspect. Critics of the educational systems of modern times point to the ancient system as the ideal and ask us to go back to former times. Indeed, we cannot sufficiently deplore the defects of our present day University system. The present age is an age of large-scale production, not only in industry, but it appears to us, in other aspects of life as well. Yearly thousands of graduates are turned out of our Universities, and just as in economic life the personal, human touch is not between the employer and the employed, in the educational world as well, the teacher and professor are daily being further and further removed from the student. Education must be "built upon the foundation of personal friendships between student and professor"; the personal contact of fellow seekers after Truth must result in the enrichment of minds, and the emancipation of thought. Above all education must make for the flowering of indivi-

[1] *The Dangers of Obedience*—Essay on *Teacher and Student*, p. 91.

duality, and the converging of the individual's personality in the common personality revealed in the universe, Humanity and Life. All this is impossible in our modern factory methods of instruction.

But let us not deceive ourself into believing that all this was possible in our ancient system of education ; and so we need only "go back". The relationship between the guru and the disciple cannot be described as truly personal ; and no "sharing" was involved either. The regulations determining the behaviour of the student towards the teacher are so artificial and conventional that they could not create warmth necessary enough for true mutuality. The teacher is placed too distant for the student to approach him at all. A gulf seems to separate them. We are not here speaking of the physical relationship. Two persons can come into very close physical contact, and yet remain leagues removed from each other.

And what was the ethical significance of the whole system, and what was its influence on the Polity? The answer that we get to these questions will enable us to arrive at our final judgment regarding the present value of our ancient educational ideals.

The ethical significance of the educational system of Ancient India lies in this that, tending as it did to the influence of authority on the one hand, and objective morality expressing itself in prescriptive observance on the other hand, it was admirably fitted to the maintenance of the existing order. The particular "ethos" necessary for an Order of Society based upon "Swa-Dharma" was thus fostered. The individual was not to question the wisdom of existing social conditions. He must accept everything on trust. He was not to question but to implicitly obey.

Thus we find the spirit of the educational system of Ancient India was admirably suited to serve the purposes of the State ; for all despotic Governments rest upon the foundation of authority. As Montesquieu has clearly recognised the laws of education will be different in each species of Government.[1] And those who were brought up in an educational atmosphere which demanded from them strict observance of rules and implicit trust in Authority would necessarily also be those who would uphold conformity and authority in matters of the State as well. The spirit of the educational system of Ancient India exactly suited and fostered the "ethos" of the Ancient Indian Polity.

The reformulation of our educational ideals is therefore essential if we have to build our future Polity on solid foundations. For it would be futile to erect institutions without providing for the necessary virtues for their success.

As this aspect of the problem is of far-reaching importance we shall return to it in our next chapter where we shall deal with it in its more general bearings.

---

[1] *Spirit of the Laws*, **Bk. IV.**

BOOK III

DE CIVITATE DEI

"But seek ye first the kingdom of God, and His righteousness, and all these things shall be added unto you."

CHAPTER X

THE IDEALS OF THE POLITY

"The realisation of the full destiny. the highest possible perfection of the human nature—this is the kingdom of God on earth."

IMMANUEL KANT

"Men must recognise and unify difference and then the moral law appears in all its majesty in concrete form. This is the Universal striving. This is the trend of all nature—the harmonious unifying of all. The call of the moral law is constantly to recognise this."

M. P. FOLLETT

"From the general formula that men call religion issues a rule of education, a basis of human brotherhood, a policy, a social economy, an art. It permeates politics in all questions of franchise, of the conditions of the masses, of nationality."

J. MAZZINI

"There is indeed to be no severance between the civitas Dei and the civitas terrana: each must interpenetrate the other and unite with it to bring forth the kingdom of God upon earth."

W. H. HADOW

A proper understanding of the Past is necessary, as we have often stated, for building up of the Polity of the Future. We look back in order to think forward. However revolutionary we would be we can never dispense with the experience of the past. "There is no true revolutionary who is not also conservative."[1] Even granting that history is the record of imperfection, the knowledge of imperfection is essential for any conscious striving after an ideal of perfection. But the Past is not mere imperfection; for it is an imperfection developing and growing into perfection, because of the gradual and infinite perfectibility of man and the world. The goal or destiny of human striving all through the ages is the greatest moral

[1] *Concerning Prayer* (Macmillan & Co., 1918), p. 383.

perfection. "The Universal end of mankind", says Kant, "is the highest moral perfection."[1] And in the pursuit of this End humanity is linked together in spiritual unity. It is a partnership of endeavour, linking up the past, the present and the future. A deep reverence for our past is the only test of our sincerity with regard to the future. And we cannot start the adventure of life without carrying along with us a mixed portion of help and hindrance from our past. And it is an adventure, too, on which we dare not start alone without taking the whole world with us "For ideal ends are nothing if they are not universal and all embracing; as soon as they are limited to the individual person or nation or interest they become worldly and lose their characteristic of spirituality."[2]

Nothing, in other words, can be truly spiritual unless it be social and universal. The merely spiritual, removed from the healthy contact of real life, and into which community with others, fellowseekers in the Great Quest, does not enter, is a false abstraction. Man is nothing, and can do nothing, apart from society. His actions can never be purely "self-regarding". At every turn, he touches various other Selves, and realises that he is his true Self only in relations with those "Others". It is only in the realisation of the significance of this relationship that the moral personality of man emerges.

The solution that we offer to the Problem of the Indian Polity, is, thus, a solution which can never be purely individual. It should seek to embrace the whole community, indeed the whole world. For morality is a universal striving. And man, as a moral being, will be more of the true individual the more he acts in conformity with the Universal Law of the Spirit. "For the greatness of a personality is not in itself", as Tagore rightly observes,

---

[1] *Lectures on Ethics*, p. 252.

[2] *Concerning Prayer*, p. 397.

but in its content, which is universal, just as the depth of a lake is judged not by the size of its cavity but by the depth of its water."[1]

The religious ideal must, in our opinion, not lead to a life of exclusive contemplation and self-centredness. True religion consists in a life of sharing, in a partnership of spiritual endeavour. Man is essentially a "social animal" and as a member of society alone he could realise the End of Life. There must therefore be the recognition of human values. The world of fact must be appraised in terms of value. We should realise that this life, Here and Now, has also its own values which would serve us in our spiritual efforts. We ought not to turn away from life. This world "serves us and fulfils our needs, but our relation to it does not end there. We are bound to it with a deeper and truer bond than that of necessity. Our soul is drawn to it ; we are attached to it with numberless threads, which extend from this earth to the stars."[2]

That is to say, this world cannot be evil in itself ; and we are not strangers in it. It is only when "a man does not realise his kinship with the world, he lives in a prison house whose walls are alien to him."

"The ideal that India tried to realise," as Tagore has rightly said, and as our own analysis of the Ancient Polity has made us to conclude "led her best men to the isolation of a contemplative life, and the treasures that she gained for mankind by penetrating into the mysteries of reality cost her dear in the sphere of worldly success."[3] But we should remember that material success was not the prime End of the Life of our ancients ; they cared more for the things of the Spirit than for the concerns of this our mundane existence. Theirs was essentially a religious temperament and a spiritual outlook. They had their own

[1] *Sadhana* (Ind. Edn.), p. 59.
[2] *Ibid.*, p. 112.
[3] *Ibid.*, p. 14.

ideal of perfection; and all human endeavour converged towards a single End, the realisation of Dharma.

There is much to be said in favour of our ancients if only we remember that some of the greatest thinkers of the world have considered a life of contemplation with special approval. And as we have often explained, we are not against true inwardness as such. What we would insist is that what is inward must be objectified in outward acts through a life of moral striving. Exclusive contemplation may result in sterility, unless the personality of man is driven to express itself in the ordering of life in which he is impelled by the Law of his Being to strive for Ends which have a universal or social significance.

"Man's life," says Miss Follett, "is one of manifold relatings."[1] True individuality cannot be abstracted from a life of activity. "The activity which produces the true individual is at the same time interviewing him and others into a real whole."[2] The doctrine of Self realisation of our ancients as the ideal of moral life, is to be reinterpreted if it is to serve our purpose. The Self or Atman, as conceived by our thinkers, is too unreal to be the object of our Quest. As we have seen, self realisation more often became in practice self repression. The Atman doctrine of emancipation, as we hold, is fundamentally defective. In the first place there is no Self which is a "thing-in-itself;" and no Self absolutely independent of "others". "The seeing of self as, with all other selves, creating, demands a new attitude and a new activity in man. The fallacy of self-and-others fades away and there is only self-in-through-others, only others so firmly rooted in the self and so fruitfully growing there that sundering is impossible."[3] And, in the second place, Life, Here and Now is not evil, and not, therefore, a hindrance. The

[1] *The New State*, p. 6.
[2] *Ibid.*, p. 7.
[3] Miss Follett: *The New State*, p. 8.

final End of human effort is not Release or Emancipation. Freedom does not mean the severance of the ties, human and so social. The more we are bound to each other, the more we are released from our mere "individuality". Our freedom lies in our bondage. The more we realise that we are knit together the greater is our realisation of Freedom. Far from being hindrances, our relationships, Here and Now, may be sublimated so that they shall serve the Ends of the Greater Life.

Above all, this our world is not apart or beside God. We cannot tear away from it with the feeling that it is "Mithya" or unreal. If it is a manifestation of God, it must participate of His Reality. God is even Here, in our very midst. We need not go in search of Him to some distant realm. He is here, immanent in our very thoughts. Just as the water that drops down from the heavens carried along by innumerable streamlets and rivers, reaches ultimately the bosom of the wide expanse of the ocean, so also the countless little deeds of man, however unconsciously performed, are already dedicated to the loving Father. We all of us seek Him, though in different ways. In the varied walks of life, we are all of us on the same Quest. He is Here, There and Everywhere. All of us have our being in His Living Presence. "For in Him we live, and move, and have our being...... For we are also his offspring."[1]

Spiritual communion, in other words, is the realising of spiritual community. We need to focus God in our everyday life. We should concentrate Him in whatever we do. We come to realise the bond that brings us together, children of a Common Father. We slowly recognise in this our Life, Here and Now, every day new values and new meanings. We become alive to the possibilities of

[1] *The Acts*, xvii, 28.

our Existence, and ultimately know that we need not cease to be human to know God. We can be men, and yet realise Him.

Our Life, Here and Now is a sacred thing. The bonds of earthly existence are sacred things. Men themselves are sacred. We should learn to see God's Living Presence in everything. He is enthroned in the shrine of our heart; He fills the vast expanse of the Universe. Every little act done in His name brings us nearer and nearer to Him. Service of man is one expression of the service of God. If we do not love men whom we see, how can we love God whom we have not seen? Service of the least of our brethren is acceptable to Him as service done unto Him. If we turn away from man, we turn away from God as well.

Ultimately we are led to the recognition of the sacredness of Humanity in each individual. Our common Parentage is the witness of our mutual relation. If we so act as to forget that we belong to a fraternity we forfeit our inheritance. We are all equal in the eyes of our Father. Why should we act towards each other on terms of superiority and inferiority? Our Father wishes us to share equally of the things he has given us. But we perpetuate in our lives the sin and the curse of Cain. Unless we do unto others as we would be done by we have no right to our inheritance. "We have all of us", says Kant, "an equal right to the good things which nature has provided. These good things have not, however, been shared out by God. He has left men to do the sharing. Everyone of us, therefore, in enjoying the good things of life must have regard to the happiness of others; they have an equal right and ought not to be deprived of it Since God's providence is universal, I may not be indifferent to the happiness of others. If, for instance, I were to find in the forest a table spread with all manner of dishes, I ought not to conclude that it is all for me; I may eat, but I should also remember to leave some for others to enjoy."[1] It is only when we behave towards each other as children of a common Father ought to, that we can inherit the Earth.

Our inheritance, moreover, is not merely of goods earthly. Ours is also a spiritual heritage, and we have claims on the legacies of the Past. The Great Men of the world do not belong to this or that country, and they are for all time. Germany can no more claim Kant exclusively for herself than India can claim Sankara. Material things may diminish in sharing but spiritual goods never. And, what is more, instead of getting poorer, we become all the richer for sharing.

Our Life on earth must, therefore, be an all-inclusive Partnership. No one, not even the least of us, shall be excluded. We seek to realise, in the manifold relations of life, the Fellowship of the Great Society. The institutions we build must be truly corporate in nature. And no institution can be corporate in spirit unless it is founded on co-operation and makes for universal coherence. The Polity that we build is not to be mere collection of individuals or groups. Society is more than an aggregate of men; and the State, which is the complex of human institutions must be a universal harmony and must seek to embrace every aspect of life. The State is not the mere political or legal organisation of the community. It is the highest, all-inclusive, institutional expression of Man.

And if the State, as we claim it is, is the highest institutional expression of Man, it is truly moral in its nature. Man as a moral being can realise the fullest stature of his personality within the State; for its "supreme function is moral ordering."[2] And morality is the "fulfilment of relation by man to man, since it is impossible to conceive an isolated man: the father and mother appear in our

---

[1] *Lectures on Ethics*, p. 192.

[2] Miss M. P. Follett: *The New State*, p. 333.

mind and with the three the whole infinite series. The State is the ordering of this infinite series into their right relations that the greatest possible welfare of the total may be worked out. This ordering of relations is morality in its essence and completeness". The State must, therefore, gather up into itself all the moral power of the Community, and must so order its life as to lead to the realisation of the Purpose of Life. The State must seek to direct all the moral force in Humanity towards the fulfilment of the Supreme End.

This conception of the State necessitates the revision of our traditional ideas of Life. Man's activity must be moral or nothing; and whatever End we visualise, whatever be the value and destiny of the human soul that we have, everything must be rooted in the idea of the infinite possibility of perfection of our Life, Here and Now, which could be made, nobler, better and more perfect through the purposive and creative activity of man. The End that mankind is seeking is the ideal of complete perfection, and every moment we are nearing, in a measure, the ideal of perfection Our End is not a remote possibility. It need not abstract us from life, and impel us to seek an elusive phantom. All our traditional ideas of life, of Karma and Samsara, and of Final Release must therefore be surrendered. Release is an empty Quest. Escape is delusion. Release or escape from what? Where shall we go in search of Him leaving Him behind! We shall glory in our bondage, for even our father is not Himself free. He is bound to us by inseparable ties.

We have so long looked upon the World as a prison of untold misery. The time has come to convert it into the shrine of our Father. Let us keep the temple precincts holy and pure so that He could be invited to stay with us for ever and ever. And we can make this a suitable abode,

---

[1] *Ibid.*

acceptable to Him, by so ordering our lives and by so directing our individual aims that this earth will become as near to Heaven as it is given to man to so make it. The civitas terrana shall become the civitas Dei. Our earthly Polity shall be the concretised embodiment of His Righteousness.

This brings us to the necessity of re-interpreting the conception of Dharma. Dharma as the End of Life, as the principle underlying the Polity, must not be conceived of in the exclusive sense it was done by our ancients. The conception of Swadharma must be surrendered. Dharma must be grounded upon true principles of Justice and Righteousness—political, social, and religious. Dharma must make for harmony; it must be the principle that integrates diverse and multiple aims into the all-inclusive Whole. It must make for Universal coherence. No element of the Polity shall be reduced to a mere "means" to serve "ends" external to itself. Dharma, in other words, should be the fulfilment of a Common or Social Purpose. The Good as the End of the State must be capable of being shared in by all. Dharma, in the last resort, must be the principle of the all-inclusive Partnership; and the Polity, as the concrete embodiment, must be the actualisation of Dharma so re-interpreted and re-visualised.

And all our ideas regarding Empirical Dharma, or the Social Order must likewise be surrendered. Our moral life is not merely of negative import and discipline of our ethical life is not merely to prepare us for Philosophical aloofness through Psychological detachment. And moreover, Dharma in its empirical significance, shall not be mere prescriptive observance; for that would perpetuate distinctions of Varna or Caste, and perpetuate likewise those influences which elevate some into masters and condemn others into slaves.

Dharma, in its Absolute sense, shall be the Idea,

complete and perfect. But Dharma, in its empirical aspect, must be conceived as capable of modification and change. It is Dharma gradually growing and developing into perfection. This means that we have to surrender again the idea of the fixity of our Social Order. Empirical Dharma is not an eternal ordering, compelling conformity. As reinterpreted by us, it is capable of infinite modification by the purposive and creative genius of man. So put, the maintenance of Dharma as the End of the State shall not be to keep the various elements of the Social Order, supposed to be fixed for all time, to the proper performance of their Swadharma, but it shall be, by a right ordering of life, to provide for Infinite perfectibility, and to enable each element by the opportunities offered, to realise and seek for itself, what is best and noblest, so that it shall occupy its appropriate Station in Life. The End of the State shall make for Progress and not fixity.

Dharma, again, must be truly universal in its nature. And if it should seek to regulate the life of man, it must primarily rest upon the idea of man's moral or ethical Personality. And no man is truly moral if he is not also free. True Freedom is the condition of true morality. The end for which man is destined is to be achieved through his own freedom. The State cannot, in other words, be the moral leader of slaves or unfree people. It cannot be that is to say, a mere relation between the Monarch on the one hand and his subjects on the other. The State must be a Fellowship of free men. The citizens in their collective capacity, as we have said, shall be the rulers, and in their individual capacity shall be citizens.

We are not, however, suggesting any particular form of Government as the best. We shall rest content merely with laying down the general principles of the Polity. "Every Government is legitimate in proportion as it stands for righteousness, if it does not do so it is null and void." We have no special preference for any particular form ; and every form of Government has had its admirers and advocates.

It was not our ancients alone who sang the praises of monarchy. Aristotle[1] also considered Absolute Monarchy to be the best. Plato[2] is of opinion that if there is an intelligent and young ruler, assisted by an able councillor even the Gods themselves could not do more for the mankind. Dante himself was in favour of monarchy ; the medieval thinkers like Bodin and Aquinas again favoured monarchical. "Although there are many types of commonwealths, it is the concensus of nearly all wise thinking men", says Erasmus, "that the best form is monarchy. That is according to the example of God that the sum of all things be placed in one individual, but in such a way that following God's example, he surpasses all others in his wisdom and goodness, and wanting nothing, may desire only to help his state."[3]

This would be in conformity with the paternal conception of the State ; the Prince is a sort of pater familias. In modern times this idea has lost its hold and democracy has been conceived as the best form of government. J. S. Mill sang the praises of representative government more than sixty years ago when he looked upon it as "the ideally best form of government", for under it "every person is able and habitually disposed to stand up for his rights". He further claimed that representative government "increases the amount and variety of personal energy enlisted in promoting the general prosperity."

By the middle decades of the nineteenth century, however, we already notice "a reaction against the uncritical faith in popular government, which characterised the writ-

---

[1] See *Politics*, Bk. III, Chs. XVI and XVII.

[2] Plato: *Laws*, Book IV, p. 92 ff.

[3] See Lester K. Born's article on *Erasmus on Political Ethics*, *Political Science Quarterly*, Vol. XLIII, Dec. 1928, Number 4, p. 528.

ings of the early utilitarians."[1] It was felt that it tended to produce "collective mediocrity" ; and Hare, in 1859, had already put forward his advocacy of the system of proportional representation. Proportional representation, however, though resulting in legislatures that reflect the nation as a whole, has led to a multiplication of parties and to chronic ministerial instability. The result has been that in all modern countries there is a remarkable decline in legislatures noticeable. "There is evidence to indicate in nearly every country some decline from that admiration of and confidence in the system of representative government which in England possessed the generation who took their constitutional history from Hallam and Macaulay and their political philosophy from J. S. Mill and Walter Bagehot."[2] And the Parliamentary system of the present day, as H. A. L. Fisher points out, "is assailed by Socialists disappointed with its achievements in the field of industry, or by high Tories like Dean Inge, who writes that the democratising of Parliament has become 'fatal to its power and prestige', and that it is 'increasingly doubtful whether its days are not numbered'. That is why more direct methods and novel devices like the Referendum and the Initiative are being advocated. These, too, however, have not proved more effective than the other democratic institutions, for the Referendum and the Initiative have tended to discredit legislatures without suppressing them altogether. Their effect on public life thus has been fatal. We are thus coming to realise that the so-called representative system of Government is a failure. We have come to realise the evils of Party life and the futility of electoral organisations. The single member

[1] Hattersley: *A Short History of Democracy*, p. 166.

[2] *Modern Democracies*: Chapter on *The Decline of Legislatives*.

[3] Articles on *The Adequacy of Parliaments* in the *Contemporary Review*.

districts and the general ticket system have both manifested certain evils that defeat the very purpose of democracy, and no electoral device has been discovered so far that would avoid the pitfalls so familiar in the working of modern democratic States.

So far every experiment in political life has left behind a keen sense of disappointment. Democracy, so far defined and actually realised, has brought us no nearer the millenium than the previous forms of Government. We are coming to recognise more and more the inherent defects of our modern democracies. In fact, there is a growing need to make democracy safe for the world. Faced as we are to-day with heaps of ruins on all sides, our enthusiasm for any particular form of political expression is bound to cool down, with the increasing knowledge that throughout we have conceived of political life in mathematical terms as if everything could be prepared according to a given formula. We thought of the human being more as a voter than a man; we reduced him thereby into a machine. The conviction is being pressed on us, with greater and greater force as our experience gets widened, that the constitution is primarily an ethical force, and that the time has come to go back to Plato and Aristotle. The constitution determines and is determined by the ethical level of the community. The particular form the Ancient Indian Polity had assumed was congruent with its social system and was influenced and moulded by the ideas of the times. And some of the most characteristic of those ideas have continued to the present day. So much so, if we try to frame a political constitution which is congruent with the social system, we shall be importing the imperfections of our social order into our Polity. "We think," as Tagore truly observes, "that our one task is to build a political miracle of freedom upon the quicksand of social slavery."[1]

[1] *Nationalism*, pp. 120-126.

Frankly speaking, therefore, we ought to surrender all those ideas which had made for particularism so far. And we should bring about radical changes in our body politic. We should revolutionise our society. To frame a constitution which shall be congruent with the present order of things is just to perpetuate our misery and slavery. The various attempts made so far to give us a constitution were bound to fail. We are of opinion that a mere political change will not suffice. Change must be effected in all other aspects of life at the same time.

Our failure so far is due to a wrong reading of the Problem. The Problem is not how to distribute seats and power to satisfy the clamouring claimants. That way spells disaster. The craze that has attacked us, of recent years, for the so-called representative institutions, for the party organisation and for the voting system is rapidly vitiating our whole life. The poison so works as to crush us into the mere parts of a soulless machine. "One man, one vote," if it be the formula to guide us in our institutional life, we shall rapidly degenerate and perish. We should surrender our numerical criteria, and build up our Polity on more solid bases. Equality, as defined by us, is not a quantitative conception ; it is essentially qualitative and so spiritual. We would, therefore, emphasise, as did Kant, on the sacredness of Humanity in each individual, and so erect our Polity that it shall be based upon principles that shall make for justice and coherence.

The life of our people is mainly non-political. The Problem of the Indian Polity is, therefore, mainly non-political. It is essentially social and racial. "To India", says Tagore, "has been given her problem from the beginning of history—it is the race problem."[1] "Our real problem", as he says elsewhere, "in India is not Political. It is social......it is the race problem."[2] We seem to

[1] *Nationalism*, p. 4.
[2] *Ibid.*, pp. 97-102.

overlook this fact because our attention is diverted from the main issues owing to the emergence of the political question. We have come to expect political emancipation to be the panacea for all our ills.

The source of the passion for political freedom however very often has its springs in superficial facts of our experience. Freedom does not mean hatred of the master and the "foreigner". We are our own slaves; and the fetters that bind us are wrought by ourselves. Those who are truly free can never be enslaved. The passion for freedom must be all embracing. Change effected in the Political life must be simultaneous with change effected in other aspects of life. If we concede freedom to the millions who are oppressed under the yoke of the inhuman caste-system and the inequality of our social order, if we eradicate the differences, communal and religious that divide us, no power on earth can keep us a moment longer enslaved. Unhappily we try to erect the edifice of political freedom on the quicksands of social slavery. That is the tragedy of our public life.

The root of the problem as we conceive it, is racial and social. We refuse to believe that the Englishman is really a "foreigner", though he has made himself such. According to us, India has not known, and shall not know hereafter any "Foreigner". Our country is that "ideal realm", to borrow the expression of Lowell, "which we represent to ourselves under the names of Religion, Duty and the like." In other words, our country is not a spatial conception, and so has no physical or territorial limits. It is a land that has no frontiers. India is the World in epitome. The Problem of India is the problem of the world. And any solution that we suggest for the Indian Polity is really valid for the world-state as well. We hold the balance of spiritual and material forces in our hands to-day and ours is a special function in the blending of the civilisations of the world. In India, the East and the West have met in a grappling embrace. The five great cultures of the world have gathered together in a vast confluence; and the current of Humanity so long distributed in sluggish innumerable, streamlets has now gathered momentum in this titanic commingling and the rising surge has overflowed the banks.

For the moment, however, we hear the loud roar of the waters, the rumbling din of the clash. Timid natures draw back frightened, now that the flood-gates have been thrown open. In this universal deluge, they see their own civilisation, which had proudly withstood the onslaughts of pitiless Time these long centuries, at last move from its hinges and go crashing down into the vortex of a phenomenal cataclysm. In this terrific impact, no idea and no institution which we have hugged so long as characteristically Indian will remain itself any longer.

The root cause of the present unrest in India is, not therefore, political or economic. It is the deep conviction that this impact is unholy and vicious. It is a protest against the "rude pressure of the political ideals of the West on the East."[1] It is the determination not to be blown off our feet, as Mahatma Gandhi has characteristically expressed it. This modern civilisation is, according to him, a disease. It is the Mahatma's deep conviction that "India has nothing to learn from anybody else." Her Dharma must be preserved from this profane contact of the West.

The political movement fathered and guided by Mahatma Gandhi is primarily to rescue Dharma from the universal wreckage. After knocking at "alien" doors, the spiritual aspirant came back to his own. He is convinced that India would be untrue to herself if she admitted "foreign" influence. And so he is exerting his whole strength to fight against the new tendencies.

---

[1] See Tagore: *Nationalism*, p. 81.

We, on the other hand, are not afraid of the impact of the West on the East. The mighty transformation that is being effected already gives us glimpses into the Coming Age. Amidst death-throes and birth-throes is the New Order being born. This New Order is not of the East and is not of the West. It is neither Hindu, nor Muslim, nor Christian. This vast commingling of culture that is going on is the greatest and noblest fact since History began. It is not a small change but a mighty Revolution. And as is inevitable in all revolutions destruction precedes construction. And the whole process is ruthless in its energy. Old world traditions and superstitions are receiving rude shocks. Whole edifices are being razed to their foundations. The conflict of the Old and the New appears indeed brutal ; but, as Victor Hugo has said, what are Revolutions, but the brutalities of progress?

We, therefore, do not draw back from the awe-inspiring spectacle before us. We hail it with hope and trust. We do not see mere conflict and struggle, for we discern the principle of harmony. Even Revolutions obey the Law of Rhythm ; there is order in their fury, reason in their madness. Out of this clash the West will not emerge as the West, neither the East as the East. When the surge of the tide has receded, the old towers and minarets will not rise up as before. The civilisation of the Future is neither Western nor Eastern. It will be the world civilisation.

It is given to India to achieve this Noble and Mighty task. We ought to rise to the occasion. Instead, we make the Great Refusal. We ought to yoke all our energies to the car of Progress instead of allowing ourselves to be crushed beneath its wheels, in a vain attempt to hinder its movement. Any movement that we shall have must raise us from our exclusiveness. It is futile to work against the revolution. Shall we not sail rather over the storm tide, and ride the whirlwind?

The India of the Future is not, and shall not be "India for the Indians". The nationalist idea is a narrow and separatist idea. There never was an "India for the Indians" in the past; as we have said, India has known no foreigner. She has been the home of every people of this world. Why should there be, we ask, an "India for Indians" to-day? Our "nationalist" school of writers have tried to prove that there was a strong sense of Nationalism in Ancient India.[1] Such a misreading of our Past is a dangerous anachronism. "India has never had a real sense of nationalism."[2] And to try to evoke it to-day is the greatest disservice done, not only to India, but to the whole world. Nationalism is a destructive and disruptive force, and its influence has been wholly for evil. It has always made for war. In its accentuated form it has revealed itself in its true colours as Imperialism. Its seeds have been veritable dragon's teeth. The existence of one nation is a standing menace to the liberties of others. When two nationalities meet, they must inevitably struggle for supremacy. "In the struggle between Nationalities one nation is the hammer and the other the anvil; one is the victor and the other vanquished."[3] There seems to be no law but force that can decide the issue between nation and nation. Our international relationships, as we have said elsewhere, are still not above the ethics of the foot-pad. "The bridges between the nations seem broken down, and no one can tell when they will be repaired."[4] Immanuel Kant as early as 1779 said: "If we look at the most enlightened portion of the world, we see the various States armed to the teeth, sharpening their weapons in

---

[1] See Radhakumud Mookerji: *Nationalism in Hindu Culture*.

[2] *Nationalism*, p. 106.

[3] Prince Bulow: Quoted by A. E. Zimmern, *Nationality and Government*, p. 18.

[4] *Ibid.*, p. 19.

time of peace the one against the other."[1] The world-position to-day is infinitely worse ; for it is a state of perpetual war. And the greatest obstacle of peace and harmony is to be found in Nationalism and National Prejudices. "The Nation has thriven long upon mutilated humanity. Men, the fairest creations of God, came out of the National manufactory in huge numbers as war-making and money-making puppets ludicrously vain of their pitiful perfection of mechanism."[2] Nationalism is "the apotheosis of selfishness" and the "interminable breed and hatred and greed, fear and hypocrisy, suspicion and tyranny." And the Logic of the nation is such that "It will never heed the voice of truth and goodness. It will go on in its ring-dance of moral corruption, linking steel unto steel, and machine unto machine, trampling under its tread all the sweet flowers of simple faith and the living ideals of man."[3]

The main source of the strength of the spirit of nationalism is selfish vanity, miscalled patriotism. Mr. Pearson assumes that "there is or ought to be a virtue of patriotism, a sense of national feeling, which binds the Englishman to England, the Frenchman to France in some special and not easily dissoluble way."[4] And the Indian nationalist, too, assumes that this virtue must similarly bind the Indian to India. Patriotism is the very definite feeling of "My country, right or wrong" ; it is the "preference for one's own people or State above all other peoples and States, and a consequent wish to get for that people or State the greatest advantages and power that can be got, things which are obtainable only

[1] *Lectures on Ethics*, p. 252.

[2] Tagore: *Nationalism*, pp. 44-46.

[3] *Ibid.*, p. 41.

[4] Quoted by Dr. Pattabhi Seeta Ramaih: *Indian Nationalism*, pp. 11-12.

at the expense of the advantages and power of other peoples and States."[1]

As a feeling, therefore, it is obvious that patriotism "is bad and harmful, and as a doctrine is stupid. For it is clear that if each people and each State considers itself the best of peoples and States, they all live in a gross and harmful delusion."

And nationalism subsists by hypnotising a whole people with this dope of the patriotic spirit. It imbues the mind of the people with the sense of their superiority to other peoples; and excites in them repulsion or dislike for the "foreigner". By rousing up a whole people to the defence of their country by the spell of the cry "the country in danger", it converts its whole citizen population into the soldiers of the field. Its "young men shall go to fight; married men shall forge weapons and transport of supplies; the women shall make tents and uniforms or serve in the hospitals; the children shall make lint; the old men shall be carried to the public square to excite the courage of soldiers."[2] The wars of modern times, since the eruption of nationality, are not wars between mere Governments but between peoples. They are wars of all against all. Nationalism has furthered ceasarism or militarism.

If the world is to survive, the time has come, we believe, for surrendering altogether this principle of nationality. Indeed its day has drawn to its close. There are already signs that herald the coming of a New Age. "The Modern World", says Zimmern, "is in fact international to the core."[3] The world is already one great

---

[1] Tolstoy: *Patriotism and Government*, Essays and Letters, p. 240.

[2] Decree of the National Convention of France, Aug. 23—(quoted by Holland Rose: *Nationality in Modern Europe*, pp. 136-137).

[3] *Nationality and Government*, p. 36.

society, as Norman Angell tells us. "For the merchant, the banker, and the stock broker political frontiers have been broken down. Trade and industry respond to the reactions of a single, world-wide nervous system". It is the stupendous fact that Graham Wallas has so well described.[1] There is no reason why the Great Society should not have a common will and a common organisation. It is only then that war could be averted and Perpetual Peace insured. Immanuel Kant had dreamt that Perpetual Peace could be established through commerce. The world-market, however, has intensified rivalry, and commerce has always been the underlying motive for war. The Imperialism to-day is essentially commercial. The principle that would bring together the different peoples of the world together in a single Commonwealth must be sought for in some other factor which shall be lasting and healthy in its influence.

The first and urgent necessity is to visualise the correct ideals that would serve the Polity of the Future. The Thought and Will of the Great Society must be organised,[2] and all ideas that hinder the realisation of the Great Society must be immediately surrendered.

Above all, our love for our little platoon, our "motherland," or "fatherland" as we call it, must urgently be surrendered. India is not the "motherland" for us ; and the other countries of the world are not, therefore, "foreign" lands. The love of the Motherland or the Fatherland conceived thus is crude and narrow. We are all children of a Common Father ; and the whole Earth is our inheritance. Our Fatherland, therefore, is the world as such, and our country is a land with no frontiers. We have no reason to think that our immediate neighbour is our brother and the distant Englishman or German is

---

[1] *The Great Society*, p. 4.

[2] See Graham Wallas: *The Great Society.*

the foreigner. The tie that binds us to our immediate neighbour is also the tie that draws us closer together with another brother thousands of miles away.

The idea that something is "foreign" to us must immediately be expunged from our consciousness. The idea, also, that we have nothing to learn from others must immediately be surrendered. We have suffered enough already by erecting rigid barriers and high walls ; and have paid too high a price for the stability of our civilisation and culture. We ought not to, even if we can, shut out the rest of the world from India. Ours is the Legacy of the World. We cannot rest content that either we or our ancestors have discovered Truth and gained knowledge for all time. Our searching analysis in the preceding pages has shown how much we could learn from the West. Truth and Knowledge are nobody's exclusive possession. We have not yet become, and we believe that we shall never become, so perfect as to dispense with the rest of the World. "Knowledge", as Delisle Burns has truly observed,[1] "cannot expand within frontiers ; for the supply of genius in any community is small and use may be found for foreign genius."

Our conception of the Polity postulates the essential truth that no people or nation can live its own life, independent of the rest ; in other words, no nation or people can live unto itself. To talk of a nation's destiny or Purpose which is not, and cannot, also be the destiny or Purpose of the whole Human Race in the result of the failure to see the wood for the trees. The destiny of India is, as we believe, the destiny of the world ; and her purpose is the Purpose of Humanity.

We ought, therefore, to surrender the particularist ideas of Swadharma, Swadeshi and Swarajya. It is an

[1] *Democracy*, p. 96.

unhappy thing that the various movements of this country have fallen into the familiar grooves that movements elsewhere have fallen. If at all we have to profit through the experience of History it is time we realise the significance of what we are doing. Almost all the thinkers of the West have come to realise "that many movements which seemed full of infinite promise have, even when successful, disappointed the hopes of their adherents."[1] The Italy that Mazzini dreamt of is not the Italy of Mussolini. Perhaps the India that Mahatmaji dreams of may not be the actual India when Swaraj is obtained.

Lest we forget, let us reiterate with all the emphasis that we can, the necessity to surrender all ideas which have a "Swa" as their prefix. We do want to be free. India dependent is a misfortune, not only to her people but to others as well. She cannot participate in the life of the world except on terms of equality. Partnership, if real, can never be on any other basis. And further it is only India, free and strong, that can help other peoples to freedom and strength.

What, however, we do insist is, that India ought not to be independent. Free Partnership in the life of the great society means that the basis of mutuality will be co-operation of service, and Interdependence in fellowship. Above all Fellowship is possible in and through Love. Let us not therefore put premium upon mere neighbourhood. The fundamental basis of our future Polity shall be the maxim that nothing is alien to us which is not foreign to Man.

That is why we insist upon the necessity of revising and revisualising our ideals. If we would avoid repeating in our life the history of Germany, Italy and the other countries which began with similar generous enthusiasms,

---

[1] Dicey: *Law and Public Opinion in England*, pp. lvi-lvii.

if we would avert the inevitable disappointment that would follow with the blighting of our hopes, if we, the oppressed of to-day would not like to become the oppressors of tomorrow, we should weed out such ideas, and prepare against such influences, which would drive our movements of emancipation, into the fatal direction which has given similar movements elsewhere the distorted results of today.

The passion for Freedom must, therefore, be pure and free from the alloy of grosser elements. We believe that we need not become a nation to gain our liberty. And freedom need not mean independence. All that which makes for mere individualism and particularism must, as we said, be surrendered. This can be done only by redefining Dharma by giving it a universal and positive content.

We should, indeed, grasp the supreme Truth that we can best preserve Dharma by vitalising the conception, freeing it from its narrow confines. Dharma shall be the principle of Justice and Righteousness.

The Doctrine of Swadharma is the root of all evil. It is dangerous, under the complex conditions in which we live at the present day, to talk of Swadharma. No people and no individual can have a Dharma which is not that of others as well. Dharma is either universal or no Dharma at all. In a country like India, especially a home of diverse peoples and multiple cultures, whose dharma do we mean whenever we talk of "Swadharma"? Are we to perpetuate our divisions by emphasising our differences?

And how can we, moreover, talk of the Swadharma of India unless by the same conception we mean something which could be vitally related to the Dharma of other countries?

To imbue the mind of a whole people with the idea of a special destiny and a special Purpose, which is not and cannot be the destiny and Purpose of the rest of Mankind is to mutilate Humanity at its most vital part. It is to ignore our common extraction.

The Doctrine of Dharma must be re-interpreted, therefore, if it is to serve as the End of the Future Polity. Dharma, if it is to be the expression of Social Justice, involves the re-shuffling of the Social Order so that artificial barriers erected by caste and by the accidents of historical religions could be overcome. All social disabilities based upon birth must be immediately removed. No individual, class or caste shall be degraded into mere instruments to serve Ends external to themselves. Every individual, or class or caste shall be at once an End and means. And Dharma, if it is to be the expression of Economic Justice must be grounded upon a righteous and equitable system of Distribution. There shall be no leisured classes on the one side and the labouring masses on the other. Leisure shall be the reward for the service rendered by labour. If Dharma, again, is to be the expression of Political Justice, it shall not further influences that train some into masters and the rest into slaves. The virtue to be fostered shall not be mere obedience, but co-operation which expresses itself in service Then only can Authority be reconciled with Freedom. The Partnership of the Great Society shall be universal. Lastly, if Dharma is to be the expression of Ethical Justice, it must make for Spiritual Harmony. It must be the principle of universal coherence and must be grounded on the ideas of the Infinite Perfectibility of Man, of his Life, Here and Now, and of the grandeur of the Moral Personality of the Individual. Moral Progress postulates the Freedom of the Will. But this is a Freedom in the exercise of which Man is bound all the more to the rest of Mankind and the universe with inseparable ties. The realisation of Dharma shall be the realisation of Man's kinship with the Universe. All the faculties of his Personality shall so converge in their efforts as to point to the fulfilment of a richer and nobler Personality, in which the distinction of the "Self" and the "Other" shall be dissolved in the vital Harmony of the Universal Self.

Our ideal postulates the Inter-dependence of all things in the Universe. Man should be knit closer to Man, and Man with Nature. The relation between Man and Man, and Man and Nature is sacred, for ultimately it is a relation between Man and God. For God is not far removed from us. And if this relation could be actualised in institutional terms, that complex of human relationships which we term the Polity shall not be alien to Man or his End. The relation between man and God, may involve, in other words, the awareness of a third entity which we term the State.

Dharma, as the End of the State, shall make for Justice and Righteousness, only when the prejudices of Swadharma are surrendered. It is only the spirit of partisanship that would lead us to set up one set of ideas and institutions into competition with others considered as "foreign". And our narrow and separatist tendencies can only be controlled and checked by the removal of limitations upon our views of the kind of Humanity which constitutes a claim upon our allegiance. First of all we must determine the kind of Life we would wish to live and then we could visualise the ideals of the Polity. And according to us, the Life we should aspire to live is nothing less than that of the Great Society which constitutes the Universal Human Fellowship. And India is eminently fitted to show to the world how this Great Society could be founded. Any constitution that we provide for her must be valid for the world State as well. The problem is, how to reconcile our differences. To recognise them and embody them in our Polity is to perpetuate our division, for they shall always be ranged against each other in opposition. No pact of interest will endure. Recognition of differences very often, in practice, become the sanction of such differences. We talk incessantly of majority rights and minority rights. Have we ever given thought to the rights of the whole to which we belong? As soon as we begin to define, in legal terms, our mutual relations, we are bound to fall out. For Life is more than what legal definitions would make it. An enduring Pact is only the union of Hearts. The relation that brings us together is, and ought to be, that of Love. Being children of a common Father we ought to love each other with all our hearts and all our souls. And the more we love one another the more do we realise our kinship with God.

In other words, the Polity shall be the Family Writ Large and the Indian Polity shall be the miniature of the world Polity. In its internal aspect it shall be the harmony of diverse shades that form its life, but a harmony born not out of haphazard conflict, but on the inter-action of Love. In its external aspect, it shall be coterminous with the world. The external relations shall make for Peace and strive to put an end to war. Dharma will reign in the State and in the Human Race only when Perpetual Peace is established.

And the blessing of Perpetual Peace will be added unto us if we seek first the Kingdom of Reason and Righteousness, as Kant insists.[1] The welter of our individual purposes and conflicting wills must be dissolved in the participation of the pursuit of a Common Good in the Great Society, through Love and Co-operation.

War is a stupid, savage thing. It cannot be justified on any ground. General Moltke says, that "Perpetual Peace is a dream and not a beautiful dream either; War is a part of the divine order of the world. During war are developed the noblest virtues which belong to man......" Treitschke talks of "the moral majesty of war" and

[1] *Perpetual Peace*, p. 178.

asserts that war is an institution ordained of God,"[1] and so "the hope of driving war out of the world is not only senseless, it is deeply immoral".[2] But the noblest minds of all ages have refused to admit such pretensions. The recognition acceded to the necessity of war is at best very grudgingly given. "Reason requires," says Hobbes "that every man ought to endeavour peace, as far as he has hope of obtaining it; and when he cannot obtain it, that he may seek, and use, all helps and advantages of war".[3] Aristotle says that war has its end in peace. Cicero also maintains that "wars are to be undertaken for this end that we may live in peace without being injured" and so "in engaging in war we ought to make it appear that we have no other view but peace". According to Erasmus, "If there be anything in the affairs of mortals which it becomes us deliberately to attack, which we ought indeed to shun by every possible means, to avert and to abolish, it is certainly war".

But the problem for us to solve is how to abolish war and make it unnecessary in the Future. And here we can call to our aid one of the most characteristic ideas of our Ancients. We have seen that Universal sovereignty was the constant ideal which was placed before the Monarch. It was considered to be the best guarantee of Peace. Universal Sovereignty involves the surrender of separate sovereignties; the absorption into a Single State the various separate states that constitute the world to-day. But Universal Sovereignty, in the sense of the One-man rule, which our ancients had thought of and which Dante dreamt of, and which Napoleon was so dangerously near accomplishing, is a dangerous thing, even if possible. By Universal Sovereignty, we mean the integrating of all our separate and exclusive existences into the membership

---

[1] *Treitschke*, p. 38.

[2] *Ibid.*, p. 41.

[3] *Leviathan*, I, Ch. XIV.

of an all-inclusive World Organisation. It is in fact, the creation of a New State which is the world State. "For the problems arising out of the contact of races and nations can never be adjusted either by the wise action of individuals or by conflict and warfare; they can only be solved by fair and deliberate statesmanship within the bosom of a single State, through the recognition by both parties of a higher claim than their own sectional interest— the claim of a common citizenship and the interest of civilisation."[1]

This means that our ideas of Sovereignty and Citizenship need an urgent revision and reformulation. Sovereignty must inhere in the whole of Humanity organised in a single Commonwealth. As Mazzini has beautifully said Sovereignty is not in "I" or in "we", but in God. Our conception of Sovereignty, in other words, is not spatial, and so we ought not to define it in physical or territorial terms. The Pluralist attack on State-Sovereignty, we admit, is perfectly justified, for the independence of the several States of the world to-day constitutes the greatest danger to the peace of the world. The world-State must be grounded upon the principle of interdependence.

Our conception of citizenship likewise must be radically revised. We are primarily citizens of the world, and we cannot love "our own" country more than others, if by "our own" country we mean the India bounded on the north by the Himalayas and on the other sides by the ocean. Our loyalty is to the country that knows no boundaries. Our highest loyalty is to Humanity but it is a loyalty that has expanded in ever-widening concentric circles. Lesser loyalties are not abrogated but are fulfilled in the higher. And no citizenship is possible, as we have so often insisted except on terms of equal Partnership. In other words, the principle of citizenship must be interpreted by

[1] Zimmern: *Nationality and Government*, p. 30.

our attitude towards our fellow men. We should do unto others as we would be done by. Only under conditions of such reciprocity is the exercise of the functions of citizenship possible.

And our loyalty is primarily to the State that insures universal Partnership in the Life of the Great Society. The Nation-State ought not and shall not demand any claims on our allegiance. Our allegiance is to the State which realises for us our ideal of Universal Human Fellowship.

The foregoing discussion brings us back direct to our problem. The object of this work is to discover principles that would serve us to build up the Polity of the Future. The need has arisen to-day to redefine the grounds of political obligation. Our study of the Ancient Indian Polity is to recover elements of value from our past which can yet serve us in our institutional efforts. The Modern Idea of the State lays primary emphasis on legal[1] and political aspects of life. Not that the legal aspect of the Ancient State is negligible in itself. But we should remember that the Ancient Polity was more than a legal community. "A supernatural presidency is supposed to consecrate and keep together all the cardinal institutions of those times, the State, the Race and the Family".[2]

Almost every idea has a religious background. And further, we should remember that the Polity is more than its mere political institutions. "The body politic is the social body plus the political organisation."[3] In all our discussions of the nature of the State we have followed the Idealistic trend of thought in refusing to identify it with its organisation. An institution as we have so often maintained, is an idea and is the embodiment of purpose.

---

[1] See Krabbe: *The Modern Idea of the State.* His thesis is that "the idea of the State must be derived from the Law".

[2] Sir Henry Maine: *Ancient Law*, p. 6.

[3] Willoughby: *The Nature of the State*, p. 2.

The State is, therefore, primarily an idea. As Fichte has put it, "the State is an essentially unseen Idea".[1] It is moreover the expression of spiritual unity. Hegel was certainly right in including all other social groups in the State, considering the State, of course, in its widest sense. The State, is to him, the unity of all other social functions.[2] Or to express it in other words, the State is the highest integrating principle of the community. It is the unified and unifying State. It is the complex of institutions without which the individual can have no life to call his own.[3]

It is really irrelevant to question the existence of the State in the abstract. Some modern writers complain that the Idea of the State is mystical. Mac Iver considers that to interpret the State as a unity—a mystical unity—is to retard "the progress of political thought" and a disservice rendered "to our understanding."[4] A grove of trees might not be a tree; and the State is not a unity in that sense. The Idealist, however, speaks of unity in the spiritual sense, not the coming together of individuals as persistent objects in space and time—for then we have only an aggregate—but a higher commingling, resulting from the contact of minds. To persist in looking upon individuals as mere individuals is the defect of those "who fail to see the wood for the trees".

Further, there seems to be a serious confusion between the idea of the State and its partial realisation in the Actual State. As we have often pointed out, no idealist contends that the State as it is, is already perfect. It is a State "developing and approaching perfection", though "the idea of the State, is the State perfect and com-

[1] *The Popular Works*, p. 151.
[2] See Watson: *The State in Peace and War*, p. 129.
[3] T. H. Green: *Political Obligation*, p. 122.
[4] See *The Modern State*, pp. 447-454.

plete".[1] The Actual is an imperfect embodiment of the Ideal. Because the Ideal has never been completely actualised, we cannot say that the Ideal is unreal. "Whether such a one exists, or ever will exist in fact, is no matter"; whether the actual State will in every respect coincide with the Ideal is an altogether different question. "Would a painter", asks Plato, "be any the worse because, after having delineated with consummate art an ideal of a perfectly beautiful man, he was unable to show that any such man could ever have lived?"[2] The ideal may be unattainable in its perfection; but we may nevertheless make an attempt to realise the ideal of the State in some measure at least. The Actual State, moreover, in spite of its imperfections is a progressive fulfilment of the ideal.

In the last analysis, we could say that any State is better than anarchy, or *Matsyanyaya*, as the Indian writers describe it. Most thinkers, in their attack on the State, identify it with the institutions through which its compelling power is exercised. But as we have often insisted, the governmental organisation is not the State. Governments may be, and in fact, are imperfect. It would not do, however, to somehow assure ourselves that though evil, because Government is necessary[3] we should tolerate its authority. It is held that "it is a tolerably well-ascertained fact that men are still selfish".[4] And so "why ask whether those in power *have* sought their own advantage in preference to that of others? With human nature as we know it, they must have done so. It is the same tendency in men to pursue gratification at the expense of their neighbours which renders government needful. Were we not selfish, legislative restraint would be

---

[1] Burgess: *Pol. Science and Const. Law*, Vol. I, pp. 49-50.

[2] *The Republic*, Bk. V, 472-D.

[3] Spencer.

[4] Spencer: *Social Statics*, pp. 52-53 (R. P. A. Cheap Reprints).

unnecessary." Constraint, in this view, is evil, but a necessary evil. Indeed, a thinker like Tolstoy does not even recognise this necessity. "The abolition of Governments", he says, "will merely rid us of an unnecessary organisation which we have inherited from the past."[1]

The suspicion of the Government and the State is based, as we understand it, on a wrong analysis of the facts of human nature, and a very narrow conception of the political life. Government is not like a policeman appointed to keep watch over convicts but the instrument through which the Purpose of the State is to be translated into the actualities of life. The whole attack on the State and its activities is, moreover, based upon misconceived ideas of Freedom and Moral Personality. Freedom is not mere absence of restraint. It can be harmonised with restraint. All Life and its Progress are the result of the conflict of these forces. Viewed as separate facts, freedom and restraint might appear to be irreconcilable; but as Hegel has shown, these apparently opposing principles can be harmonised in a higher synthesis.

In the ultimate, moreover, restraint is not a moral hindrance. In a sense, the man, as a moral personality is always free. "Since in willing a man is his own object, the will is always free. Or, more properly, a man in willing is necessarily free, since willing constitutes freedom..."[2] Paradoxical as it may appear, restraint is always self-imposed if the purpose of such restraint is related to the purpose of the volitional life of Man. We have become familiar with the truism that a man cannot be made moral through legislation against his will. But this is so if the man does not act as man, but acts as an isolated individual. If the individual is in his nature universal, as we

[1] Essay on *Patriotism and Government*, *Essays and Letters* (World's Classics).

[2] T. H. Green: Essay on the Different Senses of *Freedom* as Applied to Will and to the Moral Progress of Man.

have maintained throughout, he can so act, as what he wills will also be of a universal nature. It is in this sense that Kant would have us so act that the exercise of our will "be able to coexist with the freedom of others according to universal law". The mere individual, as possessing natural rights and natural freedom, is a myth. It is only as the member of Society that he comes to have either freedom of rights.

And "the power, which in a political society" individuals have to obey "is derived from the development and systematisation of those institutions for the regulation of a common life, without which they would have no rights at all.[1] Government in our view, is not in itself evil, and the obligation to render allegiance to the State is not merely a political obligation, but also essentially moral. It is to be grounded on the conception of the moral personality of Man. If man's will is free, and as a moral person he is able, and in fact, "is irresistibly impelled, to formulate for himself an ideal of perfection toward the attainment of which he is conscious of a moral obligation to strive",[2] this consciousness of obligation takes the form of a Categorical Imperative.

In our discussions of the grounds of political obligation, the problem to be solved is that of the opposition between the individual and the State. Why does the individual render obedience to the commands of the State? The Idealist does not see any real antagonism between the State and the individual. He only seeks to question the moral validity of the acts of Government, justifying or condemning to the extent they further or hinder the fulfilment of the Purpose of the State. We do not seek to question the existence of the State as such. Or to express our meaning in other words, in "bringing a particular

---

[1] T. H. Green: *Political Obligation*, p. 122.
[2] Willoughby: *Social Justice*, p. 244.

State to the bar of moral criticism, it is rather its activities than its own right to existence which is brought to trial."[1]

And so when we come to reformulate the grounds for political obligation the question to be answered is, why should we as moral beings obey the commands of the State, meaning by the term "State" here, not the State in the abstract but the actual and definite organisation through which it seeks to realise its Purpose. No theory that we have so far noticed will serve as adequate. The Social contract theory, as we said has no basis either in reason or in fact, the Divine Right Theory, again can never find universal acceptance. Those who do not recognise the theist's position would summarily reject this theory as sublime mysticism and nonsense. It does not, moreover, follow that every theist can unquestioningly adopt it. "All that necessarily follows from the divine theory is that political rule of some sort or other is divinely justified. No test, or suggestion of a test, is thereby afforded for determining whether any particular empiric manifestation of such order is exercised according to this divine purpose, or by the hands divinely appointed; unless, indeed, we say that the mere fact that the given state does exist and that its Government is in the hands that it is, such a condition must therefore be according to the will of Him who is omnipotent and directs all Human things."[2] This, however, amounts to a justification of the *status quo* whether just or unjust. If "the powers that be are ordained of God", as St. Paul would say, it does not mean that there is a divine right to do wrong. The ruler must "maintain a righteous order, a just order; a righteous system of life."

The Force Theory, again, we reject, as it insults our sense of moral adequacy. If people do right only when

---

[1] Willoughby: *Social Justice*, p. 230.

[2] Willoughby: *The Nature of the State*, p. 52.

under necessity they are no moral agents at all, and moreover, "the mere possession of sceptre", as Socrates pointed out long ago, "gave no claim to power". Further the mere legality of Force is not its justification. In the conception of Law at any rate as our ancients understood it, something more was involved; Law meant Dharma. And it understood it in this general sense, the observation of Duguit becomes intelligible if applied to the Ancient Indian State. "The State is founded upon force, but this force is lawful when it is exercised in accordance with law."[1] Mere force, in other words, "can never give to a rule that *ethical* element which belongs to a rule of law."[2] And the rule of law can acquire this ethical quality, "from the feeling or sense of right which is rooted by nature in the Human mind."

Ultimately, therefore, we are thrown back on moral and ethical ground for our theory of political obligation.[3] The commands of the State must be obeyed because they express a purpose which can be vitally related to our own purpose; the End the State seeks to fulfil is also the End we seek in our lives.[4]

"The only ground upon which the citizen can give or be asked to give his support for the State is upon the conviction that what it is aiming at is, in each particular again, good. We should not," as Laski truly says, "support a given State because the ideal State is patterned upon Utopia. We should not even support a given State because its intentions are sincere".[5] Our allegiance to the State is not to what it is, but to what it ought to be. Any given State, however, is an embodiment, imperfect it may be, of the State as the Ideal. The duty of the citizen

---

[1] Quoted by Hsiao: *Political Pluralism*, pp. 14-15.
[2] Krabbe: *The Modern Idea of the State*, p. 48, also p. 208.
[3] *Fichte*, pp. 158-159.
[4] See Willoughby: *Social Justice*, p. 260 ff.
[5] *The Dangers of Obedience*, p. 16.

is therefore not merely to stand outside of it and pass judgments, but to actively participate in shaping the life of the State that thereby its history will be the history of "the march of God upon earth". The State, indeed, is the vital concern of the individual ; it is short-sightedness to assume mere anti-thesis between the two.[1] We must "learn to think of our political conduct in terms of the vast reverberation of consequences on thousands and millions of lives, great and lowly, present and to come."[2] We do not of course, suggest that a conflict may not arise for we hold that loyalty can only be based upon the moral appeal of the State which essays sincerely to fulfil the good Purpose of its citizens. All that we wish to point out along with Bosanquet, is "that what makes and maintains States as States is will and not force the idea of a common good".[3] And simply because a given State does not answer the requirements of the ideal State, the individual cannot, on every flippant pretext, chose to disobey the Will of the State. Life otherwise becomes impossible. The right to revolt becomes a gospel of anarchy. There can be neither stability nor peace.

But peace and stability may be purchased at too high a price. And our analysis of the Ancient Indian State has convinced us that our ancients bartered away Freedom for Authority, and Progress for Order. The End of the State, as we have already seen was stability and not Progress ; it was to preserve Dharma, which in its empirical

---

[1] Between the individual and the State we see no fundamental conflict of purpose," writes Pipkin: (*The Idea of Social Justice*, p. 549), "and a view of the State which would to-day maintain the reality of this conflict completely fails to estimate the moral advance of mankind in raising the standards of individual duty and of collective responsibility"......

Watson: *State in Peace and War*, pp. 3-9-17.

[2] Hobhouse: *The Metaphysical Theory of the State*, p. 136.

[3] *Phil. Theory of the State*, p. 274.

manifestation was the Fixed Social Order, which therefore admitted no possibility of modification. Its scheme of Life was the mutilation of Social, Economic and political Justice; it did not aim at the "Good Life" which was "Common" for all. If "Dharma" is to serve as the principle of political obligation, we have to re-define it. It cannot be hereafter Dharma that is "Swadharma"; and all ideas regarding Varnashram must be completely surrendered.[1] If Dharma could be re-visualised as the supreme principle which is the Universal coherence, which seeks to establish a comprehensive social economy, which is itself the highest Good within the reach of even "the lowliest" and "the lost" who belong to the despised and the down-trodden, the expression of Justice which embraces in its scheme of rights and duties every component element of the Polity, it is yet possible for us to base our grounds of obligation on the ideal of Dharma. And the State, as the embodiment of Dharma, as the highest institution of man which seeks to provide for him the conditions necessary for the realisation of Dharma, will acquire and assert a moral supremacy which would justify its claim to the allegiance of every one of the citizens who live under it. The State would be the truest instrument of life and the enrichment of personality.

Our highest loyalty is, therefore, to the State that would help us realise the membership of the Great Society. The Great Society itself might yet be a far off vision. But there is nothing impracticable or impossible in the establishment of the Great Society on an organised

[1] We cannot sufficiently emphasise this view of ours, especially in view of recent tendencies which are otherwise very healthy. And the doctrine of Dharma, as relating to Varnashram, seems to acquire a new lease of life since Mahatma Gandhi, the greatest ethical force of modern times has openly advocated it. It is necessary, hence, to point out the reactionary character of the ideal of Dharma rather than its positive aspect.

basis. We can already speak of an "International Mind" as a Reality. "To argue that the international mind, required for the successful working of an international Government, is non-existent and impossible", says Hobson, "is to deny that the spirit of education has done anything to broaden the views and to expand the sympathies of men."[1] Hobson has done well in pointing out what education has achieved already. But education has still to effect much. To-day our relationships are mostly international, and yet most of our relationships are still on the machine-plane. They lack the human touch. Unless the various peoples are drawn towards each other by feelings of a tender nature, grounded on the faith of a common Parentage, the world State will not be possible. And the Education imparted to the young must prepare for the citizenship of the coming Polity. The aim of Education is to help the students "to see themselves and their neighbour in the light of the Universal."[2] And the importance of education for the success of political institutions can never be exaggerated. Plato long ago realised that it is not sufficient if we delineate the picture of the perfect Polity. The "ethos" of the institution must also be carefully fostered. Wisdom must be implanted in States, for ignorance is ruin. "It is idle to make institutions," writes Leslie Stephen, "without making the qualities by which they must be worked."[3] If education is to free the capacities of the individual and enable him to direct his life towards the realisation of social Ends it cannot be based on narrow interests. We should surrender, that is to say, all our ideals of education based upon the principle of nationalism. The aim of national education is exclusive. To imbue the mind of the people with regard for their culture and lore is not in itself unhealthy ; but to teach the

[1] *Towards International Government*, p. 199.
[2] J. J. Findlay: *The Foundations of Education*, p. 44.
[3] *Social Rights and Duties*, Vol. II, p. 206.

young that "India has nothing to learn from anybody else", and shut out the light from other quarters is the outcome of a State of mind that is incompatible with the virtues necessary for the membership of the Great Society. We are of opinion that there ought to be no such idea of National Education. "Science, Commerce and Art transcend national boundaries. They are largely international in quality and method. They involve interdependencies and co-operation among the peoples inhabiting different countries."[1] Education imparted by the nation-state restricts and corrupts its social ends. The Education imparted must be such as to enable the pupil to transcend limitations and help him to realise his kinship with Nature on the one hand and with Humanity on the other. And whatever would tend to impress the mind with particularist prejudices must be carefully expunged from the system. The prosperity of one's own country is not to be the aim, but the well-being of the whole human society. Education must be adapted to the ends of the Great Society.

Education is the only effective vehicle for the communication of ideals. We have seen the necessity for a radical revision of our traditional ideas and conceptions. If through a broad and general system of instruction we could prepare the coming generations for the citizenship of the Future Polity, by implanting in them the virtues essential for its success, we see nothing impossible of actualisation. Education, however, as a Social Process can have "no definite meaning until we define the kind of society we have in mind."

This we propose to do in the last few pages at our disposal.

[1] Dewey: *Democracy and Education*, p. 113.

CHAPTER XI

THE COMING POLITY

"The End of the State is, therefore, the vision of God."

AQUINAS

The Problem of the Indian Polity, and indeed of any Polity is primarily to visualise the kind of life which is desired to be lived. And in the light of that vision the traditional attitude to life should be revised and ideals re-formulated. This re-definition is only possible if we have an adequate understanding of human values and the worth of human Personality. Our institutional endeavour must be related to the Purpose which we wish to actualise in the Polity.

Personality and Purpose should be the two supreme principles that should interpret and determine Life. And they cannot be conceived purely in terms of the individual; for the Polity is a coherent, all-inclusive Whole. Life is a unity, the expression of a common Personality and social Purpose. The End the individual man seeks is a Social End, or no End at all. It must be an End in the pursuit of which he would be sharing with others. It is in this common End that social freedom lies, and the State would be the Actualisation of Freedom. The individual, if a good man, does not merely make use of Society and co-operate with others to satisfy his needs and interests, but he would identify himself with those "others", and would seek to merge his personality in the Common Life. He would have no End which cannot be the End of the whole to which he belongs. He would have no point of view which is not that of the whole as well. And he so acts that his conduct shall be in conformity with the coherence of the Society as a Whole. In the Common Purpose, that is to say, the opposition between the individual and the State is finally dissolved. The Individual realises his true Self in a Society of Selves which is Humanity. He is a member of the Brotherhood of Man.

The pursuit of purely particular purposes will result in incoherence and disharmony. Reality is the Harmony or coherence of the whole. True life lies in integrating the discordant elements, both in human nature and social relations. This involves on the one hand the conception that the self can only be self-conscious in Society and on the other hand the idea of mankind as a Spiritual Unity. We are members of one another. The Purpose of each is related to the other and finds its meaning in relation to the Whole. Every one is at once an end and a means. The Purpose or End of the Polity shall have equal significance to all; otherwise sharing is impossible. And Justice or Dharma cannot be realised.

Only when the End we seek is common or universal is the polity permeated through and through with the spirit of Dharma. And only then shall Dharma be the ideal we have been seeking all through the ages. We cannot and dare not limit the scope of Dharma. By limiting it we mutilate the ideal, for Dharma will not be Social Justice or Righteousness. It will only be class or caste Justice.

Dharma as regulating human relationship must therefore be the just awardment of Rights and Duties in the Polity. We cannot accept the evaluations of Society based upon the idea of Swadharma. And we cannot also accept existing conditions. For the Present Order as much as that of our Ancient Polity, is unrighteous from whatever point of view we might study it. There is an unnatural divorce between power and responsibility, functions and rewards, service and enjoyment, leisure and labour. Most of us are, indeed, parasitic. Our social opportunities are such that the rich become richer and the poor poorer.

This is so because the individual looks upon Society as something which he could make use of, and other individuals as mere instruments to minister unto his needs. That is why we are sinking lower and lower every day in materialism. We only live unto our selfish selves.

The Present Order is instinct with factors that spell imminent disaster. The need is urgent that we should reconstitute our social bases on a truly functional basis. Rights and Duties shall be determined on the principle of co-operation. It is only then that the Polity would become a coherent Whole, otherwise it would be a discordant Aggregate.

And for the Polity to become a spiritual harmony its ethical atmosphere must first undergo a vital transformation. Its ethos must be changed by a proper system of education. The Social Purpose must determine the value of educational ideals. The individual should be taught to direct all his efforts towards the realisation of the common End.

Religion is the vital principle of the Polity. We ought to spiritualise politics. Religion has always been to us the one thing that really matters. No vision of the Future will be real unless it seeks to fulfil the Soul's Quest for God. All through the ages, India has sought God, and she shall continue to seek Him, for ever and ever. Her pilgrimage shall not cease until He is enshrined in our midst.

This would only be possible in a faith grounded upon a Living God. God is not somewhere away in a supra-lunar solitude. We are one with Him in principle. "He is all which the human spirit is capable of becoming." He is our ideal of perfection and we would be even as perfect as He is. We are created in His likeness; but it is a likeness which we have always felt to be greater and better than ours. We would become as like unto Him as is possible for man only if we act according to His Principles.

For God is Love and he who loves not knows not God. Being His children if we do not learn to love each other, and forgive our mutual tresspasses neither can we expect anything from Him who knows everything.

Our Polity, must, therefore, be founded on Love. In love could everything be reconciled. It is the solvent of all our differences. Love is never selfish; it ever yields itself up, but never asks. Out of the abundance of our heart we give up spontaneously. So much of strife that we have in our life is possible only because we are greedy and miserly. We ask for safeguards, and insist on definite pacts. And ever the vicious wheel goes on revolving in its fateful rounds, crushing out all joy and happiness from our life.

We need only to know that the only safeguard that we must have is the capacity to love, and we shall immediately wake up to the infinite possibility of joy and Happiness in this our earthly existence. What better pact can we have than the bond that brings us together, as children of a common Father? The moment we recognise this sacred kinship we shall cease to enslave each other. We shall no longer rage and rave.

"In love all the contradictions of existence merge themselves and are lost." The many conflicting elements in our body-politic could be then organised for a single purpose. The Principle of unity that would yoke the complex of diverse elements to the Eternal Quest is the firm faith in the Fatherhood of God—that God is one and the same for all, and that He is our father. This was the truth preached by Nanab, Kabir, and Chaitanya. This was the truth proclaimed by Christ and Muhammad; and true religion is the Quintessence of this High Truth.

Why need we, therefore, emphasise non-essentials and fall out between ourselves? Here is the common basis for Fellowship. And the moment we try to guide our institutional life according to this idea our racial and social problem is automatically solved. Our Polity would become a true partnership. And people of widely differing temperaments and faiths could easily be bent to a single and common purpose in equal service and common devotion.

Our vision points to the establishment of a better order of society grounded upon the ideal of co-operation in service. The Social Order would then be the embodiment of Dharma, and the State, the actualisation of freedom.

Human relations have so far been regulated by principles that divide. The time has come, if civilisation is to survive, to organise them on love and fellowship. The present is a challenge to us, and we rise or sink according as we recognise its implications.

In the pursuit of the "Eternal Quest", we shall be realising DHARMA. We need only seek the Kingdom of DHARMA, and all the other conditions of our Polity shall be added unto us.

APPENDIX A

ABBREVIATIONS EMPLOYED

(Only the more important are given. The others are too familiar to be noticed here.)

Rel. and Phil. of the Veda.	Religion and Philosophy of the Veda.
Hist. of Ind. Phil.	History of Indian Philosophy.
Ind. Hist. Quarterly.	Indian Historical Quarterly.
Art.	Article.
Pub. Adm. in Anc. Ind.	Public Administration in Ancient India.
Edn.	Edition.
Phil. Theory of the State.	Philosophical Theory of the State.
Theory of Govt. in Anc. Ind.	Theory of Government in Ancient India.
Social Organ.	Social Organisation.
Camb. Hist. of Ind.	Cambridge History of India.
Anc. Ind.	Ancient India.
Vill. Com.	Village Communities.
Hist. of Ind.	History of India.

APPENDIX B

BIBLIOGRAPHY

The names of the important books consulted are included in the following list which is by no means exhaustive.

Other references will be found in the body of the text spread out in the foot-notes.

Abbott, Evelyn.	Hellenica.	Rivingtons.
Acton, Lord.	Lectures on Modern History.	Macmillan & Co., Ltd. 1920.
,, ,,	Lectures on the French Revolution.	Macmillan & Co., Ltd. 1910.
Acworth, H. A.	Ballads of the Marathas.	Longmans, Green, & Co., Ltd. 1894.
Adams, G. B.	Constitutional History of England.	Jonathan Cape, 1930.
Aiyangar, K. V. R.	Some Aspects of Ancient Indian Polity.	S. P. C. Press, Madras.
Alberuni.	India.	Kegan Paul, Trench, Trubner & Co.
Allen, Grant.	Darwin. (Edited by Andrew Long)	Longmans, Green, & Co., Ltd. 1888.
Anson, W. R.	The Law and Custom of the Constitution.	Oxford University Press.
Arbuthnot, F. F.	Arabic Authors.	William Heinemann, 1890.
Aristotle.	Athenian Constitution, (Trans. by F. G. Kenyon)	G. Bell & Sons, Ltd., 1914.
,,	A Treatise on Government. (Trans. by William Ellis)	George Routledge & Sons, Ltd., 1888.
,,	Ethics. (Trans. by Welldon)	Macmillan & Co., Ltd.
,,	Politics. (do.)	Macmillan & Co., Ltd.
Arnold, Sir E.	The Song Celestial.	Kegan Paul, Trench, Trubner & Co., 1893.
Arnold, Mathew.	Thoughts on Education.	Smith, Elder & Co. 1893.
Augustine, St.	Treatise on the City of God.	Macmillan & Co., Ltd. New York.
Austin, J.	Lectures on Jurisprudence.	John Murray, 1913.
Bacon, Francis.	The New Atlantis.	Macmillan & Co., Ltd. 1912.
,, ,,	Advancement of Learning And Novum Organum.	World's Great Classics, Colonial Press, 1900.
Baden-Powell, B. H.	Indian Village Community.	Longmans, Green & Co., Ltd. 1896.
,, ,,	Land Revenue and Tenure in British India.	Clarendon Press, 1913.

Bagehot, Walter.	The English Constitution.	Kegan Paul & Co. 1878.
,, ,,	Physics and Politics.	Kegan Paul & Co. 1878.
Baldwin, J. M. (Editor)	Dictionary of Philosophy and Psychology..	Macmillan & Co., Ltd.
Ballantyne, J.R.	The Sankhya Aphorisms of Kapila.	Bibliotheca Indica, Calcutta, 1865.
Bandhyopadhyaya, N. C.	Kautilya.	R. Cambray & Co.
Banerjea, Pramathanath.	Public Administration in Ancient India.	Macmillan & Co., Ltd. 1916.
Barker, E.	National Character.	Methuen & Co., Ltd., 1927.
,, ,,	Greek Political Theory.	Methuen & Co., Ltd.
,, ,,	Political Thought in England.	Home University Library.
Barnett.	Antiquities of India.	Philip Lee Warner.
Basu, Profulla Chandra.	Indo-Aryan Polity.	P. S. King, Ltd. 1925.
Bendell.	Siksha Samucchya.	John Murray, 1922.
Beni Prasad.	The State in Ancient India.	Indian Press, Allahabad.
,, ,,	Theory of Government in Ancient India.	,, ,,
,, ,,	History of Jehangir.	,, ,,
Bergson, Henri.	Creative Evolution.	Macmillan & Co., Ltd.
Bevan, Edwin.	Thoughts on Indian Discontent.	George Allen & Unwin, Ltd. 1929. [1914.
,, ,,	Indian N onalism.	Macmillan & Co., Ltd.
Bhandarkar, D. R.	Lectures on the Ancient History of India.	University of Calcutta, 1919.
,, ,,	Some Aspects of Ancient Hindu Polity.	Benares Hindu University, 1929.
Bhandarkar, R. G.	Early History of the Deccan.	... ...
,, ,,	A Peep into the Early History of India.	Taraporewala & Sons.
Bhasa.	Pratima Nataka.	Oriental Book Agency.
,,	Vasavadatta.	Oxford University Press, 1923.
Bhavabhuti.	Malatimadhava.	The Oriental Publishing Company 1913.
Blochman, H.	The Ain-I-Akbari.	Baptist Mission Press, Calcutta.
Bloomfield.	The Religion of the Veda.	Clarendon Press.
,, ,,	Hymns of the Atharva Veda.	Clarendon Press.
Bluntschli, J.	The Theory of the State.	Clarendon Press, Oxford.
Bosanquet, B.	The Principle of Individuality and Value.	Macmillan & Co., Ltd. 1927.
,, ,,	Education in Plato's Republic.	University Press, Cambridge, 1908.
,, ,,	The Value and Destiny of the Individual.	Macmillan & Co., Ltd. 1913.

Bosanquet, B.	The Philosophical Theory of the State.	Macmillan & Co., Ltd. 1925.
Bose, Dr. K. B.	Lord Buddha And His Doctrine.	Bharat Dharma Syndicate, Ben. 1927.
Bradley, F. H.	Ethical Studies.	Clarendon Press, Oxford, 1927.
Bradshaw, John.	Sir Thomas Munro.	,, ,, 1894.
Brihaspati.	(Trans. by Jolly J.)	Clarendon Press.
Bryce, James.	The Holy Roman Empire.	Macmillan & Co., Ltd. 1897.
,, ,,	Studies in History and Jurisprudence. 2 Vols.	Clarendon Press, Oxford, 1901.
,, ,,	Modern Democracies.	Macmillan & Co., Ltd. 1923.
Buckle, H. T.	History of Civilisation in England.	Grant Richards, London.
Buhler, George.	Sacred Laws.	Clarendon Press, 1879.
Burlingame, Eugene Watson.	Buddhist Legends.	Harvard University Press, Cambridge, 1921.
Bury, J. B.	The Idea of Progress.	Macmillan & Co., Ltd. 1920.
,, ,,	A History of Greece.	Macmillan & Co., Ltd. 1900.
Burns, C. D.	The Principles of Revolution.	George Allen & Unwin.
,, ,,	Political Ideals.	Oxford University Press.
,, ,,	The Conception of Liberty.	Macmillan & Co., Ltd.
Caird, E.	The Evolution of Religion.	James Maclehose & Sons.
,, ,,	The Critical Philosophy of Emmanuel Kant.	James Maclehose & Sons, 1889.
,,	The Evolution of Theology In the Greek Philosophers.	James Maclehose & Sons, 1893.
Caird, John, (Principal)	Introduction to the Philosophy of Religion.	James Maclehose & Sons, 1880.
Carlyle.	Representative Selections.	G. Bell & Sons, Ltd. 1913.
Carter, E. H.	The New Past.	Basil Blackwell, Oxford, 1925.
Carr, H. Wildon.	The Philosophy of Change.	T. C. & E. C. Jack Ltd. 1919.
Carr, Saunders. A. M.	Eugenics.	Williams & Norgate, London.
Carus, Paul.	The Gospel of Buddha.	The Opening Court Publishing Co.
,, ,,	Amitabha.	The Opening Court Publishing Co.
Casson, Stanley.	Ancient Greece.	Oxford University Press, 1922.
Catlin, G. E. G.	The Science And Method of Politics.	Kegan, Paul, Trench. Trubner & Co. 1927.

Cecil, Lord H.	Liberty and Authority.	Edward Arnold & Co. London.
Chamberlain, H. S.	Foundations of the Nineteenth Century.	John Lane Company.
Chirol, Sir Valantine.	India.	Ernest Benn Ltd. 1926.
Clarke, M. I.	Medieval City-State.	
Colebroke, H. T. & Wilson, H. H.	The Sankhya Karika.	Oriental Translation Fund, Oxford, 1837.
Cole, G. D. H.	Social Theory.	Methuen & Co., Ltd.
Coomaraswamy, A.	Buddha & The Gospel of Buddhism.	London.
Collingwood, R. G.	The Limits of Historical Knowledge. (An Article)	Journal of Philosophical Studies.
C. O. P. E. C., Commission Reports	The Home.	Longmans, Green & Co., Ltd. 1924.
,, ,, ,,	Politics and Citizenship.	,, ,, ,,
Comte, Auguste	The Positive Philosophy	G. Bell & Sons, Ltd. 1896.
Confucius.	The Classics of Confucius—The Book of History—(Shu King)	John Murray, Albemarle Street, 1911.
Coulanges, Fustel De.	The Ancient City.	Lothrop, Lee & Shepard & Co.
Cotton, Sir Henry John Stedmen.	New India.	Kegan Paul, Trench, Trubner & Co., Ltd.
Cowell, E. B.	The Buddha Charita of Aswaghosha.	Clarendon Press.
Craik, Sir Henry.	The State in Relation to Education.	Macmillan & Co., Ltd.
Croce, Benedetto.	Theory And History of Historiography.	George G. Harrap & Co. 1921.
,, ,,	Logic as the Science of the Pure Concept.	Macmillan & Co., Ltd. 1917.
Crump, C. C.	History and Historical Research.	George Routledge & Sons, 1928.
Curtis, Lionel.	Letters to the People of India On Responsible Government.	C. H. Harvey, Calcutta, 1917.
Cushman, H. E.	A Beginner's History of Philosophy.	G. G. Harrop & Co.
Dante.	De Monarchia.	Clarendon Press, Oxford, 1916.
Das Gupta.	A History of Indian Philosophy.	University Press, Cambridge, 1922.
Das Gupta and Lawrence Binyon.	Sakuntala.	Macmillan & Co., Ltd. 1920.
Das, A. C.	Rig-Vedic India.	University of Calcutta, 1920.
Date, Govind Trimbak.	The Art of War In Ancient India.	Oxford University Press, 1929.
Davids, T. W. Rhys.	Dialogues of the Buddha.	

Davids, Mrs. Rhys.	Psalms of the Early Buddhist "Theragatha".	Oxford University Press, 1913.
Davids, T. W. Rhys.	Buddhism.	
Davids, T. W. (Hibbert Lectures)	Lectures on the Origin and Growth of Religion.	Williams & Norgate.
Davids, Rhys.	Buddhist India.	T. Fisher Unwin, 1911.
Dawson, Christopher.	Progress and Religion.	Sheed & Ward. 1929.
Dealey, J.	The Family in its Sociological Aspects.	Houghton Mifflin Co.
,, ,,	The Development of the State.	G. G. Harrap & Co.
Deussen, Paul.	Outlines of Indian Philosophy.	
,, ,,	The Philosophy of the Upanishads.	T. & T. Clark, Edinburgh.
Dewey, Prof. John.	Education and Democracy.	
Dicey, A. V.	Law and Opinion in England.	Macmillan & Co., Ltd. 1914.
Dickinson, G. L.	The Greek View of Life.	Methuen & Co., Ltd. London,
Dickinson, G. Lowes.	Justice and Liberty.	J. M. Dent & Sons.
Dow Alexander.	The History of Hindostan.	London 1803.
Duff. J. C.	A History of the Maharathas.	
Duhler.	Laws of Manu.	
Duff Robert A.	Spinoza's Political & Ethical Philosophy.	James Maclehose & Son.
Duguit, Leon.	Laws in the Modern State.	B. W. Huebech, New York.
Dunning, W. A.	A History of Political Theories, 4 Vols.	Macmillan & Co., Ltd.
Dutt, R. C.	The History of India.	The Grolier Society.
Dutt, N. K.	The Aryanisation of India.	
Dutt, Romesh C.	The Civilisation of India.	Ballantyne Hanson & Co.
Dutt.	Santi Parva.	H. C. Das, Elyseum Press, 1903.
Eggeling, Julius.	The Sathapatha-Brahmana.	Clarendon Press, Oxford.
Elphinstone, Mountstuart.	The History of India.	John Murray.
Elphinestone, Mountstuart.	The History of India.	John Murray, London.
Emerson, Ralph Waldo.	Essays and Representative Men.	G. Bell & Sons, Ltd.
Epictetus.	The Teaching of Epictetus.	The Walter Scott Publishing Co.
Fichte, J. G.	The Popular Works.	John Chapman.
Fick, Richard.	The Social Organisation in North East India in Buddhist Time.	University—Calcutta.

Findlay.	Foundations of Education.	
Firdusi, Abul Kasim Mansur.	The Shah Nameh.	The Colonial Press. 1900.
Follett, M. P.	The New State.	Longmans Green. & Co., Ltd. 1926.
Fowler, Warde.	The City State of the Greeks and Romans.	Macmillan & Co., Ltd.
Froude. James Anthony.	Short Studies on Great Subjects.	Longmans, Green & Co., Ltd. 1892.
Garbe, Richard.	The Samkhya Pravacana Bhashya.	Harvard University, 1895.
Garratt, G. T.	An Indian Commentary.	
Geddes, P. & Thomson, J. A.	Evolution.	Williams & Norgate.
Gettell, Raymond Garfield.	Readings in Political Science.	Ginn & Company.
Gierke.	Political Theories of the Middle Ages.	University-Cambridge.
Ghose, Aurobindo	Essays on the Gita. (First and Second Series)	Arya Publishing House.
Ghosal, U. N.	A History of Hindu Political Theories.	University Press, Oxford.
Giddings, F. H.	The Responsible State.	Constable & Co.
Godwin.	The Enquiry Concerning Political Justice.	
Gooch, G. P.	Political Thought from Bacon to Halifax.	Home University Library.
,, ,,	The History of English Democratic Ideas in the Seventeenth Century.	University Press, Cambridge.
Gough, Archibald Edward.	The Philosophy of the Upanishads.	Kegan, Paul, Trench Trubner & Co., 1903.
Green, Thomas Hill.	Prolegomena to Ethics.	Clarendon Press, Oxford.
,, ,,	On the Principles of Political Obligation.	Longmans, Green & Co., Ltd.
Griffith.	Ramayana.	Trubner & Co.
,,	Hymns of the Atharva Veda.	Lazarus & Co.
,,	Hymns of the Rig-Veda.	,, ,,
Hadow.	Citizenship.	Clarendon Press.
Hafiz.	Divan-Aafiz.	The Educational Publishing Co., Karachi.
,,	Diwan The.	The Colonial Press, New York.
Haldane, J. B.	Mechanism, Life & Personality.	
Hammond, B E.	The Political Institutions of The Ancient Greeks	Cambridge University Press, 1895.
Sri Harsha Deva.	Nagananda.	The Standard Publishing Co., Bombay.
Hearn, Lafcadio.	Gleanings in Buddha Fields.	Jonathan Cape, London.

Hegel, Geory Wilhelm Friedrich.	Philosophy of History.	G. Bell & Sons, Ltd.
Hellenica.	A collection of Essays, on Greek Poetry, Philosophy, History and Religion.	Rivingtons-London.
Heras, Rev. H.	Asoka's Dharma & Religion.	An Article reprinted from the Quarterly Journal of the Mythic Soc., Bangalore.
Hetherington, Prof. H. J. W. and Muirhead, Prof. J. H.	Social Purpose.	Macmillan & Co., Ltd.
Hobbes.	Leviathan.	Everyman's Library.
Hobhouse, L. T.	Liberalism.	Williams & Norgate.
,, ,,	The Elements of Social Justice.	George Allen & Unwin, Ltd.
,, ,,	Social Development.	,, ,,
,, ,,	Social Evolution and Political Theory.	Columbia University Press, 1913.
,, ,,	The Metaphysical Theory of the State.	Macmillan & Co., Ltd.
Hobson, J. A.	Towards International Government.	
,, ,,	Work and Wealth.	Macmillan & Co., Ltd.
Hocart, A. M.	Kingship.	Oxford University Press, 1927.
Hogg, A. G.	Karma and Redemption.	The Christian Literature Society for India.
Hopkins, Washburn.	The Ethics of India.	Yale University Press, New Haven.
Hopkins, E. W.	India Old and New.	
Hopkins, E. W.	The Religions of India.	Gin & Company. 1895.
Hoyland. John S.	The Case for India.	J. M. Dent & Sons, Ltd.
Hsiao, K. C.	Political Pluralism.	Kegan, Paul, Trench, Trubner & Co., Ltd.
Hudson, W. H.	An Introduction to the Philosophy of Herbert Spencer.	Chapman & Hall Ltd.
Hume. David	Essays.	Ward Lock and Bowden.
Hume, Robert Ernest.	The Thirteen Principal Upanishads.	Oxford University Press.
Huntington, Ellsworth.	The Pulse of Progress.	Charles Scribner's Sons.
Huxley, T. H.	Evolution and Ethics.	Macmillan & Co., Ltd. 1911.
Iyer, Ananta Krishna.	Lectures on Ethnography.	University of Calcutta, 1925.
Jathar, G. B. and Beri, S. G.	Indian Economics, 2 vols.	D. B. Taraporevala Sons, Bombay.

Jayaswal, K. P.	Hindu Polity.	Butterworth & Co., Ltd., Calcutta, 1924.
Joad, C. E. N.	The Present and Future of Religion.	Ernest Benn, Ltd., 1930.
Johnson, Allen.	The Historian and Historical Evidence.	
Jolly, J.	Article on Dharma. Encyclopaedia of Religion and Ethics.	T. & T. Clark, Edinburg, 1911.
,,	The Minor Law-Books, Part 1, Narada. Brihaspati.	Clarendon Press, Oxford, 1889.
Jolly, J.	Hindu Law and Custom.	
Jolly, J. and Schmidt, R.	Arthasastra of Kautilya, A New Ed., Vol. I.. 1923.	
Jones, Sir Henry.	Principles of citizenship.	Macmillan & Co., Ltd.
,, ,,	The Working Faith of the Social Reformer.	,,
	Journal of Philosophical Studies.	Macmillan & Co., Ltd. London.
,, ,,	Journal of the Royal Asiatic Society.	
Jouvean-Dubreuil, G.	The Pallavas.	1917.
Jowett.	The Politics of Aristotle, 4 Vols.	Clarendon Press, Oxford.
Kalidasa.	Malavikagnimitra.	1918.
,,	The Vikramorvasiya.	The Oriental Publishing Co., Bombay, 1916.
,,	Sakuntala.	Macmillan & Co., Ltd. London, 1920.
Kamandaka.	Nitisara.	
Kant, Immanuel.	Lectures on Ethics.	
,, ,,	Perpetual Peace.	Swan Sonnenschein & Co., 1903.
Kautilya.	Arthasastra.	The Wesleyan Mission Press, Mysore, 1923.
Kapila.	The Sankhya Aphorisms.	Trubner & Co., London, 1885.
Keay, F. K.	Ancient Indian Education.	Oxford University Press, 1918.
Keith, A. B.	The Religion and the Philosophy of the Veda and Upanishads.	Cambridge, Massachusetts Harvard University Press, London; Humphrey Milford, Oxford University Press, 1925.
,, ,,	Buddhist Philosophy.	Clarendon Press, Oxford, 1923.
,, ,,	The Samkhya System.	Oxford University Press, London, 1924.
Kern, H.	Manual of Indian Buddhism.	Education Society's Press, Byculla, Bombay, 1918.

Kokileswar, Sastri.	An Introduction to Adwaita Philosophy.	University of Calcutta, 1926.
Krabbe, H.	The Modern Idea of the State.	D. Appleton & Co., New York, London, 1930.
Kunte. M. M.	The Vicissitudes of Aryan Civilisation.	Bombay, 1880.
Laski, H. J.	Authority in the Modern State.	Yale University Press.
Lowell, Lawrence.	The Government of England, 2 Vols. New Ed.	Macmillan & Co., Ltd. New York, 1919.
Macaulay.	Selections.	Longmans, Green & Co., Ltd. New York, Bombay, 1906.
Macdonell, A. A.	India's Past.	The Clarendon Press, Oxford, 1927.
Macdonell, and Keith.	Vedic Index of Names and Subjects, 2 vols.	John Murray, London, 1912.
Maccun, John.	Ethics of Citizenship.	James Maclehose & Sons, Glasgow, 1896.
Macgovern, Dr. W. M.	A Manual of Buddhist Philosophy.	Kegan Paul, London, 1923.
Mac Iver.	The Modern State.	1926.
McKenzie, The Rev. Dr. John.	Hindu Ethics.	Oxford University Press, 1922.
Macphail, James H.	Asoka.	Oxford University Press.
Maine, Sir Henry Sumner.	Popular Government.	1886.
do.	Village Communities in the East and the West.	John Murray, London, 1895.
do.	Early Institutions.	John Murray.
do.	Ancient Law.	Oxford.
Manu.	Laws of Manu.	Clarendon Press, Oxford, 1886.
Marcus Aurelius Antonius.	The Communings with himself.	William Heinemann, London.
Marriott, Sir John A. R.	Second Chambers.	The Clarendon Press, Oxford, 1927.
Marvin, F. S.	The Unity of Western Civilisation.	Oxford University Press, 1926.
Myres, J. L.	The Political Ideals of the Greeks.	1927.
Myres, Phillip Van Ness.	History as Past Ethics.	
Mathai, John.	Village Government in British India.	T. Fisher Unwin, Ltd.
Mazumdar, N. N.	A History of Education in Ancient India.	Macmillan & Co., Ltd.
Mazumdar, R. C.	Corporate Life in Ancient India.	1918.
Maurice.	Indian Antiquities.	
Mazzini.	Duties of Man.	

MacLenan.	The Patriarchal Theory.	Macmillan & Co., Ltd. 1885.
Mill, John Stuart.	Utilitarianism, Liberty, Representative Government.	Everyman's Library.
,, ,,	A System of Logic.	Longmans, Green & Co., Ltd.
Montesquieu, Baron De.	The Spirit of Laws.	The World's Great Classics.
Mookerjee, Radhakumud.	Local Government in Ancient India.	Clarendon Press. Oxford.
,, ,,	The Fundamental Unity of India.	Longmans, Green & Co., Ltd.
,, ,,	Nationalism in Hindu Culture.	Theosophical Publishing House, London.
Miigge, Macmillan.	Heinrich Von Treitschke.	The People's Books.
More, Sir Thomas.	The Utopia.	London, Walter Scott Ltd.
Mori, Mosatoshi Gensen.	Buddhism and Faith.	The Herald-Sha. Tokyo, 1928.
Morley, Viscount.	Notes on Politics & History.	Macmillan & Co., Ltd. 1914.
Muir, Ramsay.	The Expansion of Europe.	Constable & Co.. Ltd.
,, ,,	Nationalism and Internationalism	,, ,, ,,
Mukherji, Radha-Kamal	Democracies of the East.	P. S. King & Sons, 1923.
Muller, Max.	The Upanishads.	Panini Office, Allahabad. 1912.
,, ,,	India, What can it teach us.	Longmans. Green & Co., Ltd.
,, ,,	Selected Essays.	,, ,, ,, 1881.
,, ,,	The Six Systems of Indian Philosophy.	,, ,, ,, 1899.
Murasaki Shikib.	Genji Monogatari. (World's great classics)	The Colonial Press, N.
Nettleship, Richard Lewis.	The Theory of Education in the Republic of Plato. *(Hellenica)*	Rivington.
Nevinson, H. W.	Essays in freedom	Duckworth & Co., London.
Newman, Sir G.	Citizenship & The Survival of Civilisation.	Yale University Press, 1928.
Newman, W. L.	The Politics of Aristotle, Vol. 1.	Clarendon Press, 1897.
Nicholson, Reynold A. A.	Literary History of the Arabs.	T. Fisher Unwin Ltd.
Nordentoft, Severin.	Practical Pacifism.	Allen and Unwin Ltd.
Old, Gorn W.	The Classics of Confucius.	John Murray, 1911.
Dr. Oldenberg, Hermann.	Buddha, His Life, His Doctrine, His Order.	Williams and Norgate, London. 1882.
Omar Khayyam.	The Rubaiyat.	The Colonial Press.

B. Pattabhi Sitaramayya.	Indian Nationalism.	M. Krishnarao, 1913.
,, ,,	Indian National Education Pt. I & II	Krishna Swadesi Press, 1910.
Perry. Ralph Barton.	Present Philosophical Tendencies.	Longmans, Green & Co., Ltd. 1925.
Pipkin, C. W.	The Idea of Social Justice.	The Macmillan Co., Ltd. 1927.
Plato	The Dialogues of Plato. "Laws".	Clarendon Press.
,,	The Dialogues of Plato. "Republic."	,, ,,
Pollock, Sir Frederick.	History of the Science of Politics.	Macmillan & Co., Ltd. 1925.
Poussin, L. De La Vallie	"Nihilism" (Buddhist). An Article. (Encyclopaedia of Religion and Ethics)	T and T Clark.
,, ,,	The Way to Nirvana.	Cambridge University Press. 1917.
,, ,,	Nirvana. An Article. (Encyclopaedia of Religion and Ethics)	T. and T. Clark.
Poussin, And E. J. Thomas.	Mysticism (Buddhist). An Article. (Encyclopaedia of Religion and Ethics)	T. and T. Clark
Pritchard, F. H.	Essays of To-day.	George G. Harrap & Co.
Pringle, Pattison.	Studies in the Philosophy of Religion.	Clarendon Press, 1930.
,, ,,	The Idea of God.	Oxford University Press, 1880.
Palmer, E. H.	The Quran.	Clarendon Press, 1880.
Quick, R. H.	Essays on Educational Reforms.	Longmans, Green & Co., Ltd. 1894.
Radhakrishnan, S.	Indian Philosophy, 2. Vols.	Macmillan & Co., Ltd. 1923.
Ragozin, Z. A.	Vedic India.	T. Fisher Unwin.
Ramabai Saras-swati, Pandita.	The High Caste Hindu Woman.	Philadelphia, 1888.
Rangaswami Aiyangar.	Considerations on some Aspects of Ancient Indian Polity.	S. P. C. K. Press, University Printers, Madras, 1916.
Rashdall, Hastings.	The Theory of Good and Evil.	Clarendon Press, Oxford, 1907.
Ray. Pratap Chandra.	Karna Parva.	Bharata Press, Calcutta, 1889.
,, ,,	The Mahabharata.	,, ,,
Reed, Sir S. And Cadelt, P. R.	"India" The New Phase.	Phillip Allan & Co., London, 1928.
Ritchie D. G.	Rights.	Natural George Allen Unwin, Ltd.
Ronaldshay, Earl.	The Heart of Aryavarta.	Constable & Co. 1925.
,, ,,	"India"	,, ,,

Rose, Holland.	Nationality in Modern History.	Rivingtons, London, 1916.
Rousseau.	The Social Contract.	Everman's Library.
,,	Emile.	,, ,,
Ruskin, J.	Unto the Last & The Two Paths.	Collins Pocket Classics.
Rutherford, V. H.	Modern India.	The Labour Publishing Co., Ltd. 1927.
,, ,,	India and Labour Party.	The Labour Publishing Co. Ltd. 1928.
Sadi.	Gulistan.	Walter Scott Publishing Co.
,,	The Divine Songs of Sadi.	
Samaddar.	The Glories of Magadha.	Patna University, 1927.
Santideva.	Siksha Samucchaya.	1922.
Sardesai, G. S.	Main Currents of Maratha History.	
Sarkar, Benoy Kumar.	The Political Institutions and the Theories of the Hindus.	Verlag Von Markert and Patters, Leipzig.
Saunders, K. J.	The Heart of Buddhism.	Oxford University Press. 1915.
Schlegel, F. V.	The Philosophy of History.	G. Bell & Sons Ltd. 1908.
Schiveitzer, A.	Civilisation & Ethics.	A. & C. Black Ltd.
Sen. Ajit Kumar.	Studies in the Hindu Political Thought.	Calcutta—1926.
Sen. Surendranath.	Siva Chhatrapati.	University of Calcutta, 1920.
Senart, Emile.	Caste in India.	Metheun & Co., Ltd. 1930.
Seth, James.	Ethical Principles.	William Blackwood & Sons, Edinborough & London.
,, ,,	Essays in Ethics and Religion.	William Blackwood & Sons, Edinborough & London.
Shama Sastri.	Evolution of Indian Polity.	University of Calcutta, 1920.
Shilotri, P. S.	Indo-Aryan Thought & Culture.	1926.
Sidhanta, N. K.	The Heroic Age of India.	
Sidwick, Henry.	Outlines of the History of Ethics.	Macmillan & Co., Ltd. 1918.
,, ,,	The Elements of Politics.	,, ,, 1908.
Sircar, Mahendranath.	Comparative Studies in Vedantism.	Oxford University Press, 1927.
Smith, Vincent A.	Indian Constitutional Reforms.	Oxford University Press, 1927.
,, ,,	Oxford History of India.	
,, ,,	Early History of India.	
Spencer Herbert.	Social Statics.	Watts & Co. 1910.
,, ,,	The Man versus The State.	,, ,,

Spencer Herbert.	The Principles of Sociology.	Williams & Norgate. 1893.
Spengler, Oswald.	The Decline of the West.	Allen & Unwin. Ltd.
Stephen, Leslie.	Social Rights and Duties.	Macmillan & Co., Ltd. 1896.
Sukra Acharya.	Sukra Niti Sara.	India Press, 1913.
Sully, James.	Pessimism (2nd Ed.)	Kegan Paul. 1891.
Tagore, Rabindranath	Nationalism.	Macmillan & Co., Ltd. 1920.
Taine, A. H.	History of English Literature.	Colonial Press.
Taylor, H. O.	Ancient Ideals.	Macmillan & Co., Ltd. 1921.
Tawney. R. H.	Religion and Rise of Capitalism.	
do.	The Acquisitive Society.	G. Bell & Sons. Ltd. 1926.
Teggart, F. J.	Theory of History.	Yale University Press.
do.	Processes of History.	
Telang.	Bhagavadgita.	Clarendon Press, 1908.
do.	Anugita.	do. 1908.
do.	The Sanatsugatiya.	do. 1908.
Temperley.	Selected Essays.	University Press. 1930.
Thucydides.	History of the Peloponnesian War.	Everyman's Library.
Tod, James.	Annals and Antiquities of Rajastan.	G. Routledge & Sons, Ltd.
Tolstoy, Leo	Essays and Letters.	World's Classics.
Tiele, Prof. C. P.	Outlines of the History of Religion.	Trubner & Co. 1884.
Tocqueville, Alexio De.	Democracy in America.	The Colonial Press.
Urquehart, W. S.	The Vedanta and Modern Thought.	Oxford University Press, 1928.
Urwick, E. J.	The Social Good.	Methuen & Co., Ltd.
do.	A Philosophy of Social Progress.	do.
Vasu S. C.	The Mitaksara.	
Vaughan, C. E.	Studies in Political Philosophy.	
do.	The Political Writings of Jean Jacques Rousseau.	University Press. 1915.
Venkateswara, S. V.	Indian Culture Through The Ages.	Longmans. Green & Co., Ltd. 1928.
Wadia P. A.	Zoroastrianism and our Spiritual Heritage.	
Wadia and Joshi.	The Wealth of India.	Macmillan & Co., Ltd. 1927.
Wallace, W.	Epicureanism.	London Society for Promoting Christian Knowledge, 1880.
Wallas, Graham.	The Great Society.	Macmillan & Co., Ltd. 1925.

Wallas, Graham.	Human Nature in Politics	Constable & Co., Ltd. 1908.
Wallas, Graham.	Our Social Heritage.	Allen & Unwin.
Ward. William.	The Hindoos.	London, 1882.
Ward, P. W.	Sovereignty.	G. Routledge & Sons, Ltd.
Warren, Henry Clarke.	Buddhism in Translations.	Harvard University, 1909.
Walldon.	Aristotle-Ethics and Politics.	
Wenlay, R. M.	Aspects of Pessimism.	Blackwood & Sons.
Westcott, B. F.	Religious Thought in the West.	Macmillan & Co., Ltd. 1891.
Westermarck.	The Origin and Development of Moral Ideals.	Macmillan & Co., Ltd.
Whitehead, Bishop Henry.	Indian Problems.	Constable & Co., Ltd. 1924.
Willoughby, W. W.	Social Justice.	
do.	The Nature of the State.	
do.	The Ethical Basis of Political Authority.	
Wilson, W.	The State.	Heath & Co. 1919.
Windelband, Dr. W.	History of Ancient Philosophy.	Marston & Co. 1900.
Woodroffe, Sir John.	Is India Civilised?	Ganesh & Co. 1922.
Yajnavalkya.	Smriti.	1918.
Zimmern, A. E.	Nationality & Government.	Chatto & Windus, 1919.

INDEX